All the Presidents' Trivia

All the
Presidents'
Trivia

Peter Wrench

SMITHFIELD PRESS
NORTH RICHLAND HILLS, TEXAS

Smithfield
Press

Smithfield Press
An imprint of D. & F. Scott Publishing, Inc.
P.O. Box 821653
N. Richland Hills, TX 76182
817 788-2280
info@dfscott.com
www.dfscott.com
(see below for purchase information)

Printed in the United States of America

08 07 06 05 04   5 4 3 2 1

Library of Congress Cataloging-in-Publication Data
Wrench, Peter Yorke.
    All the presidents' trivia / Peter Y. Wrench.
        p. cm.
    Includes index.
    ISBN 1-930566-38-7 (trade paper : alk. paper)
    1. Presidents—United States—Miscellanea. I. Title.
E176.1 .W946 2003
973'.09'9—dc22

                                    2003024730

Note: The use of the seal of the president of the United States of America by
All the Presidents' Trivia does not imply, nor should the reader infer, spon-
sorship or approval of this book by the president of the United States of
America or indeed by any part of the federal government.

To purchase books, contact:

    Wrench Enterprises
    P.O. Box 142484
    Irving, Texas 75014-2484
    (972) 887-9334
    petewrench@hotmail.com

To my father

Philip

with gratitude
for his sacrifices

Also by Peter Wrench:

Kitchen Cabinets (2000)
Ladies First (1996)

"It has long been an axiom of mine that the little things are infinitely the most important."

Sir Arthur Conan Doyle
"A Case of Identity"
The Adventures of Sherlock Holmes

Contents

Contents

Contents

Contents

Preface

This book presents a fascinating collection of more than four thousand trivia questions and answers about every president of the United States, from George Washington to George W. Bush. Its approach is informal, its style non-prosaic, and its intent informative. It covers a variety of topics about each president's accomplishments and disappointments, causes and characteristics, and dozens of other topics.

From its conception in 1986 during the class "American Presidency" with renowned presidential scholar Dr. Bruce Buchanan at the University of Texas at Austin, the manuscript evolved into the most comprehensive book ever published regarding the lesser-known facts about the men who have occupied the most important political office in the world. During the last seventeen years, I worked methodically to create this book in order to share my passion for presidential trivia with the public in the most impactful manner possible.

The questions included, for the most part, are those that evoke the unique, unusual, or unknown about each of the presidents, not the commonplace or known. As such, the book contains many obscure or difficult questions that might frustrate some readers. However, one man's pedantry is another man's pedagogy, one man's uselessness another man's utility. So the author exhorts the reader to approach this book with an open mind and, if a question or set of questions leaves him or her uninterested, to simply move on to another one.

It must be stated that questions referring to a person with a specific title, such as "president" or "vice president," allude to that person at any point in his or her life unless otherwise qualified by the word "future," "incumbent," or "former." In many cases, the correct answer depends upon whether or not one of these qualifiers is present and, if so, which one is used.

Having consulted over 900 sources, I believe the information presented herein to be accurate. But as Alexander Pope quipped, "To err is human." Whether through my own fault or that of a faulty source, there might be some inaccuracies in these pages. Your corrections or suggestions, with corroboration, will ensure a more accurate product for presidential posterity.

Irving, Texas
January 1, 2004

Airplanes

1. Which president first flew in an airplane?
2. Which *incumbent* president first flew in an airplane?
3. Which president first flew in a jet airplane?
4. Which president first made an international flight?
5. What was the name of Harry Truman's presidential airplane?
6. What was the name of Dwight Eisenhower's presidential airplane?
7. Which recent president used John Kennedy's air force 707?
8. What was the name of Jimmy Carter's campaign airplane?
9. Which president nicknamed *Air Force One* "The Sacred Cow"?
10. What is the call sign of *any* aircraft that the president uses?
11. Who presided at the dedication of the first hospital airplane?
12. How much did the current *Air Force One* jumbo jets cost?
13. Which president once ordered his pilot to dive-bomb the White House to 500 feet?
14. Which president jumped from an airplane at any time in his life?
15. Which president had a chair able to be raised or lowered installed in *Air Force One*?
16. Which actor portrayed the president in the movie *Air Force One*?
17. Which president was the last one who *never* flew in an airplane during his entire lifetime?
18. Which president held a pilot's license at any time in his life?
19. Which president piloted a jet aircraft?
20. Which president saw an airplane land at the White House, after a fantastic voyage?
21. During which Administration did a plane last land at the White House?
22. Which president first banned flights over the White House?
23. Which president was instrumental in airlifting 14,000 Jews from Ethiopia to Israel?
24. Which president circumnavigated the globe in *Air Force One*?
25. Which *incumbent* president was the only one who piloted any kind of aircraft?
26. Which president made an "arrested landing" on an aircraft carrier?
27. Which president flew in the only aircraft ever designated *Navy One*?

Animals

1. Which president claimed that he had encountered a "killer rabbit" in the outdoors?
2. Which president owned a beer-drinking rabbit?
3. Which president first received animals as gifts from foreign potentates?
4. Which president had kept a coyote, five bears, and a zebra at his home?
5. Which president was given a grizzly bear?
6. Which president rode a moose?
7. Which president shipped a moose to a French naturalist to prove to him it existed?

Airplanes (answers)

1. Theodore Roosevelt (1910), in a Wright biplane, at Kinloch Field, St. Louis, Missouri.
2. Franklin Roosevelt (1943), from Miami to Port of Spain, on the way to Casablanca.
3. Dwight Eisenhower (1959), in a Boeing VC-137A, to Germany, the U.K., and France.
4. Franklin Roosevelt (1943), to attend the Teheran Conference.
5. The *Caroline*
6. The *Columbine III* (1954-1961), named for the state flower of Colorado.
7. George Bush (1989)
8. The *Peanut One* (1976-1977). The pilot's name was James Kenneth "Jimmy" Carter!
9. Harry Truman (1945), a Douglas VC-54C airplane.
10. *Air Force One*, *Army One*, *Marine One*, or *Navy One*, based upon which branch owns it.
11. President and Mrs. Harry Truman
12. $390 million. For security purposes, no person ever has solitary access to the aircraft.
13. Harry Truman, in order to scare his wife and daughter, who were on the roof.
14. George Bush (1944), from the Grumman Avenger *Barbara III*, during World War II.
15. Lyndon Johnson, so that he could raise his eye level above that of his guest or guests.
16. Harrison Ford (1997)
17. Calvin Coolidge (1872-1933)
18. Dwight Eisenhower (1939), issued by the Commonwealth of the Philippines.
19. George W. Bush (1970), a Convair F-102, in the Texas Air National Guard.
20. William Taft (1911), who saw Harry A. Atwood land on the White House lawn.
21. Bill Clinton's (1994), when Frank E. Corder crashed a stolen Cessna into the White House.
22. Franklin Roosevelt (1935), because they were disturbing his sleep.
23. George Bush (1991), in Operation Solomon.
24. Lyndon Johnson (1967), in 110 hours, visiting five countries on three continents.
25. George W. Bush (2003), when he co-piloted a Lockheed Viking S-3B jet aircraft.
26. George W. Bush (2003), aboard the USS *Abraham Lincoln*, in the same aircraft.
27. George W. Bush (2003), in the same aircraft, with John "Skip" Lussier as pilot.

Animals (answers)

1. Jimmy Carter (1979), resulting in mocking tabloid headlines.
2. John Kennedy
3. George Washington
4. Theodore Roosevelt
5. Thomas Jefferson
6. Calvin Coolidge
7. Thomas Jefferson, to Georges Louis Leclerc de Buffon.

8.   For whom was the "Teddy Bear" named?
9.   Which president was the first one who had been an avid fox hunter?
10. Which president received an antelope and a donkey named "Ebenezer"?
11. Which president, as a child, owned a pet pig that he taught to play "hide and seek"?
12. Which president was the first one who had raised sheep, deer, or mules?
13. Which president, a Republican, received an elephant from the president of Sri Lanka?
14. Who first used the elephant as the symbol of the Republican Party?
15. Which presidents had witnessed bullfights?
16. Which president received the first salmon of the year caught in the Penobscot River?
17. Which president received a hippopotamus from the Firestone rubber plantation?
18. Which president thought he was destined to become a famous zoologist?
19. Which president classified a species of animals, sorting bones at the White House?
20. For which president was the largest American elk species named?
21. Which president was allergic to animal fur?
22. Which president helped form the American Bison Society?
23. Which president had spent many mornings in swamps for the Audubon Society?

Appointments

1.   Which president first hired a female private secretary?
2.   Which president appointed Winston Lord, a Pillsbury heir, as ambassador to China?
3.   Which president appointed Thomas Nast to a diplomatic post?
4.   Which president had been appointed as the first ambassador to Colombia?
5.   Which president's director of OMB had been queried by anti-Communist police?
6.   Which president appointed one of the founders of Houston to a diplomatic post?
7.   Which president's national security advisor had dropped out of Stanford University?
8.   Which former Reagan advisor made an unsuccessful suicide attempt?
9.   Which president was the first one whose appointee was rejected by the Senate?
10. Which president appointed author Washington Irving as minister to Spain?
11. Which president appointed Brigham Young as governor of Utah Territory?
12. Which ambassador insisted that the U.S.A. not aid England as Nazis bombed her?
13. Which president appointed the author of *Ben Hur* to a diplomatic post?
14. Which president did Meriwether Lewis serve as private secretary?
15. Which president appointed the only recipient of the four highest U.S. military honors?
16. Which president appointed the first female White House chief of protocol?
17. Which president had been dismissed as head of New York City Customs?
18. Which presidents appointed actresses as delegates to the United Nations?
19. Which two national security advisors taught a course at Harvard?

8. Theodore Roosevelt, for not shooting a bear cub. The original is in the Smithsonian.
9. George Washington
10. Theodore Roosevelt
11. Abraham Lincoln
12. George Washington
13. Ronald Reagan, appropriately since the elephant is the mascot of the Republican Party.
14. Political cartoonist Thomas Nast (1874). Before then, the bull had been the mascot.
15. Ulysses Grant (Mexico) and John Kennedy (France). Grant left when the bull bled.
16. William Taft (1912), beginning a long tradition.
17. Calvin Coolidge (1927), from the plantation in Liberia, named "Billy."
18. Theodore Roosevelt
19. Thomas Jefferson (*Mammuthus jeffersonii* and *Megalonyx jeffersonii*)
20. Theodore Roosevelt (*Cervus Rooseveltii*)
21. John Kennedy
22. Theodore Roosevelt (1905), to save that animal from extinction.
23. George Bush (1947)

Appointments (answers)

1. James Polk (1845-1849). His secretary was Sarah Polk, his wife.
2. Ronald Reagan (1985)
3. Theodore Roosevelt (1902), as U.S. consul in Guayaquil, Ecuador, where he died.
4. William Henry Harrison (1828), only to be recalled a month later.
5. Ronald Reagan's, David Stockman (1968), while attending Michigan State University.
6. Zachary Taylor, who appointed Augustus Allen.
7. Ronald Reagan's, William Clark, who also flunked law school and failed the bar exam.
8. National Security Advisor Robert McFarlane (1987)
9. George Washington (1789), who had chosen Benjamin Fishbourn for a post in Savannah.
10. James Polk (1842)
11. Millard Fillmore (1850)
12. Joseph P. Kennedy (1940), who had been appointed by Franklin Roosevelt.
13. James Garfield (1881), to Constantinople, hoping he would write again about the Bible.
14. Thomas Jefferson (1801), before leaving to explore the Louisiana Territory.
15. Franklin Roosevelt (1941), who appointed "Wild Bill" Donovan as director of the OSS.
16. Gerald Ford (1976), who appointed Shirley Temple Black.
17. Chester Arthur (1878), fired by Rutherford Hayes for rampant corruption.
18. Dwight Eisenhower (Irene Dunn) and Richard Nixon (Shirley Temple Black)
19. McGeorge Bundy and Henry Kissinger, who taught "The United States in World Affairs."

20. Which president appointed the first black chairman of the Civil Rights Commission?

21. Which Reagan appointee admitted having fabricated quotations attributed to Reagan?

22. Which presidential staff was ten times larger than his predecessor's twenty years earlier?

23. Which president's appointee became editor of *U.S. News and World Report*?

24. Which president first appointed congressional liaisons within the White House?

25. Which president regularly had his advisors debate in front of him?

26. Which president's appointee coined the term "supply-side economics"?

27. Which president nominated a livery-stable supervisor as minister to Belgium?

28. Which president first appointed a female ambassador?

29. Which president first appointed a female ambassador to a major country?

30. Which president appointed a female ambassador to the Court of St. James's?

31. Which president appointed the first black U.S. consul?

32. Which journalist was an aide to Woodrow Wilson at the Versailles Peace Conference?

33. Which president appointed Harry Guggenheim as ambassador to Cuba?

34. Which president appointed William Waldorf Astoria as ambassador to Italy?

35. Which presidential appointee first stole $1 million from the federal government?

36. Which president appointed the first ambassador to China?

37. What was the nickname of Gerald Ford's government re-organization?

38. Which presidential appointee had been #1 in his class and commandant of cadets?

39. Which president's physical-fitness program did the father of Princess Grace head?

40. Which president ordered his personnel chief to count Jews in a government agency?

41. Which president first appointed J. Edgar Hoover as director of what became the FBI?

42. Which president appointed the grandfather of Rush Limbaugh to a diplomatic post?

43. Which president appointed the son of Francis Scott Key as a U.S. attorney?

44. Which president fired every single U.S. attorney in the country, without precedent?

45. Which president appointed the first female to the U.S. Foreign Service?

46. Which president first received congressional appropriation for a presidential secretary?

47. Which president appointed the highest percentage of cronies to ambassadorships?

48. Which president first appointed a Jew to a federal post?

49. Which president first appointed a U.S. consul to Palestine?

50. Which president was offered a ministerial cabinet post in the British government?

51. Which president said that each appointment created "nine enemies and one ingrate"?

Assassinations

1. Which items did Abraham Lincoln carry "on him" the night of his assassination?

2. Who was handcuffed to Lee Harvey Oswald when Jack Ruby shot Oswald?

3. Who made the famous "home video" of Kennedy's assassination?

20. Ronald Reagan (1981), who appointed Clarence Pendleton, Jr.
21. Larry Speakes, White House spokesman.
22. Franklin Roosevelt's
23. Ronald Reagan's director of communications, David Gergen (1989).
24. Dwight Eisenhower, in order to interact with that branch of government.
25. Ronald Reagan, placing him in "chairman of the board" status.
26. Richard Nixon's chairman of the Council of Economic Advisers, Dr. Herbert Stein (1976).
27. Ulysses Grant (1869), who chose Joseph Russell Jones.
28. Harry Truman (1949), who appointed Eugenie Anderson as ambassador to Denmark.
29. Dwight Eisenhower (1953), who appointed Clare Boothe Luce as ambassador to Italy.
30. Gerald Ford (1976), who appointed Anne Armstrong.
31. Andrew Johnson (1866), who appointed John Seys as U.S. consul to Liberia.
32. Walter Lippmann (1919)
33. Herbert Hoover (1929)
34. Chester Arthur (1882)
35. New York Port Collector Samuel Swartwant, appointed by Martin Van Buren (1838).
36. John Tyler (1844), who appointed Caleb Cushing.
37. The "Halloween Massacre" (1975), hiding Nelson Rockefeller's decision not to run.
38. John Poindexter (1958), appointed by Ronald Reagan as national security advisor.
39. Franklin Roosevelt's. His name was Jack Kelly.
40. Richard Nixon (1971), in the Bureau of Labor Statistics, for supposedly undermining him.
41. Calvin Coolidge (1924)
42. Dwight Eisenhower, who appointed Rush H. Limbaugh as ambassador to India.
43. James Buchanan (1853), who appointed Philip Barton Key to the District of Columbia.
44. Bill Clinton (1993), allegedly to stop an investigation into him by a single U.S. attorney.
45. Warren Harding (1922), who appointed Louise Curtis as legation secretary in Bern.
46. James Buchanan (1857), who received $2,500 in the federal budget.
47. Ronald Reagan (37%), followed by John Kennedy (36%) and Bill Clinton (33%).
48. Thomas Jefferson (1801), appointing Reuben Etting as U.S. marshal for Maryland.
49. John Tyler (1844), who appointed Warder Cresson.
50. Herbert Hoover (1919), for his humanitarian efforts to rebuild Europe after World War I.
51. William Taft

Assassinations (answers)

1. A pair of spectacles, a handkerchief, a pocketknife, an eyeglass cleaner, and a wallet.
2. Dallas Police Detective Jim Leavelle. Ruby's real name was Jack Leon Rubinstein.
3. Abraham Zapruder, a dress manufacturer, using a Bell & Howell video camera.

4. Did Abraham Lincoln eat supper on the night of his assassination?
5. Which president was shot at a public hand-shaking reception?
6. Besides Lincoln, which other officials were targeted for assassination at the same time?
7. If Andrew Johnson had been assassinated too, who would have become president?
8. Who was present at or near the assassination of three U.S. presidents?
9. Which president was the target of the first assassination attempt?
10. Which president was the first one assassinated?
11. Where was James Garfield going when he was shot?
12. Since which assassination have the Secret Service protected every U.S. president?
13. Which president was assassinated on Good Friday?
14. Where was Abraham Lincoln's bodyguard when Lincoln was assassinated?
15. What was James Garfield's only official act during his brief convalescence?
16. For which president's recovery did the navy create the world's first air conditioner?
17. Which famous inventor visited James Garfield's bedside?
18. Whom did John Kennedy call to congratulate on his ninety-fifth birthday?
19. How long after John Kennedy's assassination was Lyndon Johnson sworn in?
20. Which president-elect donned a disguise in order to foil an assassination attempt?
21. In what was Abraham Lincoln sitting when he was assassinated?
22. Which one of James Garfield's doctors had the surname of a future vice president?
23. Where was Theodore Roosevelt when he heard of William McKinley's assassination?
24. Which president scrawled "Am I dead?" to an aide after being shot?
25. After which assassination did Congress reform the federal civil service?
26. Which president did Puerto Rican nationalists from New York City try to assassinate?
27. Whom did Abraham Lincoln invite to join him and Mrs. Lincoln at Ford's Theater?
28. Who were Abraham Lincoln's theater guests instead that evening?
29. Which president received 860 death threats during his first year in office alone?
30. Where is the speech that saved Theodore Roosevelt's life?
31. How fast was John Kennedy's presidential limousine traveling when he was shot?
32. Which presidents signed executive orders prohibiting political assassination?
33. Which president's corpse was exhumed recently to test an assassination theory?
34. Did Abraham Lincoln arrive on time to the play on the night of his assassination?
35. At what time was it announced that John Kennedy had died?
36. Which president was saved by a "prominent figure in the gay community"?
37. To which group had Ronald Reagan just finished speaking when he was shot?
38. Which line was said as Booth shot Abraham Lincoln, a line chosen for loud applause?
39. Which three figures in the Kennedy assassination all died at Dallas's Parkland Hospital?
40. Which president, when shot, pleaded that his assassin be saved?
41. Which president kept an envelope entitled "Assassinations" in his desk drawer?

4. No

5. William McKinley (1901), in Buffalo, New York.

6. Vice President Andrew Johnson and Secretary of State William Seward

7. Senator Lafayette S. Foster (R-CT), the president pro tempore of the Senate.

8. Abraham Lincoln's son, Robert Todd Lincoln (1843-1926).

9. Andrew Jackson (1835), by Richard Lawrence.

10. Abraham Lincoln (1865)

11. To his twenty-fifth anniversary college reunion (1881)

12. William McKinley's (1901), although Abraham Lincoln had created it much earlier (1865).

13. Abraham Lincoln (1865)

14. John F. Parker was next door to Ford's Theater at Taltavull's bar, having a drink.

15. Signing an extradition paper sent by the State Department (1881)

16. James Garfield's (1881). The "air conditioner" sent air past towels wet with iced water.

17. Alexander Graham Bell tried to find the bullet, using the world's first metal detector.

18. Former Vice President John Nance Garner, just hours before Kennedy was shot.

19. Ninety-nine minutes

20. Abraham Lincoln (1865), on the way to his inauguration from Baltimore, Maryland.

21. A rocking chair

22. Dr. D. Hayes Agnew

23. On Isle La Motte in Lake Champlain, with the Vermont Fish and Game League.

24. Ronald Reagan (1981), to Michael Deaver.

25. James Garfield's (1881), because his assassin was a disgruntled civil-service applicant.

26. Harry Truman (1950). Instead, they killed Leslie Coffelt, Truman's guard.

27. General and Mrs. Ulysses Grant, who declined.

28. Major Henry R. Rathbone and Miss Harris, in Box 7.

29. John Kennedy (1961), more than two per day!

30. The Smithsonian Institution. The folded speech in his pocket blocked a bullet.

31. Twenty-five miles per hour

32. Gerald Ford (1976), Jimmy Carter (1978), and Ronald Reagan (1982)

33. Zachary Taylor's (1991), on the theory that pro-slavery Southerners had killed him.

34. No

35. Approximately 1:00 P.M. Central Standard Time (CST)

36. Gerald Ford (1975), by Oliver Sipple, from assassination by Sara Jane Moore.

37. The Construction Trades Conference, in Washington, DC (1981)

38. "I know enough to burn you inside out, you sockdologizing old mantrap!"

39. John Kennedy, Lee Harvey Oswald, and Jack Ruby

40. William McKinley (1901), saying, "Let no one hurt him."

41. Abraham Lincoln, obsessively keeping written death threats made to him.

42. Which president-*elect* was the only one against whom an attempt was made?
43. Which *former* president was the only one against whom an attempt was made?
44. Which army general tended to two presidential assassination victims?
45. Which president was present at his predecessor's assassination?
46. How long of his life sentence did Dr. Samuel Mudd serve?
47. Which three persons were wounded by John Hinckley, Jr.'s assassination attempt?
48. Where was Abraham Lincoln taken after being shot in Ford's Theater?
49. Which president told his wife, "Sorry, honey, I forgot to duck," after an attempt on his life?
50. Why did Abraham Lincoln not want to see *Our American Cousin*?

Assassins

1. Who was the doctor jailed for setting the leg of Lincoln's assassin?
2. Where was Lee Harvey Oswald murdered?
3. When did Abraham Lincoln last see John Wilkes Booth before the day of his death?
4. Who shot James Garfield?
5. Who was the anarchist who shot William McKinley?
6. Who shot Lincoln's assassin, John Wilkes Booth, during Booth's escape attempt?
7. Which presidential assassin willingly paid extra money for his murder weapon?
8. Which famous Civil-War era figure's hanging did John Wilkes Booth witness?
9. Which presidential assassin said his act was necessary to unite Republicans?
10. Which would-be presidential assassin said William McKinley ordered him to do it?
11. Which presidential assassin said God made him do it?
12. Which Latin phrase did John Wilkes Booth shout after shooting Abraham Lincoln?
13. What were John Wilkes Booth's last words?
14. Which presidential assassin had worked hard in his victim's presidential campaign?
15. Who was the only foreign leader's child arrested for threatening to kill a U.S. president?
16. Which assassin, while in jail pending trial, was the target of an attempted murder?
17. Which would-be assassin plotted to kill the Italian king and three U.S. presidents?
18. Which assassin spent time in the Oneida Community, a bizarre spiritual commune?
19. Who was the first woman executed by the federal government?
20. Which would-be assassin misfired twice, the odds of which are calculated at 125,000-1?
21. Where was assassin Lee Harvey Oswald found after he had shot John Kennedy?
22. What was the name of John Wilkes Booth's famous brother, who was also an actor?
23. Why did James Garfield's assassin shoot him?
24. Which president was the first one who a woman attempted to assassinate?
25. Which assassin had been a United States Marine?
26. What did James Garfield's assassin shout after shooting his target?

42. Franklin Roosevelt (1933), by Giuseppe Zangara, in Miami, Florida.
43. Theodore Roosevelt (1912), by John Nepomuk Schrank, in Milwaukee, Wisconsin.
44. General Joseph K. Barnes, aiding Abraham Lincoln (1865) and James Garfield (1881).
45. Lyndon Johnson (1963), following closely behind John Kennedy in Dallas, Texas.
46. Three years, seven months, and twelve days
47. James Brady, Secret Service Agent Timothy McCarthy, and Officer Thomas Delahanty
48. To a boarding house at 435 Tenth Street, NW, Washington, DC.
49. Ronald Reagan (1981), paraphrasing Jack Dempsey after being defeated by Gene Tunney.
50. He had seen the play once before.

Assassins (answers)

1. Dr. Samuel Mudd, as in "His name is Mudd."
2. In the basement of the Dallas Police Department in Dallas, Texas.
3. On November 9, 1863, in Ford's Theater, to watch him perform in *The Marble Heart!*
4. Charles Guiteau
5. Leon Czolgosz, a Polish ironworker.
6. Cavalryman Boston Corbett, who claimed that he took his order from God.
7. Charles Guiteau (1881), because he thought it would become a museum piece.
8. Abolitionist John Brown's execution (1859) for murdering five pro-slavery men in Kansas
9. Charles Guiteau
10. John Nepomuk Schrank, allegedly in a dream.
11. Charles Guiteau
12. "*Sic semper tyrannis*," the state motto of Virginia, which means "Thus ever to tyrants."
13. "Useless! Useless!"
14. Charles Guiteau
15. Panamanian President Demetrio B. Lakas's son Otto, who threatened George Bush.
16. Charles Guiteau, by an army guard later acquitted on the grounds of insanity.
17. Giuseppe Zangara targeted Franklin Roosevelt, Calvin Coolidge, and Herbert Hoover.
18. Charles Guiteau
19. Mary Surratt (1865), for harboring men who had plotted to kill Abraham Lincoln et al.
20. Richard Lawrence (1835)
21. Inside the Texas Theatre in Dallas, Texas.
22. Edwin Thomas Booth
23. Because Garfield had denied him U.S. consulships in Vienna, Austria, and Paris, France.
24. Gerald Ford (1975), shot at by Lynette Alice "Squeaky" Fromme, in Sacramento.
25. Lee Harvey Oswald
26. "I am a Stalwart, and [Vice President Chester] Arthur is president now!"

27. Which would-be presidential assassin was denied his right to vote?
28. Which presidential assassin's partial skeleton is displayed in Walter Reed Hospital?
29. Which would-be presidential assassin came from a wealthy family in Colorado?
30. With what name did Leon Czolgosz register at a hotel before committing his crime?
31. Who were given life sentences for assassination attempts?
32. Which assassin bought his weapon from a Sears, Roebuck and Co. catalog?
33. Was Jack Ruby innocent of killing Lee Harvey Oswald at the time of Ruby's death?

Astrology

1. Which presidents were born under the sign Capricorn?
2. Which presidents were born under the sign Aquarius?
3. Which presidents were born under the sign Pisces?
4. Which presidents were born under the sign Aries?
5. Which presidents were born under the sign Taurus?
6. Which president was born under the sign Gemini?
7. Which presidents were born under the sign Cancer?
8. Which presidents were born under the sign Leo?
9. Which presidents were born under the sign Virgo?
10. Which presidents were born under the sign Libra?
11. Which presidents were born under the sign Scorpio?
12. Which presidents were born under the sign Sagittarius?
13. Which president frequently consulted the zodiac during stressful political situations?

Autobiographies

1. Which president first wrote his autobiography?
2. Which president died only four days after completing his autobiography?
3. Which famous author published Ulysses Grant's two-volume autobiography?
4. Which future president wrote an autobiography entitled *Looking Forward*?
5. Which book did Harry Truman say was the best one he had read in the White House?
6. Which president wrote an autobiography entitled *Why Not the Best?*
7. Which president failed to mention his own wife *even once* in his autobiography?

Automobiles

1. Which president first rode in an automobile?
2. Which *incumbent* president first owned an automobile?
3. Which president first rode in a motorcade?

27. John Hinckley, Jr., who tried to register to vote in the District of Columbia.
28. John Wilkes Booth's
29. John Hinckley, Jr.
30. "John Doe"
31. Lynette "Squeaky" Fromme and John Hinckley, Jr.
32. Lee Harvey Oswald
33. Yes, the trial had not begun by the time of his death.

Astrology (answers)
1. Millard Fillmore, Andrew Johnson, Woodrow Wilson, and Richard Nixon
2. W. H. Harrison, Abraham Lincoln, William McKinley, Franklin Roosevelt, and Ronald Reagan
3. George Washington, James Madison, Andrew Jackson, and Grover Cleveland
4. Thomas Jefferson and John Tyler
5. James Monroe, James Buchanan, Ulysses Grant, and Harry Truman
6. John Kennedy
7. John Quincy Adams, Calvin Coolidge, Gerald Ford, and George W. Bush
8. Benjamin Harrison, Herbert Hoover, and Bill Clinton
9. William Taft and Lyndon Johnson
10. Rutherford Hayes, Chester Arthur, Dwight Eisenhower, and Jimmy Carter
11. John Adams, James Polk, James Garfield, Theodore Roosevelt, and Warren Harding
12. Martin Van Buren, Zachary Taylor, and Franklin Pierce
13. Andrew Johnson, especially during his intense trial in the Senate.

Autobiographies (answers)
1. John Adams (1807)
2. Ulysses Grant (1902), whose widow earned $440,000 in royalties.
3. Mark Twain (1885), who re-wrote and polished the manuscript.
4. George Bush (1987), in anticipation of his campaign for president in 1988.
5. *Tallulah* (1952), by Tallulah Bankhead, about her life on stage, radio, and television.
6. Jimmy Carter (1975), who had been asked that question by Admiral Hyman Rickover.
7. Martin Van Buren (1920). The book was published decades after his death.

Automobiles (answers)
1. William McKinley (1899), in an F. O. Stanley steam carriage.
2. William Taft (1909)
3. William Taft (1909), followed by Secret Service agents on motorcycles.

4. Which president wanted to arrest anybody traveling more than twenty miles per hour?
5. Which president first drove an automobile?
6. Which president ordered that White House cars be designed for top hats?
7. Which president ordered the creation of "bubbletop" presidential limousines?
8. Which president first received congressional appropriation for motor vehicles?
9. Which president made a lengthy automobile trip to the Central Plains?
10. What make and model was the limousine in which John Kennedy was assassinated?
11. Which other presidents used John Kennedy's Lincoln Continental?
12. Which president first joined the American Automobile Association?
13. Which president owned three cars with right-side steering?
14. Which president last utilized automobiles with right-side steering?
15. Which president was the first one who had received a driver license?
16. Which president's automobile first featured Secret Service license plates?
17. Which president's automobile first featured bulletproof tires and armor?
18. Which president first drove an electric automobile?
19. Which president used an electric car as a newlywed?
20. Which departing president bought his presidential limousine for private use?
21. Which president had driven a Ford Model "T" while in high school?
22. Which president ordered that all federal-government cars be of U.S. manufacture?
23. Which president drove a Chrysler sedan during his diplomatic appointment overseas?
24. Which president converted the White House stables into a four-car garage?
25. Which *incumbent* president attended an Indianapolis 500 race?
26. Which president wanted to race in the Indianapolis 500 himself?
27. Which president was a member of the Stock Car Racing Association?
28. Who said, "Nothing has spread socialistic feeling more than the automobile"?
29. Which president said his car was the only thing his wife "did not have a desire to run"?

Baseball

1. Which president had played Little League baseball in his youth?
2. Which president tossed the first pitch at a game of a Little League World Series?
3. Which president had played in the first College World Series?
4. Which *incumbent* president attended a game of the College World Series?
5. Which position had William Taft played on his college baseball team?
6. Which position had Dwight Eisenhower played on his college baseball team?
7. For which major-league baseball team did Ronald Reagan broadcast games?
8. Which position had George Bush played on his college baseball team?
9. Which president first watched a baseball game?

4. Woodrow Wilson, who considered them "reckless speeders."
5. Warren Harding (1921)
6. Harry Truman
7. Dwight Eisenhower (1954), which cars he personally designed.
8. William Taft (1909)
9. Theodore Roosevelt (1910), to the Badlands of South Dakota.
10. A blue Lincoln Continental (1963)
11. Lyndon Johnson, Richard Nixon, Gerald Ford, and Jimmy Carter
12. Woodrow Wilson (1919)
13. William Taft, who owned two Pierce Arrows and one white steamer.
14. Woodrow Wilson (1919)
15. William Taft, in Connecticut. Warren Harding was the first licensed driver elected president.
16. Herbert Hoover's Pierce Arrow, whose plates read "U.S.S.S."
17. Franklin Roosevelt's 1937 Lincoln (1942), after Pearl Harbor.
18. William Taft
19. Dwight Eisenhower (1916)
20. Woodrow Wilson (1919), who bought his Pierce Arrow for $3,000.
21. Gerald Ford (1930)
22. Lyndon Johnson
23. George Bush (1974), as ambassador to the People's Republic of China.
24. William Taft (1909)
25. Gerald Ford (1979). George Bush (2003) and Bill Clinton (2003) also attended one.
26. George Bush, "as a macho man going around the bank at 130 miles an hour."
27. Jimmy Carter
28. Woodrow Wilson (1906), when only the rich could afford an automobile.
29. Warren Harding

Baseball (answers)

1. George W. Bush (1954), as a catcher, in Midland, Texas.
2. George W. Bush (2001), in Williamsport, Pennsylvania.
3. George Bush (1947), as captain of the Yale team that lost to California, 2-0.
4. George W. Bush (2003), who watched Stanford defeating Tulane, in Omaha, Nebraska.
5. Second base
6. Outfielder
7. The Chicago Cubs (1933)
8. First base
9. Andrew Johnson (1865), at the "White Lot," Washington, DC.

10. Which president first watched a major-league baseball game?

11. Which president first watched a major-league baseball game at night?

12. Which president first watched a major-league baseball game outside Washington, DC?

13. Which *incumbent* president first watched a major-league doubleheader and tripleheader?

14. Which *incumbent* president probably watched the most major-league baseball games?

15. Which *incumbent* president first watched a major-league baseball game in his hometown?

16. Which *incumbent* president first watched a major-league baseball game from the dugout?

17. Which *incumbent* president first watched a major-league baseball game with his veep?

18. Which president turned on the lights at the first major-league night baseball game?

19. Which president first tossed the first pitch on baseball's Opening Day?

20. Which president is the only one since then *not* to toss the first pitch on Opening Day?

21. Which president first tossed the first pitch on Opening Day outside of Washington, DC?

22. Which president first tossed the first pitch on Opening Day in a foreign country?

23. Which president first tossed two opening pitches, left-handed and right-handed?

24. Who tossed the first pitch at the game when Babe Ruth made his "called-shot" home run?

25. Which *incumbent* president first attended baseball's All-Star Game?

26. Which *incumbent* president first tossed the first pitch at an All-Star Game?

27. Which *incumbent* president first attended baseball's All-Star Game at night?

28. Which *incumbent* president first tossed the first pitch at a night All-Star Game?

29. Which presidents were the first and last ones who attended a World Series?

30. Which presidents were the first and last ones who tossed the first pitch at a World Series?

31. Which president first tossed the first pitch at Game One of a World Series?

32. Which president especially enjoyed baseball's Opening Day?

33. Which foreign leader attended a baseball game on Opening Day with a president?

34. Which president inadvertently invented the "seventh-inning stretch"?

35. Which president had played sandlot baseball with his future wife in their youth?

36. Which president had organized a racially-integrated softball tournament?

37. What was the middle name of Jackie Robinson, the first black major-leaguer?

38. Which president threw a baseball left-handed but batted right-handed?

39. Which president made Benjamin Harrison pay a fare after entering a baseball park?

40. Which president's boyhood baseball hero was New York Yankee Lou Gehrig?

41. Which *incumbent* president met Babe Ruth?

42. Which athlete probably first earned more money than the president?

43. Which president first dedicated a baseball stadium?

44. Which president first attended a major-league exhibition baseball game?

45. Which president was offered a position in major-league baseball?

46. Which president had worn a major-league uniform?

47. Which president was considered "for inclusion on the Hall of Fame veterans' ballot"?

10. Benjamin Harrison (1892), at Swampoodle Grounds in Washington, DC.
11. Harry Truman (1948), at Griffith Stadium in Washington, DC.
12. William Taft (1909), at Forbes Field in Pittsburgh, Pennsylvania.
13. Woodrow Wilson (1913), at Griffith Stadium in Washington, DC.
14. William Taft (14)
15. William Taft (1912), at Redland Field in Cincinnati, Ohio.
16. Ronald Reagan (1984), at Memorial Stadium in Baltimore, Maryland.
17. Bill Clinton (1995), at Camden Yards in Baltimore, Maryland, with Al Gore.
18. Franklin Roosevelt (1935), at Crosley Field in Cincinnati, Ohio, by remote control.
19. William Taft (1910), at Griffith Stadium in Washington, DC.
20. Jimmy Carter (1977-1980)
21. Richard Nixon (1973), at Anaheim Stadium in Anaheim, California.
22. George Bush (1990), at the SkyDome in Toronto, Ontario, Canada.
23. Harry Truman (1950), at Griffith Stadium in Washington, DC.
24. Franklin Roosevelt (1932), at Wrigley Field in Chicago, Illinois.
25. Franklin Roosevelt (1937), at Griffith Stadium in Washington, DC.
26. Franklin Roosevelt (1937), at that same game.
27. Richard Nixon (1970), at Memorial Stadium in Baltimore, Maryland.
28. Richard Nixon (1970), at that same game.
29. Woodrow Wilson (1915) and George W. Bush (2001), respectively.
30. Woodrow Wilson (1915) and George W. Bush (2001), respectively. Bush's was a strike.
31. Calvin Coolidge (1924), at Griffith Stadium in Washington, DC.
32. Harry Truman
33. Hosni Mubarak (1989), with George Bush, at Camden Yards in Baltimore, Maryland.
34. William Taft (1910), when he stood up at Griffith Stadium in Washington, DC.
35. Harry Truman
36. George Bush (1966), who created the "George Bush All Stars" when it was impolitic.
37. Roosevelt
38. George Bush
39. Herbert Hoover, after Harrison had neglected to buy a ticket at Stanford's ballpark.
40. George Bush's
41. Calvin Coolidge (1924). George Bush (1948) also met him at the College World Series.
42. Babe Ruth (1930), who earned $80,000, more than President Herbert Hoover.
43. Lyndon Johnson (1965), who dedicated the Astrodome, in Houston, Texas.
44. Lyndon Johnson (1965), at that same game.
45. Richard Nixon (1965), with the Major League Baseball Players Association.
46. Ronald Reagan (1952), in *The Winning Team*, portraying Grover Cleveland Alexander.
47. George W. Bush (2003)

48. Which president had a baseball field built on the White House lawn?
49. Which president said, "I never leave a game before the last pitch"?
50. Which president had been a part owner of a professional baseball team?
51. Which president first welcomed an organized baseball team to the White House?
52. Which president first welcomed a professional baseball team to the White House?
53. Which president first welcomed a major-league baseball team to the White House?

Bibles

1. Which president produced a version of the Bible in his spare time?
2. Which book other than the Bible was the only one Millard Fillmore owned?
3. Which president had a "clipped Bible"?
4. Where does George Washington's famous Bible permanently reside?
5. Which president had compiled a New Testament?
6. Which president had been the first leader of the American Bible Society?

Biographies

1. Which temperance activist wrote a biography of Abraham Lincoln?
2. About which president did author Washington Irving write a biography?
3. Which author wrote a "campaign biography" for Franklin Pierce?
4. Which author wrote a campaign biography for Abraham Lincoln?
5. Which author wrote campaign biographies for two presidents?
6. About which president have more biographies been published than any other?
7. Which president had written a biography of Senator Thomas Hart Benton (R-MO)?
8. Which president had written a biography of George Washington?
9. Which president had written a biography of Oliver Cromwell?
10. Which president is the only one about whom a biography has *not* been written?

Birds

1. Which president had a talking parrot that could whistle "Yankee Doodle"?
2. Which president kept a pet mockingbird named "Bill" in his study?
3. Which animal was the mascot of the Democratic Party before the donkey?
4. What is "the Coolidge effect" as it relates to animals?
5. Which president supposedly taught his parrot how to differentiate men from women?
6. Which president had collected birds when he was eleven years old?
7. Which president owned two singing Harz Mountain canaries named "Nip" and "Tuck"?
8. Which president kept a coop of turkeys at the White House?

48. Abraham Lincoln (1861), called the "White Lot," on the Ellipse in Washington, DC.
49. Richard Nixon, because in baseball, as in politics, "you never know what will happen."
50. George W. Bush (1989-1994), who held a 1.8% stake in the Texas Rangers.
51. Andrew Johnson (1865), a "delegation of the National Base Ball Club."
52. Ulysses Grant (1869), the Cincinnati Red Stockings.
53. Chester Arthur (1883), the Cleveland Forest Citys.

Bibles (answers)

1. Thomas Jefferson (1819-1820), which Bible became known as the "Jefferson Bible."
2. A dictionary
3. Thomas Jefferson, purging all passages that did not reflect Christ's ethical teachings.
4. In a Masonic lodge in New York City, and used occasionally for presidential inaugurations.
5. Thomas Jefferson
6. John Adams (1816)

Biographies (answers)

1. Ida Tarbell (1895), founder of the American Temperance Society.
2. George Washington (1855-1859)
3. Nathaniel Hawthorne, whom Pierce appointed U.S. consul in Liverpool (1853).
4. William Dean Howells, whom Lincoln appointed U.S. consul in Venice (1861).
5. General Lew Wallace, for Rutherford Hayes (1876) and Benjamin Harrison (1888).
6. Abraham Lincoln, about whom at least sixty biographies have been written.
7. Theodore Roosevelt (1887)
8. Woodrow Wilson (1896)
9. Theodore Roosevelt (1900)
10. Chester Arthur

Birds (answers)

1. William McKinley
2. Thomas Jefferson. The bird perched on one's shoulder *à la* Long John Silver.
3. The rooster
4. The re-arousal of a male animal by a new female
5. William McKinley
6. Franklin Roosevelt
7. Calvin Coolidge
8. Warren Harding

9.   Which president had collected stuffed birds while an undergraduate student?
10. Which president owned a white canary named "Snowflake"?
11. Which president owned several parrots, an eagle, and a barn owl?
12. Which president was given a goose named "Enoch"?
13. Which president was the first one who had raised turkeys and geese?
14. Which president had a macaw named "Eli Yale"?
15. Which president taught his pet mockingbird to eat food from his lips?
16. Which president's bird attended his funeral?
17. Which president had arranged a military funeral for a bird?

Birth Geography

1.   Which president was born farthest north?
2.   Which president was born farthest south?
3.   Which president was born farthest east?
4.   Which president was born farthest west?
5.   Which president was the first one born west of the Allegheny Mountains?
6.   Which president was the first one born west of the Mississippi River?
7.   Which president was the first one born west of the Rocky Mountains?
8.   Which president was the first one born in the U.S.A.?
9.   Which president was the last one born a British subject?
10. Which president was the first one born outside the original thirteen colonies?
11. Which president and his vice president were born closest geographically?
12. Which president and his major-party opponent were born closest geographically?
13. In which region of the country have the plurality of presidents been born?

Birth States

1.   Which president had been born in Arkansas?
2.   Which president had been born in Connecticut?
3.   Which president had been born in Illinois?
4.   Which president had been born in Kentucky?
5.   Which president had been born in Massachusetts?
6.   Which president had been born in Missouri?
7.   Which president had been born in New Hampshire?
8.   Which president had been born in New Jersey?
9.   Which president had been born in New York?
10. Which president had been born in North Carolina?
11. Which president had been born in Ohio?

9.   Theodore Roosevelt, at Harvard University.
10. Calvin Coolidge
11. Theodore Roosevelt
12. Calvin Coolidge
13. George Washington
14. Theodore Roosevelt. Ironically, he was a graduate of Harvard University, Yale's archrival.
15. Thomas Jefferson
16. Andrew Jackson's (1845)
17. Ulysses Grant (1848), to impress his future wife, Julia Dent.

Birth Geography (answers)

1.   Chester Arthur (1830), in Fairfield, Vermont.
2.   Lyndon Johnson (1908), near Stonewall, Texas.
3.   John Quincy Adams (1767), in Braintree, Massachusetts, feet farther east than his father.
4.   Richard Nixon (1913), in Yorba Linda, California.
5.   Andrew Jackson (1767), near Waxhaw, South Carolina.
6.   Herbert Hoover (1874), in West Branch, Iowa.
7.   Richard Nixon (1913), in Yorba Linda, California.
8.   Martin Van Buren (1782), in Kinderhook, New York.
9.   William Henry Harrison (1773), in Charles City County, Virginia.
10. Abraham Lincoln (1809), in Hardin County, Kentucky.
11. William Henry Harrison (1773) and John Tyler (1790), twelve miles apart in Virginia.
12. George Bush (1924) and Michael Dukakis (1933), 7.5 miles apart in Massachusetts.
13. The South

Birth States (answers)

1.   Bill Clinton (1946), in Hope, Arkansas.
2.   George W. Bush (1946), in New Haven, Connecticut.
3.   Ronald Reagan (1911), in Tampico, Illinois.
4.   Abraham Lincoln (1809), in Hardin County, Kentucky.
5.   John Adams (1735), in Braintree, Massachusetts.
6.   Harry Truman (1884), in Lamar, Missouri.
7.   Franklin Pierce (1804), in Hillsboro, New Hampshire.
8.   Grover Cleveland (1837), in Caldwell, New Jersey.
9.   Martin Van Buren (1782), in Kinderhook, New York.
10. James Polk (1795), in Mecklenburg County, North Carolina.
11. Ulysses Grant (1822), in Point Pleasant, Ohio.

12. Which president had been born in Pennsylvania?
13. Which president had been born in Texas?
14. Which president had been born in Vermont?
15. In which state had the most presidents been born?
16. Which president was the first one who had *not* been born in Virginia or Massachusetts?
17. Which three consecutive presidents had been born in Virginia?
18. Which three consecutive presidents had been born in Ohio?
19. In which state besides Ohio and the first thirteen states have most presidents been born?
20. Which president's birthplace was claimed by two different states?
21. Which state is the most populous one without a native-born U.S. president?
22. In which of the original thirteen states has *no* U.S. president been born?

Birth Towns
1. Which president was born in Staunton, Virginia, the site of Staunton Military Academy?
2. Which two presidents were the only ones born in big cities?
3. At what address in Lamar, Missouri, was Harry Truman born?
4. Which president was born a few doors down from where his father had been born?
5. Which president did not know where he was born until he was elected president?
6. Which president was born in the same town as actress Ginger Rogers?

Birthplaces
1. Which president was born in a rented house near some railroad tracks?
2. Which presidents were the first and last ones born in a log cabin?
3. Which president told a foreign leader that he had been "born in a manger"?
4. Which president was the first one born in a hospital?
5. Which president's birthplace burned to the ground?
6. Which president's birthplace includes a Greek Revival building?
7. Which president's birthplace includes a steeplechase course?
8. Which president's birthplace was restored by the United Auto Workers union?
9. Which president's birthplace is now located on the campus of Mercersburg Academy?

Births
1. In which month were no presidents born?
2. In which month were the most presidents born?
3. Which president had no full siblings?
4. Which presidents were born earliest and latest in the eighteenth century?

12. James Buchanan (1791), near Mercersburg, Pennsylvania.
13. Dwight Eisenhower (1890), in Denison, Texas.
14. Chester Arthur (1830), in Fairfield, Vermont.
15. Virginia, giving that state the unofficial nickname "Mother of the Presidents."
16. Andrew Jackson (1767), in Waxhaw, South Carolina.
17. Thomas Jefferson (1743), James Madison (1751), and James Monroe (1758)
18. Ulysses Grant (1822), Rutherford Hayes (1822), and James Garfield (1831)
19. Texas, where Dwight Eisenhower (1890) and Lyndon Johnson (1908) were born.
20. Andrew Jackson's (1767), claimed by both North Carolina and South Carolina.
21. Florida
22. Delaware, Maryland, and Rhode Island

Birth Towns (answers)
1. Woodrow Wilson (1856)
2. William Taft (Cincinnati, Ohio) and Theodore Roosevelt (New York, New York)
3. 1009 Truman Place, although at the time of his birth (1884) there was no street name.
4. John Quincy Adams (1767)
5. Dwight Eisenhower (1890), who thought he had been born in Tyler, Texas.
6. Harry Truman (1884), born in Lamar, Missouri.

Birthplaces (answers)
1. Dwight Eisenhower (1890), in Denison, Texas.
2. Andrew Jackson (1767) and James Garfield (1831), respectively.
3. Lyndon Johnson, after having been asked if he had been born in a log cabin.
4. Jimmy Carter (1924), in Plains, Georgia.
5. Thomas Jefferson's
6. Woodrow Wilson's
7. James Madison's
8. Harry Truman's
9. James Buchanan's

Births (answers)
1. None
2. October (6)
3. Bill Clinton, who had a half-brother, Roger Clinton. No president has been an only child.
4. George Washington (1732) and Millard Fillmore (1800), respectively.

5. Which presidents were born earliest and latest in the nineteenth century?
6. Which presidents were born earliest and latest in the twentieth century?
7. In which years were the most presidents born?
8. Which presidents were born British subjects?
9. What is the most common first name for presidents?
10. Which president's birthday was a legal holiday in every state of the Union?
11. Which president first changed his name?
12. Which president was the first one who had been the eldest child in his family?
13. Which president had been a youngest child?
14. Which president had been born on a national holiday?
15. Which president's birthday is a holiday in the U.S. Virgin Islands but not in the U.S.A.?
16. Which presidents were born posthumously (after their fathers' deaths)?
17. Which president was the first one born after the American Revolution had ended?
18. Which president was the first one born after the Civil War had ended?
19. Which president was the first one born after World War II had ended?
20. Which two presidents were the only two born on the same day of the year?
21. Which president greeted visitors at the White House on his sixty-sixth birthday?
22. Where did George Washington spend his last birthday?
23. Which president did not have a name for three months after his birth?
24. What happened on Harry Truman's sixty-first birthday?
25. Which president's birthday was voted a holiday by his hometown's city council?
26. For which president's birthday did the Liberty Bell peal for the last time?
27. Which president first turned seventy years old in the White House?
28. When is Presidents' Day, which combines Washington's and Lincoln's birthdays?
29. Which president was named for the doctor who delivered him at birth?
30. Which president shared a birthday with English naturalist Charles Darwin?
31. Which president do some historians claim was born on a ship?
32. Which president once thought that he was an illegitimate child?
33. Which president was born at the stroke of midnight?

Boats

1. What were the names of the two sailboats regularly used by the Kennedy family?
2. Which president first rode on a steamboat?
3. Which president had once owned boats named *Half Moon* and *Full Moon*?
4. Which president owned a twenty-eight-foot "Cigarette" speedboat named *Fidelity*?
5. What was the name of Franklin Roosevelt's forty-five-foot sailboat?
6. Which ship's sinking did Theodore Roosevelt say was "murder on the high seas"?

5. Franklin Pierce (1804) and Dwight Eisenhower (1890), respectively.
6. Lyndon Johnson (1908) and Bill Clinton (1946), respectively.
7. 1767, 1822, 1913, 1924, and 1946, each with two presidents' births.
8. All of them before Martin Van Buren, and William Henry Harrison.
9. James (6)
10. George Washington's (February 22), before Presidents' Day was created.
11. Ulysses Grant (1839), from Hiram Ulysses Grant to Ulysses Simpson Grant, at West Point.
12. John Adams (1735)
13. Andrew Jackson (1767)
14. Calvin Coolidge (1872), born on Independence Day.
15. Franklin Roosevelt's (January 30)
16. Andrew Jackson (1767) and Bill Clinton (1946)
17. Martin Van Buren (1782)
18. Warren Harding (1865)
19. George W. Bush (1946), but Bill Clinton was the first Baby Boomer president elected.
20. James Polk (1795) and Warren Harding (1865) were both born on November 2.
21. Dwight Eisenhower (1956)
22. Gadsby's Tavern, in Alexandria, Virginia (1799).
23. Lyndon Johnson (1908), because his parents could not decide on one.
24. V-E Day (May 8, 1945), the date Allies achieved victory in Europe during World War II.
25. Richard Nixon's (January 9), by Yorba Linda, California.
26. George Washington's (1846)
27. Dwight Eisenhower (1960)
28. The third Monday in February
29. Chester Arthur
30. Abraham Lincoln (February 12, 1809)
31. Andrew Jackson (1767), which if true would have made him ineligible to be president.
32. Abraham Lincoln
33. James Madison

Boats (answers)

1. The *Tenofus* and the *Onemore*
2. James Monroe (1819), who rode on the *Savannah*.
3. Franklin Roosevelt
4. George Bush
5. *Amberjack II*
6. The *Lusitania*'s (1915)

Books

1. Which president first published a book?
2. What was the title of the only book that James Buchanan wrote?
3. Which presidents claimed to have read every book in their hometown libraries?
4. Which president, vice president, and secretary of state were "The Three Musketeers"?
5. Which president called *Common Sense* "a malicious, short-sighted, crapulous mass"?
6. Which president obtained the freedom from prison of Thomas Paine?
7. Which president's only book was *Discourse On the Aborigines Of the Valley Of Ohio*?
8. Which president was profiled in John Kennedy's book *Profiles in Courage*?
9. About which president was a book first written alleging that he was of mixed blood?
10. Which president wrote a naval history of the War of 1812?
11. Which president, fittingly, enjoyed reading books about King Arthur as a child?
12. Which president wrote a book about the presidency as an institution?
13. Who wrote *Why England Slept*, about British unpreparedness before World War II?
14. Which president wrote *Mr. Citizen*?
15. Who wrote *42 Years in the White House*?
16. Which two presidents wrote books that were made into television movies?
17. Which president's clean-up of the civil service forced Nathaniel Hawthorne from his job?
18. Which president wrote a book about fishing?
19. What were the six incidents to which Richard Nixon referred in his book *Six Crises*?
20. Who was writing *My First Days in the White House* when he was assassinated?
21. Which president's favorite book as a child was *The Arabian Nights*?
22. Which president often claimed that he had read only one book in his entire life?
23. Which president wrote *American Individualism*?
24. Which president wrote *Portrait of an Assassin*?
25. Which president wrote a comparative vocabulary study of American Indian languages?
26. Which president wrote a college textbook that was utilized for *sixty* years?
27. Which president wrote *Through the Brazilian Wilderness*?
28. After a defeat at the polls, which president wrote a book entitled *This Country of Ours*?
29. Which president wrote *Mandate for Change*?
30. Who first published an account of an affair she claimed to have had with a president?
31. Which president liked *War and Peace* but thought Shakespeare was "very dense"?
32. In which book did Ronald Reagan call George Bush "a Preppy, a Yalie, a sissy"?
33. Which president's advisor pseudonymously wrote *Philip Dru: Administrator*?
34. Which president used a literary pseudonym?
35. Which president wrote *An Outdoor Journal*, about his life as a fisherman and hunter?
36. Which book was Woodrow Wilson's favorite as a child?
37. Which president always kept a book on a pedestal near the main White House door?

Books (answers)

1. John Adams (1776), who published *Thoughts on Government*.
2. *Mr. Buchanan's Administration on the Eve of the Rebellion* (1866)
3. Harry Truman (1898) and Jimmy Carter (1938), each by the age of fourteen years.
4. Theodore Roosevelt, William Taft, and Elihu Root
5. John Adams
6. James Monroe (1794), after Paine had been jailed for supporting King Louis XVI.
7. William Henry Harrison's (1839)
8. John Quincy Adams (1956)
9. Warren Harding
10. Theodore Roosevelt (1880), in *Naval War of 1812*, still the definitive work on the topic.
11. John Kennedy, whose Administration became known as "Camelot."
12. Theodore Roosevelt (1910), who wrote *The Presidency*.
13. John Kennedy (1939)
14. Harry Truman (1960), describing his life as president.
15. Irwin H. "Ike" Hoover, the first and longest White House chief usher (1891-1933).
16. Dwight Eisenhower (*Crusade in Europe*) and John Kennedy (*Profiles in Courage*)
17. Zachary Taylor's (1857). Hawthorne immediately began writing *The Scarlet Letter*.
18. Herbert Hoover (1950), entitled *Fishing is Fun*.
19. Alger Hiss, finances, Ike's health, Venezuela, Khrushchev, and the 1960 campaign
20. Louisiana Governor Huey P. Long (1935)
21. John Quincy Adams's
22. Andrew Jackson
23. Herbert Hoover (1922)
24. Gerald Ford (1976), about Lee Harvey Oswald.
25. Thomas Jefferson (1816)
26. Herbert Hoover (1909), who wrote *Principles of Mining*.
27. Theodore Roosevelt (1914)
28. Benjamin Harrison (1897), about the federal government.
29. Dwight Eisenhower (1963)
30. Nan Britton (1927), who wrote *The President's Daughter*, saying her child was Harding's.
31. George Bush
32. *The Preppy Handbook* (1980), the same year Bush became Reagan's running mate.
33. Woodrow Wilson's, Edward M. House (1912), about a bureaucrat who becomes dictator.
34. Franklin Roosevelt (1937), who wrote part of a novel, *The President's Mystery Story*.
35. Jimmy Carter (1988)
36. *The Life of Washington* (1800), by Parson Weems.
37. Theodore Roosevelt, to read a few pages at a time while waiting for guests to arrive.

38. Which president read western novels for relaxation?
39. Which president was a good friend of American novelist Owen Wister?
40. Which president was fascinated with Ian Fleming's James Bond novels?
41. Which president wrote *Waging Peace*?
42. Which president wrote *Have Faith in Massachusetts*?
43. Which president translated Agricola's *De Re Metallica*?
44. Which president wrote *The Origin and Course of Political Parties in the United States*?
45. Which president does *Bartlett's Quotations* list more than any other?
46. From which book did Theodore Roosevelt originate "Speak softly and carry a big stick"?
47. Which president wrote *Years of Decision* and *Years of Trial and Hope*?
48. Which president did William Makepeace Thackeray use as a character in *The Virginians*?
49. Which president began a book comparing the U.S.A. to ancient Greece and Rome?
50. Which president wrote a serious history of the Roman Empire *after* leaving office?
51. Which president asked his aides to locate all the books about King Charles I of England?
52. Which president published a book on oratory that was utilized for decades?
53. Which presidents published books about children's letters that they had received?
54. Which president was the most voracious reader, reading whenever he got a chance?

Boxing

1. Which president-elect fought former middleweight boxing champion Mike Donovan?
2. Which president lost the sight in his left eye after a blow from an army boxer?
3. Which future president's hands were too small as a child to learn boxing?
4. Which president was a good friend with legendary boxer John L. Sullivan?
5. Which president coined the phrase "My hat's in the ring"?

Breakfasts

1. Which president's favorite breakfast was cucumbers soaked in vinegar?
2. Who liked to have his head massaged and covered with petroleum jelly at breakfast?
3. Which president enraged Congressmen after inviting them to breakfast then billing them?
4. Which president regularly had an eight-ounce breakfast steak?
5. Which president often ate quail for breakfast?
6. Which president toasted his own English muffins in the morning?
7. Which president liked to have grapefruit juice and raw eggs for breakfast?
8. Which president started the interdenominational White House Prayer Breakfast?
9. Which president attended the first annual National Hispanic Prayer Breakfast?
10. Which president first announced his intention to run at the Christian Science Monitor Breakfast?
11. Which president made a famous apology at a White House breakfast, surrounded by clergy?

38. Dwight Eisenhower
39. Theodore Roosevelt
40. John Kennedy, who read them in the White House.
41. Dwight Eisenhower (1966)
42. Calvin Coolidge (1919)
43. Herbert Hoover (1912). He got a Mining and Metallurgical Society Gold Award for it.
44. Martin Van Buren (1867), published posthumously.
45. Abraham Lincoln
46. *The McGuffey Reader*
47. Harry Truman (1955 and 1956)
48. George Washington (1859)
49. James Monroe
50. Harry Truman
51. Andrew Jackson, delighting that those condemning the king to die met untimely deaths.
52. John Quincy Adams (1810), who wrote *Lectures on Rhetoric and Oratory*.
53. Herbert Hoover (*On Growing Up*) and John Kennedy (*Kids' Letters to President Kennedy*)
54. Abraham Lincoln, carrying a book most everywhere and walking miles to borrow one.

Boxing (answers)
1. Theodore Roosevelt
2. Theodore Roosevelt
3. Theodore Roosevelt's
4. Theodore Roosevelt
5. Theodore Roosevelt. The saying began when a man wanted to enter a boxing match.

Breakfasts (answers)
1. Ulysses Grant's
2. Calvin Coolidge
3. Jimmy Carter
4. William Taft
5. Franklin Roosevelt
6. Gerald Ford
7. Woodrow Wilson
8. Dwight Eisenhower (1953)
9. George W. Bush (2002), at the Capital Hilton, in Washington, DC.
10. Jimmy Carter (1973), something several other candidates have done as well.
11. Bill Clinton (1998), for his sins.

Bridges

1. What is the longest vertical-lift bridge in the United States?
2. From which bridge did boxer Muhammad Ali throw his 1960 Olympic Gold Medal?
3. Who was the first person to walk across the Brooklyn Bridge, on the day it was opened?
4. Which bridges in the District of Columbia are named for presidents?
5. Which two "presidential" routes go from one side of the Hudson River to the other?

Buildings

1. Which president laid the cornerstone of the Capitol Building in Washington, DC?
2. Which president laid the cornerstone of the CIA building in Langley, Virginia?
3. Which president dedicated the National Geographic Society headquarters in Washington?
4. Which president remotely turned on 80,000 lights at the Woolworth Building?
5. Which president ordered the Treasury Building placed where it is today?
6. What are the names of the three main buildings of the Library of Congress?
7. In honor of which president was the Parthenon illuminated?
8. In which building is the Office of Presidential Management located?
9. In which building was part of the Central Intelligence Agency located?
10. In which building is the Department of Commerce located?
11. In which building is the Department of State located?
12. For which other presidents are federal buildings named?

Burial Geography

1. Which president was buried farthest north?
2. Which president was buried farthest south?
3. Which president was buried farthest east?
4. Which president was buried farthest west?
5. Which president was buried inside the District of Columbia?
6. In which state were the most presidents buried?
7. Which president was buried farthest from his place of birth?
8. Which president's exact grave site is not known?
9. Which president was buried in the town where the Football Hall of Fame is located?
10. Which presidents were buried in the same place they had been born?
11. Which three presidents were buried in towns ending in "ville"?
12. Which seven presidents were buried in towns consisting of two words?
13. Which two presidents literally were buried next to each other?
14. Which president's remains lie inside a church?
15. Which president was buried outside the contemporary borders of the U.S.A.?

Bridges (answers)

1. The 360-foot long Benjamin Harrison Memorial Drawbridge (James River, Virginia).
2. The Jefferson County Bridge, in Louisville, Kentucky.
3. Chester Arthur (1883)
4. The Theodore Roosevelt, William H. Taft, and Woodrow Wilson Memorial Bridges
5. The George Washington Bridge and the Lincoln Tunnel

Buildings (answers)

1. George Washington (1793)
2. Dwight Eisenhower (1959)
3. Lyndon Johnson (1964)
4. Woodrow Wilson (1913), at the time the world's tallest building.
5. Andrew Jackson (1836), in the middle of old Pennsylvania Avenue.
6. The John Adams, Thomas Jefferson, and James Madison Buildings
7. Ulysses Grant (1902)
8. The Theodore Roosevelt Federal Building
9. The Woodrow Wilson Federal Building
10. The Herbert Hoover Federal Building
11. The Harry S Truman Federal Building
12. John Kennedy (Boston), Gerald Ford (Grand Rapids), and Ronald Reagan (Santa Ana)

Burial Geography (answers)

1. Calvin Coolidge (1933), in Plymouth, Vermont.
2. Lyndon Johnson (1973), near Stonewall, Texas.
3. John Adams (1826), in Quincy, Massachusetts, just feet from his son in the same crypt.
4. Richard Nixon (1994), in Yorba Linda, California.
5. Woodrow Wilson (1924)
6. New York (Van Buren, Fillmore, Grant, Arthur, and both Roosevelts)
7. Ulysses Grant (1885), born in Point Pleasant, Ohio, and buried in New York City.
8. John Tyler's, because his tombstone was moved a long time ago.
9. William McKinley (1901), in Canton, Ohio.
10. George Washington (Mount Vernon) and Richard Nixon (Yorba Linda)
11. James Polk (Nashville), Zachary Taylor (Louisville), and Andrew Johnson (Greeneville)
12. Washington, William Henry Harrison, Grant, both Roosevelts, Hoover, and Nixon
13. James Monroe (1831) and John Tyler (1862), in Hollywood Cemetery, Richmond, Virginia.
14. Woodrow Wilson's (1924), entombed in Washington National Cathedral.
15. None

Burials

1. Which president asked that a copy of the Constitution prop his head when he was buried?
2. Which president was buried on his son's third birthday?
3. Which president's undertaker claimed he never got paid?
4. Who came up with the idea for John Kennedy's "eternal flame"?
5. Which religious figure presided at Lyndon Johnson's burial?
6. Which president was offered a chance to be buried in a Roman emperor's sarcophagus?
7. Which president, contrary to his instructions, was "embalmed and hermetically sealed"?
8. During which president's funeral did the Associated Press teletype stop?
9. Which president first wrote his own epitaph?
10. Which president's epitaph reads, "His faith in the American people never wavered"?
11. Which president who died in office was the first one *not* to have a formal state burial?
12. Which president was denied a chance to be a pallbearer for his ex-fiancée?
13. Which president's funeral escort included 2,000 Knights Templar?
14. Which president first had a Masonic burial?
15. Which two royal figures walked in John Kennedy's funeral procession?
16. Which president's corpse was exhumed multiple times?
17. How many presidents were cremated?
18. At which president's burial did the chaplain of the House of Representatives preside?
19. Which president's corpse was draped in the Confederate flag before being buried?
20. Which president's pallbearers included Lewis Cass, Henry Clay, and Daniel Webster?
21. Which president's pallbearers included Charles Tiffany and Cornelius Vanderbilt?
22. Which president's funeral was first broadcast by radio?
23. For which presidents' burials did the stock market close for the entire day?

Business

1. Which president had Montgomery Ward denied a position as sporting-goods manager?
2. Which president practically acted as an agent for the construction firm Brown & Root?
3. Which president had been a spokesman for General Electric Company?
4. Which president had been CEO of a zeppelin company that went bankrupt?
5. Which president had been CEO of Citra-Frost, a marketer of frozen orange juice?
6. Which president had owned a shoeshine shop?
7. Which president had been a warehouse sweeper for Dresser Industries?
8. Which presidents had been bank officers?
9. Which president formed one of the nation's first offshore oil-drilling companies?
10. Which *former* president accepted a position on a corporation's board of directors?
11. Which president started a lead-and-zinc mining operation that eventually failed?

Burials (answers)

1. Andrew Johnson (1875)
2. John Kennedy (1963)
3. James Garfield's (1881)
4. Jackie Kennedy, from a similar memorial at the Arc de Triomphe in Paris, France.
5. Reverend Billy Graham (1973)
6. Andrew Jackson (1845)
7. Franklin Roosevelt (1945)
8. John Kennedy's (1963). All planes and trains stopped too, an unprecedented gesture.
9. Thomas Jefferson, who did not mention his having been president!
10. Andrew Jackson's (1845)
11. Zachary Taylor (1850)
12. James Buchanan (1819). She had committed suicide after their broken engagement.
13. William McKinley's (1901)
14. James Buchanan (1868). Harry Truman (1972) also had a Masonic burial.
15. King Baudouin of Belgium and Queen Frederika of Greece (1963)
16. Abraham Lincoln's, to verify that it had not been stolen.
17. None
18. John Quincy Adams's (1848), by Reverend R. R. Gurley.
19. John Tyler's (1862)
20. Zachary Taylor's (1850)
21. Chester Arthur's (1886)
22. William Taft's (1930)
23. Franklin Roosevelt's, Kennedy's, Truman's, Lyndon Johnson's, Eisenhower's, and Nixon's

Business (answers)

1. Ronald Reagan
2. Lyndon Johnson
3. Ronald Reagan
4. Franklin Roosevelt
5. Richard Nixon (1940)
6. Lyndon Johnson (1917), who owned Johnson Shoe Shine Shop.
7. George Bush (1949)
8. Calvin Coolidge (Northampton Savings) and Franklin Roosevelt (Fidelity & Deposit)
9. George Bush (1953), who formed Zapata Off-Shore and named it for Emiliano Zapata.
10. Gerald Ford, as director of Texas Commerce Bancshares, Inc.
11. Harry Truman (1916)

12. Which president became known as the "trust buster" president for breaking monopolies?
13. Which president first required federal contractors to establish goals for hiring minorities?

Campaign Finances

1. Which president first pushed for public financing of presidential campaigns?
2. Which presidential campaign was the first one with disclosure requirements in effect?
3. Which opposing presidential nominees first disclosed their financial statements?
4. What is the current limit for a personal contribution to a presidential campaign?
5. What is the current limit for a PAC contribution to a presidential campaign?
6. Which president offered naval contracts to his friend in return for campaign contributions?
7. Which president wanted to ban contributions before the presidential election year?
8. Which corporation spent $1 million trying to defeat Franklin Roosevelt in 1936?
9. Which presidential election first featured PACs playing an influential role?
10. Which black woman first placed her name on the ballots of every state in the Union?
11. Which presidential election first featured large dinner fund-raisers?

Campaign Managers

1. Who was the first presidential campaign manager, albeit unofficially?
2. Who was the first female presidential campaign manager?
3. Which famous financier managed William Henry Harrison's presidential campaign?
4. Which presidential campaign manager was blind?
5. Which presidential campaign manager quit after being investigated for cocaine use?
6. Which presidential nominee had been co-chairman of another presidential campaign?
7. Which campaign manager had been the first female president of the *Harvard Law Review*?
8. Which presidential campaign manager ended up being nominated for president himself?

Campaign Media

1. Which presidential campaign first featured nationwide partisan newspapers?
2. Which presidential election was first broadcast by stereopticon?
3. Which president made the first paid political television appearance?
4. Which presidential campaign first featured national television coverage of the primaries?
5. Which presidential campaign first featured political television ads?
6. Which presidential campaign first featured negative television ads?
7. Which presidential campaign first featured color television ads?
8. Which presidential campaign first featured "slice of life" television ads?
9. Which presidential campaign first featured "documentary" television ads?

12. Theodore Roosevelt, although William Taft waged twice as many anti-trust suits.
13. Richard Nixon

Campaign Finances (answers)

1. Theodore Roosevelt
2. The 1972 presidential campaign
3. Dwight Eisenhower and Adlai Stevenson (1952)
4. $4,000 ($2,000 for the primary election, $2,000 for the general election)
5. $5,000 ($2,500 for the primary election, $2,500 for the general election)
6. James Buchanan (1856), to George Plitt.
7. Gerald Ford (1975)
8. The DuPont Corporation. Ironically, its CEO's relative married Franklin Roosevelt, Jr.!
9. The 1944 presidential election
10. Lenora Fulani (1988), also the first who got funds from the Federal Election Commission.
11. The 1936 presidential election

Campaign Managers (answers)

1. Alexander Hamilton (1799), for John Adams.
2. Susan Estrich (1988), for Michael Dukakis.
3. Nicholas Biddle (1840), telling him not to say "what you think . . . or what you will do."
4. Senator Thomas Gore (D-OK) (1912), for Woodrow Wilson.
5. Tim Kraft (1980), for Jimmy Carter.
6. Walter Mondale (1968), for Hubert Humphrey.
7. Susan Estrich (1988), also the first woman to teach criminal law at Harvard Law School.
8. James Garfield (1880), who had managed James Sherman's campaign that year.

Campaign Media (answers)

1. The 1840 presidential campaign
2. The 1872 presidential campaign, on top of a building in New York City.
3. Harry Truman (1948), in Jersey City, New Jersey.
4. The 1952 presidential campaign
5. Dwight Eisenhower's (1952)
6. The 1964 presidential campaign
7. The 1968 presidential campaign
8. Gerald Ford's (1976), featuring typical Americans responding to questions.
9. Ronald Reagan's (1980), listing achievements and giving data about the candidate.

10. Which journalist moderated the first presidential debate, between Kennedy and Nixon?
11. Which network estimated the odds of John Kennedy's beating Richard Nixon at 100-1?
12. Which president last conducted a "front-porch" campaign?
13. Which presidential campaign first featured campaign literature printed in Yiddish?

Campaign Mudslinging
1. Which presidential campaign first brought out political "mudslinging"?
2. Which presidential campaign said its opponent got American girls for the Russian czar?
3. Which presidential campaign was between two known "draft dodgers"?
4. Which presidential campaign said its opponent was the "son of a mulatto"?
5. Which president's opponents said he was un-Christian for living in a two-family house?
6. Which president's opponents said he took more baths than a normal man ought to take?
7. Which president had been attacked politically for an unpaid tailor's bill in Troy, New York?
8. Which president's opponents accused him of branding his slaves for identification?

Campaign Paraphernalia
1. Which presidential campaign first featured mass-distributed campaign materials?
2. Which presidential campaign used pamphlets and orators to woo the German vote?
3. Which presidential campaign published pamphlets in eight languages?
4. Which city houses the Presidential Museum, which collects campaign memorabilia?
5. When did Congress outlaw the use of the American flag as a political advertisement?
6. Which presidential campaign popularized suspenders as a campaign item?
7. Which presidential campaign button was the second most expensive one ever purchased?
8. Which presidential campaign first featured political "ferrotypes"?
9. Which president probably was first burned in effigy on repeated occasions?
10. Which presidential campaign first featured metal license-plate attachments?
11. Which presidential campaign first featured celluloid pin-back buttons?
12. Which presidential campaign first featured lithographed campaign buttons?
13. Which diptych campaign button, a button showing running mates, is the most expensive?
14. Which presidential campaign first featured a campaign cartoon?

Campaign Posters
1. Which presidential nominee first used campaign posters?
2. Which president's campaign posters adoringly compared him to Jesus Christ?
3. Which presidential campaign first featured negative campaign posters?
4. Which presidential campaign first featured foreign-language campaign banners?

10. Howard K. Smith (1960)
11. NBC (1960)
12. Calvin Coolidge (1924), delivering speeches and entertaining the media in his home.
13. William McKinley's (1896)

Campaign Mudslinging (answers)

1. The 1796 presidential campaign
2. Andrew Jackson's (1828)
3. The 1884 presidential campaign, between Grover Cleveland and James Blaine.
4. John Quincy Adams's (1828), and that his opponent's wife was "a common prostitute."
5. John Tyler's (1840)
6. Martin Van Buren's (1836)
7. James Garfield (1880)
8. James Polk (1844)

Campaign Paraphernalia (answers)

1. The 1828 presidential campaign
2. Abraham Lincoln's (1860)
3. William McKinley's (1900)
4. Odessa, Texas.
5. At the turn of the twentieth century
6. Franklin Roosevelt's (1932)
7. Theodore Roosevelt's, whose 1904 button entitled "T.R. at the Gate" sold for $14,640.
8. Abraham Lincoln's (1860)
9. Andrew Johnson (1868)
10. The 1936 presidential campaign
11. The 1896 presidential campaign
12. The 1920 presidential campaign
13. The 1920 Cox-Roosevelt button costs more than $3,000.
14. The 1824 presidential campaign

Campaign Posters (answers)

1. Andrew Jackson (1828)
2. Jimmy Carter's (1976)
3. The 1828 presidential campaign
4. Abraham Lincoln's (1860)

5. Which presidential campaign first featured political banners?
6. Which presidential campaign first featured campaign posters with the platform on them?

Campaign Songs

1. Which president first had a campaign theme song?
2. What was the name of Theodore Roosevelt's 1904 campaign theme song?
3. What was the name of Franklin Roosevelt's 1932 campaign theme song?
4. What was the name of Dwight Eisenhower's 1952 campaign theme song?
5. What was the name of John Kennedy's 1960 campaign theme song?
6. Which president has been featured in more songs than any other?

Campaign Travels

1. Which presidential candidate first campaigned actively, visiting voters around the country?
2. Which president first campaigned *after* being re-nominated?
3. Which presidential nominee campaigned in all fifty states?
4. Which *incumbent* president probably campaigned hardest for his party's candidates?
5. Who is probably the only state legislator campaigned against by two presidents?
6. Which presidential candidate first used automobiles in a campaign?
7. Which president had used a 1920 Fiat to campaign for the Senate?
8. Which president used a bright red Maxwell touring car in his first political campaign?
9. Which president probably was the only one *never* to mention his opponent's name?
10. Which Republican presidential nominee first stumped hard in the Deep South?

Campaigns

1. During which presidential campaign did the term "OK" originate?
2. During which presidential campaign did the word "booze" become popular?
3. Which president first had a female opponent for president?
4. Which president lost the most campaigns before actually becoming president?
5. Which presidential campaign's primary results first dictated the nominee?
6. Which Republican presidential nominee most intensely courted the blue-collar vote?
7. Which president first hired an advertising firm to help him win?
8. Which president first personally campaigned in German?
9. Which president first exalted his humble origins during a campaign?
10. Which president had been the first "dark horse" presidential candidate?
11. Which presidential candidate was first endorsed by a major labor organization?
12. Which president first sought a third term aggressively?

5.   William Henry Harrison's (1840)
6.   Abraham Lincoln's (1860)

Campaign Songs (answers)

1.   Thomas Jefferson (1800), entitled "Fair and Free Elections."
2.   "A Hot Time in the Old Town"
3.   "Happy Days Are Here Again"
4.   "I Like Ike," composed by Irving Berlin.
5.   "High Hopes"
6.   Abraham Lincoln, in about 500 songs.

Campaign Travels (answers)

1.   William Henry Harrison (1840)
2.   William Taft (1912)
3.   Richard Nixon (1960), which maybe cost him the election for spreading himself too thin.
4.   Gerald Ford (1976), who campaigned fifty-three out of sixty-four days in thirty states.
5.   State Representative David Duke (R-LA) (1992), by Ronald Reagan and George Bush.
6.   Theodore Roosevelt (1912)
7.   John Kennedy (1958)
8.   Franklin Roosevelt (1910), campaigning for New York state senator.
9.   Herbert Hoover (1932)
10. Dwight Eisenhower (1951). For a century, the Deep South had been blindly Democratic.

Campaigns (answers)

1.   Martin Van Buren's (1836), known as "Old Kinderhook" for his birthplace in New York.
2.   William Henry Harrison's (1840), when E. C. Booz made spirits for him.
3.   Ulysses Grant (1872)
4.   Abraham Lincoln (1860), who had lost eight political campaigns.
5.   Jimmy Carter's (1976)
6.   Ronald Reagan (1980)
7.   Dwight Eisenhower (1952)
8.   James Garfield (1880)
9.   William Henry Harrison (1840), with miniature log cabins, in order to try to win votes.
10. James Polk (1844). In racing, it means a horse about which nobody knows anything.
11. Franklin Roosevelt (1932)
12. Ulysses Grant (1876)

13. Which two persons were nominated for national office by a major party five times?
14. Which presidents first and last ran for re-election during a war?
15. Which presidential candidate first openly solicited votes in person?
16. Which incumbent president was the last one who did *not* solicit votes in person?
17. Which future president climbed a tree to watch a parade for Grover Cleveland?
18. Where did John Kennedy and Richard Nixon finish their campaigns, respectively?
19. Which president often quipped, "I'll never tell a lie," during campaign appearances?
20. For what did critics say "T.A.F.T." stood?
21. Which president was the first one who had never lost a political campaign?
22. What were the only two political races that George Washington lost?
23. Which third-party nominee last gained access to the ballot in all fifty states?
24. Which presidential campaign first featured a ticker-tape parade?
25. Which *incumbent* president first participated in a presidential debate?
26. Which president had run a campaign as candidate for mayor of New York City?
27. Which president had lost a campaign after declining to provide free whiskey to voters?
28. During which president's campaign did one of his staff say "Public office is a public trust"?
29. Which president, opposing travel, said he minded "being dragged over half a continent"?
30. When was the last time no incumbent president *or* vice president ran for national office?

Carriages

1. Which president owned an ornate green state coach?
2. Which president fired a groom for escorting guests in the White House carriage?
3. Which president was given a carriage made of wood from the USS *Constitution*?
4. From which cabinet member did John Tyler purchase his presidential carriage?
5. Which president left his carriage at the White House for use by his successor?
6. Which president put his coat-of-arms on his carriage and ordered laprobes for it?
7. Which president went riding every day from 4:00 P.M. until 6:00 P.M.?
8. Which president enjoyed an evening "drive" with his wife to relax?
9. Which presidents last used horse-drawn carriages at the White House and in DC?
10. Which presidents owned monogrammed harnesses?
11. Which president had suffered a carriage accident at the age of two years?

Cats

1. Which president first had a cat in the White House?
2. Which presidents were also ailurophiles?
3. Which president had a six-toed cat named "Slippers"?
4. Which president had a cat named "Blackie"?

13. Franklin Roosevelt and Richard Nixon
14. James Madison (1812) and George W. Bush (2004), respectively.
15. Winfield Scott (1852), before which time it had been considered undignified to do so.
16. William McKinley (1900)
17. Franklin Roosevelt (1892)
18. Boston, Massachusetts, and Detroit, Michigan (1960).
19. Jimmy Carter (1976)
20. "Take Advice From Theodore," after Roosevelt coached William Taft in his campaign.
21. Zachary Taylor. Garfield, Wilson, and Eisenhower also never lost an election.
22. Two races for the Virginia House of Burgesses (1755 and 1757)
23. Ross Perot (1992)
24. The 1888 presidential campaign
25. Gerald Ford (1976)
26. Theodore Roosevelt (1886), who lost to Abram S. Hewitt.
27. James Madison (1778), running for the Virginia House of Burgesses.
28. Grover Cleveland's (1884)
29. Theodore Roosevelt (1904)
30. 1952

Carriages (answers)
1. Martin Van Buren
2. Andrew Johnson
3. Andrew Jackson
4. James K. Paulding, secretary of the navy (1838-1841).
5. Rutherford Hayes, but James Garfield returned it to him.
6. Chester Arthur
7. Benjamin Harrison
8. William McKinley
9. Theodore Roosevelt and Woodrow Wilson, respectively.
10. Chester Arthur, William McKinley, and Theodore Roosevelt
11. Richard Nixon, which incident left him susceptible to motion sickness.

Cats (answers)
1. Rutherford Hayes, called "Siam."
2. Theodore Roosevelt, Wilson, Coolidge, Truman, Kennedy, Carter, and Clinton
3. Theodore Roosevelt
4. Calvin Coolidge

5. Which president had a lion, a hyena, and a wildcat?
6. Which president had a Siamese cat named "Shan"?
7. Which president killed several cougars by hand while on a hunting trip in Colorado?
8. Which president had a bobcat named "Smoky"?
9. Which president's favorite cat was named "Tom Kitten"?
10. Which president asked local radio stations to issue a "missing cat" bulletin?

Celebrities
1. Which president was one of Gertrude Stein's heroes?
2. Who was Calvin Coolidge's favorite celebrity?
3. Who was Dwight Eisenhower's favorite celebrity?
4. Who was Lyndon Johnson's favorite celebrity?
5. Who was Richard Nixon's favorite celebrity?

Cemeteries
1. Which presidents were buried in Arlington National Cemetery?
2. Which other two presidents were buried in the same cemetery?
3. Which president and the first Public Enemy #1 were buried in the same cemetery?
4. Which president was buried in New York City's Marble Cemetery but later re-interred?
5. Which presidents were buried in cemeteries later named for them?
6. Which two of John Kennedy's relatives were buried next to him?

Characteristics
1. Which president had the greatest difference in age compared with his predecessor?
2. Which president was the poorest?
3. Which president was the first one who was a Mason?
4. Which president held the highest degree in the Masonic Order?
5. Which president was first accused of homosexuality?
6. Which president could toss an iron bar farther than anybody in town, even in old age?
7. Which president was last in office when sixty-five years old?
8. Which president refused to deposit a check for more than $15,000 because it was off?
9. Which presidents had unusual knacks for remembering people's names and faces?
10. Which presidents had been adopted as children?
11. Which president had a habit of rubbing his glasses repeatedly while speaking?
12. Which president supposedly had a penchant for having his bath water perfumed?
13. Which president never laughed aloud?

5. Theodore Roosevelt
6. Gerald Ford
7. Theodore Roosevelt
8. Calvin Coolidge
9. John Kennedy's
10. Calvin Coolidge, after his striped alley cat disappeared.

Celebrities (answers)
1. Ulysses Grant
2. Will Rogers
3. Robert Montgomery
4. Carol Channing
5. Pearl Bailey

Cemeteries (answers)
1. William Taft (1930) and John Kennedy (1963)
2. James Monroe (1831) and John Tyler (1862), in Hollywood Cemetery, Richmond.
3. Benjamin Harrison (1901) and John Dillinger (1963), in Crown Hill Cemetery, Indianapolis.
4. James Monroe (1831)
5. Taylor (1850), Andrew Johnson (1875), and Hoover (1964)
6. His children Arabella (1956) and Patrick (1963)

Characteristics (answers)
1. John Kennedy (1961), twenty-seven years younger than Dwight Eisenhower.
2. Andrew Johnson
3. George Washington. Andrew Johnson was the first Knight Templar and first Scottish Rite.
4. Harry Truman
5. James Buchanan
6. George Washington
7. George Bush (1989)
8. James Buchanan. The check was off by ten cents!
9. William McKinley and George W. Bush
10. Gerald Ford (1916) and Bill Clinton (1962)
11. Woodrow Wilson
12. Millard Fillmore
13. Herbert Hoover, according to his major domo, Ike Hoover.

14. Which president wore pencils down to stubs in order to get maximum usage?
15. Which president's tendency to mumble was described by his wife as "an awful habit"?
16. Which modern president was notorious for his cursing?
17. Which president do many historians believe was manic-depressive?
18. Which president was one of the 100 richest persons in America compared to GNP?
19. Which president, a steadfast Christian, forbade the discussion of politics on Sundays?
20. Which "enlightened" president believed in white supremacy?
21. Which president did John Dos Passos say had a "headmaster's admonishing voice"?
22. Which president's chuckle was described as "one of our great American institutions"?

Cities
1. Which town was the first one to be named for George Washington?
2. Which incorporated city was the first one to be named for George Washington?
3. Which town was the first one to be named for a *future* president?
4. Which suburb of Dallas was founded in 1845 and originally named "Fillmore"?
5. Which town with a presidential surname is the least populous?
6. Which town named for a president is closest to the geographical center of the U.S.A.?
7. Which state has the most cities or towns with presidential first names?
8. Which deceased president probably is the only one without a namesake town?
9. Which state has towns named "President" and "White House"?
10. For which president did the citizens of Paris, France, name a major avenue?
11. Which president was born in a town named for a presidential candidate?
12. Which future president and future chief justice were attacked in a brawl in Berlin?
13. Which cities named for presidents are the first and last ones in zip-code order?
14. Which world capital besides Washington, DC, is named for a U.S. president?
15. In which foreign countries are there towns named Taft and Bush?
16. In which president's hometown is the Greyhound Hall of Fame located?
17. Which town did Franklin Roosevelt pick to launch his "March of Dimes" campaign?
18. Where can one find streets named "Rooseveltlaan" and "President Kennedylaan"?
19. Which state capitals were named for presidents?
20. By what name was Cincinnati, Ohio, formerly known?

City Names
1. Which states have cities named George and Washington?
2. Which states have cities named Thomas and Jefferson?
3. Which state has cities named James and Madison?
4. Which states have cities named Franklin and Pierce?

14. Gerald Ford
15. Herbert Hoover's
16. Harry Truman
17. John Adams
18. George Washington (59th), with wealth equivalent to 1/777th of contemporary GNP.
19. William Henry Harrison
20. Woodrow Wilson
21. Franklin Roosevelt
22. William Taft's

Cities (answers)

1. Washington, North Carolina (1775)
2. Washington, Georgia (1780)
3. Jackson, Mississippi (1821)
4. Plano, Texas.
5. Probably Johnson Village, Colorado, with about 300 residents.
6. Hoover, South Dakota.
7. Pennsylvania (8)
8. Dwight Eisenhower
9. Pennsylvania
10. John Kennedy, for whom "Avenue du President Kennedy" was named.
11. Rutherford Hayes (1822), born in Frémont, Ohio, named for John C. Frémont.
12. John Kennedy and Byron R. "Whizzer" White
13. Adams, Massachusetts (01220) and Roosevelt, Washington (99356), respectively.
14. Monrovia, Liberia, for James Monroe. There is also a Buchanan, Liberia.
15. Iran and Egypt, respectively.
16. Dwight Eisenhower's, Abilene, Kansas.
17. Dimebox, Texas (1944).
18. Amsterdam, The Netherlands.
19. Jackson, Mississippi; Jefferson City, Missouri; Lincoln, Nebraska; and Madison, Wisconsin.
20. Fort Washington

City Names (answers)

1. Iowa and Texas
2. Ohio, Oklahoma, Pennsylvania, South Dakota, and Texas
3. Mississippi
4. Idaho, Kentucky, and Nebraska

5. Which state has cities named Ulysses and Grant?
6. Which states have cities named Chester and Arthur?
7. Which states have cities named Grover and Cleveland?
8. Which state has cities named Theodore and Roosevelt?
9. Which states have cities named Woodrow and Wilson?
10. Which states have cities named Warren and Harding?
11. Which states have cities named Franklin and Roosevelt?
12. Which state has cities named Franklin, Delano, and Roosevelt?
13. Which states have cities named Lyndon and Johnson?
14. Which state has cities named James and Carter?

Civil War
1. Which president was wounded during the Civil War?
2. Which president had served under another president during the Civil War?
3. Which president intentionally excluded the media from a military invasion?
4. Which president had fought at the Battles of Shiloh and Chickamauga?
5. Which *former* president supported Lincoln's military strategy?
6. Where was Ulysses Grant when the Civil War erupted?
7. Which future president hired a Polish immigrant to fight for him during the Civil War?
8. From which building did Abraham Lincoln observe hot-air balloon military maneuvers?
9. Which president convinced his state legislature to end slavery and re-join the Union?
10. Whom did Abraham Lincoln promote for "gallant and meritorious services"?
11. Which president had been the youngest brigadier general in the Union Army?
12. Which president had driven a food wagon during the bloody Battle of Antietam?
13. Which president was criticized for hanging Robert E. Lee's portrait in the Oval Office?
14. Which Civil War battle did Abraham Lincoln watch in person from afar?
15. Which president organized the Union Continentals when the Civil War began?

Clothes
1. What was the name of George Washington's life-long valet?
2. Which president first had a full-time, professional valet?
3. Which president wore a miniature portrait of his wife around his neck for years?
4. Which president had a predilection for wearing gloves outdoors?
5. Which president insisted on wearing white gloves whenever he went fishing?
6. Which president last wore knee breeches?
7. Which president was famous for his very stiff, high shirt collars?
8. Which president was famous for his fancy monogrammed shirts?

5. Nebraska
6. Illinois, Iowa, Nebraska, and West Virginia
7. North Carolina, South Carolina, and Utah
8. Alabama
9. North Carolina, Pennsylvania, and Texas
10. Illinois, Massachusetts, and Minnesota
11. Alabama, Minnesota, New Jersey, and Texas
12. Minnesota
13. Illinois, Kansas, New York, and Vermont
14. Mississippi

Civil War (answers)

1. Rutherford Hayes, in the Battles of South Mountain (1862) and Cedar Creek (1864).
2. William McKinley (1862), who had served under Rutherford Hayes.
3. Ronald Reagan (1983), during the invasion of Grenada.
4. James Garfield (1862-1863), for the Union.
5. Martin Van Buren
6. Earning $50 per day in his father's leather store in Galena, Ohio.
7. James Garfield (1861-1862)
8. The "Castle" Building of the Smithsonian Institution (1861)
9. Andrew Johnson (1865). Johnson was military governor of Tennessee (1862-1864).
10. William McKinley (1864), for the Battles of Opequan, Cedar Creek, and Fisher's Hill.
11. James Garfield (1862), at thirty-one years old.
12. William McKinley (1862), praised for delivering hot coffee and meat to his comrades.
13. Dwight Eisenhower (1953), who did not give in to the criticism.
14. The Battle of Fort Stevens, Kentucky (1864).
15. Millard Fillmore (1861), comprised of militia volunteers more than forty-five years old.

Clothes (answers)

1. Billy Lee
2. Andrew Jackson
3. Benjamin Harrison
4. Calvin Coolidge
5. Chester Arthur
6. Andrew Jackson
7. Herbert Hoover
8. Franklin Roosevelt

9. Which president owned monogrammed stockings?
10. Which president posed wearing George Washington's Masonic apron and sash?
11. Which president's jacket became a popular women's fashion in his time?
12. Which president had the saying "The Buckaroo Stops Here" on his favorite belt buckle?
13. Which president always wore black and was known for his somber demeanor?
14. Which president always wore black clothes while in Washington, DC?
15. Which president missed an opening session of Parliament?
16. Which president made his own clothes?
17. Which president first wore trousers habitually?
18. Which president first wore a modern necktie frequently?
19. Which president imported the first Merino wool, from Spain?
20. Which president had an unusual predilection for extra baggy underwear?
21. Which presidents had the smallest and largest shoe sizes?
22. Which manufacturer has made shoes for all presidents since Zachary Taylor?
23. Which president told Elvis Presley, "Boy, you sure do dress kind of wild, don't you?"
24. Which president said, "Every time I see a girl in slacks, it reminds me of China"?
25. Which president said that if he could re-live his life, "I would be a shoemaker"?
26. Which custom clothing store fitted George W. Bush for his inauguration?

Clubs

1. Which president led the Military Order of the Loyal Legion of the United States?
2. Which presidents were members of the Baker Street Irregulars?
3. Which president had been one of the original Sons of Liberty who fought British rule?
4. Which president said his rejection by a club was one of his greatest disappointments?
5. Which president founded a university club called "The Orthogonians"?
6. Which president had been a member of the Alligator Eating Club?
7. Which president had been elected president of the American Philosophical Society?
8. Which president had been president of the prestigious Northampton Literary Club?
9. Which president had been elected president of the Albemarle County Agriculture Club?
10. Which president had joined the Ku Klux Klan?
11. Which president had been a member of the Whig Society at college?
12. Which president was a member of the Aztec Club?
13. Which *former* president became president of the American Antiquarian Society?
14. Which president was a member of the Knights of Columbus?
15. Which president started the Ananias Club in college?
16. Which president's supporters formed the Cuff Links Club?
17. Which president was a life member of Sons of Revolutionary Sires?

9. Thomas Jefferson

10. William Taft, initiated at Kilwinning Lodge #365, Cincinnati, Ohio (1909).

11. Dwight Eisenhower's army jacket

12. Ronald Reagan

13. John Quincy Adams

14. Andrew Jackson

15. James Buchanan, because he could not decide what to wear.

16. Andrew Johnson

17. James Madison. Before Madison's time, it was fashionable to wear "knee breeches."

18. Theodore Roosevelt

19. Thomas Jefferson

20. Calvin Coolidge

21. Calvin Coolidge (7½C) and Bill Clinton (13C), respectively.

22. Johnston & Murphy

23. Richard Nixon (1970)

24. Richard Nixon

25. John Adams

26. Oxxford Clothes (2001), founded in Chicago, Illinois, in 1916.

Clubs (answers)

1. Rutherford Hayes

2. Franklin Roosevelt and Harry Truman, members of the club promoting Sherlock Holmes.

3. John Adams

4. Franklin Roosevelt, who had been rejected by Porcellian at Harvard.

5. Richard Nixon, at Whittier College, after being rejected by the Franklin Club.

6. Woodrow Wilson, at Princeton University.

7. Thomas Jefferson, who served in that capacity until his death thirty years later.

8. Calvin Coolidge

9. James Madison

10. Harry Truman (1922)

11. Woodrow Wilson

12. Franklin Pierce. The club was for veterans of the Mexican War.

13. Calvin Coolidge

14. John Kennedy

15. Theodore Roosevelt. The only prerequisite was that each member be a liar.

16. Franklin Roosevelt's

17. Woodrow Wilson. The SRS is the pioneer of hereditary patriotic societies.

Codes

1. Which president was better known as Agent T-10 to the FBI?
2. What were the code names of John Kennedy's two alleged mistresses?
3. Who were "Lancer," "Lace," "Lyric," and "Lark," to the Secret Service?
4. What was the military code name for the Yalta Conference?
5. Which president was known during wartime as "Cargo"?
6. What was Jimmy Carter's Secret Service code name?
7. What was the Secret Service code name for Richard Nixon's secretary?
8. What was Gerald Ford's Secret Service code name?
9. What was George Bush's Secret Service code name?
10. Which president did his mistress give the code name "Tim Slade"?
11. What was George W. Bush's code name in Skull and Bones at Yale University?

Coins

1. Which U.S. coin first featured a president's likeness?
2. Which president is pictured on the penny?
3. When did the Lincoln Memorial first appear on the reverse of the Lincoln penny?
4. Which president is pictured on the nickel?
5. Which president met the three "models" for the Indian head of the buffalo nickel?
6. Which president is pictured on the dime?
7. To which president did the Lone Ranger ask children to send dimes?
8. Which president is pictured on the quarter?
9. Which president is pictured on the half-dollar?
10. Which president was depicted on a U.S. coin while still alive?
11. Which president was pictured on the dollar coin?
12. Which president authorized the minting of the largest and heaviest silver dollar?
13. On which president's birthday was a coin honoring him released?
14. Which president ordered all 445,000 newly-minted "Double Eagle" coins destroyed?
15. Which president faces right on a U.S. coin?
16. Which U.S. coin first portrayed a president's image on both sides?
17. Which U.S. coin most recently portrayed a president's image on each side?
18. Which U.S. coin will first portray *the same* president's image on both sides?

Colleges

1. Which future president had lived next door to the president of his college?
2. Which president had attended Stanford University?

Codes (answers)

1. Ronald Reagan, while active in the Screen Actors Guild (SAG) in the late 1940s.
2. "Fiddle" and "Faddle"
3. John Kennedy; Jackie Kennedy; Caroline Kennedy; and John Kennedy, Jr.
4. "Argonaut"
5. Franklin Roosevelt
6. "Deacon"
7. "Strawberry"
8. "Searchlight" or "Passkey"
9. "Timberwolf"
10. Warren Harding, by Nan Britton.
11. "Temporary"

Coins (answers)

1. The Lincoln penny
2. Abraham Lincoln (1909–)
3. 1959
4. Thomas Jefferson (1938–)
5. Theodore Roosevelt (1911), who met Iron Tail, Big Tree, and Two Moons.
6. Franklin Roosevelt (1946–), because of his work with the March of Dimes.
7. Franklin Roosevelt, who received more than three million dimes!
8. George Washington (1932–)
9. John Kennedy (1964–)
10. Calvin Coolidge (1926), on the sesquicentennial half-dollar.
11. Dwight Eisenhower (1971-1978)
12. Ronald Reagan (1985)
13. Franklin Roosevelt's (1946)
14. Franklin Roosevelt (1933). Ten of the $20 pieces "escaped," one later sold for millions!
15. Abraham Lincoln, on the penny (1909–).
16. The sesquicentennial half-dollar (1926), with George Washington and Calvin Coolidge.
17. The Illinois quarter (2003), with George Washington and Abraham Lincoln.
18. The South Dakota quarter (2006), with images of George Washington on both sides.

Colleges (answers)

1. George Bush, who lived next door to Yale University President Charles Seymour.
2. Herbert Hoover (1895-1898)

3. What was Ronald Reagan's college mascot?

4. Which president had co-founded Vincennes University Junior College?

5. Which president was the first one who had been a college dropout?

6. Which president contributed funds to what became George Washington University?

7. Which president signed the act allowing Gallaudet University to confer degrees?

8. Which president refused to attend a ceremony at Harvard College, his alma mater?

9. Which president had attended Amherst College?

10. Which president had attended Geauga Seminary in Chester, Ohio?

11. Which presidents were appointed chancellors of William and Mary College?

12. Which presidents had graduated at the top of their college classes?

13. Which president had graduated second in his college class?

14. Which president was on the board of trustees of Western Reserve Eclectic Institute?

15. Which future president claimed to have studied under socialist professor Harold Laski?

16. Which president founded an Institute on War, Revolution, and Peace at his alma mater?

17. Which president had to leave college *and* graduate school because of jaundice?

18. Which two presidents had been editors-in-chief of their college newspapers?

19. Which president had been a Rhodes Scholar?

20. Which president had graduated magna cum laude in political science?

21. Which president had led the campus drive for the United Negro College Fund?

22. Which president had been responsible for expelling Eugene O'Neill from college?

23. Which president had been a classmate of future New York City Mayor John Lindsay?

24. Which president had taught Sunday school while in college?

25. Which president was named Boylston Professor of Oratory and Rhetoric at Harvard?

26. Which three presidents had graduated from Yale University?

27. Which presidents had been elected to Phi Beta Kappa while undergraduates?

28. Which president had studied medicine?

29. Which president was the last one who had never attended college?

30. Which presidents had attended college but did not graduate?

31. Which president was the first one who had married a college graduate?

32. Which president had been a classmate of Longfellow's and Nathaniel Hawthorne's?

33. Which president refused to send his stepson to Princeton University?

34. Which president had begun the system of course electives to higher education?

35. Which president was the first one who had majored in history and government?

36. At which university do all students receive financial aid from a former president?

37. Which president had given his college valedictory address in Latin?

38. Which president's name was misspelled on his college commencement program?

39. Which college was named for two U.S. presidents?

40. Which president had studied Hebrew in college?

3. The Golden Tornado (Eureka College)

4. William Henry Harrison (1806), in Vincennes, Indiana.

5. James Monroe (1776), who quit William and Mary College to fight in the Revolution.

6. John Quincy Adams (1821), to Columbian College in Washington, DC.

7. Abraham Lincoln (1864), to what is now the premier college for deaf students.

8. John Quincy Adams (1833), when it gave an honorary degree to Andrew Jackson.

9. Calvin Coolidge (1891-1895)

10. James Garfield (1849-1851)

11. George Washington (1788) and John Tyler (1859), with nobody serving between them.

12. James Polk (The University of North Carolina) and James Garfield (Williams College)

13. William Taft (1878), at Yale University.

14. James Garfield, at what later became Hiram College.

15. John Kennedy (1935), at the London School of Economics.

16. Herbert Hoover (1919), at Stanford University.

17. John Kennedy (1935)

18. Franklin Roosevelt (*The Harvard Crimson*) and Lyndon Johnson (*The College Star*)

19. Bill Clinton (1968-1970). Jimmy Carter (1946) applied too but was declined.

20. John Kennedy (1940), at Harvard University.

21. George Bush (1946), at Yale University.

22. Woodrow Wilson (1907), while president of Princeton University.

23. George Bush (1946), at Yale University.

24. Theodore Roosevelt

25. John Quincy Adams (1804)

26. William Taft (1878), George Bush (1948), and George W. Bush (1968)

27. John Quincy Adams, Chester Arthur, Theodore Roosevelt, William Taft, and George Bush

28. William Henry Harrison (The University of Pennsylvania), under Dr. Benjamin Rush.

29. Harry Truman

30. James Monroe, William Henry Harrison, and William McKinley

31. Rutherford Hayes, whose wife graduated from Ohio Wesleyan Women's College (1851).

32. Franklin Pierce (Bowdoin College), in Brunswick, Maine.

33. George Washington, calling Princeton "a nest of Presbyterians."

34. Thomas Jefferson, a system still used in most colleges.

35. Woodrow Wilson (1879), at the College of New Jersey (later Princeton University).

36. Washington and Lee University, from George Washington, through interest on land sales.

37. James Polk (1818)

38. Benjamin Harrison's (1852)

39. Washington & Jefferson College (1781), in Washington, Pennsylvania.

40. James Madison (1770-1771), at the College of New Jersey (later Princeton University).

41. Which president had well known rows with Brander Matthews of Columbia University?
42. Which president finished graduate studies in reactor technology and nuclear physics?
43. Which president had received a Ph.D.?
44. Which president had attended Georgetown University?
45. Which college have more presidents attended than any other?
46. Which president had been the leader of his debate team while in college?
47. Which president entered college as a sophomore because of academic qualifications?
48. Which college in Santa Ana, California, was named for a president?
49. Which college in Seneca Falls, New York, was named for a president?
50. Which president became president of a university's board of trustees?
51. Which president became president of a university?
52. Which president had been the oldest student at his college?
53. Which president had graduated from college in only two years?
54. Which president had been president of his freshman and sophomore college classes?
55. Which president had studied economics in college?
56. Which president had taken a degree from a foreign university?
57. Which presidents became rectors at the University of Virginia?
58. Which president taught at the Harvard Business School?

Commissions and Committees

1. Which president had been a member of the Warren Commission?
2. Which president had been a member of the Mississippi River Commission?
3. Which president had chaired the Doolittle Committee to survey the executive branch?
4. Which president had been part of the Rockefeller Commission?
5. Which presidents had helped design the Great Seal of the United States?
6. Which presidents formed a blue-chip panel entitled "The American Agenda"?

Congress

1. Which president addressed the first joint session of Congress?
2. Which president first addressed Congress in writing?
3. Whom did Congress send to Woodrow Wilson's bedside?
4. Which president asked for a constitutional amendment to create an income tax?
5. Which *incumbent* presidents testified before Congress?
6. Who were the first and last presidents who had *not* served in or run for Congress?
7. Which Democratic president had voted against every civil-rights bill as a Congressman?
8. Which president had been elected to the First Congress?
9. Which president had been the first member of Congress to enlist after Pearl Harbor?

41. Theodore Roosevelt, about "simplified spelling."
42. Jimmy Carter (1952-1953), at Union College, in Schenectady, New York.
43. Woodrow Wilson (1886), from Johns Hopkins University.
44. Bill Clinton (1964-1968), the first president who had graduated from a Catholic university.
45. Harvard University (both Adamses, both Roosevelts, and John Kennedy)
46. Lyndon Johnson (Southwest Texas State Teacher's College)
47. James Polk (1816)
48. William Howard Taft University (1976–)
49. Eisenhower College (1969-1982)
50. Grover Cleveland (Princeton University)
51. Dwight Eisenhower (1948), of Columbia University.
52. James Garfield (Williams College)
53. James Madison (1771), half a year faster than George Bush.
54. Bill Clinton (1964-1965)
55. Ronald Reagan (Eureka College)
56. John Quincy Adams (1780), at the University of Leyden, The Netherlands.
57. John Adams, Thomas Jefferson, and James Madison
58. Herbert Hoover

Commissions and Committees (answers)
1. Gerald Ford (1963-1964), charged with the "official" report on Kennedy's assassination.
2. Benjamin Harrison (1879), appointed by Rutherford Hayes.
3. Herbert Hoover (1954). He did so well that it was renamed the Hoover Commission.
4. Ronald Reagan (1975), reviewing CIA activities within the United States.
5. John Adams and Thomas Jefferson (1776-1782), relying upon the Bible and mythology.
6. Gerald Ford and Jimmy Carter (1988), to make suggestions for the new president.

Congress (answers)
1. John Adams (1800), in the new Capitol Building.
2. Thomas Jefferson (1801), beginning a tradition lasting until Woodrow Wilson (1913).
3. William Jennings Bryan (1919), Wilson's life-long, hated political enemy.
4. William Taft (1909). It was ratified in 1913 by the requisite number of states (36).
5. George Washington (1789), Abraham Lincoln (1863), and Gerald Ford (1974)
6. Zachary Taylor and Ronald Reagan, respectively.
7. Lyndon Johnson, during an eleven-year stretch, even against one to end lynching.
8. James Madison (1789)
9. Lyndon Johnson (1941)

10. Which president asked Congressmen who had rushed to war to return?
11. Which president's message to Congress caused the fastest Pony Express ever?
12. Which president first met regularly with congressional leaders?
13. Which president, during his first six years in Congress, introduced only one bill?
14. When were there eight members of Congress named for George Washington?
15. Which *incumbent* presidents were subpoenaed for testimony or information?
16. Which president's address to Congress was first broadcast over live television?
17. Which president's speech is the only one read annually in Congress?
18. Which *former* president ran for both U.S. representative and U.S. senator?
19. Which president said, "The people are responsible for the character of their Congress"?
20. Which Democratic president was elected at the same time as a Republican Congress?
21. When did Democrats first win a post-Civil War majority in both houses of Congress?

Congressional Composition

1. Which president's political party held a majority in the House but *not* the Senate?
2. Which presidents first and last held majorities in the Senate but *not* the House?
3. Which presidents first and last held veto-proof majorities in *both* houses of Congress?
4. Which presidents held majorities in *neither* the House nor the Senate?
5. Which presidents held majorities in *neither* house *throughout their entire tenures*?

Constitution

1. Which president declined an invitation to help write the French Constitution?
2. Which president first had seen the Constitution's verbiage in a foreign country?
3. Which president had opposed the ratification of the Constitution without a Bill of Rights?
4. What is the Constitution's viewpoint on presidents' accepting gifts?
5. Which president wrote a constitutional amendment that was approved 203 years later?
6. Which president had drafted a state's constitution?
7. Which president wrote nine of the ten articles in the Bill of Rights?
8. Who was the last living signer of the Constitution?
9. Which presidents had signed the Constitution?
10. Which president's "brain trust" included R. G. Tugwell, who wrote a new Constitution?
11. Which president's journal gave the most insight into the Constitutional Convention?
12. Which president first supported an amendment to allow eighteen-year-olds to vote?
13. For how many years must a candidate for president reside in the U.S.A.?
14. How many words are in the presidential oath of office as specified by the Constitution?
15. What is the maximum period of time that a person can serve as president?
16. Which presidents each served less than two months' time after an inauguration?

10. Franklin Roosevelt (1942), so they could be of more use to the nation.
11. Abraham Lincoln's (1861). The cross-country ride took seven days, seventeen hours.
12. Franklin Roosevelt (1933)
13. Lyndon Johnson (1943), to make a job for himself by merging the NYA and the CCC.
14. During Grover Cleveland's Administration
15. James Monroe (1818), Richard Nixon (1974), and Ronald Reagan (1988)
16. Harry Truman's (1947)
17. George Washington's "Farewell Address," read annually since 1893 by alternating parties.
18. Andrew Johnson, for the Senate (1871) and the House (1872), both unsuccessfully.
19. James Garfield
20. Bill Clinton (1996), elected with 227 House Republicans and 55 Senate Republicans.
21. 1892, twenty-seven years after the Civil War had ended.

Congressional Composition (answers)

1. Grover Cleveland's (1893-1897)
2. John Tyler (1841-1845) and Ronald Reagan (1987-1989), respectively.
3. Thomas Jefferson (1801-1809) and Lyndon Johnson (1965-1969), respectively.
4. John Quincy Adams (1825-1829) and Bill Clinton (1995-2001), respectively.
5. Millard Fillmore, Richard Nixon, Gerald Ford, and George Bush

Constitution (answers)

1. Thomas Jefferson (1789)
2. John Adams (1787), in France.
3. James Monroe (1788), as a delegate to the Virginia Ratifying Convention.
4. It forbids any "present, emolument, office, or title" without congressional approval.
5. James Madison (1789), the Twenty-Seventh Amendment, ratified in 1992.
6. John Adams (1779), who wrote the Massachusetts Constitution.
7. James Madison (1790), based upon the Massachusetts Bill of Rights.
8. James Madison (1836)
9. George Washington and James Madison (1787)
10. Franklin Roosevelt's. The new Constitution, obviously, was never approved.
11. James Madison's (1787), because reporters and the public were barred.
12. Dwight Eisenhower
13. Fourteen years before inauguration
14. Located in Article II, Section 1, it is thirty-five words long.
15. Ten years (two years as VP succeeding to president and two terms as president)
16. William Henry Harrison (1841) and Abraham Lincoln (1865)

17. Which president served a full term in office that was less than four years long?
18. After how many days does a bill become law if the president does not sign it?
19. How long did Founding Father George Washington predict the Constitution would last?
20. Which president suspended the writ of habeus corpus?
21. Which president sponsored a constitutional amendment to protect pre-born children?
22. What is the constitutional age requirement for a president?

Convention Ballots
1. Which president was first nominated on the first ballot of a national convention?
2. Which Republican candidate was first nominated *unanimously* on the first ballot?
3. Which Republican candidate was the last one who needed more than one ballot?
4. Through 1972, which party won more times with first-ballot nominees?
5. How many total convention ballots have Republicans and Democrats had since 1856?
6. What is the record number of ballots for a Republican National Convention?
7. What is the record number of ballots for a Democratic National Convention?
8. During which national convention was an automatic-voting machine first used?
9. How many ballots did it take to nominate Woodrow Wilson in 1912?

Convention Cities
1. In which city have more national conventions been held than any other?
2. In which city have more Republican National Conventions been held than any other?
3. In which city have more Democratic National Conventions been held than any other?
4. Which cities held *both* major-party national conventions in the same year?
5. Which two presidents were nominated in two different churches in the same city?
6. Which national ticket held national conventions in the same city *and* were re-elected?
7. Which national convention adjourned without nominating a presidential candidate?
8. Where in the South did Democrats first hold a national convention after the Civil War?

Convention Media
1. Which national convention was first broadcast by telegraph?
2. Which national convention was first broadcast on television?
3. Which national convention was first broadcast live on television?
4. Which national convention was first broadcast live and nationwide on television?
5. Which national convention was first broadcast on closed-circuit cable television?
6. Which national convention first televised by its own proceedings?
7. Which national convention was first broadcast in real-time coverage on its Web site?

17. Franklin Roosevelt, his first term was shortened by the Twentieth Amendment.
18. Ten
19. Twenty years
20. Abraham Lincoln (1861), due to the Civil War, probably his most controversial act.
21. Ronald Reagan (1988)
22. At least thirty-five years old on Inauguration Day

Convention Ballots (answers)
1. Andrew Jackson (1828)
2. Ulysses Grant (1868)
3. Thomas Dewey (1948), nominated on the third ballot.
4. The Republicans
5. 106 and 263, respectively.
6. Thirty-six ballots (1880 Republican National Convention)
7. 103 ballots (1924 Democratic National Convention)
8. The 1908 Democratic National Convention
9. Forty-six. At the next convention, Wilson got every single delegate vote except one.

Convention Cities (answers)
1. Chicago, Illinois, which has held twenty-four national conventions.
2. Chicago, Illinois, which has held fourteen Republican National Conventions.
3. Chicago, Illinois, which has held ten Democratic National Conventions.
4. Chicago (1884, 1932, 1944, 1952), Philadelphia (1948), and Miami Beach (1972)
5. Martin Van Buren (1840) and William Henry Harrison (1840), in Baltimore, Maryland.
6. Richard Nixon and Spiro Agnew (1972), in Miami Beach, Florida.
7. The 1860 Democratic National Convention, which moved from Charleston to Baltimore.
8. Houston, Texas (1928).

Convention Media (answers)
1. The 1844 Democratic National Convention, between Baltimore and Washington, DC.
2. The 1928 Republican National Convention
3. The 1948 Republican National Convention, broadcast live from Richmond to Boston.
4. The 1952 Democratic National Convention
5. The 1964 Democratic National Convention
6. The 1996 Republican National Convention, on a cable channel called "GOP-TV."
7. The 1996 Republican National Convention

8. Which national convention was first Internet enabled?
9. Which national convention was first broadcast live on HDTV?
10. Which national convention first featured an Intranet for press updates?

Convention Speeches

1. Which president first traveled to his party's national convention?
2. Who was the last person to make an acceptance speech away from the convention?
3. With which president's quotation did Ronald Reagan finish his acceptance speech?
4. Which Republican presidential nominee first made an acceptance speech?
5. At which convention did a "nominating speech" first appear?
6. Which president memorized and recited his national-convention address?
7. What were Jimmy Carter's first words to the 1976 Democratic National Convention?
8. Which president delivered a national-convention address on his birthday?
9. Which president's convention speech gave Sweden an undeserved reputation of suicide?
10. Which president had won national prominence supporting Barry Goldwater's candidacy?
11. When did Abraham Lincoln declare, "A house divided against itself cannot stand"?

Convention Women

1. Which major-party national convention first voted to require 50% female delegates?
2. Which major-party national convention last had 50% or more female delegates?
3. Which major-party national convention did a woman first address?
4. Which major-party national convention first featured female alternates?
5. Which major-party national convention first featured female delegates?
6. Which major-party national convention first featured a female committee chairman?
7. Which major-party national convention first featured a female nominator?
8. Which major-party national convention first featured a female candidate nominated?
9. Which major-party national convention first featured a female keynote speaker?
10. Who seconded Theodore Roosevelt at the Progressive Party National Convention?
11. Which national convention placed in nomination Judge Sarah T. Hughes?
12. Who promised revolt if a woman was not chosen at the Democratic National Convention?

Conventions

1. Which national convention was the shortest one ever?
2. Which Republican National Convention was the shortest ever?
3. Which national convention was the longest one for either major political party?
4. Which Ohio politician masterminded Warren Harding's national-convention victory?

8. The 2000 Republican National Convention
9. The 2000 Republican National Convention, by Japan Broadcasting Corporation.
10. The 2000 Republican National Convention, to distribute convention information.

Convention Speeches (answers)

1. Franklin Roosevelt (1932), to make an acceptance speech.
2. Alfred Smith (1928), from the State Capitol in Albany, New York.
3. Franklin Roosevelt's (1980)
4. Thomas Dewey (1944)
5. The 1831 National Republican Convention in Baltimore, as "an address to the people."
6. Franklin Pierce (1852)
7. "My name is Jimmy Carter, and I'm running for president," his first words on the stump.
8. Lyndon Johnson (1964)
9. Dwight Eisenhower's (1960), referring to a socialist country where "suicide has gone up."
10. Ronald Reagan (1964), at the Republican National Convention.
11. At the 1858 Illinois Republican State Convention

Convention Women (answers)

1. The 1980 Democratic National Convention, for all future conventions.
2. The 1988 Democratic National Convention (52%)
3. The 1892 Republican National Convention (Ellen Foster)
4. The 1892 Republican National Convention (Therese Jenkins and Cora Carleton)
5. The 1900 Republican National Convention (Frances Warring)
6. The 1928 Republican National Convention (Mabel Willenbrandt)
7. The 1940 Republican National Convention (Gladys Pyle)
8. The 1964 Republican National Convention (Margaret Chase Smith, for president)
9. The 1972 Republican National Convention (Anne Armstrong)
10. Jane Addams (1912)
11. The 1952 Democratic National Convention. She would swear in Lyndon Johnson.
12. The National Organization for Women (1984)

Conventions (answers)

1. The 1844 Whig National Convention (1 day)
2. The 1972 Republican National Convention (16 hours, 59 minutes)
3. The 1924 Democratic National Convention (14 days)
4. Harry Daugherty, whose "wait-em-out" tactic gave rise to the term "smoke-filled room."

5. Which Republican National Convention first featured full Southern delegations?

6. Which national convention required that the chairmanship alternate between sexes?

7. Which *incumbent* presidents sought re-nomination but were *denied*?

8. Which president was the first one who had been nominated by a national convention?

9. Why did Andrew Jackson convene the first Democratic National Convention?

10. Which national convention was held in winter?

11. At which Republican National Convention did managers forge admission slips?

12. Which Democratic National Convention did supporters with bogus passes pack?

13. Which likely presidential nominee first named his running mate *before* the convention?

14. Which presidential nominee first introduced his running mate to the convention?

15. Which black first received a bloc of delegates at a major-party national convention?

16. Which president had been a page at the 1900 Democratic National Convention?

17. Which national convention had a rostrum protected by barbed wire?

18. Which presidents were the first and last ones nominated by the caucus system?

19. Which president was last nominated over seven months before the election?

20. In which campaign were both major-party national conventions last held before June?

21. Between 1864 and 1952, when did Democrats hold their national convention first?

22. Which political party first created a central or national committee to organize itself?

23. Which national convention did *not* nominate a candidate for vice president?

24. Which national convention first nominated their presidential candidate by acclamation?

25. Which national convention first conducted business in committees?

26. Which Democratic National Convention abolished the two-thirds rule?

27. Where did the short-lived States' Rights Party hold its only national convention?

28. Which president met his running mate for the first time *after* the national convention?

29. Which national convention was held earliest in the year?

30. Which national convention was held latest in the year?

31. When was a major-party national convention last deadlocked?

32. Which national convention first elected a black as temporary convention chairman?

33. Which national convention chose a House leader as permanent convention chairman?

34. What probably squelched Theodore Roosevelt's chances for re-nomination?

35. Which national convention first used computers to project vote totals?

36. At which national convention did the first pre-meditated delegate demonstration occur?

37. Who nominated four men for vice president or president all named Charles?

38. Which Democratic ticket's nominees shared the same first name?

39. Which Republican ticket's nominees shared the same first name?

40. Which president attended his national convention wearing a huge Mexican sombrero?

41. Who seconded Democrat Averill Harriman's nomination for president in 1956?

42. Which president declined to address a women's suffrage national convention?

All the Presidents' Trivia

5. The 1868 Republican National Convention
6. The 1972 Democratic National Convention
7. Franklin Pierce (1856), Ulysses Grant (1876), and Chester Arthur (1884)
8. Andrew Jackson (1832)
9. Because he wanted to "dump" his vice president, John Calhoun (1832).
10. The 1831 National Republican Convention, in Baltimore. Many delegates arrived late.
11. The 1860 Republican National Convention, by Abraham Lincoln's campaign managers.
12. The 1940 Democratic National Convention, by Henry Wallace's supporters.
13. Walter Mondale (1984), who showcased Geraldine Ferraro.
14. Lyndon Johnson (1964 Democratic National Convention)
15. Jesse Jackson (1988 Democratic National Convention)
16. Harry Truman
17. The 1912 Republican National Convention, because the Roosevelt-Taft split was so acute.
18. James Madison (1808) and John Quincy Adams (1824), respectively.
19. Martin Van Buren (1836), so that more opposition could not mount against him.
20. The 1868 presidential campaign
21. 1888
22. The Democrats (1844), followed by the Whigs (1852) and the Republicans (1856).
23. The 1840 Democratic National Convention, because they opposed Vice President Johnson.
24. The 1831 Anti-Masonic National Convention
25. The 1831 Anti-Masonic National Convention
26. The 1936 Democratic National Convention, requiring Southern support for nomination.
27. Houston, Texas (1948), where Strom Thurmond and Fielding Wright were nominated.
28. Abraham Lincoln (1860), who had never met Hannibal Hamlin!
29. The 1860 Democratic National Convention (April 23-May 3, 1860)
30. The 2004 Republican National Convention (August 30-September 2, 2004)
31. The 1952 Democratic National Convention, which nominated Adlai Stevenson for president.
32. The 1884 Republican National Convention (Representative John Roy Lynch)
33. The 1932 Republican National Convention (Representative Bertrand Snell)
34. The re-allotment of delegates due to a Republican decline in the South (1912)
35. The 1960 Republican National Convention
36. The 1860 Republican National Convention, designed to benefit Abraham Lincoln.
37. The Republican Party (1904-1932), Messrs. Fairbanks, Hughes, Dawes, and Curtis.
38. George McClellan and George Pendleton (1864)
39. Charles Hughes and Charles Fairbanks (1916)
40. Theodore Roosevelt (1912)
41. Harry Truman, maybe the only time an ex-president seconded a person who did not win.
42. James Garfield (1872)

43. Who said that Democrats should avoid "the longhairs, the feminists, and the crazies"?
44. At which national convention did the balloons set to cascade onto delegates get stuck?
45. Who was one vote shy of becoming Abraham Lincoln's running mate in 1864?

Corpses
1. Which president's corpse was first exhumed and moved?
2. Which president's corpse did Congress vote to move to Washington, DC?
3. Which president's corpse was moved the most number of times?
4. Which president allegedly requested to be embalmed in whiskey?
5. Which president's corpse was first placed on a "funeral train"?
6. Which president escorted Abraham Lincoln's corpse from Batavia to Buffalo?
7. Which First Lady talked to her husband's corpse for hours before it was buried?
8. Which president's skull did a drunken workman try to steal?
9. Whose death more than any other convinced Americans of the benefits of embalming?
10. Which First Lady refused to allow her husband's corpse to be embalmed?
11. Which president first stipulated death guarantees?

Counties
1. In which county is George, Washington, located?
2. Which one of Texas's counties has the best record for selecting presidential winners?
3. Which county has voted for every presidential winner since 1896?
4. In which county were more presidents born than any other?
5. Which counties named for a president are the least and most populous?
6. In which county named for a president did the Battle of Antietam take place?
7. In which county named for a president can one find the Paw Paw River?
8. In which county named for a president was novelist Mark Twain born?
9. In which county can one find the geographical center of North America?
10. In which county can one find Des Moines?
11. In which counties can one find parts of Portland and St. Paul?
12. In which counties can one find Birmingham, Denver, New Orleans, and St. Louis?
13. For which top-three presidents are the most counties named?
14. Which states have the most counties named for presidents?
15. Where is McKinley County?
16. Where is Millard County?
17. What percentage of the counties' popular votes did George W. Bush win in 2000?
18. Which president failed to carry his home county in each of his presidential elections?
19. Which counties were "Ground Zero" during the Florida Recount in 2000?

43. John Connally (1968)
44. The 1980 Democratic National Convention
45. Representative Green Clay Smith (R-KY), who would have become president.

Corpses (answers)

1. William Henry Harrison's (1841), from Washington, DC, to North Bend, Ohio.
2. George Washington's, wanting to bury him underneath the new Capitol Building.
3. Abraham Lincoln's, seventeen times!
4. George Washington
5. Abraham Lincoln's (1865)
6. Millard Fillmore (1865)
7. Florence Harding (1923)
8. George Washington's, but he actually stole the skull of George Washington's nephew.
9. Abraham Lincoln's, because it allowed millions to see his corpse on its way to burial.
10. Margaret Taylor (1850)
11. George Washington, such as the draining of blood and removal of organs.

Counties (answers)

1. Grant County
2. Reagan County (almost 90%)
3. Palo Alto County, Iowa, through twenty-six straight elections.
4. Norfolk County, Massachusetts (4), both Adamses, John Kennedy, and George Bush.
5. Arthur County, Nebraska (556) and Jefferson County, Kentucky (684,793), respectively.
6. Washington County, Maryland.
7. Van Buren County, Michigan.
8. Monroe County, Missouri.
9. Pierce County, North Dakota.
10. Polk County, Iowa.
11. Washington Counties
12. Jefferson Counties
13. George Washington (30), Thomas Jefferson (25), and Abraham Lincoln (23)
14. Iowa and Nebraska (12), Missouri and Texas (11), and Georgia and Kentucky (10)
15. New Mexico
16. Utah
17. He won the countywide popular vote in 2,434 out of 3,111 counties (78.2%).
18. Franklin Roosevelt (Duchess County, New York)
19. Miami-Dade and Palm Beach Counties, Florida.

Countries

1. Which president settled a dispute between businessmen and the country of Peru?
2. Which president first sent armed escorts of freed American slaves back to Africa?
3. Which president led the American Colonization Society?
4. Which country named one of its departments (states) for a U.S. president?
5. Which president had an honorary citizenship from San Marino, Europe's smallest country?
6. Which president tried hard to "acquire" the Republic of Santo Domingo?
7. Which president ardently opposed the annexation of the Philippines?
8. Which president recognized a foreign country after it was only twelve minutes old?
9. Which president refused to recognize white insurrectionists who had seized Hawaii?
10. From which country did John Kennedy remove missiles to settle the Cuban Missile Crisis?
11. To which president is ground dedicated at Runnymede?
12. Which royal emblem incorporated the U.S. flag?
13. Which president wanted to buy Cuba from Spain?
14. Which president claimed, "Poland is not under Soviet domination"?
15. Which president first failed to make a proclamation during Captive Nations Week?

Currency

1. Which president wanted to have the motto "In God We Trust" removed from U.S. currency?
2. Which president signed an act allowing the use of the national motto on all U.S. currency?
3. Which presidents appeared on foreign currency?
4. Which presidents appeared on food coupons issued by the Department of Agriculture?
5. Which president devised the decimal system of currency still in use today in the U.S.A.?
6. Which presidents *never* carried credit cards and cash, respectively?
7. Which president forever removed the dollar from the "gold standard"?
8. Which president last introduced a *foreign* currency?
9. During which president's tenure was the dollar strongest against most currencies?

Dams

1. Where is the Madison Dam?
2. Where is the Buchanan Dam?
3. Where is the Lake Lincoln Dam?
4. Where is the Theodore Roosevelt Dam?
5. Where is the Coolidge Dam?
6. Where is the Hoover Dam?
7. Where is the Truman Dam?
8. Where is the Eisenhower Dam?

Countries (answers)

1. Millard Fillmore (1850), over guano deposits.
2. James Monroe (1822), leading to the creation of Liberia in 1847.
3. James Madison (1836-1849), whose purpose was to re-settle American slaves in Africa.
4. Paraguay, which country named Presidente Hayes for Rutherford Hayes.
5. Abraham Lincoln
6. Ulysses Grant
7. Grover Cleveland (1901), after the Spanish-American War.
8. Harry Truman (1948), who recognized Israel.
9. Grover Cleveland (1893). The rebels had seized control from Queen Lili'uokalani.
10. Turkey
11. John Kennedy, where King John I of England had signed the Magna Carta.
12. Yap's
13. James Buchanan (1857)
14. Gerald Ford (1976), at the height of the Cold War, damaging his chances of re-election.
15. Bill Clinton (1996). The week seeks the freedom of China, Cuba, and North Korea.

Currency (answers)

1. Theodore Roosevelt, because he thought it was unconstitutional and blasphemous.
2. Dwight Eisenhower (1955). The 1957 $1 silver certificate was the first money to bear it.
3. George Washington (1903-1949) and William McKinley (1916-1937), in the Philippines.
4. John Adams and Thomas Jefferson
5. Thomas Jefferson
6. Dwight Eisenhower and John Kennedy
7. Richard Nixon (1971), letting the dollar float freely against other currencies.
8. George W. Bush (2003), who introduced the new Iraqi dinar, without Hussein's portrait.
9. Ronald Reagan's (1981-1983)

Dams (answers)

1. Madison County, Montana, on the Madison River.
2. One hour northwest of Austin, Texas, although it was not named for James Buchanan.
3. Just northwest of St. Louis, Missouri, near the Mississippi River.
4. Near Phoenix, Arizona, on the Salt River.
5. In Southeast Arizona, on the Gila River.
6. Nevada and Arizona
7. Warsaw, Missouri, near Clinton, Missouri.
8. Lake Texoma, on the border between Oklahoma and Texas.

Death Geography

1. Which president died the farthest north?
2. Which president died the farthest south?
3. Which president died the farthest east?
4. Which president died the farthest west?
5. Which president died at Walter Reed Hospital, in Washington, DC?
6. Which president died in the air?
7. Which president died twenty-seven years before his wife died, in the *same* hotel?
8. Which presidents died inside the White House?
9. Which president died just feet from where he had been inaugurated?
10. Which president "was present at the accidental death of a prostitute during a wild party?"

Death Timing

1. Which president died in the eighteenth century?
2. Which presidents died earliest and latest in the nineteenth century?
3. Which presidents died earliest and latest in the twentieth century?
4. In which month have the most presidents died?
5. In which month has no president died?
6. Which three presidents died on the same day of the year?
7. Which presidents died the shortest and longest periods of time after their tenures?
8. Which president died in the year of his age?
9. In which two years have there been three presidents?
10. What is the greatest number of presidents ever alive at one time?
11. After which president's death did London's Big Ben toll every minute for an hour?

Deaths

1. For which presidents' deaths was the White House draped in black?
2. Which presidents' deaths did doctors probably hasten, unintentionally?
3. Which president, ironically, died the youngest from natural causes?
4. Which presidents lied in state in the Capitol Rotunda, all on the same black catafalque?
5. Which presidents were the first and last ones who lied in state at the White House?
6. Which president was the youngest at death and which one will be the oldest at death?
7. Which other presidents have reached at least ninety years of age?
8. What was John Quincy Adams doing when he suffered a fatal heart attack?
9. Which president's death was completely ignored by the federal government?
10. Which president's death prompted ten days of mourning in France?

Death Geography (answers)

1. Franklin Pierce (1869), in Concord, New Hampshire.
2. Lyndon Johnson (1973), in Johnson City, Texas.
3. John Adams (1826), in Braintree, Massachusetts.
4. Warren Harding (1923), in San Francisco, California.
5. Dwight Eisenhower (1969)
6. Lyndon Johnson (1972), in a helicopter, bound for a hospital in San Antonio, Texas.
7. John Tyler (1866), in Richmond, Virginia.
8. William Henry Harrison (1841) and Zachary Taylor (1850)
9. John Quincy Adams (1848), who was inaugurated and died in the House chamber.
10. Warren Harding

Death Timing (answers)

1. George Washington (1799)
2. John Adams (1826) and Rutherford Hayes (1893), respectively.
3. Benjamin Harrison (1901) and Richard Nixon (1994), respectively.
4. July (7)
5. May
6. John Adams, Thomas Jefferson, and James Monroe (July 4)
7. James Polk (123 days) and Herbert Hoover (31 years, 231 days), respectively.
8. Millard Fillmore (1874), at the age of seventy-four years.
9. 1841 and 1881
10. Six (Nixon through Clinton, inclusive, and Ford through George W. Bush, inclusive)
11. John Kennedy's

Deaths (answers)

1. William Henry Harrison's (1841) and Abraham Lincoln's (1865), who both died in office.
2. George Washington's (1799) and James Garfield's (1881)
3. Theodore Roosevelt (1919), at the age of sixty years, ironic because he was so active.
4. Lincoln, Garfield, McKinley, Harding, Taft, Kennedy, Hoover, Eisenhower, and Johnson
5. William Henry Harrison (1841) and Lyndon Johnson (1972), respectively.
6. John Kennedy (46 years, 177 days) and Ronald Reagan (over 92 years), respectively.
7. John Adams (1825), Herbert Hoover (1964), and Gerald Ford (2003)
8. Making a speech against U.S. entrance into the Mexican War (1848)
9. John Tyler's (1862), due to his support for the Confederacy.
10. George Washington's (1799)

11. Which presidents were the first and last ones who died in office?
12. Who was the first person to succeed to the presidency?
13. After which president's death did Richard Nixon say he cried?
14. Which president last lost consciousness while alone and later died?
15. Which president dreamed of his death and even related his dream to the Senate?
16. Who advised Vice President John Tyler of William Henry Harrison's death?
17. After which president's death was the Panama Canal closed?
18. Of which president's face was a death mask made?
19. Who said that he wanted the president pro tempore of the Senate to succeed him?
20. After which president's death did networks broadcast for seventy-one hours?
21. Which president wore mourning attire for six months for his immediate predecessor?
22. Which president had been administered last rites after a back operation?
23. What is it customary for the public to do when a president or former president dies?
24. After which president's death did veterans nail the U.S. flag to the door of an embassy?
25. Which president refused to leave his bedroom for a month after his wife had died?
26. Which president's funeral was attended by five incumbent or former U.S. presidents?
27. Which president was not a United States citizen at the time of his death?

Declaration of Independence
1. Which president loaned the original Declaration of Independence to Philadelphia?
2. Whose first draft of the Declaration of Independence abolished slavery?
3. Which president was given the Czechoslovakian Declaration of Independence?
4. What fraction of Thomas Jefferson's original Declaration of Independence was re-worded?
5. Did George Washington sign the Declaration of Independence?
6. How long did it take Thomas Jefferson to write the Declaration of Independence?

Delegates
1. Which delegate announced the death of Calvin Coolidge, Jr.?
2. Which Southern state had the only delegation at the first Republican National Convention?
3. Which Republican nominee selected the runner-up in delegates to be his running mate?
4. How many delegates did John Connally get at the 1980 Republican National Convention?
5. Which Republican presidential candidate received zero delegate votes against him?
6. Who was the oldest delegate at the 1980 Republican National Convention?
7. Who pioneered guerrilla tactics in delegate selection, taking control from party leaders?
8. Who threatened his delegates not to run if they denied his vice presidential choice?
9. Which political party first considered delegate credentials carefully?
10. Which presidential nominee had been a delegate to a Progressive National Convention?

11. William Henry Harrison (1841) and John Kennedy (1963), respectively.
12. John Tyler (1841), after the death in office of William Henry Harrison.
13. Dwight Eisenhower's (1969)
14. Lyndon Johnson (1972)
15. Abraham Lincoln (1865)
16. Fletcher Webster (1841), son of Daniel Webster.
17. John Kennedy's (1963)
18. John Tyler's (1866)
19. Chester Arthur, in case anything were to happen to him.
20. John Kennedy's (1963), without a single commercial.
21. Chester Arthur (1881-1882), for James Garfield.
22. John Kennedy (1954)
23. Enter thirty days' mourning, or as dictated by the flags on the Capitol Building.
24. Woodrow Wilson's (1924), at the German Embassy, after it had refused to lower its flag.
25. Thomas Jefferson (1782)
26. Richard Nixon's (1994)
27. John Tyler (1866), after renouncing his U.S. citizenship. Jimmy Carter restored it to him.

Declaration of Independence (answers)

1. Ulysses Grant (1876), for its Centennial Exposition.
2. Thomas Jefferson's (1776), but it was removed due to "popular pressure."
3. Woodrow Wilson (1919), at the Paris Peace Conference, by nationalist Tomas Masaryk.
4. One-third
5. No
6. About two weeks

Delegates (answers)

1. Franklin Roosevelt (1924), at the Democratic National Convention.
2. Kentucky (1856)
3. Ronald Reagan (1980), who selected George Bush, the only time that has happened.
4. One (Ada Mills of Alaska)
5. Ronald Reagan (1984), although there were two abstentions.
6. Hamilton Fish (91), who said Reagan was the best campaigner he had seen since TR.
7. William Rusher and F. Clifton White
8. Franklin Roosevelt (1936), at the Democratic National Convention.
9. The Anti-Masonic Party
10. George McGovern (1948), nominated for president by the Democrats (1972).

11. Since when have national committees created the temporary roll of delegates?
12. Which national convention first instituted a party-loyalty provision for future conventions?
13. Which political party first nominated a candidate by acclamation *after* the delegate vote?
14. Who was the last surviving delegate to the Virginia Constitutional Convention of 1776?
15. Which presidents met each other at a Boys' Nation conference?
16. Who hired detectives to prevent each other from bribing delegates to the convention?
17. At which national convention did a delegate try to nominate "Joe Smith" for president?
18. Which black first received a delegate for president at a major-party national convention?
19. Which future president received two delegates at a national convention?
20. Which major-party national convention first modified its delegate-allocation method?
21. Which major-party national convention first instituted a bonus system?
22. Which Republican National Convention first had delegates from every state?
23. What is the largest delegation that any state has ever sent to a national convention?
24. Which national convention started the "majority-rules" tradition within a state delegation?
25. Which presidents were the first and last ones who had been national delegates?

Diaries

1. Which president first kept a diary?
2. Which president wrote in his diary, "I am the hardest-working man in the country"?
3. Who had the diaries of Franklin Roosevelt "edited" to remove discrediting comments?
4. Which president was the most dedicated diarist?
5. Which president wrote in his diary that he hated doling federal patronage?
6. Which president made an entry in his diary for *every day* of his life during two decades?
7. Which president wrote in his diary, "The Jews, I find are very, very selfish"?
8. Which president first created an Office of the Presidential Diary?
9. Which president wrote in his diary that he would be "rooting for" his successor?

Dinners

1. Who were always served first at Andrew Jackson's dinner table?
2. Which president probably served more food at a time than any other?
3. Which president usually spent two or three hours at the dinner table?
4. Which president began celebrating Thanksgiving on the last Thursday of November?
5. Which president was served "fragrant meat" that was really "the upper lip of a wild dog"?
6. Which president was treated to two seventy-course meals by the Chinese government?
7. Which president served steaks, baked potatoes, and pecan pie on the White House roof?
8. Which president broke a tradition excluding women from the Alfalfa Club Dinner?
9. Which president occasionally ate from White House guests' dinner plates?

11. The 1852 presidential campaign
12. The 1956 Democratic National Convention
13. The Anti-Masonic Party. Delegates still do so today to unite behind their nominee.
14. James Madison (1836)
15. John Kennedy and Bill Clinton (1963)
16. William Taft and Theodore Roosevelt (1912)
17. The 1956 Republican National Convention. The delegate was from Nebraska.
18. Frederick Douglass (1888), on the fourth ballot, by the Republican Party.
19. Ronald Reagan (1968). The delegates were from Texas.
20. The 1916 Republican National Convention, reducing delegates from Southern states.
21. The 1924 Republican National Convention, by which states were rewarded for loyalty.
22. The 1880 Republican National Convention
23. The California delegation (433) to the 2000 Democratic National Convention
24. The 1832 Democratic National Convention
25. Abraham Lincoln (1848) and George W. Bush (1996), respectively.

Diaries (answers)
1. George Washington (1765)
2. James Polk (1845)
3. J. Edgar Hoover, even *after* the diaries had been deposited in libraries!
4. John Quincy Adams, who kept a diary for seventy years!
5. Warren Harding
6. John Quincy Adams
7. Harry Truman (1947), the man who recognized the country of Israel in record time.
8. Ronald Reagan (1991), at his presidential library, to provide access to his diary.
9. George Bush (1993), after a bitter defeat at the polls.

Dinners (answers)
1. Children
2. Ulysses Grant, up to twenty-nine courses for a state dinner!
3. Chester Arthur
4. George Washington (1789)
5. George Bush (1972), in China.
6. Ulysses Grant (1879), during a world tour after leaving office.
7. Lyndon Johnson
8. Bill Clinton (1994), by bringing his wife. The tradition had stood for ninety years.
9. Lyndon Johnson

Diseases and Afflictions

1. Which president proudly pointed to the scar left after his gall-bladder operation?
2. Which president's face was scarred by smallpox, which he had contracted as a child?
3. Which president almost died of dengue fever that he had contracted overseas?
4. Which president suffered life-long bouts of "melancholia," or extreme depression?
5. Which presidents were afflicted with hemorrhoids?
6. Which president caught influenza during a worldwide epidemic of the virus?
7. Which president suffered repeatedly from acute constipation?
8. Which president suffered from acute indigestion and used a stomach pump on himself?
9. Which president was the only one who died from any form of cancer?
10. Which president's family suffered genetically from pancreatic cancer?
11. Which president officially declared war on cancer?
12. Which president was asthmatic?
13. Which president coughed so often that he thought he had tuberculosis?
14. Which president almost died of diphtheria as a child?
15. Which president suffered from Addison's Disease?
16. Which presidents suffered from Bright's Disease?
17. Which president suffered from chronic sinusitis?
18. Which president bathed his feet in cold water every morning?
19. Which president had psychosomatic seizures similar to epilepsy?
20. Which president first suffered a heart attack while in office?
21. Which president survived a gallstone operation *without* anesthesia or antiseptics?
22. Which president suffered from bursitis and ileitis?
23. Which president do some historians believe had syphilis?
24. Which president was struck with poliomyelitis, crippling him for life?
25. Which presidents suffered debilitating strokes?
26. Which president had an adrenal deficiency?
27. Which president suffered from deafness at a late age, and became deaf in one ear?
28. Which president had had malaria, smallpox, pleurisy, and dysentery?
29. Which president almost died after catching a fever in Japan?
30. Which president was among the first Americans inoculated for smallpox?
31. Of what did William Henry Harrison die?
32. Which president almost died of viral pneumonia while in his thirties?
33. Which president likely had Marfan Syndrome, whose victims grow tall and gangly?
34. Which president caught malaria, suffered from hideous abscesses, and lost fifty pounds?
35. Which president suffered from gallstones?
36. Which presidents suffered from terrible bouts of rheumatism?
37. Which president suffered from Alzheimer's disease?

Diseases and Afflictions (answers)

1. Lyndon Johnson (1965)
2. George Washington's
3. William Taft
4. Abraham Lincoln
5. Gerald Ford and Jimmy Carter
6. Woodrow Wilson (1919), at the Paris Peace Conference.
7. Abraham Lincoln
8. Woodrow Wilson
9. Ulysses Grant (1885), who died from throat cancer.
10. Jimmy Carter's. Pancreatic cancer killed his father, brother, and sister.
11. Richard Nixon (1971)
12. Theodore Roosevelt
13. Calvin Coolidge
14. Harry Truman
15. John Kennedy
16. James Garfield and Chester Arthur
17. Franklin Roosevelt
18. Thomas Jefferson, believing it kept away colds.
19. James Madison
20. Dwight Eisenhower (1955), in Denver, Colorado.
21. James Polk (1813), at the age of seventeen years.
22. Dwight Eisenhower
23. Abraham Lincoln
24. Franklin Roosevelt (1921), at his island home of "Campobello" in Maine.
25. George Washington and Woodrow Wilson
26. John Kennedy
27. Theodore Roosevelt, after developing mastoiditis. Herbert Hoover also became deaf.
28. Abraham Lincoln, all before he was thirty years old!
29. John Kennedy
30. Thomas Jefferson (1766)
31. Pneumonia, after not protecting himself adequately from cold weather at his inauguration.
32. Ronald Reagan
33. Abraham Lincoln
34. Theodore Roosevelt (1914), after an expedition to the Amazon River.
35. James Polk
36. Thomas Jefferson and James Madison
37. Ronald Reagan

38. Which president became addicted to cocaine?

39. Which president suffered from maniaphobia, the fear of going insane, as a youth?

Dogs

1. Which president recorded a duet with his dog titled "Dogs Have Always Been My Friends"?

2. What was the *full* name of Franklin Roosevelt's inseparable black Scottie?

3. Which president had a black Scottie named "Spunky" while in the military?

4. What was the name of Herbert Hoover's favorite dog, which nobody was allowed to pet?

5. Which president had a Llewellyn setter named "Winks"?

6. Which president had a golden retriever named "Liberty," who would pounce on visitors?

7. Which president's Airedale terrier was issued Washington Dog License #1?

8. Who became livid upon learning that sailors had cut hair from his dog for souvenirs?

9. Which president was allergic to dog hair?

10. Which president had a Scotch terrier named "Meggie," who liked to sleep in fireplaces?

11. What was the name of John Kennedy's favorite dog?

12. Which president's dog was sent to Marine training school to gain discipline, but failed?

13. What was the name of the dog that Richard Nixon ardently defended in a famous speech?

14. Which president enjoyed training dogs to sit on chairs and perform at cabinet meetings?

15. Which president's bull terrier chewed a hole in the pants of the French ambassador?

16. Which president's buff and black German shepherd bit a British prime minister?

17. Which president had a Chesapeake retriever named "Sailor Boy"?

18. Which president saved a dog's life by getting a judge to reverse his condemnation order?

19. Which president revealed that he showered with his dog about once a week?

20. Which president had a large, shaggy English sheepdog named "Tiny"?

21. Which president had bred dogs named "Mopsey," "Taster," "Cloe," and "Forester"?

22. Which president had a wolfhound named "Wolf"?

23. Which president's dog wore boots in the rain and dressed in a "coat" for a wedding?

24. Which president had an Irish cocker spaniel named "Shannon"?

25. Which president's dogs included a Shetland sheepdog and a reddish-brown chow?

26. Which president's dog delivered the newspaper to his master every morning?

27. Which president caused the greatest outrage over a president's handling of his pet?

28. Which president had a huge Great Dane named "President"?

29. For whom was the Bushes' dog, "Millie," named?

30. Which president had a white English bulldog named "Oh Boy"?

31. Which president's Weimeraner was "exiled" to a farm after urinating in the White House?

32. Which president's dog's house had a parquet floor and flagpole?

33. Which president's dog stood on its hind legs whenever the national anthem was played?

38. Ulysses Grant, after taking it for medicinal purposes.
39. Rutherford Hayes

Dogs (answers)

1. Lyndon Johnson, with "Yuki."
2. "Murray, the Outlaw of Fallahill," or "Fala" for short.
3. Dwight Eisenhower
4. "King Tut"
5. Franklin Roosevelt. The dog was buried in a dog cemetery in Silver Spring, Maryland.
6. Gerald Ford
7. Warren Harding's, "Laddie Boy."
8. Franklin Roosevelt, from "Fala."
9. John Kennedy
10. Franklin Roosevelt
11. "Charlie"
12. Calvin Coolidge's, "Paul Pry."
13. "Checkers," named by Nixon's daughters, Tricia and Julie.
14. Warren Harding
15. Theodore Roosevelt's
16. Franklin Roosevelt's, who bit British Prime Minister Ramsay MacDonald.
17. Theodore Roosevelt
18. Warren Harding
19. George Bush
20. Franklin Roosevelt
21. George Washington
22. John Kennedy
23. Lyndon Johnson's, "Yuki."
24. John Kennedy, from Irish Prime Minister Eamon de Valera.
25. Calvin Coolidge's
26. Herbert Hoover's, "King Tut."
27. Lyndon Johnson, by pulling his dog "Him" up in the air by its ears.
28. Franklin Roosevelt
29. "Mildred Kerr Bush" was named for Mildred Kerr, wife of friend Baine P. Kerr.
30. Warren Harding
31. Dwight Eisenhower's
32. Ronald Reagan's
33. Franklin Roosevelt's, "Fala."

34. Which president had a Japanese poodle?
35. Which president's dog appeared in almost every newspaper in the Free World?
36. Which president's family dog was named "Black Jack"?
37. Which president quipped, "If you want a friend in this life, get a dog"?
38. Which president's dog traveled more than any other president's animal?
39. Which president fed his dog in the White House State Dining Room?
40. Which president was given a dog named "Pushinka"?
41. Which president was given a dog named "Edgar"?
42. Which president had a white collie named "Rob Roy" for a Highland outlaw?
43. Which president returned his military opponent's dog to him under a flag of truce?
44. Which president dressed his dogs for the annual Easter Egg Hunt at the White House?
45. Which president, who became known for his cat, actually had owned a dog first?
46. Who said that he "who does not like dogs . . . does not deserve to be in the White House"?
47. Which president had a handsome chocolate Labrador named "Buddy"?
48. Which president named his dog "Veto" as a hint to Congress to pass his agenda?
49. Which presidential candidate first campaigned with his dog?
50. Which president had a dog named "Spot," the only second-generation presidential pet?
51. Which journalist called George Bush a "lap dog [with] a thin, tinny 'Arf'"?

Drink

1. Whose favorite drink was an old-fashioned, for which he kept secret caches of bourbon?
2. Which presidents liked Madeira wine and often served it to their guests?
3. Which president did Texas hero Sam Houston say drank too much water?
4. Which president served alcohol in the White House only once?
5. Who did hatchet-wielding teetotaler Carry Nation claim appeared to her in "visions"?
6. Which president helped popularize the daiquiri?
7. Which president liked the taste of daiquiris and often served them at the White House?
8. For which soft drink did Lyndon Johnson install special dispensers in the White House?
9. Who was our greatest milk-drinking president?
10. Who was our greatest beer-drinking president?
11. Who allegedly coined the phrase "Good to the Last Drop" for Maxwell House Coffee?
12. Which president enjoyed sipping Chinese green tea?
13. What was George Washington's liquor bill for his first year in office?
14. Who persuaded Richard Nixon to steer Nikita Khrushchev to the Pepsi booth?
15. Who would say that he was going to church but instead buy a "cask of 'Old J.B. Whiskey'"?
16. Which frugal president often served ice water in plain paper cups to his guests?
17. Which president do most historians consider to have been an alcoholic?

34. Grover Cleveland
35. Franklin Roosevelt's, "Fala."
36. Theodore Roosevelt's
37. Harry Truman
38. Franklin Roosevelt's, "Fala."
39. Calvin Coolidge, where state banquets were held.
40. John Kennedy. "Pushinka" was the child of "Strelka," the first Soviet animal in space.
41. Lyndon Johnson, from FBI Director J. Edgar Hoover.
42. Calvin Coolidge
43. George Washington, to British General William Howe.
44. Calvin Coolidge
45. Bill Clinton, named "Zeke." The dog tragically had been run over by an automobile driver.
46. Calvin Coolidge
47. Bill Clinton (1998), named for that president's favorite uncle.
48. James Garfield
49. William Henry Harrison (1840)
50. George W. Bush (2001–)
51. Columnist George Will (1988)

Drink (answers)

1. Harry Truman's. During Prohibition, Hoover stopped at the Belgian Embassy for martinis.
2. George Washington and James Buchanan
3. James Polk
4. Rutherford Hayes, after the State Department said doing so would help Russian relations.
5. William McKinley, giving her "a license" to smash saloons.
6. Theodore Roosevelt
7. John Kennedy
8. Fresca
9. Andrew Johnson
10. Grover Cleveland, once grudgingly restricting himself to four glasses daily.
11. Theodore Roosevelt, while at Andrew Jackson's homestead, The Hermitage.
12. Herbert Hoover. John Adams never drank tea again after the Boston Tea Party (1774).
13. $2,000, a sum conservatively equivalent to $500,000 today!
14. Pepsi-Cola executive Donald Kendall (1959), at a trade exhibit in Moscow, Russia.
15. James Buchanan
16. Calvin Coolidge
17. Franklin Pierce

18. Who encouraged Italian growers to settle in his home state and reproduce their grapes?
19. Who mixed the first drink in the White House after Prohibition had been repealed?
20. Which president, upon leaving office, said, "There's nothing [to do] . . . but to get drunk"?
21. For which president was a drink named?

Economics

1. Which presidents first and last attended an Economic Summit of Industrialized Nations?
2. Which presidents first and last hosted an Economic Summit of Industrialized Nations?
3. Which president first took steps to deal with an economic depression?
4. What was the name of John Kennedy's ten-year program of aid for Latin America?
5. Who told the unemployed they were "too damn dumb" to fathom the Great Depression?
6. Which president first visited the World Economic Forum in Davos, Switzerland?

Education

1. Which president *never* had attended any school of formal education?
2. Which president could understand French, Greek, Irish Gaelic, Italian, Latin, and Spanish?
3. Which presidents had been taught to read and write by their wives?
4. Who created the idea that academics' guiding two-way discussion is mutually beneficial?
5. Which president called the governors to a meeting addressing a single national issue?
6. Which *incumbent* president taught Sunday school fourteen times?
7. Which president received the degree of Master of Business Administration (M.B.A.)?

Elections

1. Which two native sons did Southerners overwhelmingly *reject* for the White House?
2. Which Republican presidential nominee finished third on Election Day?
3. Which president received the smallest share of votes from eligible citizens in an election?
4. Which president was elected in a year ending in an odd number?
5. Which single person decided the victor in the 1824 presidential election?
6. How many presidents have failed to win re-election during wartime?
7. Which presidential election was contested among three newspapermen?
8. Which two presidents never had voted until their own presidential elections?
9. Which presidents were the youngest and oldest ones at the time of election, respectively?
10. Which political party first formed a national committee to help its nominee win election?
11. During which presidential election did the highest percentage of eligible voters "turn out"?
12. In which other presidential elections did more than 80% of eligible voters participate?
13. Which president was re-elected after a major financial crisis?

18. Thomas Jefferson, in Virginia. Jefferson installed the first wine cellar in the White House.

19. Franklin Roosevelt (1933), who made a martini.

20. Franklin Pierce

21. William McKinley (1896). The "McKinley" was born at the Republican National Convention.

Economics (answers)

1. Gerald Ford (1975) and George W. Bush (2004), respectively.

2. Gerald Ford (1976) and George W. Bush (2004), respectively.

3. Herbert Hoover (1930). His predecessor largely had ignored them.

4. "Alliance for Progress"

5. Calvin Coolidge (1928)

6. Bill Clinton (2000)

Education (answers)

1. Millard Fillmore

2. Thomas Jefferson

3. Millard Fillmore and Franklin Pierce

4. Woodrow Wilson

5. George Bush (1989), addressing education.

6. Jimmy Carter (1977-1980), at the First Baptist Church in Washington, DC.

7. George W. Bush (1975), at Harvard University.

Elections (answers)

1. Zachary Taylor (1848) and Jimmy Carter (1980)

2. William Taft (1912), against Woodrow Wilson and Theodore Roosevelt.

3. Martin Van Buren (1836), with 11.4%.

4. George Washington (1789), in the first presidential election.

5. Representative Stephen van Rensselaer (R-NY), the deciding vote in his state delegation.

6. None

7. The 1920 presidential election, among Warren Harding, James Cox, and Robert Macauley.

8. Zachary Taylor (1848) and Dwight Eisenhower (1952)

9. John Kennedy (43 years, 236 days) and Ronald Reagan (73 years, 272 days)

10. The Democratic-Republicans (1804)

11. The 1876 presidential election (86%)

12. The 1840 and 1860 presidential elections

13. James Monroe (1820)

14. Which president was elected to two non-consecutive terms?
15. In which presidential election did Americans first vote along geographically sectional lines?
16. In which elections did more than one, ten, fifty, and 100 million persons first vote?
17. On how many Southern states' ballots did Abraham Lincoln appear in 1860?
18. Which president was the only one elected unanimously in the Electoral College?
19. By federal law, when is the presidential Election Day?
20. In which year was the first national Election Day recognized?
21. Which presidential election was described as the "Battle of the Standards"?
22. Which president was the first "minority president"?
23. In which presidential election were computers first used to project final returns?
24. Which president was the first one defeated for re-election?
25. Which Democratic presidents were defeated for re-election?
26. Which Republican presidents were defeated for re-election?
27. No incumbent president has been defeated in an election year ending in which number?
28. Which president probably got the highest percentage of new voters?
29. Which president won a presidential election after three previous attempts at nomination?
30. Which presidents had lost a presidential election before winning one?
31. Who was vice president and later president, but was not elected to either office?
32. Which Democratic nominee since 1945 carried a majority of white voters?
33. Which three presidential elections were not held in a leap year?
34. Which presidential election first featured the "Australian ballot"?
35. Which presidential election first featured voting machines?
36. Which president was the first one who had advocated "female suffrage"?
37. Who won the first presidential election in which women voted?
38. In which presidential election did women first vote in greater numbers than men?
39. Which presidential election pitted two incumbent senators against two former senators?
40. In which presidential election was the term "GOP" first used widely?
41. In which presidential election did the Deep South first go entirely Republican?
42. How many times have incumbent Congressmen squared off in a presidential contest?
43. Of the world's leading democracies, where did the U.S.A. place in voter participation?
44. In which presidential election did blacks first vote?
45. Which Republican nominee last received a significant amount of the black vote?
46. Which presidential election first featured absentee voting by civilians?
47. In which presidential election did more persons vote than any other?
48. What has every president except two elected in a year ending in zero done?
49. How many presidents have been elected to serve two terms?
50. Which president probably was the only one who conceded before all the polls had closed?
51. Which president was elected on his birthday?

14. Grover Cleveland (1884 and 1892)
15. The 1860 presidential election
16. The 1828, 1884, 1940, and 1992 presidential elections, respectively.
17. None
18. George Washington (1789 and 1792)
19. On the first Tuesday after the first Monday of November
20. 1845
21. The 1896 presidential election, referring to the gold and silver standards.
22. John Quincy Adams (1824), with 31.8% of electoral votes and 29.8% of popular votes.
23. The 1960 presidential election
24. John Adams (1800)
25. Grover Cleveland (1888) and Jimmy Carter (1980)
26. Harrison (1892), Taft (1912), Hoover (1932), and Bush (1992)
27. Four (Gerald Ford is the only one who has been defeated in an election year ending in "6")
28. Lyndon Johnson (88%)
29. James Buchanan (1856), after attempts in 1844, 1848, and 1852.
30. Thomas Jefferson, Andrew Jackson, Grover Cleveland, and Richard Nixon
31. Gerald Ford (1974-1977)
32. Lyndon Johnson (1964)
33. The 1789, 1800, and 1900 presidential elections
34. The 1888 presidential election. The secret ballot is publicly funded and lists candidates.
35. The 1892 presidential election, in Lockport, New York.
36. Abraham Lincoln (1832)
37. Warren Harding (1920)
38. The 1972 presidential election
39. The 1960 presidential election (Kennedy and Johnson vs. Nixon and Lodge)
40. The 1880 presidential election
41. The 1972 presidential election
42. Three (1796, 1836, and 1860), although never the top two candidates.
43. Twenty-third out of twenty-four
44. The 1868 presidential election; 500,000 voted, the margin was about 200,000 votes.
45. Dwight Eisenhower (1956), with about 40% of the black vote.
46. The 1896 presidential election, by Vermont.
47. The 2000 presidential election (105,405,100 votes)
48. Die in office. Ronald Reagan (1980) and George W. Bush (2000) are the exceptions.
49. 15 out of 42 (35.7%)
50. Jimmy Carter (1980), who had conceded before polls closed on the West Coast.
51. Warren Harding (1920), elected on his fifty-fifth birthday.

52. Who defeated two *future* presidents and two *former* presidents in presidential elections?
53. Who is the only person who was, in a row, vice president, private citizen, and president?
54. Which president last failed to attract a serious primary opponent for re-nomination?
55. Which political family has had the most generations in a row *elected* to federal office?

Electoral College

1. Why did the framers of the Constitution create the Electoral College?
2. How many states have cast electoral votes in every presidential election?
3. Which three presidents called for the abolition of the Electoral College?
4. Which electoral vote did a Democratic National Committee chairman predict exactly?
5. Which president was first elected after the Twelfth Amendment had been ratified?
6. Which president said he was a "dropout from the Electoral College"?
7. Which president learned his electoral results later than any other one?
8. Which president helped award all disputed electoral votes to Rutherford Hayes in 1877?
9. Which presidential elections were the first and last ones with third-party electoral votes?
10. Which third-party nominee received the most electoral votes in a single election?
11. Which third-party nominees since World War I received any electoral votes?
12. When did the Electoral College make its most lopsided reversal from the prior election?
13. Who would have become president with a shift of only 10,000 popular votes?
14. Which *incumbent* president made the worst showing in the Electoral College?
15. Who lost two national elections by the largest combined electoral vote in history?
16. Which presidential nominee received the highest electoral vote in a losing effort?
17. Which president received the highest electoral vote?
18. Which presidential election resulted in the closest electoral vote?

Electoral College - Democrats

1. Which Democratic nominees were the first and last ones who won Alabama?
2. Which Democratic nominees were the first and last ones who won Alaska?
3. Which Democratic nominees were the first and last ones who won Arizona?
4. Which Democratic nominees were the first and last ones who won Arkansas?
5. Which Democratic nominees were the first and last ones who won California?
6. Which Democratic nominees were the first and last ones who won Colorado?
7. Which Democratic nominees were the first and last ones who won Connecticut?
8. Which Democratic nominees were the first and last ones who won Delaware?
9. Which Democratic nominees were the first and last ones who won Florida?
10. Which Democratic nominees were the first and last ones who won Georgia?
11. Which Democratic nominees were the first and last ones who won Hawaii?

52. George Washington (1792) and Woodrow Wilson (1912), respectively.
53. Richard Nixon (1961-1969)
54. George W. Bush (2004)
55. The Taft Family (4), followed by the Adams, Bush, and Harrison Families (3).

Electoral College (answers)

1. As a compromise between election of the president by the people and by Congress.
2. Seven (CT, DE, MD, MA, NH, NJ, and PA)
3. James Polk (in his maiden speech in the House), Harry Truman, and Jimmy Carter
4. The 1936 presidential election (523-8), by James A. Farley.
5. Thomas Jefferson (1804), after electors voted apart for president and vice president.
6. Richard Nixon, "because [he had] flunked debating."
7. Rutherford Hayes (1877), just *three* days before his inauguration on March 5!
8. James Garfield (1877), who served on the electoral commission deciding the matter.
9. The 1856 and 1968 presidential elections, respectively.
10. George Wallace (1968), with forty-nine (49) electoral votes.
11. Robert LaFollette (1924), Strom Thurmond (1948), and George Wallace (1968)
12. The 1932 presidential election (from 444-87 for Republicans to 472-59 for Democrats)
13. Gerald Ford (1976), in Hawaii and Ohio.
14. William Taft (1912), with only eight (8) electoral votes.
15. Walter Mondale (1,014-62), for vice president (1980) and president (1984).
16. Al Gore (2000), with 266 electoral votes, just four electoral votes shy of a majority.
17. Ronald Reagan (1984), with 525 electoral votes.
18. The 1876 presidential election (185-184), between Rutherford Hayes and Samuel Tilden.

Electoral College - Democrats (answers)

1. Andrew Jackson (1828) and Jimmy Carter (1976), respectively.
2. Lyndon Johnson (1964) and Lyndon Johnson (1964), respectively.
3. Woodrow Wilson (1912) and Harry Truman (1948), respectively.
4. Martin Van Buren (1836) and Bill Clinton (1996), respectively.
5. Franklin Pierce (1852) and Bill Clinton (1996), respectively.
6. William Bryan (1896) and Bill Clinton (1992), respectively.
7. Martin Van Buren (1836) and Al Gore (2000), respectively.
8. Franklin Pierce (1852) and Al Gore (2000), respectively.
9. Franklin Pierce (1852) and Bill Clinton (1996), respectively.
10. Andrew Jackson (1828) and Bill Clinton (1992), respectively.
11. John Kennedy (1960) and Al Gore (2000), respectively.

12. Which Democratic nominees were the first and last ones who won Idaho?
13. Which Democratic nominees were the first and last ones who won Illinois?
14. Which Democratic nominees were the first and last ones who won Indiana?
15. Which Democratic nominees were the first and last ones who won Iowa?
16. Which Democratic nominees were the first and last ones who won Kansas?
17. Which Democratic nominees were the first and last ones who won Kentucky?
18. Which Democratic nominees were the first and last ones who won Louisiana?
19. Which Democratic nominees were the first and last ones who won Maine?
20. Which Democratic nominees were the first and last ones who won Maryland?
21. Which Democratic nominees were the first and last ones who won Massachusetts?
22. Which Democratic nominees were the first and last ones who won Michigan?
23. Which Democratic nominees were the first and last ones who won Minnesota?
24. Which Democratic nominees were the first and last ones who won Mississippi?
25. Which Democratic nominees were the first and last ones who won Missouri?
26. Which Democratic nominees were the first and last ones who won Montana?
27. Which Democratic nominees were the first and last ones who won Nebraska?
28. Which Democratic nominees were the first and last ones who won Nevada?
29. Which Democratic nominees were the first and last ones who won New Hampshire?
30. Which Democratic nominees were the first and last ones who won New Jersey?
31. Which Democratic nominees were the first and last ones who won New Mexico?
32. Which Democratic nominees were the first and last ones who won New York?
33. Which Democratic nominees were the first and last ones who won North Carolina?
34. Which Democratic nominees were the first and last ones who won North Dakota?
35. Which Democratic nominees were the first and last ones who won Ohio?
36. Which Democratic nominees were the first and last ones who won Oklahoma?
37. Which Democratic nominees were the first and last ones who won Oregon?
38. Which Democratic nominees were the first and last ones who won Pennsylvania?
39. Which Democratic nominees were the first and last ones who won Rhode Island?
40. Which Democratic nominees were the first and last ones who won South Carolina?
41. Which Democratic nominees were the first and last ones who won South Dakota?
42. Which Democratic nominees were the first and last ones who won Tennessee?
43. Which Democratic nominees were the first and last ones who won Texas?
44. Which Democratic nominees were the first and last ones who won Utah?
45. Which Democratic nominees were the first and last ones who won Vermont?
46. Which Democratic nominees were the first and last ones who won Virginia?
47. Which Democratic nominees were the first and last ones who won Washington?
48. Which Democratic nominees were the first and last ones who won West Virginia?
49. Which Democratic nominees were the first and last ones who won Wisconsin?

12. William Bryan (1896) and Lyndon Johnson (1964), respectively.

13. Andrew Jackson (1828) and Al Gore (2000), respectively.

14. Andrew Jackson (1828) and Lyndon Johnson (1964), respectively.

15. Lewis Cass (1848) and Al Gore (2000), respectively.

16. William Bryan (1896) and Lyndon Johnson (1964), respectively.

17. Andrew Jackson (1828) and Bill Clinton (1996), respectively.

18. Andrew Jackson (1828) and Bill Clinton (1996), respectively.

19. Andrew Jackson (1832) and Al Gore (2000), respectively.

20. Franklin Pierce (1852) and Al Gore (2000), respectively.

21. Woodrow Wilson (1912) and Al Gore (2000), respectively.

22. Martin Van Buren (1836) and Al Gore (2000), respectively.

23. Franklin Roosevelt (1932) and Al Gore (2000), respectively.

24. Andrew Jackson (1828) and Jimmy Carter (1976), respectively.

25. Andrew Jackson (1828) and Bill Clinton (1996), respectively.

26. William Bryan (1896) and Bill Clinton (1992), respectively.

27. William Bryan (1896) and Lyndon Johnson (1964), respectively.

28. Winfield Hancock (1880) and Bill Clinton (1996), respectively.

29. Andrew Jackson (1832) and Bill Clinton (1996), respectively.

30. Andrew Jackson (1832) and Al Gore (2000), respectively.

31. Woodrow Wilson (1912) and Al Gore (2000), respectively.

32. Andrew Jackson (1832) and Al Gore (2000), respectively.

33. Andrew Jackson (1828) and Jimmy Carter (1976), respectively.

34. Woodrow Wilson (1912) and Lyndon Johnson (1964), respectively.

35. Andrew Jackson (1828) and Bill Clinton (1996), respectively.

36. William Bryan (1908) and Lyndon Johnson (1964), respectively.

37. Horatio Seymour (1868) and Al Gore (2000), respectively.

38. Andrew Jackson (1828) and Al Gore (2000), respectively.

39. Martin Van Buren (1836) and Al Gore (2000), respectively.

40. Andrew Jackson (1828) and Jimmy Carter (1976), respectively.

41. William Bryan (1896) and Lyndon Johnson (1964), respectively.

42. Andrew Jackson (1828) and Bill Clinton (1996), respectively.

43. Lewis Cass (1848) and Jimmy Carter (1976), respectively.

44. William Bryan (1896) and Lyndon Johnson (1964), respectively.

45. Lyndon Johnson (1964) and Al Gore (2000), respectively.

46. Andrew Jackson (1828) and Lyndon Johnson (1964), respectively.

47. William Bryan (1896) and Al Gore (2000), respectively.

48. Samuel Tilden (1876) and Bill Clinton (1996), respectively.

49. Lewis Cass (1848) and Al Gore (2000), respectively.

50. Which Democratic nominees were the first and last ones who won Wyoming?
51. Which Democratic nominees were the first and last ones who won District of Columbia?

Electoral College - Republicans

1. Which Republican nominees were the first and last ones who won Alabama?
2. Which Republican nominees were the first and last ones who won Alaska?
3. Which Republican nominees were the first and last ones who won Arizona?
4. Which Republican nominees were the first and last ones who won Arkansas?
5. Which Republican nominees were the first and last ones who won California?
6. Which Republican nominees were the first and last ones who won Colorado?
7. Which Republican nominees were the first and last ones who won Connecticut?
8. Which Republican nominees were the first and last ones who won Delaware?
9. Which Republican nominees were the first and last ones who won Florida?
10. Which Republican nominees were the first and last ones who won Georgia?
11. Which Republican nominees were the first and last ones who won Hawaii?
12. Which Republican nominees were the first and last ones who won Idaho?
13. Which Republican nominees were the first and last ones who won Illinois?
14. Which Republican nominees were the first and last ones who won Indiana?
15. Which Republican nominees were the first and last ones who won Iowa?
16. Which Republican nominees were the first and last ones who won Kansas?
17. Which Republican nominees were the first and last ones who won Kentucky?
18. Which Republican nominees were the first and last ones who won Louisiana?
19. Which Republican nominees were the first and last ones who won Maine?
20. Which Republican nominees were the first and last ones who won Maryland?
21. Which Republican nominees were the first and last ones who won Massachusetts?
22. Which Republican nominees were the first and last ones who won Michigan?
23. Which Republican nominees were the first and last ones who won Minnesota?
24. Which Republican nominees were the first and last ones who won Mississippi?
25. Which Republican nominees were the first and last ones who won Missouri?
26. Which Republican nominees were the first and last ones who won Montana?
27. Which Republican nominees were the first and last ones who won Nebraska?
28. Which Republican nominees were the first and last ones who won Nevada?
29. Which Republican nominees were the first and last ones who won New Hampshire?
30. Which Republican nominees were the first and last ones who won New Jersey?
31. Which Republican nominees were the first and last ones who won New Mexico?
32. Which Republican nominees were the first and last ones who won New York?
33. Which Republican nominees were the first and last ones who won North Carolina?

50. William Bryan (1896) and Lyndon Johnson (1964), respectively.
51. Lyndon Johnson (1964) and Al Gore (2000), respectively.

Electoral College - Republicans (answers)

1. Ulysses Grant (1868) and George W. Bush (2000), respectively.
2. Richard Nixon (1960) and George W. Bush (2000), respectively.
3. Warren Harding (1920) and George W. Bush (2000), respectively.
4. Ulysses Grant (1868) and George W. Bush (2000), respectively.
5. Abraham Lincoln (1860) and George Bush (1988), respectively.
6. Rutherford Hayes (1876) and George W. Bush (2000), respectively.
7. John Frémont (1856) and George Bush (1988), respectively.
8. Ulysses Grant (1872) and George Bush (1988), respectively.
9. Ulysses Grant (1868) and George W. Bush (2000), respectively.
10. Barry Goldwater (1964) and George W. Bush (2000), respectively.
11. Richard Nixon (1972) and Ronald Reagan (1984), respectively.
12. Theodore Roosevelt (1904) and George W. Bush (2000), respectively.
13. Abraham Lincoln (1860) and George Bush (1988), respectively.
14. Abraham Lincoln (1860) and George W. Bush (2000), respectively.
15. John Frémont (1856) and Ronald Reagan (1984), respectively.
16. Abraham Lincoln (1864) and George Bush (1992), respectively.
17. Calvin Coolidge (1924) and George W. Bush (2000), respectively.
18. Rutherford Hayes (1876) and George W. Bush (2000), respectively.
19. John Frémont (1856) and George Bush (1988), respectively.
20. Abraham Lincoln (1864) and George Bush (1988), respectively.
21. John Frémont (1856) and Ronald Reagan (1984), respectively.
22. John Frémont (1856) and George Bush (1988), respectively.
23. Abraham Lincoln (1860) and Richard Nixon (1972), respectively.
24. Ulysses Grant (1872) and George W. Bush (2000), respectively.
25. Abraham Lincoln (1864) and George W. Bush (2000), respectively.
26. Benjamin Harrison (1892) and George W. Bush (2000), respectively.
27. Ulysses Grant (1868) and George W. Bush (2000), respectively.
28. Abraham Lincoln (1864) and George W. Bush (2000), respectively.
29. John Frémont (1856) and George W. Bush (2000), respectively.
30. Ulysses Grant (1872) and George Bush (1988), respectively.
31. Warren Harding (1920) and George Bush (1988), respectively.
32. John Frémont (1856) and Ronald Reagan (1984), respectively.
33. Ulysses Grant (1868) and George Bush (1992), respectively.

34. Which Republican nominees were the first and last ones who won North Dakota?
35. Which Republican nominees were the first and last ones who won Ohio?
36. Which Republican nominees were the first and last ones who won Oklahoma?
37. Which Republican nominees were the first and last ones who won Oregon?
38. Which Republican nominees were the first and last ones who won Pennsylvania?
39. Which Republican nominees were the first and last ones who won Rhode Island?
40. Which Republican nominees were the first and last ones who won South Carolina?
41. Which Republican nominees were the first and last ones who won South Dakota?
42. Which Republican nominees were the first and last ones who won Tennessee?
43. Which Republican nominees were the first and last ones who won Texas?
44. Which Republican nominees were the first and last ones who won Utah?
45. Which Republican nominees were the first and last ones who won Vermont?
46. Which Republican nominees were the first and last ones who won Virginia?
47. Which Republican nominees were the first and last ones who won Washington?
48. Which Republican nominees were the first and last ones who won West Virginia?
49. Which Republican nominees were the first and last ones who won Wisconsin?
50. Which Republican nominees were the first and last ones who won Wyoming?
51. Which Republican nominees were the first and last ones who won District of Columbia?

Electoral States

1. For whom did New York and Rhode Island cast electoral votes in the first election?
2. Which president had traveled to the states in dispute during the 1876 electoral fight?
3. Which state last chose electors by its state legislature instead of by popular vote?
4. Which states were the first ones that split their electoral votes?
5. Which state split its electoral votes among four different candidates?
6. Which presidential nominees received all electoral votes from New England states?
7. In which election did every state east of the Mississippi cast identical electoral votes?
8. Which presidents first and last received all electors from west of the Mississippi River?
9. When between 1880 and 1944 did former Confederate states' electors *not* vote alike?
10. Since 1820, which Democratic nominees received Vermont's electoral votes?
11. Since 1852, which four Democratic nominees received Maine's electoral votes?
12. Since 1872, which four Republican nominees received Arkansas's electoral votes?
13. Which states have the lowest and highest percentages of picking presidential winners?
14. Which state first held Election Day on the "Tuesday after the first Monday of November"?
15. Which state's electors supported a Democrat in nine of the last eleven elections?
16. Which Democratic presidential nominee was the only one who won Alaska's electors?
17. Which Republican presidential nominees were the only ones who won Hawaii's electors?

34. William McKinley (1896) and George W. Bush (2000), respectively.
35. John Frémont (1856) and George W. Bush (2000), respectively.
36. Warren Harding (1920) and George W. Bush (2000), respectively.
37. Abraham Lincoln (1860) and Ronald Reagan (1984), respectively.
38. Abraham Lincoln (1860) and George Bush (1988), respectively.
39. John Frémont (1856) and Ronald Reagan (1984), respectively.
40. Ulysses Grant (1868) and George W. Bush (2000), respectively.
41. Benjamin Harrison (1892) and George W. Bush (2000), respectively.
42. Ulysses Grant (1868) and George W. Bush (2000), respectively.
43. Herbert Hoover (1928) and George W. Bush (2000), respectively.
44. William McKinley (1900) and George W. Bush (2000), respectively.
45. John Frémont (1856) and George Bush (1988), respectively.
46. Ulysses Grant (1872) and George W. Bush (2000), respectively.
47. Benjamin Harrison (1892) and Ronald Reagan (1984), respectively.
48. Abraham Lincoln (1864) and Ronald Reagan (1984), respectively.
49. John Frémont (1856) and Ronald Reagan (1984), respectively.
50. Benjamin Harrison (1892) and George W. Bush (2000), respectively.
51. No Republican presidential nominee has ever won the District of Columbia.

Electoral States (answers)

1. Nobody, because their electors had not been selected yet.
2. James Garfield (1876), in defense of Rutherford Hayes.
3. West Virginia (1916), switching to direct election by the people.
4. Maryland, North Carolina, Pennsylvania, and Virginia (1796)
5. New York (1824)
6. Lyndon Johnson (1964), Ronald Reagan (1984), and Bill Clinton (1992, 1996)
7. The 1792 presidential election
8. James Madison (1812) and Richard Nixon (1972), respectively.
9. The 1920 and 1928 presidential elections
10. Lyndon Johnson (1964), Bill Clinton (1992), and Al Gore (2000)
11. Woodrow Wilson, Lyndon Johnson, Hubert Humphrey, and Bill Clinton
12. Richard Nixon, Ronald Reagan, George Bush, and George W. Bush
13. Alabama (52.3%) and New Mexico (95.2%), respectively.
14. New York, later standardized nationwide.
15. Minnesota's
16. Lyndon Johnson (1964)
17. Richard Nixon (1972) and Ronald Reagan (1984)

18. Which states have cast the fewest and the most total electoral votes?
19. Which state has cast the most electoral votes for third-party candidates?
20. Which nominees first and last formed a coast-to-coast swath of states' electors?
21. Which nominees first and last won the presidency without winning California?
22. Which nominees first and last won the presidency without winning Illinois?
23. Which nominees first and last won the presidency without winning New York?
24. Which nominees first and last won the presidency since 1804 without winning Ohio?
25. Which states' electors voted for a major-party nominee that their adjacent states did not?
26. Which two states opposed Franklin Roosevelt five times?
27. Which state has the streak for supporting the winner in presidential elections?
28. Which nominees were the first and last ones who won the Great Lakes states' electors?
29. When did North Dakota's and South Dakota's electors *not* vote alike?
30. When since 1820 did Alabama's and Mississippi's electors *not* vote alike?
31. When between 1860 and 1928 did Maine's and Rhode Island's electors *not* vote alike?
32. When since 1892 did Idaho's and Montana's electors *not* vote alike?
33. Which two states are tied for supporting the same party's presidential nominee?
34. Which state holds the record for *not* supporting the same party twice in a row?
35. Which nominees were the first and last ones who won all Atlantic Seaboard electors?
36. Which nominee since 1792 won all states through which the Mississippi River runs?
37. Which two states do not go by the rule of "winner take all" in awarding their electors?
38. Which states were the first ones that cast electoral votes before entering the Union?
39. Which state is the only one carried by every Republican presidential nominee since 1952?
40. Which two presidents carried the most states on Election Day?
41. Which state last wielded as much electoral power as California now does?
42. Which Democratic nominee won the presidency without carrying Texas's electoral votes?
43. Which Republican nominee won the presidency without carrying Ohio's electoral votes?
44. Which Democratic nominee won the presidency without a majority of Southern states?
45. Which presidential election last featured two major-party nominees from the same state?

Electors
1. How many electors failed to vote in the first meeting of the Electoral College, in 1789?
2. Which presidential election was the first one in which all electors cast votes?
3. Which election was the first one in which most electors had been elected by popular vote?
4. Which election was the first one in which *all* electors had been elected by popular vote?
5. Which elector cast a vote for a Libertarian presidential nominee?
6. Which Republican elector cast a vote for a Democratic presidential nominee?
7. Who was one vote shy of being unanimously elected in the Electoral College?

18. Hawaii (24) and New York (893), respectively.
19. Pennsylvania (38)
20. William Jennings Bryan (1896) and George Bush (1988), respectively.
21. James Garfield (1880) and George W. Bush (2000), respectively.
22. John Quincy Adams (1824) and George W. Bush (2000), respectively.
23. James Madison (1812) and George W. Bush (2000), respectively.
24. John Quincy Adams (1824) and John Kennedy (1960), respectively.
25. WV (1988); IN, MT (1992); FL, IN (1996); and NH, NM, ME (2000).
26. Maine and Vermont, once for vice president and four times for president.
27. New Mexico (16), although the streak has ended.
28. George Washington (1789) and Richard Nixon (1972), respectively.
29. The 1912 and 1916 presidential elections
30. The 1840 presidential election
31. The 1928 presidential election
32. The 1892 and 1992 presidential elections
33. Arkansas and Georgia (23), for the Democrats, although not up to the present day.
34. Louisiana (1944-1980), through ten presidential elections.
35. George Washington (1792) and Ronald Reagan (1984), respectively.
36. Richard Nixon (1972)
37. Maine and Nebraska
38. Indiana (1816) and Missouri (1820)
39. Arizona (1952-2000)
40. Richard Nixon (1972) and Ronald Reagan (1984), who each won forty-nine states.
41. New York (1872), with 12.2% of electors. California now has 10.2% of electors.
42. Bill Clinton (1992 and 1996)
43. None
44. Bill Clinton (1992 and 1996)
45. The 1944 election, between Franklin Roosevelt and Thomas Dewey of New York.

Electors (answers)

1. Four (two from Maryland and two from Virginia)
2. The 1792 presidential election
3. The 1816 presidential election, rather than appointed by state legislatures.
4. The 1872 presidential election
5. John Hospers (1972), of Virginia, for Roger L. MacBride.
6. Henry D. Irwin (1960), of Oklahoma, for Senator Harry F. Byrd (D-VA).
7. James Monroe (1820). An elector ensured Washington stayed the only one so chosen.

8. Whom does the Constitution prohibit from being an elector?
9. How many electors is each state entitled to send to the Electoral College?
10. Which state currently has the largest delegation of electors in the Electoral College?
11. Which president was the first one who had been a presidential elector?
12. Which *former* presidents became presidential electors?

Employment

1. Which president had worked as a barker at "Slippery Gulch Rodeo" in Prescott, Arizona?
2. Which president had worked a summer job at Yellowstone Park?
3. Which president had worked as a mule driver and a bargeman?
4. Which two presidents had been indentured servants?
5. Which president owned forty-nine slaves?
6. Which president was the last one who had owned slaves?
7. Which president was caught in the middle of the Boxer Rebellion in Tientsin, China?
8. Which presidents were the first and last ones who had been ranchers?
9. Which president was the first one who had a profession other than the military or the law?
10. Which president had been a saloon keeper?
11. Which president had owned a mill?
12. Which president had lifted blocks of ice in a creamery?
13. Which president had been a postmaster?
14. Which president had worked in tire rationing for the Office of Price Administration?
15. Which president had been in charge of the first federal census?
16. Which president had been a census enumerator?
17. Which president waited tables to help pay for his undergraduate studies?
18. Which president, as a lifeguard, had saved seventy-seven persons from drowning?
19. Which president had worked in China, Russia, New Zealand, and Australia?
20. Which president had been a state comptroller?
21. Which president had been the chief clerk of the Tennessee State Senate?
22. Which president had been a ferry worker?
23. Which presidents were the first and last ones who had served as mayors?
24. Which president had been a radio announcer at WOC, in Davenport, Iowa?
25. Which president was the first one who had become a self-made millionaire?
26. Which president resigned from more political positions than any other?
27. Which president had helped design the town of Alexandria, Virginia?
28. Which president had worked in a cotton gin, tending a big steam boiler?
29. Which president had been the first full-time politician?
30. Which president, like his father and grandfather, had been a volunteer fireman?

8. Any federal office-holder
9. A number equivalent to one for each senator plus one for each representative
10. California (55)
11. William Henry Harrison (1820 and 1824), for James Monroe and Henry Clay.
12. John Adams (1816, for James Monroe) and Martin Van Buren (1852, for Franklin Pierce)

Employment (answers)
1. Richard Nixon, during his high-school years.
2. Gerald Ford (1936), feeding animals, giving directions to visitors, and directing traffic.
3. James Garfield (1845), on the Erie Canal.
4. Millard Fillmore and Andrew Johnson, working as a mercer and tailor, respectively.
5. George Washington
6. Zachary Taylor
7. Herbert Hoover (1900), where he was working for the Chinese Bureau of Mines.
8. Theodore Roosevelt (1901) and George W. Bush (2005), respectively.
9. Andrew Johnson (1865), who was a tailor.
10. Abraham Lincoln (1833), at "Berry and Lincoln," in Springfield, Illinois.
11. Calvin Coolidge
12. Dwight Eisenhower
13. Abraham Lincoln (1833-1836), in New Salem, Illinois.
14. Richard Nixon (1942)
15. Thomas Jefferson (1790)
16. Harry Truman (1920)
17. Herbert Hoover
18. Ronald Reagan (1927-1932)
19. Herbert Hoover, as a mining engineer.
20. Millard Fillmore (1848-1849), in New York.
21. James Polk (1823)
22. Abraham Lincoln, on the Mississippi River.
23. Andrew Johnson (1830) and Grover Cleveland (1882), respectively.
24. Ronald Reagan (1932), for five dollars per week.
25. Herbert Hoover, who was worth about $4 million.
26. Andrew Johnson, as state solicitor and U.S. attorney, representative, and senator.
27. George Washington (1749)
28. Lyndon Johnson
29. William Henry Harrison
30. Franklin Roosevelt, for the Duchess County Rescue Hook and Ladder Company.

31. Which president hired a reader for fifty cents per day to read to him while he worked?
32. Which president covered the Potsdam Conference as a special correspondent?
33. Which president said, given a choice, he would rather be a gardener?
34. Which former president became president of the National Prison Association?
35. Which president had been a janitor?
36. Which president had established the Black Republican Alliance?
37. Which president had pushed a cart at Reward Mine Company in Nevada City, California?
38. Which president would awake at 4:00 A.M. to work in a grocery store and filling station?
39. Which president entered a Democratic meeting and walked out a mayoral candidate?
40. Which president was the first one who had been a religious minister?
41. Which president had worked as a grape picker, dishwasher, and auto mechanic?
42. Which presidents had been surveyors?
43. Which president had been a highly successful engineer?
44. Which president had managed a billiards hall?
45. Which president had washed dishes in a sorority house to help pay college expenses?
46. Which president had worked for the Santa Fé Railroad?
47. Which presidents were the first and last ones who had been state representatives?
48. Which presidents had been speakers of their state houses of representatives?
49. Which presidents had been state senators?
50. Which presidents had been state attorneys general?
51. Which presidents had been lieutenant governors?
52. Which presidents had been educators at the college or university level?
53. Which president had owned a naillery?

Engagements
1. Which president had been engaged to Ann Rutledge?
2. Which president had been engaged to the daughter of a signer of the Declaration?
3. Which president married after a four-year engagement?
4. Which president married after a five-year engagement?
5. Which president and his fiancée decided to keep their engagement a secret?
6. Which president remained a bachelor all his life?
7. Which words did Franklin Roosevelt use to propose to his girlfriend Eleanor?

Eulogies
1. Which presidents delivered orations at the funerals of other presidents?
2. Who delivered the eulogy for George Washington?
3. Who delivered the eulogy for Nathaniel Hawthorne?

31. Benjamin Harrison
32. John Kennedy (1945), for the International News Service.
33. Thomas Jefferson
34. Rutherford Hayes (1883-1893)
35. James Garfield, at the Western Reserve Eclectic Institute.
36. George Bush (1963), as Harris County (Texas) Republican Party chairman.
37. Herbert Hoover
38. Richard Nixon
39. Grover Cleveland (1882), in Buffalo, New York.
40. James Garfield
41. Lyndon Johnson
42. George Washington, John Adams, and Abraham Lincoln
43. Herbert Hoover, voted the second greatest engineer in U.S. history after Edison (1964).
44. Ulysses Grant
45. Ronald Reagan
46. Harry Truman, as a timekeeper.
47. George Washington (1758-1773) and Theodore Roosevelt (1882-1884), respectively.
48. Franklin Pierce (1832-1833) and John Tyler (1839-1840)
49. John Quincy Adams (1803-1808) and Jimmy Carter (1963-1966)
50. Martin Van Buren (1815-1819) and Bill Clinton (1977-1979)
51. Warren Harding (1904-1906) and Calvin Coolidge (1916-1919)
52. James Garfield, Woodrow Wilson, and Bill Clinton
53. Thomas Jefferson

Engagements (answers)
1. Abraham Lincoln, but she caught malaria and died.
2. James Madison, to Catherine Floyd, daughter of William Floyd of New York.
3. James Garfield (1858), during which time he saw his future wife only once!
4. John Tyler (1813), during which time he kissed his fiancée only once, *on the hand*!
5. Grover Cleveland and Frances Folsom, until she had returned from a trip to Europe.
6. James Buchanan, although he had been engaged to the daughter of a wealthy iron mogul.
7. "Miss Roosevelt, Mr. Roosevelt . . . [asks] you to become Mrs. Roosevelt."

Eulogies (answers)
1. John Tyler (1826), for Thomas Jefferson, and Bill Clinton (1994), for Richard Nixon.
2. Richard "Light Horse Harry" Lee (1799), the father of Robert E. Lee.
3. Former classmate Franklin Pierce (1864)

4. Who delivered the eulogy for the Marquis de Lafayette, French hero of the Revolution?
5. Who delivered the eulogy for Benjamin Harrison?

Eyes
1. Which president had been kept out of West Point due to bad eyesight?
2. Which president was nearsighted in one eye and farsighted in the other?
3. Which president first wore contact lenses?
4. Which president wore a contact lens in his right eye for reading?
5. Which president was blinded in one eye but kept it a secret until his death?
6. Which president had a cataract in his right eye that blinded it?
7. Which other president was partially blind and almost completely blind at death?
8. Which president wore pince-nez to resolve his acute myopia?
9. Which president's poor eyesight made him order what we now know as bifocals?
10. Which president had different-colored eyes?
11. Which president wore glasses from the age of eight years?

Favorites
1. Which president was notoriously addicted to folk humor?
2. Which president owned an elk-horn chair in which he liked very much to sit?
3. Which president owned a favorite branding iron?
4. Which president was Richard Nixon's favorite?
5. Which international leader did Jimmy Carter say he most respected and tried to emulate?
6. Which president's favorite British prime minister was William Gladstone?
7. Which president's favorite color was fuchsia?
8. Which color was Lyndon Johnson's favorite?

Floats
1. In which president's inaugural parade were "floats" introduced?
2. In which president's inaugural parade did Helen Keller sit on a float?
3. In which president's inaugural parade did a float appear with a girl from every state?
4. In which president's inaugural parade did the longest float appear?
5. In which president's inaugural parade did organized labor first march and enter floats?

Flowers
1. Which president's favorite flower was the purple lilac?
2. Which president's favorite flower was the yellow ball mum?

4.   John Quincy Adams (1834)
5.   Poet James Whitcomb Riley (1901)

Eyes (answers)

1.   Harry Truman
2.   James Buchanan, causing him to slant his head forward and sideways when talking.
3.   Ronald Reagan (1945)
4.   Jimmy Carter
5.   Theodore Roosevelt (1904), during a boxing match with an assistant.
6.   Andrew Jackson
7.   Woodrow Wilson
8.   Theodore Roosevelt
9.   Thomas Jefferson's
10. James Buchanan, who had blue and brown eyes.
11. Woodrow Wilson

Favorites (answers)

1.   Abraham Lincoln
2.   Rutherford Hayes
3.   Theodore Roosevelt
4.   Woodrow Wilson
5.   Egyptian President Anwar Sadat
6.   Woodrow Wilson's
7.   Millard Fillmore's
8.   Yellow

Floats (answers)

1.   James Buchanan's (1857), including a full-rigged miniature of the USS *Constitution*.
2.   Woodrow Wilson's (1913)
3.   Abraham Lincoln's (1861)
4.   Dwight Eisenhower's (480 feet)
5.   Harry Truman's (1949)

Flowers (answers)

1.   Franklin Pierce's
2.   Lyndon Johnson's

3. Which president's favorite flower was the Delicate violet?
4. Which president's favorite flower was the day lily?
5. Which president's favorite flower was the orchid?
6. Which president's favorite flower was the peonie?
7. Which president's favorite flower was the pink gladiolus?
8. Which president's favorite flower was the pansie?
9. Which president's favorite flower was the daisy?
10. Which president's favorite flower was the blue iris?
11. Which president's favorite flower was the white rose?
12. Which president's favorite flower was the pink garden rose?
13. Which presidents' favorite flower was the red rose?
14. Which president's favorite flower was the Hawthorn?
15. Which president's favorite flower was the red carnation?
16. Which president's favorite flower was the blue corn flower?
17. Which president was probably the only one for whom a variety of flower was named?

Food

1. Which president observed meatless and wheatless days?
2. Which president liked peanuts and ate a few bowls' worth daily?
3. Which president said the only two things he could never give up were coffee and tobacco?
4. Which president was fond of squirrel broth?
5. Which dish was Franklin Roosevelt's favorite, which he often cooked for friends or guests?
6. What was John Kennedy's favorite food?
7. What was Lyndon Johnson's favorite food?
8. What was Andrew Jackson's favorite food?
9. Which president reportedly ate pie at every meal?
10. Which president liked apple pie and just about any type of cake?
11. Which dish was Grover Cleveland's favorite?
12. What was Richard Nixon's favorite snack food?
13. What was one of Richard Nixon's favorite meals?
14. Which president insisted that grace be said before every meal, even at state banquets?
15. Which president liked fettuccini?
16. Which snack did Ronald Reagan supposedly start eating to help him quit smoking?
17. Which president's favorite dessert was prune whip?
18. Which president installed the first cast-iron stove in the White House?
19. Which president was first responsible for the creation of a popular food product?
20. Which president wanted to know what happened to leftovers at the White House?

3. Millard Fillmore's
4. Ulysses Grant's
5. Woodrow Wilson's
6. Andrew Jackson's
7. Franklin Roosevelt's
8. Grover Cleveland's
9. Warren Harding's
10. James Madison's
11. John Quincy Adams's
12. Zachary Taylor's
13. Lincoln's, Hayes's, Garfield's, Arthur's, Benjamin Harrison's, and Theodore Roosevelt's
14. Harry Truman's, the state flower of Missouri.
15. William McKinley's, the state flower of Ohio.
16. John Kennedy's, which he often wore as a boutonniere.
17. Herbert Hoover, for whom varieties of the blue sweet pea were named.

Food (answers)

1. Woodrow Wilson, as a symbolic gesture while the nation was at war.
2. Franklin Roosevelt
3. Andrew Jackson
4. Thomas Jefferson
5. Scrambled eggs
6. Cole slaw
7. Chili
8. Turkey hash
9. George Washington
10. Franklin Roosevelt
11. Corned beef and cabbage
12. Cottage cheese and ketchup
13. Meat loaf
14. Franklin Pierce
15. John Kennedy
16. Jelly beans. Blueberry Jelly Bellies were created for Reagan.
17. Dwight Eisenhower's
18. Millard Fillmore, ending meals cooked over an open fire.
19. George Washington, for his Mount Vernon flour.
20. Calvin Coolidge

21. Which president was the first North American to grow a tomato?
22. Which president often had sauerkraut-and-mashed-potatoes parties at his home?
23. Which president liked sweet potatoes?
24. Which president invented Baked Alaska?
25. Which president invented chicken à la king?
26. Which president first brought his chef with him to the nation's capital?
27. Which president's cook in the White House was named Jimmy Carter?
28. What was the name of Lyndon Johnson's personal female cook at the White House?
29. Which president had a personal barbecuer named Walter Jettou?
30. Which president liked sliced beef, ribs, ham, and links, with potato salad and beans?
31. Which president liked eating frog legs and pig knuckles?
32. Which president had a mint garden?
33. Which president's favorite California dish was casserole with crabmeat and artichokes?
34. Which president served hot dogs in his home to the King and Queen of England?
35. Which president was sent a poisoned fish from Cuba but did not eat it?
36. Which president was our most famous McDonald's aficionado?
37. Which president hosted the first presidential barbecue?
38. Which president introduced ice cream, waffles, and macaroni to the U.S.A.?
39. Which president and First Lady often ate alone and in complete silence?
40. Which president was a member of the Adult Peanut Butter Lovers Fan Club?
41. Which president first popularized the term "nutrition"?
42. Which president ate crackers and preserves as a snack?
43. Which president liked grapes so much that he maintained an arbor at the White House?
44. Which president served a 1,600-pound cheese at receptions for four years?
45. Which president first tasted the common Chinese dish chop suey?
46. Which president had a well publicized aversion to broccoli?
47. Which president was a "chocoholic"?
48. Which president maintained a potato crop in his retirement?
49. Which president was the most capable with a spittoon?
50. Which president would "never eat anything that went on two legs"?

Football

1. Which president had been voted most valuable player of his college football team?
2. Which president had been a punt kicker for his college football team until a knee injury?
3. Which president was selected part of *Sports Illustrated*'s twenty-fifth All-American team?
4. Which president attended a football game and was oblivious to what was happening?
5. Which president had played in a college football All-Star Game?

21. Thomas Jefferson

22. James Buchanan

23. Theodore Roosevelt

24. Thomas Jefferson, consisting of cake topped with ice cream covered with meringue.

25. Andrew Jackson, consisting of baked chicken on rice with a light, creamy sauce.

26. George Washington, who brought Hercules, a black chef.

27. Franklin Roosevelt's

28. Zephyr Wright

29. Lyndon Johnson

30. George Bush

31. Franklin Roosevelt

32. Theodore Roosevelt

33. Ronald Reagan's

34. Harry Truman

35. Franklin Roosevelt

36. Bill Clinton, often stopping in after a morning jog.

37. George Washington (1793)

38. Thomas Jefferson

39. President and Mrs. Calvin Coolidge

40. Gerald Ford

41. James Garfield

42. Calvin Coolidge

43. James Buchanan

44. Thomas Jefferson

45. Grover Cleveland

46. George Bush

47. John Kennedy

48. Martin Van Buren

49. Zachary Taylor

50. Ulysses Grant

Football (answers)

1. Gerald Ford (1934), who played center and wore #48.

2. Dwight Eisenhower (1911), while playing for West Point. He played against Jim Thorpe.

3. Gerald Ford (1935)

4. William McKinley

5. Gerald Ford (1935)

6.   Which president first attended a professional football game?
7.   Which president had been "the most spirited bench-warmer" of his college football team?
8.   Which president became renowned for having played college football without a helmet?
9.   Which president had *The New York Times* said was "one of the most promising backs"?
10. Which high school produced two Heisman Trophy winners?
11. Which president threw the football left-handed?
12. Which president played football at Harvard University but then became a cheerleader?
13. Which president became famous for playing touch football with his family?
14. Which president first watched a Super Bowl on television?
15. Which *incumbent* president first participated in a coin toss for a Super Bowl?
16. Which president first personally made the coin toss at a Super Bowl?
17. Which president last watched an Army-Navy football game in person?
18. During which Administration was the annual Commander-in-Chief's Trophy established?
19. Which president said Gerald Ford "played too much football with his helmet off"?

Fraternities

1.   Which presidents had been members of Delta Kappa Epsilon fraternity?
2.   Which president had been a member of Phi Delta Phi legal fraternity?
3.   Which president had been a member of Phi Gamma Delta fraternity?
4.   Which president had been a member of Tau Kappa Epsilon fraternity?
5.   Which president and his vice president had been members of the same fraternity?
6.   Which president had been a member of the Barbarians?
7.   Which president had been a member of the Interfraternity Council?

Geography

1.   During which Administration was the U.S. Land Office created?
2.   Which president never saw a map of the U.S.A. until he was nineteen years old?
3.   Near which drive is the United Nations located in New York City?
4.   Where is Lincoln Gulch?
5.   Where is Eisenhower Memorial Tunnel?
6.   Where is Fort Benjamin Harrison?
7.   What was the previous name of Lafayette Square, in front of the White House?
8.   Which president first committed the U.S.A. to a two-state solution in the Middle East?
9.   Which president first endorsed China's unequivocal position on sovereignty over Taiwan?
10. In which state with two time zones did TV networks significantly affect voter turnout?
11. During which Administration was the Canadian boundary set from Maine to Minnesota?
12. Which president did Mormons petition to create the State of Deseret?

6.   Lyndon Johnson (1966), between the Baltimore Colts and the Washington Redskins.
7.   Richard Nixon
8.   Gerald Ford (1933-1935)
9.   Dwight Eisenhower (1912)
10. Woodrow Wilson High School, which produced Davey O'Brien and Tim Brown.
11. George Bush
12. Franklin Roosevelt
13. John Kennedy
14. Lyndon Johnson (1967), who watched Super Bowl I.
15. Ronald Reagan (1985), in Super Bowl XIX, via satellite from the White House.
16. George Bush (2002), at Super Bowl XXXVI, in New Orleans.
17. Bill Clinton (1996)
18. Richard Nixon's (1972). The trophy has gone to Air Force (14), Army (6), and Navy (5).
19. Lyndon Johnson

Fraternities (answers)
1.   Gerald Ford and George Bush, at Yale University.
2.   Gerald Ford, at the University of Michigan.
3.   Calvin Coolidge, at Amherst College.
4.   Ronald Reagan, at Eureka College.
5.   George Bush and Dan Quayle, members of Delta Kappa Epsilon, but at different colleges.
6.   Herbert Hoover. The group was for men too poor to join regular fraternities.
7.   George Bush

Geography (answers)
1.   James Madison's
2.   Millard Fillmore
3.   Franklin Roosevelt Drive
4.   Deer Lodge, Montana.
5.   One hour west of Denver, Colorado.
6.   Indianapolis, Indiana.
7.   President's Square
8.   George W. Bush (2001)
9.   Bill Clinton (1998)
10. Florida (2000), by incorrectly "calling" the state for Gore, affecting Panhandle voters.
11. John Tyler's (1842), in the Webster-Ashburton Treaty, including the Mesabi Iron Range.
12. Millard Fillmore (1849), which would have included most of Nevada, Utah, and Arizona.

Gettysburg Address

1. How did the Gettysburg Address begin?
2. From what was Abraham Lincoln suffering when he gave the Gettysburg Address?
3. How long did Abraham Lincoln's Gettysburg Address last?
4. Where are Abraham Lincoln's two drafts of the Gettysburg Address?
5. Where is the original, final copy of the Gettysburg Address?
6. Where is the only signed, dated copy of the Gettysburg Address?
7. From whom did Lincoln borrow the words "of the people, by the people, for the people"?
8. Which president said, "The world will little note nor long remember what we say here"?

Gifts

1. Which president did Charles DeGaulle present with an alligator desk set?
2. For which president was the Gobelin tapestry "The Marriage of Psyche" especially woven?
3. Which president received a desk made from the HMS *Resolute*?
4. Which president received the original working proof for a Rembrandt etching?
5. Which president received a chrome-plated Colt .45 replica from Elvis Presley?
6. After which president's assassination were dozens of his busts donated to his family?
7. Which president liked to give sterling-silver book boxes engraved with his seal?
8. Which president's gifts for visitors showed the most thoughtfulness?
9. Which president first had a strict rule of not accepting gifts from any public officials?
10. Which president received a priceless fourteenth-century painting from Pope Paul VI?

Golf

1. Which president had a heart attack at the Cherry Hills Country Club in Denver, Colorado?
2. Which president sponsored his archrival for membership in a golf club?
3. Which president received the Ben Hogan Trophy?
4. Which president received the William D. Richardson Award?
5. Which presidents participated in PGA tournament pro-ams?
6. Which Democratic president was the only one who considered golf a hobby?
7. Which president became known for knocking out bystanders with errant golf shots?
8. Which president bet $1,000 that he could shoot under 100 on a very difficult course?
9. Who had a putting green at the White House and walked indoors with spikes?
10. Which president established an invitational golf tournament?
11. Which president first took up golf regularly?
12. Which presidents shot at least one hole-in-one?
13. Which president bet the most money on his golf game and regularly shot in the 90s?

Gettysburg Address (answers)

1. "Four score and seven years ago . . .," meaning eighty-seven years.
2. Smallpox
3. Less than three minutes. It was 272 words long.
4. In the Smithsonian Institution, Washington, DC.
5. In the Library of Congress, Washington, DC.
6. In the Lincoln Bedroom of the White House
7. Minister and abolitionist Theodore Parker, who had used it thirteen years earlier.
8. Abraham Lincoln, at Gettysburg, after delivering one of the most famous speeches ever.

Gifts (answers)

1. John Kennedy (1961), who reciprocated with a letter from Lafayette to Washington.
2. Woodrow Wilson (1895)
3. Rutherford Hayes (1880), from Queen Victoria.
4. Dwight Eisenhower
5. Richard Nixon (1970)
6. John Kennedy's (1963)
7. Lyndon Johnson
8. John Kennedy's
9. John Quincy Adams (1825)
10. Lyndon Johnson. He reciprocated by offering a cheap bust of . . . himself.

Golf (answers)

1. Dwight Eisenhower (1955), who used a golf club as a cane during his convalescence.
2. Richard Nixon, who sponsored John Kennedy at the Burning Tree Golf Club in Maryland.
3. Dwight Eisenhower (1955), for his inspirational recovery from his heart attack.
4. Dwight Eisenhower (1955), for his outstanding contribution to golf.
5. Gerald Ford (1975), in Florida, and George Bush (1990), in Texas.
6. Woodrow Wilson
7. Gerald Ford
8. William Taft. He shot a 98.
9. Dwight Eisenhower (1953). The U.S. Golf Association installed the green.
10. Gerald Ford, who started the Jerry Ford Invitational, in Vail, Colorado.
11. William Taft (1912)
12. Gerald Ford (3) and Dwight Eisenhower (1), who called it "the thrill of a lifetime."
13. Warren Harding

14. Which president had courted his future wife on the golf links?

15. Which president had played on his college golf team and usually shot in the 70s there?

16. Which president sarcastically said that he could play four golf courses simultaneously?

17. Which president always played golf by himself?

18. Which president was such an avid golfer that it became detrimental to his campaign?

19. Which president often played eighteen holes in the morning and nine in the afternoon?

20. Who said golf looked like "good exercise" but asked, "What is the little white ball for?"

21. Which president painted golf balls black or red in order to play "snow golf"?

22. Which president first played golf with comedian Bob Hope?

23. Which president probably played more golf than any other, sometimes six times a week?

24. Which president was easily bored by playing golf?

25. Which president eliminated squirrels at the White House after they disrupted his golf?

26. Which president rarely played golf because he could not bend over to place the ball?

27. Which president formally ended a war in his golf clothes?

28. Which president refused to give up his golf game to meet the president of Chile?

29. Which president likely was the only one who was a member of Augusta National Golf Club?

30. Which president played golf left-handed?

31. Which president had a legitimate handicap in the single digits?

32. What did Gerald Ford do on the first day after leaving office?

Governors

1. Which presidents were the first and last ones who had been a state governor?

2. Which presidents were the first and last ones who had been a territorial governor?

3. Which two presidents had been governors of Louisiana Territory?

4. Which president had originated the concept of "environmental-impact studies"?

5. Who were the first and last *incumbent* governors elected president?

6. Which president had been the youngest governor in the nation since Harold Stassen?

7. Which president had been the first three-term governor of Ohio?

8. Which president had suppressed a slave revolt as governor of Virginia?

9. Which president had been re-elected governor of New York by the largest majority?

10. Which president had lost two gubernatorial elections to the same man?

11. Which president had defeated Patrick Henry's descendant in a gubernatorial race?

12. Which *former* president first ran for governor?

13. Which president succeeded and was succeeded by a father and son, respectively?

14. In which presidential election did a former New York governor defeat an incumbent one?

15. Who defeated two former New York governors in separate presidential elections?

16. When were two incumbent governors nominated by the two major parties?

14. Woodrow Wilson
15. John Kennedy
16. Gerald Ford
17. Richard Nixon
18. William Taft
19. Richard Nixon
20. Ulysses Grant, after seeing a golfer for the first time, a beginner hacking at the fairway.
21. Woodrow Wilson, including on the White House lawn.
22. George Bush
23. Woodrow Wilson. He played golf on the day Congress declared war against Germany!
24. Lyndon Johnson
25. Dwight Eisenhower, with orders to kill the squirrels on sight.
26. William Taft
27. Warren Harding (1921). After signing papers, he said, "That's all" and went back to golf.
28. William Taft, saying, "I'll be damned if I give up my game of golf to see this fellow."
29. Dwight Eisenhower, who lived there in "Eisenhower Cottage," next to "Ike's Pond."
30. Calvin Coolidge
31. John Kennedy
32. He played in a golf tournament in California.

Governors (answers)
1. Thomas Jefferson (1779-1781) and George W. Bush (1995-2000), respectively.
2. Andrew Jackson (1821) and William Taft (1900-1904), respectively.
3. William Henry Harrison (1801-1812) and Zachary Taylor, respectively.
4. Ronald Reagan (1969), as governor of California.
5. Rutherford Hayes (1876) and George W. Bush (2000), respectively.
6. Bill Clinton (1978), elected governor of Arkansas at the age of thirty-two years.
7. Rutherford Hayes (1868-1872 and 1876-1877)
8. James Monroe (1802)
9. Franklin Roosevelt (1930), by more than 750,000 votes.
10. Andrew Jackson, to George C. Jones, for governor of Tennessee.
11. Andrew Johnson (1850), who defeated Gustavus Henry for governor of Tennessee.
12. John Quincy Adams (1833), for governor of Massachusetts.
13. Ronald Reagan, as governor of California, by Jerry Brown and Jerry Brown, Jr.
14. The 1944 presidential election (Franklin Roosevelt defeated Thomas Dewey)
15. Woodrow Wilson (Theodore Roosevelt in 1912 and Charles Hughes in 1916)
16. The 1876 presidential election (Rutherford Hayes of Ohio and Samuel Tilden of New York)

17. Who quipped, when asked how he could greet visitors and still work, "You talk back?"
18. Which journalist asked Lyndon Johnson to appoint him as governor of American Samoa?

Grade Schools
1. Which president had bragged to first-grade classmates that he would become president?
2. Which president had been chauffeured to school as a child in the family limousine?
3. Which president had attended Campbelltown Academy with future Justice John Marshall?
4. Which president had attended Passy Academy near Paris, France?
5. In which school did Lyndon Johnson begin his formal education?
6. Which president had been principal of an academy in North Pownal, Vermont?
7. Which president had taught grade school to impoverished Mexican children?
8. Which president had taught at an elementary school in Hebron, Maine?

Gridiron Club
1. Which president first attended a Gridiron Club dinner?
2. Which president since then has *not* attended a Gridiron Club dinner?
3. Who said the Gridiron Club dinner was like "throwing cowshit at the village idiot"?
4. Who said the Gridiron Club dinner was "the most elegant lynching I've ever seen"?
5. Who always has the last say at the Gridiron Club roast?
6. Which president first performed in a skit at a Gridiron Club dinner?
7. Which First Couple danced the jitterbug at a Gridiron Club dinner?

Hair
1. Which presidents were considered bald?
2. Which president last wore a queue?
3. Which presidents had moustaches?
4. Which presidents had sideburns?
5. Which presidents had beards?
6. Who was the eleven-year-old girl who advised Abraham Lincoln to grow a beard?
7. Which presidents were the first and last ones who had right-side parts in their hair?
8. Which president changed his hair part while in office, from the right side to the left side?
9. Which president last parted his hair in the middle?
10. Which president inherited his premature gray hair from his father's family?
11. What do Winston Churchill, Andrew Jackson, and Thomas Jefferson have in common?
12. Which president last faced a major-party opponent with facial hair in a general election?

17. Calvin Coolidge, as governor of Massachusetts.
18. Hunter Thompson (1966), who later withdrew after Johnson's bombing of Vietnam.

Grade Schools (answers)

1. Lyndon Johnson (1914)
2. George Bush (1936-1938)
3. James Monroe (1769-1774)
4. John Quincy Adams (1778-1780), with some of Benjamin Franklin's grandsons.
5. The Junction School (1912), in Stonewall, Texas.
6. Chester Arthur (1851-1852). James Garfield taught penmanship there three years later!
7. Lyndon Johnson (1927), at the Welhausen School in Cotulla, Texas.
8. Franklin Pierce (1825), at Hebron Academy.

Gridiron Club (answers)

1. Benjamin Harrison
2. Grover Cleveland
3. Lyndon Johnson
4. Ronald Reagan
5. The president of the United States
6. Ronald Reagan (1983)
7. President and Mrs. Jimmy Carter (1979)

Hair (answers)

1. John Quincy Adams, Martin Van Buren, and Dwight Eisenhower
2. James Madison
3. Chester Arthur, Grover Cleveland, Theodore Roosevelt, and William Taft
4. Martin Van Buren and Chester Arthur. Martin Van Buren had sideburns only.
5. Abraham Lincoln, Ulysses Grant, Rutherford Hayes, James Garfield, and Benjamin Harrison
6. Grace Bedell (1860), saying "All the ladies like whiskers."
7. John Tyler (1841) and Ronald Reagan (1989), respectively.
8. Jimmy Carter (1979), supposedly to emulate John Kennedy.
9. Herbert Hoover (1933)
10. Bill Clinton
11. They were redheads.
12. Franklin Roosevelt (1944), who faced mustachioed Thomas Dewey.

Handwriting

1. Which president was famous for doodling at his desk instead of writing?
2. Where is Abraham Lincoln's original, handwritten Emancipation Proclamation?
3. Which president probably had the worst handwriting?
4. Which presidents could take shorthand?
5. Which president often wrote in the third person?
6. Which president penned his wife's epitaph?
7. Which writer told Franklin Pierce, "I pity you . . . from the bottom of my heart"?
8. Which president's White House staff measured his incoming personal mail by the yard?
9. Which president could write Latin with one hand and Greek with the other, *simultaneously*?
10. Which president was ambidextrous only while standing?
11. Which president first used the abbreviation "U.S." in correspondence?
12. Which president had the most "effeminate" handwriting?
13. Which president's chief requirement for his staff was that they have excellent handwriting?
14. What is the largest sum ever paid at auction for a piece of presidential handwriting?
15. Which president signed 1,000 autographs in a period of three and one-half hours?

Hats

1. Which president frequently tossed his hat into the crowd at campaign stops?
2. Which president last wore a top hat regularly?
3. Which president-elect renewed interest in the Homburg?
4. Which president liked to wear a battered straw hat?
5. Which president-elect first wore a fedora to his inauguration?
6. Which president last wore a cocked hat?
7. Which president wore the same hat for ten years?
8. Which president hated wearing hats and started the custom of men's not wearing them?
9. Which president had the largest hat size?

Health

1. Which presidents became notorious for their bad migraine headaches?
2. What immediately cleared Ulysses Grant of an exceptionally painful headache?
3. Which president received neck massages from his wife for his headaches?
4. Which president said he got a headache when he did not "have a woman for three days"?
5. Which president's mistress said he was impotent?
6. Which two presidents became famous for campaigning on crutches?
7. Which dead president's tissue samples did a government museum recently want to clone?

Handwriting (answers)

1. Herbert Hoover
2. It was destroyed in the Great Chicago Fire of 1871.
3. John Kennedy
4. James Madison, John Quincy Adams, and Woodrow Wilson
5. Thomas Jefferson
6. Harry Truman, even though he would die ten years before she did.
7. Nathaniel Hawthorne (1852), after his election.
8. Franklin Roosevelt's
9. James Garfield, a classics man.
10. Gerald Ford
11. George Washington (1796)
12. Grover Cleveland, even though he was one of the most masculine presidents.
13. George Washington's
14. $1,500,000 (1992), for a page of the draft of Abraham Lincoln's "house divided" speech.
15. Calvin Coolidge (1926)

Hats (answers)

1. Lyndon Johnson, whose aide was responsible for retrieving it each time.
2. Franklin Roosevelt (1945)
3. Dwight Eisenhower (1953), when he substituted it for the top hat at his inauguration.
4. Zachary Taylor
5. Lyndon Johnson (1965)
6. James Monroe (1825)
7. John Quincy Adams
8. John Kennedy
9. James Garfield (7¾)

Health (answers)

1. Thomas Jefferson, Ulysses Grant, and Woodrow Wilson
2. Reading the surrender note of General Robert E. Lee
3. Woodrow Wilson
4. John Kennedy
5. Dwight Eisenhower's
6. Franklin Roosevelt, as a campaign manager, and John Kennedy, as a candidate.
7. Abraham Lincoln's, in order to answer persistent questions about his health.

8.   Which president was in a coma?

9.   Which *incumbent* president first released his medical report?

10. Which president carried a lead ball just two inches from his heart for nearly forty years?

11. Which president became president of a hospital?

12. Who was issued Medicare Card #1?

13. What did Lyndon Johnson start drinking regularly after his heart attack?

14. Which president shaved three times a day to avoid the "five-o'clock shadow"?

15. Which two presidents traveled to France to enjoy the salubrious waters of a famous spa?

16. Which president often stood on soda bottles and rolled back and forth on his arches?

17. Which president wore a prosthesis?

18. Which president liked taking cold baths and swimming in the icy Potomac River?

19. Which president first used nitrous oxide, otherwise known as "laughing gas"?

20. Which president forbade his wife to keep the soap given her by a manufacturer?

21. Which president had scar tissue that caused an extreme curvature of his ring finger?

22. Which president had to sleep for months at a time in a chair?

23. Which *former* president *rejected* Secret Service protection, the only one who did so?

24. Which president last received lifetime protection by the Secret Service?

25. Which president detested the constant Secret Service presence more than any other?

26. Which president approved the hiring of the first female Secret Service officers?

27. Which president's personal doctor created the first White House dispensary?

28. Which president had received a huge radiation dosage in eighty-nine seconds?

29. Which president had once spent time in the Battle Creek Sanitarium?

30. Which naval officer and future president carried a bucket with him when standing watch?

31. Which president was denied nomination partly because he might have had a pedicure?

32. How much below average is the life expectancy of a president?

33. Which president had the first in-house female physician in the White House?

34. Which president had gotten blood poisoning and was told his leg might be amputated?

35. Which president took steroids and amphetamines?

36. Which presidents were the first ones who wore a hearing aid in one and both ears?

37. Which president suffered from advanced osteoporosis?

38. Who told his father, "I see no need of a wife so long as I have my health"?

Helicopters

1.   Which president first traveled in a helicopter?

2.   Which outgoing president's last request was that his helicopter circle the Capitol?

3.   Which president first campaigned by helicopter?

4.   Which president started the custom of using helicopter rides for short presidential trips?

8. John Adams, for five days.
9. Dwight Eisenhower (1956)
10. Andrew Jackson, from a duel with Charles Dickinson at Harrison's Mills, Kentucky.
11. Millard Fillmore (1870), of Buffalo General Hospital, in Buffalo, New York.
12. Harry Truman (1965)
13. 7-Up
14. Richard Nixon
15. Thomas Jefferson and Martin Van Buren
16. Jimmy Carter, because he thought flat feet would keep him out of the Naval Academy.
17. Grover Cleveland, in his jaw, after surgery.
18. John Quincy Adams
19. Grover Cleveland, during surgery to remove a cancerous growth from his mouth.
20. Woodrow Wilson
21. Ronald Reagan, which was especially noticeable when he waved.
22. Ulysses Grant, to avoid choking after surgery on his throat.
23. Richard Nixon (1974)
24. Bill Clinton (2001), after a law was passed limiting such protection to ten years.
25. Woodrow Wilson
26. Richard Nixon (1970)
27. Harry Truman's, Dr. Wallace H. Graham.
28. Jimmy Carter, when he disassembled a reactor core.
29. Warren Harding (1894), sent there by his wife.
30. Jimmy Carter, because he was frequently seasick.
31. Chester Arthur (1884)
32. Three years, according to *Trivial Pursuit*®.
33. John Kennedy, whose doctor was Dr. Janet Travell.
34. Dwight Eisenhower
35. John Kennedy, so much that his wife feared that he would become an addict.
36. Dwight Eisenhower and Ronald Reagan, respectively.
37. John Kennedy
38. Calvin Coolidge (1902), who was married only three years later.

Helicopters (answers)

1. Dwight Eisenhower (1957)
2. Gerald Ford's (1977)
3. Lyndon Johnson (1948), when he ran for the Senate.
4. Dwight Eisenhower

5.   What is the name of the president's helicopter when he is on board?
6.   What is arguably the most famous helicopter trip in U.S. history?
7.   Which president ordered the famous evacuation by helicopter of a U.S. embassy?
8.   What was Operation Eagle Claw, which involved a helicopter and a plane?

High Schools

1.   Who duplicated a trip made to his high school 200 years earlier by George Washington?
2.   Which president did his high-school classmates elect "Most Likely to Succeed"?
3.   Which president graduated second in his high-school class?
4.   Which president's yearbook predicted that his brother would become president?
5.   Which former president sold his shoes for $150 a pair?
6.   Which president graduated from high school at the age of fifteen years?
7.   Which president had once been a trustee of his high school?
8.   Which prestigious preparatory school had Franklin Roosevelt attended?
9.   Which president failed chemistry in high school but excelled in baseball and football?
10. Which president had been voted "Most Popular" high-school senior?
11. Which president had run away from high school with a classmate?
12. Which president had run away from home one summer after school was out?
13. Whom did his classmates vote "Most Respected," "Most Popular," and "Most Athletic"?
14. Which president had invited a mother-daughter prostitute team to a school dance?
15. What is the most popular name given to a high school in the U.S.A.?
16. Which president had taught public speaking to high-school students?
17. Which president had been a football coach at a military academy?
18. Which president had been an assistant teacher in an institute for the blind?
19. Which president had attended the same boarding school as his father?

Home States

1.   Which incumbent Democratic presidents lost their home states' popular votes?
2.   Which incumbent Republican president lost his home state's popular vote?
3.   Which incumbent president lost his home state's popular vote *but* won the election?
4.   Which other nominees since 1952 have not carried their home states?
5.   Who is the only person who would have won the presidency if he had won his home state?
6.   Which president was the first one since the Civil War from a Confederate state?
7.   Which winning national tickets hailed from contiguous states?
8.   Which state has had three times as many presidential nominees as any other state?
9.   Which state's presidential nominees lost four in a row in the 1800s?
10. How many times since 1856 have the two national tickets carried their four home states?

5. *Marine One*
6. Richard Nixon's departure from the White House lawn following his resignation (1974)
7. Gerald Ford (1975), symbolizing the end of the Vietnam War.
8. Jimmy Carter's aborted mission to free the U.S. hostages in Iran (1980)

High Schools (answers)
1. George Bush (1989), to Phillips Academy, in Andover, Massachusetts.
2. Jimmy Carter (1942)
3. William Taft (1874), who had attended Woodward High School in Cincinnati, Ohio.
4. Dwight Eisenhower's. Eisenhower was predicted to become a history professor.
5. Jimmy Carter, in order to help finance the refurbishment of his high school.
6. Lyndon Johnson (1923), the youngest ever from that school.
7. George Bush (1967-1979), of Phillips Academy, in Andover, Massachusetts.
8. The Groton School, in Groton, Connecticut, as had fifteen other Roosevelts.
9. George Bush
10. Gerald Ford (1934)
11. Franklin Roosevelt, to fight in the Spanish-American War. He was turned down.
12. Lyndon Johnson
13. George Bush
14. Andrew Jackson
15. Lincoln High School (726), according to a computer analysis.
16. Lyndon Johnson (1930-1932), at Sam Houston High School in Houston, Texas.
17. Dwight Eisenhower (1915-1919), at Peacock Military Academy, in San Antonio, Texas.
18. Grover Cleveland, in New York, New York.
19. George W. Bush (1960-1964), at Phillips Academy, in Andover, Massachusetts.

Home States (answers)
1. Martin Van Buren (1840), Grover Cleveland (1888), and Woodrow Wilson (1916)
2. Herbert Hoover (1932), who lost California.
3. Woodrow Wilson (1916), who lost New Jersey.
4. Adlai Stevenson (1952 and 1956), George McGovern (1972), and Al Gore (2000)
5. Al Gore (2000), who lost Tennessee by only 80,229 votes.
6. Lyndon Johnson (1963), almost 100 years!
7. Grant (OH) and Colfax (IN) in 1868, and Clinton (AR) and Gore (TN) in 1992 and 1996.
8. New York, but not a single one since 1948.
9. New York's, as well as three in a row in the 1900s.
10. Four

Homes

1. Who shared a home with Martin Van Buren when he was minister in London, England?
2. Which president was given Culzean Castle for the remainder of his life?
3. For whom was Mount Vernon named?
4. On which president's estate did the first Thanksgiving take place?
5. Where did Abraham Lincoln go to avoid the oppressive summer heat in Washington, DC?
6. Which president owned an estate in McLean, Virginia, called "Hickory Hill"?
7. Which president's mansion did Dr. William Thornton, the designer of the Capitol, design?
8. Which president began designing his future home as a young boy?
9. Which presidents' residences are located on streets named for them?
10. Which president's residence is the only one located on a street named for his First Lady?
11. Which president invented double doors that open simultaneously?
12. Which president's home was neutral territory during the Civil War?
13. Which president banned the Celtic tradition of placing Christmas trees in his home?
14. Which president's house is considered the oldest three-story brick house in Virginia?
15. Which president's home is the largest frame residence in the U.S.A.?
16. Which president donated his retreat in the Blue Ridge Mountains?
17. Why did John Tyler name his home "Sherwood Forest"?
18. Which president's home was used after his death as a church?
19. Which presidents' residences mean "little mountain" and "tall mountain"?
20. Which president's home first featured Venetian blinds?
21. Which president's residence had been designed by a previous president?
22. Which president's home do iron gates that had protected the White House guard?
23. Which president's first home is now part of the Anheuser-Busch brewery in St. Louis?
24. Which president's farm and home was called "Peacefield"?
25. Where did Harry Truman live during extensive renovations to the White House?
26. Which president owned a summer home named "Shadow Lawn"?
27. Which president's home is on the reverse of the nickel?
28. Which presidents, throughout their entire lives, each owned only one house?
29. Which president held meetings of a secret organization in his personal library?
30. Which president had built the first brick house in Indiana?
31. Which president's home was later occupied by the Burmese Embassy?
32. Which president's "summer White House" was in Rapid City, South Dakota?
33. Which president lived at Octagon House?
34. Which talk-show host had grown up next door to the Kennedys?
35. Which president planted on his estate an oak tree from each state in the Union?
36. Which presidents' homes were the only ones that appeared on U.S. postage stamps?
37. Which president owned a farm in Gettysburg, Pennsylvania?

Homes (answers)

1. American writer Washington Irving
2. Dwight Eisenhower, by Scotland, for his efforts during World War II.
3. George Washington's half-brother Laurence Washington's commander, Admiral Vernon.
4. William Henry Harrison's (1619), "Berkeley Plantation."
5. "Old Soldiers' Home," north of Washington, DC.
6. John Kennedy
7. James Madison's ("Montpelier")
8. Thomas Jefferson ("Monticello")
9. John Adams's (135 Adams Street) and Rutherford Hayes's (1337 Hayes Avenue)
10. Andrew Jackson's (4580 Rachel's Lane)
11. Thomas Jefferson. The doors are used to separate a hall from a parlor.
12. George Washington's ("Mount Vernon")
13. Theodore Roosevelt, because he opposed the unnecessary felling of trees.
14. William Henry Harrison's ("Berkeley Plantation")
15. John Tyler's ("Sherwood Forest"), at more than 300 feet long.
16. Gerald Ford, to the Shenandoah National Park.
17. Because he likened himself to Robin Hood, who lived in Sherwood Forest in England.
18. Franklin Pierce's, for a Swedish Baptist congregation.
19. Thomas Jefferson's ("Monticello") and James Madison's ("Montpelier"), respectively.
20. George Washington's ("Mount Vernon")
21. James Monroe's ("Oak Hill"), designed by Thomas Jefferson.
22. Rutherford Hayes's
23. Ulysses Grant's
24. John Quincy Adams's
25. Blair House, across Pennsylvania Avenue from the White House.
26. Woodrow Wilson, on the New Jersey shore.
27. Thomas Jefferson's ("Monticello")
28. Abraham Lincoln (1809-1865) and Dwight Eisenhower (1890-1969)
29. Millard Fillmore, where the Order of the Star-Spangled Banner met.
30. William Henry Harrison (1803), named "Grouseland."
31. Herbert Hoover's, in Washington, DC.
32. Calvin Coolidge's
33. James Madison
34. Morton Downey, Jr., and played baseball with the Kennedy brothers.
35. James Monroe, at "Oak Hill."
36. George Washington's, Thomas Jefferson's, John Tyler's, and Franklin Roosevelt's
37. Dwight Eisenhower, near the site of the famous Civil War battlefield.

38. Which president had a huge peach grove at his home?
39. Which president lived in a boardinghouse where the Library of Congress now stands?
40. Which president's first home after marrying was half a trailer home?
41. Since George Washington had no descendants, who inherited Mount Vernon?
42. To which estate did James Madison escape after the British invasion of Washington, DC?
43. Where was Dr. Jonas Salk's discovery of the polio vaccine announced?
44. Which president's home has 300-million-year-old dinosaur tracks on the grounds?
45. What was the name of Ulysses Grant's farmhouse?
46. Which president's home became the official residence for a university president?
47. Which president changed his address to 668 St. Cloud Road from a similar address?
48. From which president's home did Count von Zeppelin make his maiden balloon flight?
49. Which president had a home built on the thirteenth green of a golf course?
50. Which president named trees in his front yard for famous visitors?
51. After visiting which home did Washington Irving create *The Legend of Sleepy Hollow*?
52. Which First Couple first divided their time between official residences?
53. In which president's home is there nothing to keep the visitor from the actual furnishings?
54. Which president's home had been a shipyard during the American Revolution?
55. Which president's residence is the only U.S. national park located in another country?
56. Which president moved twenty-nine times in his first forty-four years of marriage?
57. Who invented "Lincoln Logs," the miniature brown logs children use?
58. What is the name of the Bush compound in Kennebunkport, Maine?
59. Which president observed Scottish custom by giving his new wife a key and some sod?
60. Which president's home did William du Pont purchase in 1901?
61. At which president's home did General Daniel Butterfield compose the tune "Taps"?
62. At which president's residence has the peacock become the symbol of the estate?
63. What is the name of Ronald Reagan's California ranch?
64. Which *former* president lived in Washington, DC, instead of returning to his home state?
65. Which president named his home for the American Indian who had lived on that land?
66. Which president created an air shaft to freshen his outhouse?
67. Which president had been raised on a farm in the Finger Lakes region of New York State?
68. Which president's residence was a campsite for the entire Union Army?
69. Where was Richard Nixon's "Western White House"?
70. Which president's home was last heated only by burning wood, not gas or electricity?

Honors

1. Who was only the fifty-eighth U.S. citizen awarded a knighthood by a British monarch?
2. Which president had been elected Most Outstanding State Senator of his state?

38. Thomas Jefferson, at Monticello.
39. Abraham Lincoln
40. George Bush's, near Odessa, Texas.
41. His nephew, Bushrod Washington.
42. "Salona," in McLean, Virginia.
43. At Franklin Roosevelt's "Little White House," in Warm Springs, Georgia (1955).
44. James Monroe's ("Oak Hill")
45. "Hardscrabble," in St. Louis, Missouri.
46. Herbert Hoover's, for Stanford University's president, in Palo Alto, California.
47. Ronald Reagan, from a number associated with evil forces.
48. William Henry Harrison's ("Berkeley Plantation"), in the *Intrepid*.
49. Richard Nixon, in Palm Springs, California.
50. Rutherford Hayes
51. Martin Van Buren's ("Lindenwald")
52. President and Mrs. Grover Cleveland
53. Harry Truman's
54. William Henry Harrison's ("Berkeley Plantation")
55. Franklin Roosevelt's ("Campobello"), partly located in Canada.
56. George Bush
57. John Lloyd Wright, son of architect Frank Lloyd Wright, fashioned after Lincoln's log cabin.
58. "Walker's Point," in the family since 1899.
59. Woodrow Wilson (1915), from their new home.
60. James Madison's ("Montpelier")
61. William Henry Harrison's ("Berkeley Plantation")
62. James Monroe's ("Ash Lawn")
63. "Rancho del Cielo," where he often chopped wood and rode horses.
64. Woodrow Wilson (1919-1924)
65. Theodore Roosevelt ("Sagamore Hill")
66. Thomas Jefferson
67. Millard Fillmore
68. William Henry Harrison's ("Berkeley Plantation"), during the summer of 1862.
69. San Clemente, California.
70. Ronald Reagan's ranch house in California

Honors (answers)

1. Ronald Reagan (1989)
2. Jimmy Carter

3. Which president had been awarded the Grand Cross of the French Legion of Honor?
4. Which president established the Medal of Freedom as a wartime honor?
5. Which living presidents were the only ones who won Presidential Medals of Freedom?
6. Which president awarded a Presidential Medal of Freedom to a former opponent?
7. Which president won an essay contest by the Sons of the American Revolution?
8. Which president was the first American citizen who won a Nobel Prize of any kind?
9. Which other presidents also received Nobel Peace Prizes?
10. Which president was awarded Columbia University's Alexander Hamilton Medal?
11. Which president had been a member of the Order of the Coif, an honorary legal fraternity?
12. Which president had received an Horatio Alger Award?
13. Which president won the Pulitzer Prize?
14. Which president's biography won the Pulitzer Prize?
15. Which president was made an honorary citizen of the Free University of Berlin?
16. Which president first made an award to a conscientious objector?
17. Which presidents were the first and last ones who had earned a Phi Beta Kappa key?
18. Which presidents were the first and last ones who earned honorary Phi Beta Kappa keys?
19. Who awarded the National Geographic Society's Hubbard Medal to Charles Lindbergh?
20. Who awarded the National Geographic Society's Hubbard Medal to Admiral Robert Peary?
21. Which president had been awarded Denmark's Order of the Elephant?
22. Who were the first and last presidents in the Academy of Moral and Political Sciences?
23. Which president had won an Intercollegiate Extemporaneous Speaking tournament?
24. Which president made Winston Churchill an honorary citizen of the U.S.A.?
25. Which president was the first foreigner awarded the Order of Victory medal?
26. For which president was the expansion wing of the National Gallery named?
27. Which president was nominated for a Grammy?
28. Which presidents were the first and last ones awarded Congressional Gold Medals?
29. Which president was honorary president of the National Horseshoe Pitching Association?
30. Which president hated ribbons and awards and spurned every one except one?
31. Which president first received an honorary degree?
32. Which presidents received and declined honorary degrees from Oxford University?
33. Which president received fifty-two honorary degrees during his lifetime?
34. Which First Couple received simultaneous honorary degrees?
35. Why was Harry Truman denied an honorary degree from Baylor University, in 1945?
36. Which president was inducted into the Newspaper Carriers Hall of Fame?
37. Which president inaugurated the World Exposition in St. Louis?
38. Which president had been chairman of the Boys Club of America?
39. Which award established by Congress was named for a president?
40. Which presidents officially created Mother's Day and Father's Day?
41. Which president received the John F. Kennedy Profile in Courage Award?

3. Dwight Eisenhower (1943)
4. Harry Truman (1945). John Kennedy named it the Presidential Medal of Freedom.
5. Ronald Reagan (1992), Jimmy Carter (1999), and Gerald Ford (1999)
6. Bill Clinton (1997), who awarded it to Bob Dole.
7. Calvin Coolidge, whose essay was "Principles Fought for in the American Revolution."
8. Theodore Roosevelt (1906), for negotiating after the Russo-Japanese War of 1905.
9. Woodrow Wilson (1919) and Jimmy Carter (2002)
10. Dwight Eisenhower (1963), for distinguished service and accomplishment.
11. Richard Nixon (1936)
12. Ronald Reagan (1969), for a person whose feats are amazing given modest beginnings.
13. John Kennedy (1957), for biography.
14. John Quincy Adams's biography (1950), written by Samuel Flagg Bemis.
15. John Kennedy (1963), on the same date he said "Ich bin ein Berliner."
16. Harry Truman (1945)
17. John Quincy Adams (1787) and George Bush (1948), respectively.
18. Martin Van Buren and Dwight Eisenhower, respectively.
19. Calvin Coolidge (1927)
20. Theodore Roosevelt (1906), for Peary's 87°6' "farthest north" drive to the North Pole.
21. Dwight Eisenhower (1947)
22. Thomas Jefferson and Ronald Reagan (1989), respectively. It is a French organization.
23. Richard Nixon (1934)
24. John Kennedy (1963)
25. Dwight Eisenhower (1945), by the USSR. He is also the only *American* to receive it.
26. John Kennedy
27. Richard Nixon (1977), in the Best Spoken Word category, for an interview by David Frost.
28. George Washington (1776) and Ronald Reagan (2000), respectively.
29. Warren Harding (1917)
30. Woodrow Wilson, who *did* accept the Polish Order of the White Eagle (1922).
31. George Washington (1776), from Harvard University.
32. Harry Truman (1956) and Millard Fillmore (1855), because it was in Latin, respectively.
33. Herbert Hoover (1874-1964)
34. Lyndon Johnson and Lady Bird Johnson (1964), from the University of Texas at Austin.
35. The Texas Baptist Convention denies one to anybody who has drunk or played poker.
36. Dwight Eisenhower
37. Theodore Roosevelt (1904), by turning a key in the East Room of the White House.
38. Harry Truman (1936)
39. The Theodore Roosevelt Award (1920), given to a law-enforcement officer.
40. Woodrow Wilson (1914) and Richard Nixon (1972), respectively.
41. Gerald Ford (2001), for his decision to pardon Richard Nixon after Watergate.

Horses

1. Which president kept a stable of racehorses at the White House?
2. Which two presidents pitted their horses against each other?
3. What was the name of John Tyler's favorite horse?
4. Which president received a jackass named "Royal Gift" from King Carlos III of Spain?
5. What was the name of the horse that bore George Washington to Yorktown?
6. What was the name of George Washington's favorite horse?
7. Which president had a horse named "Old Whitey" whose tail was plucked for souvenirs?
8. Which president's coach horses were named "Caesar" and "Cleopatra"?
9. Which president named a horse "Truxton," for the commodore of the USS *Constitution*?
10. Which president had a horse named "Traveller," as did Robert E. Lee?
11. Which president liked to ride his horse at night to relax?
12. What was the name of the pony that Theodore Roosevelt rode at San Juan Hill?
13. How many times did George Washington fall from a horse in his entire life?
14. Which president wrote an obituary for his horse?
15. Which president's groom talked and ate with the animals *à la* Dr. Doolittle?
16. Which president permanently closed the White House stables?
17. For which president did Wild Bill Cody name his famous white horse?
18. Which president irked the Society for Indecency to Naked Animals (SINA)?
19. Which president tied a man to a post for six hours for beating a horse mercilessly?
20. Which president's legs were so short that he needed help mounting his horses?
21. Which president's horse was used as a model for a huge statue near the Capitol?
22. Which president installed an electric horse in the White House and rode it daily?
23. Which president had two of his horses killed in battle?
24. What was the name of the horse that walked in John Kennedy's funeral procession?
25. Which president ordered that his six horses have their teeth brushed daily?

Hotels

1. Which president had a hotel in Washington, DC, install a special elevator for him?
2. Which president checked his mistress into hotels, saying she was his niece?
3. In which hotel room did Harry Truman regularly hold private poker games?
4. Which presidents were inaugurated in the Indian Queen and Kirkwood House Hotels?
5. In which hotel near the Alamo did Grant, McKinley, Taft, Eisenhower, and Nixon all sleep?
6. Which future president rented a room at the Norwood Hotel until he became president?
7. In which famous hotel did John Kennedy stay the night before his assassination?
8. Which president retired to the Waldorf Towers in New York City?
9. Where is the original "smoke-filled" room, come to epitomize clandestine political dealing?

Horses (answers)

1. Andrew Jackson (1829-1837), who entered them in several match races.
2. George Washington and Thomas Jefferson, an Arabian stallion versus a roan colt.
3. "The General"
4. George Washington. He was taken to Mount Vernon for breeding.
5. "Nelson"
6. "Lexington"
7. Ulysses Grant
8. John Adams's
9. Andrew Jackson
10. George Washington
11. Franklin Pierce
12. "Texas"
13. Once
14. John Tyler
15. Ulysses Grant's, Albert.
16. Herbert Hoover
17. William McKinley ("McKinley")
18. John Kennedy, for not "clothing" his horses.
19. Ulysses Grant
20. Zachary Taylor's. Taylor got help from his military orderly.
21. Ulysses Grant's
22. Calvin Coolidge
23. George Washington
24. "Black Jack." The horse marched riderless, in very poignant fashion.
25. George Washington

Hotels (answers)

1. Franklin Roosevelt, so he could enter without letting anybody see him crippled.
2. Warren Harding
3. Room #D-406 of the Shoreham Hotel, in uptown Georgetown.
4. John Tyler (1841) and Andrew Johnson (1865), respectively.
5. The Menger Hotel, in San Antonio, Texas.
6. Calvin Coolidge (1923)
7. The Rice Hotel, in Houston, Texas.
8. Herbert Hoover (1933)
9. Suite #404-406 of the Blackstone Hotel, in Chicago, Illinois.

10. Which president died in a hotel?
11. Where was Millard Fillmore living when he learned that he had become president?
12. In which hotel's bar did Theodore Roosevelt recruit many of his Rough Riders?
13. In which hotel did Ronald Reagan watch the election returns from his landslide victories?
14. Which president lived in the Neil Hotel while serving as governor?
15. Which president missed supper after his inauguration when his hotel restaurant closed?
16. At which hotel did John Nepomuk Schrank attempt to assassinate Theodore Roosevelt?
17. In which hotel did Dustin Hoffman's character have an affair in the movie *The Graduate*?
18. At which hotel did Sara Jane Moore attempt to assassinate Gerald Ford?
19. In which hotel, ironically, did the Republican Party set up its national headquarters?
20. Which hotel first catered solely to women?
21. In which hotel did Marilyn Monroe occasionally visit John Kennedy?
22. Outside which hotel was Ronald Reagan shot?
23. Which president spent the night of his inauguration in a hotel?
24. From which hotel did Richard Nixon direct his transition to power?
25. In which hotel did Roosevelt and Taft meet, by accident, for the first time since their rift?
26. Which president coined the term "lobbyist"?
27. Which president sat in a hotel distributing $5 bills to anybody who would vote for him?
28. In which hotel did Bill Clinton allegedly proposition Paula Jones?
29. Which hotel hosted ten presidents in succession as they awaited their inaugurations?
30. In which hotel did American bandmaster John Philip Sousa die?
31. Which president made an appearance in a nightclub act in Las Vegas, Nevada?

House of Representatives

1. Which president was the first one who had been a representative?
2. Which presidents had served in *both* the House and the Senate?
3. Which *incumbent* U.S. representative became president?
4. Which presidents had been members of the powerful House Ways and Means Committee?
5. Which president did the House censure?
6. Who promised to work on a dairy farm if he won a race for U.S. representative?
7. Which president had not uttered a single word during four years as a U.S. representative?
8. Which president first openly opposed the re-election of a speaker of the House?
9. Which presidents had served only one two-year term in the House?
10. Which president had financed his first campaign for the House with his wife's inheritance?
11. Which president had been speaker of the House?
12. Which president refused to take his seat in the House unless the Civil War ended?
13. Which incumbent representative first ran for president?

10. Warren Harding (1923), in the (Sheraton) Palace Hotel, in San Francisco, California.

11. The Willard Hotel, in Washington, DC.

12. The Menger Hotel's, in San Antonio, Texas.

13. The Century Plaza Hotel, in Los Angeles, California.

14. William McKinley (1892-1896), in Columbus, Ohio.

15. Thomas Jefferson (1801)

16. The Gilpatrick Hotel, in Milwaukee, Wisconsin.

17. The Taft Hotel, in San Francisco, California.

18. The St. Francis Hotel, in San Francisco, California.

19. The Roosevelt Hotel, in New York, New York.

20. The Martha Washington Hotel (1903), in New York, New York.

21. The Hotel Carlyle, in New York, New York.

22. The Washington Hilton (1981), in Washington, DC.

23. Franklin Pierce (1853), at the Willard Hotel, since there was no room in the White House!

24. The Pierre Hotel (1968), in New York, New York.

25. The Blackstone Hotel (1916), in Chicago, Illinois.

26. Ulysses Grant, to describe men who sought favors in the lobby of the Willard Hotel.

27. Lyndon Johnson (1936), in the Plaza Hotel, in San Antonio, Texas.

28. The Excelsior Hotel, in Little Rock, Arkansas.

29. The Willard Inter-Continental Hotel (Pierce to Wilson, inclusive), in Washington, DC.

30. The Abraham Lincoln (now Lincoln Plaza) Hotel, in Reading, Pennsylvania (1932).

31. Ronald Reagan (1954), at the Last Frontier Hotel, with a pair of rowdy chimpanzees.

House of Representatives (answers)

1. James Madison (1789-1797)

2. Andrew Jackson, John Kennedy, Lyndon Johnson, and Richard Nixon

3. James Garfield (1880), also an elected but un-inaugurated senator, from Ohio.

4. James Polk, Millard Fillmore (who was chairman), John Kennedy, and George Bush

5. Andrew Jackson (1834), for removing deposits from the Bank of the United States.

6. Gerald Ford (1948)

7. Lyndon Johnson (1937-1939 and 1943-1945), at least not for the record.

8. Thomas Jefferson (1805), because Nathaniel Macon did not want to annex Florida.

9. Andrew Jackson (1795-1797) and Abraham Lincoln (1847-1849)

10. Lyndon Johnson (1936)

11. James Polk (1835-1839)

12. Rutherford Hayes (1865). The Civil War ended a few months later.

13. Henry Clay (1824), who placed fourth.

14. Which president, during eleven years in the House, had not passed a single bill of note?
15. Which president, during fourteen years in the House, had been absent for *one* vote?
16. Which president testified before the House Un-American Activities Committee?
17. Which president was elected to office in the Confederacy?
18. Which president had spent more time in the House than any other?
19. Who took the House floor more than any other representative during the First Congress?
20. Which state representative once jumped out of a window in order to prevent a quorum?
21. Which *former* president became a member of the House?
22. Which two presidents had been elected to the House in 1946?
23. Which speaker resigned because he distrusted the president with whom he would work?
24. Which president advocated a term limit on representatives of eight years?
25. Which president gave his House salary to charity each year?
26. When did Richard Nixon first visit the House after that body threatened to impeach him?
27. In favor of what did Richard Nixon and John Kennedy cast their first votes in the House?
28. Which president's idol was Sam Rayburn, the second man elected speaker uncontested?
29. Which Democratic and Republican presidents last gained House seats in off-year voting?
30. Who predicted that the House would decide 95% of all presidential elections?
31. From which candidates may the House select when they decide a presidential election?
32. How are the votes allocated when the House decides a presidential election?
33. Which president had been the first U.S. representative from Tennessee?
34. Which president had defeated his presidential successor in a race for U.S. representative?
35. Which president had been the youngest representative ever to preside over the House?
36. Who led the House to adopt the title "President of the United States of America"?
37. Which speaker said, "I never served *under* any president, I served *with* eight"?
38. Who were the first and last presidents who faced articles of impeachment in the House?
39. Which *elected* president was the only one ever impeached by the House?
40. Which *unelected* president was the only other president ever impeached by the House?
41. Which president's wife awoke him, saying, "I think there are burglars in the house"?

House Composition

1. Which presidents were the first and last ones with a majority in the House?
2. Which presidents were the first and last ones *without* a majority in the House?
3. Which presidents were the first and last ones with a veto-proof majority in the House?
4. Which presidents were the first and last ones *without* a veto-proof majority in the House?
5. Which presidents were the only ones with a veto-proof majority of the opposition party?
6. Which Democratic presidents had the fewest and most House Democrats?
7. Which Democratic presidents had the fewest and most House Republicans?

14. Lyndon Johnson (1938-1949)
15. James Polk (1825-1839)
16. Ronald Reagan (1947). Richard Nixon was a member of that committee.
17. John Tyler (1861), elected to the Confederate Provisional Congress.
18. Gerald Ford (1949-1973), more than twenty-four years.
19. James Madison (1789-1791), who took the floor 124 times.
20. Abraham Lincoln (1840), on a bill to require banks to make payment in gold or silver.
21. John Quincy Adams (1831-1848)
22. John Kennedy and Richard Nixon
23. Thomas Reed (1899), who distrusted William McKinley.
24. Richard Nixon
25. John Kennedy (1947-1953)
26. 1990, sixteen years later.
27. Aid for Greece and Turkey, to thwart Soviet communist influence.
28. Lyndon Johnson's
29. Bill Clinton (1998) and George W. Bush (2002), respectively.
30. James Madison (1787), at the Constitutional Convention. It has decided 3.7% of them.
31. The top three vote-getters in the Electoral College
32. Each state's *entire* delegation gets one vote, no matter how many representatives it has.
33. Andrew Jackson (1797)
34. James Madison (1789), who defeated James Monroe in a race for the First Congress.
35. Richard Nixon (1947), at the age of thirty-four years, 186 days.
36. James Madison (1789). John Adams preferred "His Most Benign Highness."
37. Sam Rayburn
38. John Tyler (1843) and Bill Clinton (1998), respectively.
39. Bill Clinton (1998), for perjury and obstruction of justice.
40. Andrew Johnson (1868), for charges including making speeches against Congress!
41. Grover Cleveland's. He replied, "In the Senate maybe, but not in the House."

House Composition (answers)
1. George Washington (1789-1791) and George W. Bush (2001-2005), respectively.
2. John Quincy Adams (1827-1829) and Bill Clinton (1995-2001), respectively.
3. Thomas Jefferson (1803-1809) and Jimmy Carter (1977-1979), respectively.
4. George Washington (1789-1791) and George W. Bush (2001-2005), respectively.
5. Benjamin Harrison (1891-1893) and Gerald Ford (1975-1977)
6. Franklin Pierce (83) and Franklin Roosevelt (331), respectively.
7. Franklin Roosevelt (89) and Harry Truman (245), respectively.

8. Which Republican presidents had the fewest and most House Democrats?
9. Which Republican presidents had the fewest and most House Republicans?
10. Which Democratic presidents had the tiniest and largest portions of House Democrats?
11. Which Democratic presidents had the tiniest and largest portions of House Republicans?
12. Which Republican presidents had the tiniest and largest portions of House Democrats?
13. Which Republican presidents had the tiniest and largest portions of House Republicans?
14. Which president first dealt with a House majority from states outside the Civil War Union?

Inaugural Addresses

1. Which presidents delivered the shortest and longest inaugural addresses, respectively?
2. Which presidents did *not* make an inaugural address?
3. Which president gave part of his address, took the oath, and then finished his address?
4. Which president first went to church immediately after his inaugural address?
5. Which president-elect made the first "extra" by giving his inaugural address to a reporter?
6. Which president first delivered an inaugural address *before* being inaugurated?
7. Which president first delivered his inaugural address in person to a crowd?
8. Which inaugural address was first amplified onto the Capitol grounds?
9. Which inaugural addresses began with the word "I"?
10. Which president used the word "I" more times than any other in an inaugural speech?
11. Which inaugural address did *not* mention the word "I"?
12. Which inaugural address first mentioned the word "God"?
13. Which inaugural addresses ended with the word "God"?
14. How many times did Bill Clinton mention the word "change" in his first inaugural address?
15. Which inaugural address was first circulated as campaign literature?
16. Which inaugural address was the first one *not* delivered on Inauguration Day?
17. Which inaugural address was the first one *not* delivered on the current Inauguration Day?
18. Which president first mentioned a former president in his inaugural address?
19. Which inaugural address ended with the name of another president?
20. Which inaugural address first included a salutation to the American people?
21. Which inaugural address was first broadcast by radio?
22. Which president last made an inaugural address while wearing his hat?
23. Which president made the shortest speech ever after being sworn in?
24. Which president started the most sentences in his inaugural address with the word "and"?
25. Which inaugural address did Richard Nixon consider among the best?
26. Which president did not read an inaugural address but did make an impromptu oration?
27. Which presidents first and last delivered their inaugural addresses bareheaded?
28. Which inaugural address did Daniel Webster help write, deleting classical references?

130   All the Presidents' Trivia

8. Abraham Lincoln/Andrew Johnson (42) and Gerald Ford (291), respectively.
9. Benjamin Harrison (88) and Warren Harding (300), respectively.
10. Grover Cleveland (29.5%) and Franklin Roosevelt (76.4%), respectively.
11. Franklin Roosevelt (20.1%) and Grover Cleveland (68.5%), respectively.
12. Abraham Lincoln/Andrew Johnson (22.0%) and Benjamin Harrison (70.8%), respectively.
13. Benjamin Harrison (26.5%) and Andrew Johnson (74.5%), respectively.
14. Ronald Reagan (1983)

Inaugural Addresses (answers)

1. George Washington (1793), at 135 words, and W. H. Harrison (1841), at 8,445 words.
2. John Tyler, Millard Fillmore, Andrew Johnson, and Chester Arthur, unelected one-termers.
3. William Henry Harrison (1841)
4. George Washington (1789), who went to St. Paul's Church.
5. Thomas Jefferson (1801), to the *National Intelligencer*.
6. George Washington (1793)
7. James Monroe (1817)
8. Warren Harding's (1921)
9. Washington's (1793), Monroe's (1821), Buchanan's (1857), and Roosevelt's (1933)
10. William Henry Harrison (1841), forty-five times.
11. Theodore Roosevelt's (1905)
12. James Monroe's (1821)
13. Roosevelt's (1905), Coolidge's (1925), Roosevelt's (1941), and Eisenhower's (1953)
14. Nine
15. George Washington's (1789)
16. James Monroe's (1821)
17. Dwight Eisenhower's (1957)
18. William Henry Harrison (1841), who mentioned Thomas Jefferson and James Madison.
19. Theodore Roosevelt's (1905), which ended with Abraham Lincoln's name.
20. Thomas Jefferson's (1801), which started with "Friends and Fellow Citizens."
21. Calvin Coolidge's (1925)
22. Woodrow Wilson (1917)
23. Lyndon Johnson (1963), limiting his comments to eighteen words.
24. George Bush (1989), four times more than in any other inaugural address.
25. James Polk's (1845)
26. Franklin Pierce (1853)
27. Theodore Roosevelt (1905) and George W. Bush (2001), respectively.
28. William Henry Harrison's (1841)

29. Which inaugural address first mentioned women?
30. Which inaugural address was first filmed and recorded for audio?
31. From whom did John Kennedy borrow the question "Ask not what your country . . ."?
32. From whom did Franklin Roosevelt borrow "The only thing we have to fear is . . . fear itself"?

Inaugural Balls

1. Which president held the first inaugural ball?
2. Which president refused to attend his own inaugural ball?
3. Which president held the first inaugural ball held on the same day as his inauguration?
4. Which president held an inaugural ball in the Smithsonian's Museum of American History?
5. Which president canceled his inaugural ball?
6. Which inaugural ball was halted when his wife had an epileptic seizure?
7. Which president first held an inaugural ball in his own honor?
8. Which inauguration first had more than one inaugural ball to satisfy public demand?
9. Which inaugural balls were held in the Pension Building at 4th and G Streets?
10. Which president's inaugural ball was held in the new Pension Office Building?
11. Which inaugural ball was held in such cold that pipes froze and guests wore heavy coats?
12. Which inaugural ball was the first one that turned a profit?
13. Which inaugural ball was the first one held with electricity?
14. Which inaugural ball was first lighted by colored electric lights?
15. At which inaugural ball did a woman die from a bronchial infection due to the lack of heat?
16. Which presidents held "Black Tie and Boots" inaugural balls?
17. At which inaugural festivities, famous for its raucousness, were there no police on duty?
18. Where were all inaugural balls from John Quincy Adams's to James Buchanan's held?
19. Which inaugural ball was held in the Arts and Industries Building?
20. Who called James Madison "a withered little Apple-John" after attending his inaugural ball?
21. Which president held more inaugural balls than any other?
22. Which inaugural ball was broadcast to thirty-two other ballroom sites around the country?
23. Which president first invited presidential electors to his inaugural ball?
24. Which president first included an official presidential dinner as part of inaugural festivities?
25. Which president's inaugural ball was held on May 7?
26. Which president first held an inaugural ball in Washington, DC?
27. Which president's inaugural ball was first held in a legislative building?

Inaugural Bibles

1. Which president-elect did *not* use a Bible at his inauguration?
2. Which president had not been sworn in with a Bible because one could not be found?

29. Woodrow Wilson's (1913)
30. William McKinley's (1897)
31. Oliver Wendell Holmes, Warren Harding, and his headmaster at Choate Academy
32. Francis Bacon, the Duke of Wellington, and Winston Churchill

Inaugural Balls (answers)

1. George Washington (1789), in the City Assembly Rooms, in New York, New York.
2. Franklin Roosevelt (1945), because he was sick.
3. James Madison (1809)
4. Richard Nixon (1969)
5. Woodrow Wilson (1913)
6. William McKinley's (1897)
7. James Madison (1809)
8. Harry Truman's (1949). Others had had more than one ball, but not by public demand.
9. Grover Cleveland's (1885 and 1893)
10. William McKinley's (1897)
11. Rutherford Hayes's (1877)
12. James Polk's (1845). The profits were donated to orphan asylums.
13. James Garfield's (1881)
14. Grover Cleveland's (1893)
15. Ulysses Grant's (1873)
16. George Bush (1993) and George W. Bush (2001), for well-wishers from Texas.
17. Andrew Jackson's (1829)
18. Carusi's Assembly Rooms, on the site where the IRS headquarters now stands.
19. James Garfield's (1881), in what became the Smithsonian Institution.
20. American author Washington Irving (1809)
21. Bill Clinton (1997), who held fourteen balls.
22. Ronald Reagan's (1981), by satellite television.
23. Franklin Roosevelt (1933)
24. Ronald Reagan (1981)
25. George Washington's (1789), Inauguration Day being on April 30.
26. James Madison (1809)
27. Ronald Reagan's (1981), in the Rayburn House Office Building in Washington, DC.

Inaugural Bibles (answers)

1. Franklin Pierce (1853), because he believed his son's death was punishment for his sins.
2. Theodore Roosevelt (1901), sworn in at Ansley Wilcox's library in Buffalo.

3. Which president-elect placed his hand on a Catholic Gutenberg Bible at his inauguration?
4. Which president-elect placed his hand on a Catholic Douay Bible at his inauguration?
5. Which president-elect first bent and kissed his inaugural Bible after taking the oath?
6. Which president-elect's Bible was the most elaborate one ever used in an inauguration?
7. Which president-elect used his mother's Bible at his inauguration?
8. Which president used the same Bible to take the oath as vice president and president?
9. Which president used the same Bible four times when taking an oath of office?
10. Which president-elect recited the oath from a book of laws and forewent a Bible?
11. Which presidents-elect used two Bibles simultaneously during their inaugurations?
12. Which president-elect used an inaugural Bible printed in a modern foreign language?
13. Which president-elect used the White House Bible during his inauguration?
14. Which president-elect's inaugural Bible was the oldest one?
15. Which president-elect's inaugural Bible is the last one whose whereabouts are unknown?
16. Which president-elect's Bible stated "This is the spot" where he was to place his hand?
17. Which president's inaugural Bible is the only one in the Smithsonian Institution?
18. After George Washington's, which inaugural Bible is the earliest one still in existence?
19. Which president-elect's inaugural Bible also was present at his funeral?
20. Which inaugural Bible last contained a seal of the Supreme Court?
21. Which inaugural Bible had been a gift from the African Methodist Episcopal Church?
22. Besides George Washington himself, which presidents-elect have used his Bible?
23. Which president-elect was the first one whose wife held the Bible at his inauguration?

Inaugural Clothes

1. Which president-elect wore wool breeches to his inauguration?
2. Which president-elect first wore long pants to his inauguration instead of breeches?
3. Which president-elect first wore a modern business suit to his inauguration?
4. Which president-elect first wore all American-made clothes to his inauguration?
5. Which president-elect wore black to his inauguration to mourn his recently-deceased wife?
6. Who held Abraham Lincoln's stovepipe hat at Lincoln's first inauguration?
7. Which president-elect last wore a silk top hat at his inauguration?
8. Which president-elect was the first one who did *not* wear formal attire to his inauguration?
9. Which president-elect was the last one who *did* wear formal attire to his inauguration?

Inaugural Dates

1. Which president-elect's inauguration occurred longest after his predecessor's departure?
2. Which presidents-elect were not publicly inaugurated on Inauguration Day?
3. Which president-elect was first inaugurated on March 3?

3. Harry Truman (1949)
4. John Kennedy (1961)
5. George Washington (1789), his 1767 King James Bible. Franklin Pierce broke the trend.
6. William McKinley's (1897)
7. Jimmy Carter (1977)
8. Lyndon Johnson (1961 and 1965)
9. Franklin Roosevelt (1933, 1937, 1941, and 1945)
10. John Quincy Adams (1825)
11. Truman (1949), Eisenhower (1957), Nixon (1969), and Carter (1977)
12. Franklin Roosevelt (1933, 1937, 1941, and 1945), whose Bible was printed in Dutch.
13. Harry Truman (1949)
14. Franklin Roosevelt's, whose Dutch Bible was printed in 1686.
15. Herbert Hoover's (1929)
16. Rutherford Hayes's (1877)
17. James Buchanan's (1853)
18. James Polk's (1845)
19. George Washington's (1789)
20. William Taft's (1909)
21. William McKinley's (1897)
22. Harding (1921), Eisenhower (1953), George Bush (1989), and George W. Bush (2001)
23. Lyndon Johnson (1965)

Inaugural Clothes (answers)

1. James Madison (1809)
2. John Quincy Adams (1825)
3. Lyndon Johnson (1963)
4. George Washington (1789)
5. Andrew Jackson (1829)
6. Political nemesis Stephen Douglas (1861), whom Lincoln had defeated for president.
7. John Kennedy (1961)
8. Franklin Roosevelt (1945)
9. Ronald Reagan (1985)

Inaugural Dates (answers)

1. John Tyler's (1841). For fifty-three hours, the nation literally had no leader.
2. James Monroe (1821) and Zachary Taylor (1849), both inaugurated one day later.
3. Rutherford Hayes (1877), one day early.

4. Which president-elect was inaugurated on Ash Wednesday?
5. Which day did former senator Howard Baker believe should be Inauguration Day?
6. Who proposed a constitutional amendment to make November 15 Inauguration Day?
7. Which president-elect's inauguration was held on Super Bowl Sunday?

Inaugural Geography

1. Which president-elect was first inaugurated in Washington, DC?
2. Which president-elect was first inaugurated on the East Portico of the Capitol?
3. Which president-elect was first inaugurated on the East Front of the Capitol?
4. Which president-elect was first inaugurated on the West Terrace of the Capitol?
5. Which president-elect was first inaugurated on the Capitol steps?
6. Which president-elect was inaugurated inside the Capitol Rotunda?
7. Which president-elect was inaugurated on the South Portico of the White House?
8. Which president-elect was sworn in at the White House?
9. Which other presidents had been sworn in at the White House?
10. Which president-elect was inaugurated in two different cities?
11. Which president-elect was inaugurated inside a city hall?
12. Which president-elect was first inaugurated on a platform constructed for that purpose?
13. Which president had been sworn in at home?
14. Which president-elect was first inaugurated outdoors?
15. Which president-elect was first inaugurated immediately before the vice president-elect?
16. Who was inaugurated as vice president and president, both outside of Washington, DC?
17. Where was Richard Nixon when Gerald Ford was sworn in as president?
18. Which two presidents were sworn in twice in the same year?
19. Which president-elect was first inaugurated in the Senate chamber?
20. Which presidents-elect were inaugurated in the Senate chamber in Washington, DC?
21. Which president-elect was last inaugurated in the House chamber?
22. Which president was sworn in on board an airplane?

Inaugural Guests

1. Which inauguration did British author William Makepeace Thackeray attend?
2. Which presidents-elect's parents attended their inaugurations?
3. Which vice president-elect did not attend his boss's inauguration?
4. Which president-elect was upset when his inaugural guests looked at his predecessor?
5. Which president-elect first used recycled paper for his inaugural invitations?
6. Which First Lady was the first one who did *not* attend her husband's inauguration?
7. Which living presidents did *not* attend their successors' swearings-in?

4.   Andrew Jackson (1829)
5.   July 4 (Independence Day)
6.   Senator Claiborne Pell (D-RI), in order to reduce the lame-duck part of a presidency.
7.   Ronald Reagan's (1985), during Super Bowl XIX in Palo Alto, California.

Inaugural Geography (answers)

1.   Thomas Jefferson (1801)
2.   James Monroe (1817), because Congress could not agree in which house to hold it.
3.   John Kennedy (1961)
4.   Ronald Reagan (1981), to accommodate more persons.
5.   Andrew Jackson (1829)
6.   Ronald Reagan (1985), due to extremely frigid weather outside.
7.   Franklin Roosevelt (1945)
8.   Rutherford Hayes (1877), in a private ceremony.
9.   Harry Truman (1945) and Gerald Ford (1974), neither one of whom was president-elect.
10. George Washington (1789 and 1793), in New York City and Philadelphia, respectively.
11. George Washington (1789), in New York City Hall, which had become Federal Hall.
12. James Monroe (1817)
13. Chester Arthur (1881)
14. James Monroe (1817). Washington's inauguration is considered an indoor inauguration.
15. Franklin Roosevelt's (1937), instead of in the Senate or House chambers.
16. John Adams (1793 and 1797), both times in Philadelphia, Pennsylvania.
17. 33,000 feet high in a plane thirteen miles southwest of Jefferson City, Missouri (1974).
18. Rutherford Hayes (1877) and Chester Arthur (1881), in private and public ceremonies.
19. George Washington (1793), in the Senate Chamber of the Federal Hall in Philadelphia.
20. Thomas Jefferson (1805) and William Taft (1913)
21. Andrew Jackson (1833), in Washington, DC.
22. Lyndon Johnson (1963), on board a Boeing 707 at Love Field, in Dallas, Texas.

Inaugural Guests (answers)

1.   Franklin Pierce's (1853)
2.   Ulysses Grant's (1869), John Kennedy's (1961), and George W. Bush's (2001)
3.   Rufus King (1853), who was recuperating from a health problem, in Havana, Cuba.
4.   John Adams (1797)
5.   Jimmy Carter (1977)
6.   Martha Washington (1789)
7.   John Adams, John Quincy Adams, Andrew Johnson, and Richard Nixon

8.   Which president-elect refused to attend his own inauguration if his predecessor did?
9.   Which four future presidents attended Abraham Lincoln's inauguration in 1861?
10. Which presidents witnessed a son's inauguration as president?
11. Which president's son and wife contracted pneumonia at his successor's inauguration?
12. Which president-elect's inauguration was first attended by royalty?
13. Which president-elect first invited the nation's governors to attend his inauguration?
14. Which group of people is it customary *not* to invite to a presidential inauguration?
15. Which president, incensed by his defeat, refused even to *look* at his successor?
16. Which president-elect accidentally received an invitation to his own inauguration?
17. Which inauguration did four former First Ladies first attend?
18. Which inauguration first featured official programs for guests and well-wishers?
19. Which president-elect said women should skip his inaugural since "bullets may be flying"?

Inaugural Media

1.   Which inauguration was the first one news of which was transmitted by telegraph?
2.   Which inauguration was the first one of which an illustration is known to exist?
3.   Which inauguration was first recorded and copied on gramophone records?
4.   Which inauguration was first captured on motion pictures?
5.   Which inauguration first featured telephones installed on the Capitol grounds?
6.   Which inauguration was first broadcast nationwide by radio?
7.   Which inauguration was first broadcast by short-wave radio around the world?
8.   Which inauguration was first filmed with talking newsreel?
9.   Which inauguration was first broadcast on live television?
10. Which inauguration was first broadcast in color television?
11. Which inauguration first featured a press gallery and television "risers"?
12. Which inauguration was first broadcast with closed captioning for the hearing impaired?
13. Which inauguration was first broadcast from within the presidential limousine?
14. Which inauguration was first broadcast live on the Internet?

Inaugural-Oath Administrators

1.   Which president-elect did a cousin inaugurate?
2.   Which president-elect did a Supreme Court chief justice first inaugurate?
3.   Which president-elect did a Supreme Court chief justice *not* inaugurate?
4.   Which Supreme Court chief justice administered the most presidential oaths of office?
5.   Which presidents-elect did a former Confederate soldier inaugurate?
6.   When did the Supreme Court chief justice revive the tradition of wearing a black skullcap?
7.   Which president-elect did his predecessor in another office inaugurate?

8. Ulysses Grant (1869), who had antipathy towards Andrew Johnson.
9. Rutherford Hayes, James Garfield, Chester Arthur, and Benjamin Harrison
10. John Adams (1825) and George Bush (2001)
11. Millard Fillmore's (1853). The son died ten days later, the wife more than a year later.
12. William McKinley's (1901), by former Queen Lili'oukalani of Hawaii.
13. Ulysses Grant (1873)
14. Foreign dignitaries
15. Herbert Hoover (1933)
16. Franklin Roosevelt, replying that "I . . . think I may be able to go."
17. John Kennedy's (1961), by Mmes. Wilson, Roosevelt, Truman, and Eisenhower.
18. Martin Van Buren's (1837)
19. Abraham Lincoln (1865), and was quite serious about it.

Inaugural Media (answers)

1. James Polk's (1845). The inventor of Morse Code sent the news himself to Baltimore.
2. James Polk's (1845), in the *Illustrated London News*.
3. William McKinley's (1897), after which the recording was available in an amusement' hall.
4. William McKinley's (1897), by Thomas Edison.
5. Theodore Roosevelt's (1905)
6. Calvin Coolidge's (1925)
7. Herbert Hoover's (1929)
8. Herbert Hoover's (1929)
9. Harry Truman's (1949), with an estimated ten million viewers.
10. John Kennedy's (1961), on NBC.
11. Lyndon Johnson's (1965)
12. Ronald Reagan's (1981)
13. Ronald Reagan's (1985), from the Capitol to the White House.
14. Bill Clinton's (1997)

Inaugural-Oath Administrators (answers)

1. Abraham Lincoln (1865), by distant cousin Supreme Court Chief Justice Salmon P. Chase.
2. John Adams (1797), by Supreme Court Chief Justice Oliver Ellsworth.
3. George Washington (1789 and 1793), by Robert Livingston, chancellor of New York.
4. John Marshall (8), to five different presidents, from Jefferson through Jackson, inclusive.
5. Woodrow Wilson (1913 and 1917) and Warren Harding (1921), by Edward D. White.
6. William Rehnquist (1989), for George Bush's inauguration.
7. Franklin Roosevelt (1933), by Charles Evans Hughes, governor of New York before him.

8. Which president-elect did a former college classmate inaugurate?
9. Which president had been sworn in by his father, a justice of the peace?
10. Who was the only woman who swore in a president?
11. Which president-elect did a former president inaugurate?
12. Which president-elect was described as "a galvanized corpse" while being inaugurated?
13. Which president-elect did a Masonic Grand Master inaugurate?
14. Which president-elect did his former cabinet member inaugurate?
15. Whom does the Constitution state must administer the oath of office to a president-elect?

Inaugural Oaths

1. Which president-elect first included additional words in his oath of office?
2. Which president said the presidential oath of office was "an oath registered in Heaven"?
3. Who was so nervous at his swearing-in that he had to read his oath of office from paper?
4. Which president-elect chose to "solemnly affirm" that he would uphold the Constitution?
5. Which president-elect promised to "preserve, maintain, and protect" the Constitution?
6. Which two presidents-elect wrote their oaths of office instead of reciting them?
7. Who took the oath of office twice for vice president and twice for president?
8. Which presidents-elect signed an official copy of their oaths of office?

Inaugural-Parade Reviews

1. Which president needed only sixteen guards for his inaugural parade and review?
2. Which president first reviewed an inaugural parade from a platform near the White House?
3. Which president first reviewed an inaugural parade from a glass-enclosed platform?
4. Which president reviewed an inaugural parade from a replica of Andrew Jackson's home?
5. Which president first reviewed an inaugural parade from behind bulletproof glass?
6. Which president wanted dignitaries at his inaugural parade to arrive by helicopter?

Inaugural Parades

1. Which president technically participated in the first inaugural parade?
2. Which president held the first inaugural parade as we know it?
3. Which president was the first one whose wife sat next to him during his inaugural parade?
4. In which president's inaugural parade did sappers and miners precede his carriage?
5. Which presidents walked down Pennsylvania Avenue during their inaugural parades?
6. In which president's inaugural parade did blacks first participate?
7. Which president first brought his dog to an inaugural parade?
8. During which inaugural parade did the press print a newspaper while in the parade?

8. James Monroe (1817 and 1821), by John Marshall, his classmate at William and Mary.
9. Calvin Coolidge (1923), in Plymouth Notch, Vermont, by the light of a kerosene lantern.
10. Judge Sarah T. Hughes (1963), who swore in Lyndon Johnson after Kennedy's death.
11. Calvin Coolidge (1925), by Supreme Court Chief Justice William Taft.
12. Abraham Lincoln (1865), described thus by Supreme Court Chief Justice Salmon P. Chase.
13. George Washington (1789), by Robert R. Livingston of New York.
14. Abraham Lincoln (1865), by Supreme Court Chief Justice Salmon P. Chase.
15. It does not specify.

Inaugural Oaths (answers)
1. George Washington (1789), who added, "I swear, so help me God!"
2. Abraham Lincoln
3. Harry Truman (1945)
4. Franklin Pierce (1853), instead of "solemnly swear," either one of which is permissible.
5. Herbert Hoover (1929), instead of "preserve, protect, and defend."
6. John Tyler (1841) and Andrew Johnson (1865)
7. Richard Nixon (1953 and 1957 for vice president and 1969 and 1973 for president)
8. John Tyler, Andrew Johnson, Rutherford Hayes, William Taft, and Woodrow Wilson

Inaugural-Parade Reviews (answers)
1. Franklin Pierce (1853), who spent only $332 for his reviewing stand.
2. Ulysses Grant (1869)
3. William McKinley (1897)
4. Franklin Roosevelt (1937)
5. Lyndon Johnson (1965). Franklin Roosevelt did so too initially but removed it.
6. John Kennedy (1961), to save time.

Inaugural Parades (answers)
1. Thomas Jefferson (1801), when he walked back to his boarding house with a well-wisher.
2. William Henry Harrison (1841), when bands, militia units, and floats of paper took part.
3. William Taft (1909)
4. Abraham Lincoln's (1861)
5. Jimmy Carter (1977), George Bush (1989), and Bill Clinton (1993), Carter the whole way.
6. Abraham Lincoln's (1865), by companies of black troops and black Odd Fellows.
7. Lyndon Johnson (1965)
8. Abraham Lincoln's (1865)

9.   Which inaugural parade was canceled because it was uncertain who would be president?
10. Which inaugural parade first featured representation from a U.S. dependency?
11. Which inaugural parade first featured Secret Service protection?
12. Who rode bareheaded in an open car in driving rain during his inaugural parade?
13. In which inaugural parade did women first participate formally?
14. Which group has participated in every inaugural parade since formation on July 11, 1798?
15. Which inaugural parade first made accommodations for the handicapped?
16. Which inaugural parade first offered full wheelchair access?
17. In which inaugural parade did American Indians Geronimo and Quanah Parker ride?
18. Who revived the tradition of a president's personally leading his inaugural parade?
19. Which president had marched in Woodrow Wilson's inaugural parade as a young man?
20. Which inaugural parade was canceled due to the extreme cold?
21. Which inaugural parade was perhaps the most colorful?
22. Which inaugural parade included the greatest air display ever made for such a parade?
23. Which inaugural parade included the largest band ever to march *in any parade*?
24. Which inaugural parade theme was "There'll Be a Hot Time in the Ol' Town Tonight"?
25. In which presidential inaugural parade did Bob Hope make his only appearance?
26. Which president first rode in a car during his own inaugural parade?
27. Which inaugural parade was first broadcast by television in color?
28. Which inaugural parade first featured official gay and lesbian groups?
29. In which inaugural parade did Buffalo Bill ride?
30. Which inaugural parade first featured official military contingents?
31. Which president did a cowboy during his inaugural parade rope?
32. Which inaugural parade first went from the Capitol to the White House *after* inauguration?
33. During which inaugural parade did 300 members of the Electoral College march?

Inaugural Transportation
1.   Which president-elect first walked to his inauguration?
2.   Who set the precedent of going from the Capitol to the White House after inauguration?
3.   Which president-elect first rode to his inauguration in an automobile?
4.   Which president-elect first arrived by train for his inauguration?
5.   Which president-elect borrowed money to make a trip to his inauguration?
6.   Which president never had been to the nation's capital before his inauguration?
7.   Which president-elect first rode to his inauguration in an armored automobile?
8.   Which president-elect's inauguration first featured an airplane flying overhead?
9.   Which president-elect's inauguration first featured a blimp flying overhead?
10. Which president-elect's inauguration first featured a dirigible flying overhead?

9. Rutherford Hayes's (1877). The president was not known until three days beforehand.
10. William McKinley's (1901), by Puerto Rico.
11. Theodore Roosevelt's (1905)
12. Franklin Roosevelt (1937)
13. Woodrow Wilson's (1917)
14. The "President's Own" Marine Corps Band, missing only 1789, 1793, and 1797.
15. Jimmy Carter's (1977)
16. Bill Clinton's (1993)
17. Theodore Roosevelt's (1905)
18. Harry Truman (1949)
19. Dwight Eisenhower (1913), as a West Point cadet.
20. Ronald Reagan's (1985)
21. Theodore Roosevelt's (1905), which included 1,000 Rough Riders and 15,000 flags.
22. Harry Truman's (1949)
23. Richard Nixon's (1973), by the "Spirit of '76 Parade Band," with 1,976 bandsmen.
24. Theodore Roosevelt's (1905)
25. George Bush's (1989)
26. Warren Harding (1921)
27. John Kennedy's (1961)
28. Bill Clinton's (1993)
29. Benjamin Harrison's (1889)
30. William Henry Harrison's (1841)
31. Dwight Eisenhower (1953)
32. William Henry Harrison's (1841), not from the hotel to the Capitol *before* inauguration.
33. Franklin Roosevelt's (1933), at his request.

Inaugural Transportation (answers)

1. George Washington (1789), from Wall Street to Cherry Street in New York City.
2. Thomas Jefferson (1801), although he did not have a formal parade.
3. Warren Harding (1921)
4. William Henry Harrison (1841), from Vincennes, Ohio.
5. George Washington (1789)
6. Grover Cleveland (1885)
7. Lyndon Johnson (1963)
8. Calvin Coolidge's (1925)
9. Herbert Hoover's (1929), named the *Los Angeles*.
10. Herbert Hoover's (1929), belonging to the navy.

11. Who broke the precedent that the president escorts his successor to an inauguration?
12. Which president first rode to and from his inauguration in an automobile?
13. Which presidents-elect rode to their inaugurations in open carriages in heavy rain?
14. Who rode to an inauguration in a phaeton made of wood from the USS *Constitution*?
15. Which president-elect re-enacted Washington's arrival in New York City for inauguration?
16. Which president fussed about seedy shops and lots from the Capitol to the White House?
17. At the feet of which president-elect did persons throw flowers on his way to inauguration?
18. Who addressed persons along the parade route from a microphone inside his limousine?
19. Which president-elect arrived at the Capitol in the car in which John Kennedy had died?
20. Which car model made its first public appearance at a presidential inauguration?
21. Which outgoing president first departed an inaugural ceremony by helicopter?

Inaugural Weather

1. At which presidents-elect's inaugurations did it rain and snow the most?
2. Which presidents-elect's inaugurations were the coldest and warmest ever recorded?
3. Which president delivered an inaugural address in a blinding snowstorm?
4. Which president-elect's inaugural spectators stood ankle deep in mud and downpour?
5. Which president-elect said he "knew it would be a cold day when I got to be president"?
6. Whose Inauguration Day was so cold that cooked turkeys had to be cut with hatchets?
7. For which inauguration did army soldiers use flame-throwers to clear massive snowdrifts?

Inaugurations

1. Who was the youngest person ever sworn in as U.S. president?
2. Which other presidents were the youngest ones ever sworn in contemporaneously?
3. Which president-elect was drunk at his swearing-in?
4. Which presidential inauguration was the costliest?
5. Which inauguration was the first one of which a contemporary rendition exists?
6. What was the purpose of the first joint congressional committee?
7. Which president-elect's inauguration first featured fireworks celebrations?
8. Which president-elect wore two pairs of glasses at his inauguration?
9. In which inauguration did a rabbi first participate?
10. During which inauguration did the District of Columbia first participate as a corporation?
11. During which inauguration did bands first play "Hail to the Chief"?
12. Which president-elect was first inaugurated using his nickname?
13. Who received a cane made from the wood of Washington's coach as an inauguration gift?
14. Which black entertainer first performed at a presidential inauguration?
15. Which president-elect's mother first watched her own son's inauguration?

11. Theodore Roosevelt (1909). The tradition had started in 1837.
12. Woodrow Wilson (1917)
13. George Washington (1793), W. H. Harrison (1841), and Benjamin Harrison (1889)
14. Andrew Jackson (1845), as a former president.
15. Benjamin Harrison (1889), and spoke from where Washington had been inaugurated.
16. John Kennedy (1961)
17. George Washington (1789)
18. Bill Clinton (1993), although few could discern what he was saying due to the crowds.
19. Lyndon Johnson (1965). A steel roof and bulletproof glass had been added.
20. The Cadillac Eldorado Biarritz (1953), when Dwight Eisenhower rode in it.
21. Gerald Ford (1977)

Inaugural Weather (answers)
1. Abraham Lincoln's (1865) and William Taft's (1909), respectively.
2. Ronald Reagan's (1985), at -4°, and Ronald Reagan's (1981), at 55°, respectively.
3. Franklin Roosevelt (1937)
4. Abraham Lincoln's (1865). George W. Bush's inauguration (2001) was also very muddy.
5. William Taft (1909), after seeing that he would be inaugurated in a snowfall of ten inches.
6. Ulysses Grant's (1869)
7. John Kennedy's (1961)

Inaugurations (answers)
1. Theodore Roosevelt (1901), at 42 years, 320 days.
2. Washington (57), Van Buren (54), Tyler (51), Polk (49), Pierce (48), and Grant (46)
3. Andrew Johnson (1865)
4. Ronald Reagan's (1985)
5. George Washington's (1789), the first inauguration, of which a lithograph still exists.
6. To confer on the ceremony and titles of a presidential inauguration
7. George Washington's (1789). Grover Cleveland's (1885) was first with modern fireworks.
8. Andrew Jackson (1829), one for reading and one for looking at the crowd.
9. Harry Truman's (1949)
10. Andrew Jackson's (1833), when the mayor and council escorted him to the White House.
11. Martin Van Buren's (1837)
12. James E. "Jimmy" Carter (1977)
13. William Henry Harrison (1841)
14. Lionel Hampton, at Harry Truman's (1949).
15. James Garfield's (1881)

16. Who was inaugurated immediately after dining with his predecessor and his wife?
17. Which president-elect first gave a prayer at his inauguration?
18. Which president-elect first prayed at the chapel off Lafayette Square on Inauguration Day?
19. What does an outgoing president customarily leave the incoming president?
20. At which inaugurations did Marian Anderson sing "The Star-Spangled Banner"?
21. Which inaugural guard was changed because there were no blacks in it?
22. Which presidents-elect stood on the left side of the podium while taking the oath of office?
23. Which president-elect's grandmother was alive at the time of his inauguration?
24. Which president-elect was inaugurated *after* the vice president-elect, and days apart?
25. Which president-elect made a popular low bow to the people before his inauguration?
26. Who is president after a term ends but before the president-elect takes the oath of office?
27. What was the first official U.S. federal holiday?
28. Who set the tradition of hosting a luncheon as the first official event after inauguration?
29. For which inauguration was the Capitol Dome first illuminated?

Instruments

1. Which president had played the cornet and trombone in his youth?
2. Which president had courted his wife by playing duets with her?
3. Which president had played the "mouth harp" in his youth?
4. Which president liked to sit serenely and listen to the harp?
5. Which president played the harmonica?
6. Which president played the violin very well?
7. Which president owned a Stradivarius violin?
8. Which president had played flute in his college band?
9. Which president had won a statewide saxophone contest?

Intelligence

1. Which president ordered that Soviet codes bought clandestinely be returned unopened?
2. Which president enthusiastically approved the Huston Plan?
3. Which president had an affair with Inga Arvad, a Danish reporter and reputed Nazi spy?
4. Which president ordered the CIA to investigate the ending of *Gone with the Wind*?
5. Which president's advisor do historians say was an unwitting accomplice of the KGB?
6. Who offered to head the CIA after John Kennedy's botched invasion of the Bay of Pigs?
7. Which president had been a director of central intelligence (DCI)?
8. Whose aide had been a conscientious objector and was Jimmy Carter's choice for DCI?
9. Who appointed as DCI a man who became the most hated person in that position?
10. Which president's codes did cryptanalyst Herbert Yardley break before other countries'?

16. Rutherford Hayes (1877)
17. Dwight Eisenhower (1953), one that he had written that day.
18. Thomas Jefferson (1801), starting a precedent that several of his successors followed.
19. A personal note in the desk inside the Oval Office
20. Dwight Eisenhower's (1957) and John Kennedy's (1961)
21. John Kennedy's (1961)
22. Lyndon Johnson, Richard Nixon, George Bush, Bill Clinton, and George W. Bush
23. John Kennedy's (1961), ninety-six-year-old Mrs. John Fitzgerald.
24. George Washington (1789), nine days after John Adams had been inaugurated!
25. Andrew Jackson (1829)
26. The president-elect, whose term begins at noon, no matter when he is inaugurated.
27. George Washington's Inauguration (1889), on its centennial.
28. William McKinley (1897), a tradition continued to the present time, with a few exceptions.
29. William Taft's (1909)

Instruments (answers)

1. Warren Harding
2. Thomas Jefferson, he on the violin and she on the harpsichord.
3. Abraham Lincoln
4. George Washington
5. Calvin Coolidge, for relaxation.
6. Thomas Jefferson
7. William Taft
8. John Quincy Adams
9. Bill Clinton, and he personally played that instrument on the night of his inauguration.

Intelligence (answers)

1. Franklin Roosevelt (1944)
2. Richard Nixon (1970), calling for espionage at foreign embassies in Washington, DC.
3. John Kennedy (1937). She had close ties with Hitler, Goebbels, and Göring.
4. Harry Truman, to know if the authoress had revealed what happened after the ending.
5. Franklin Roosevelt's, Harry Hopkins.
6. Robert Kennedy (1961)
7. George Bush (1975-1977)
8. John Kennedy's, Ted Sorensen.
9. Jimmy Carter (1977), who appointed Stansfield Turner (1977-1981).
10. Woodrow Wilson's (1917). Yardley founded the infamous "Black Chamber" in that year.

11. Who informed Martin Luther King about surveillance of civil-rights activists by the FBI?
12. Which president gave the Office of Strategic Services (OSS) ten days to disband?
13. Which president ordered the destruction of CIA stockpiles of deadly shellfish toxin?
14. Which president created the Foreign Intelligence Advisory Board (FIAB)?
15. Who created the Central Intelligence Agency (CIA) and exempted it from supervision?
16. Which president created the National Security Agency (NSA) to gather intelligence?

Internet

1. Which president hired the first "Internet press secretary"?
2. Which inauguration first featured an official presence on the World Wide Web?
3. Which president first challenged the nation to connect every single school to the Internet?
4. Which president communicated with an American base in Antarctica by the Internet?
5. Which *incumbent* president first participated in an interactive, online chat?
6. Which president first addressed a technology trade show?
7. Which president instituted the first regular online chat program from the White House?

Justice

1. Which president had been a police chief?
2. Which president had been a justice of the peace?
3. Which president had been a deputy sheriff?
4. Which president had been a presiding county judge?
5. Which president had been elected chief justice of the Superior Court of Massachusetts?
6. Which president had been reporter of decisions for the Indiana Supreme Court?
7. Which president had applied to work for the FBI but was turned down?
8. Which president had provided architectural designs for two courthouses?
9. Which president personally had executed two convicted murderers?
10. Which president authorized the public hanging of twenty-six Minnesota Sioux Indians?
11. Which president was arrested for picking flowers on the Mall in Washington, DC?
12. Who ended the American Bar Association's role in recommending federal jurists?
13. Which *incumbent* president testified as a defendant in a lawsuit?
14. Which *incumbent* president was last subpoenaed to produce physical evidence?
15. Which *incumbent* president was subpoenaed to testify before a federal grand jury?
16. Which *future* president, among others, provided testimony in a criminal trial?
17. Which *incumbent* presidents provided verbal testimony in a criminal trial?
18. Which other incumbent president provided testimony in a criminal trial?
19. Which *former* presidents provided testimony in criminal trials?
20. Which president nominated the first two blacks to the U.S. Court of Appeals?

11. John Kennedy (1963)
12. Harry Truman (1945), but also became the first president to authorize covert operations.
13. Richard Nixon (1970)
14. Gerald Ford (1976), as oversight for the intelligence community.
15. Harry Truman (1949), by signing the Central Intelligence Agency Act.
16. Harry Truman (1952), by a still classified presidential executive order.

Internet (answers)
1. Bill Clinton (1996)
2. Bill Clinton's (1997), offering historical data and information.
3. Bill Clinton (1998)
4. Bill Clinton (1999)
5. Bill Clinton (2000), interviewed by Wolf Blitzer.
6. Bill Clinton (2000), at Comdex, in Chicago, Illinois.
7. George W. Bush (2001), called "Ask the White House."

Justice (answers)
1. Theodore Roosevelt, commissioner of police for New York City (1895-1897).
2. Thomas Jefferson (1753 and 1766)
3. Theodore Roosevelt (1883), in western Dakota Territory.
4. Harry Truman (1922-1924 and 1926-1934), in Jackson County, Missouri.
5. John Adams
6. Benjamin Harrison (1860-1862)
7. Richard Nixon (1946)
8. Harry Truman (1932), because he was in charge of building them.
9. Grover Cleveland (1870), as sheriff of Erie County, New York, by hanging.
10. Abraham Lincoln (1862), in Mankato, Minnesota, as reprisal for massacres in New Ulm.
11. William Taft
12. George W. Bush (2001)
13. Bill Clinton (1994), sued for sexual harassment by Paula Jones.
14. Richard Nixon (1974), by Prosecutor Archibald Cox, to produce the "White House tapes."
15. Bill Clinton (1998), subpoenaed by independent counsel Kenneth Starr.
16. Richard Nixon (1948), of Alger Hiss.
17. Gerald Ford (1975), of "Squeaky" Fromme, and Jimmy Carter (1978), of Robert Vesco.
18. Thomas Jefferson (1807), of Aaron Burr, in written form.
19. Richard Nixon (1975), about Watergate, and Ronald Reagan (1990), of John Poindexter.
20. John Kennedy (1961), who nominated Thurgood Marshall and William Hastie.

Labor

1. Which president first suppressed physical violence in a labor dispute?
2. Which president first seized and temporarily operated industrial property?
3. Which president made more industrial seizures than any other president?
4. Which president last threatened to seize and temporarily operate industrial property?
5. Which president first forced production against the wishes of the disputing parties?
6. Which president seized Montgomery Ward with military troops?
7. Which president volunteered to serve on a labor-arbitration panel?
8. Which president first sought a settlement in the White House of a labor dispute?
9. Which president broke a Pullman railroad strike?
10. Which president last got an injunction under the Taft-Hartley Act to end a labor dispute?
11. Which president had been a union president, and lifetime member of the AFL-CIO?

Law

1. Which president became Kent Professor of Constitutional Law at Yale University?
2. Which president had been prosecuting attorney for the Western District of North Carolina?
3. Which president had been a city solicitor in Cincinnati, Ohio?
4. Which president had been district attorney for Lebanon County, Pennsylvania?
5. Which two presidents had been law partners?
6. Which president was disbarred from practicing law?
7. Which other president had his law license suspended by his home state?
8. Which president had been president of the American Bar Association?
9. Which president had been associated with three different law firms?
10. Which president had campaigned to abolish a law requiring witnesses to believe in God?
11. Which president had defended the British "redcoats" who fired upon Crispus Attucks?
12. How many U.S. presidents were lawyers?
13. Which president had practiced law by the age of fifteen and won a case a year later?
14. Which presidents had studied law with future U.S. attorneys general?
15. Which president had studied law with George Wythe, the first U.S. professor of law?
16. Which president signed a bill mandating the sterilization of all retarded citizens?
17. Who said, "I have looked up the law, senator, and you don't have to go [to Hell]"?

Law Schools

1. Which presidents first and most recently had graduated from law school?
2. Which presidents had interacted with each other in law school?
3. Which presidents had graduated from Yale Law School?

Labor (answers)

1. Andrew Jackson (1834), when he sent troops to the Chesapeake & Ohio Canal.
2. Abraham Lincoln (1864), when he seized the Pennsylvania & Reading Railroad.
3. Franklin Roosevelt (38)
4. John Kennedy
5. Abraham Lincoln (1863), with soldiers to load and unload ships at piers in New York City.
6. Franklin Roosevelt (1944), twice.
7. Grover Cleveland (1902), during the anthracite labor strike.
8. Theodore Roosevelt
9. Grover Cleveland (1894), promising to use the military "to deliver a postcard in Chicago."
10. George W. Bush (2002), to end a longshoremen's strike in ports along the West Coast.
11. Ronald Reagan (1947-1953), of the Screen Actors Guild.

Law (answers)

1. William Taft (1913-1921)
2. Andrew Jackson (1790-1796)
3. Rutherford Hayes (1858-1861)
4. James Buchanan (1817-1819)
5. Rutherford Hayes and William Taft
6. Richard Nixon (1976), from the New York State Bar, for his role in Watergate.
7. Bill Clinton (2001), for providing "misleading" information under oath in a lawsuit.
8. William Taft (1913-1914)
9. Abraham Lincoln (Stuart and Lincoln, Logan and Lincoln, and Lincoln and Herndon)
10. Millard Fillmore (1829-1831), as a member of the New York State Assembly.
11. John Adams (1770), as well as others, after the Boston Massacre.
12. 25 out of 42 (59.5%)
13. Martin Van Buren (1797)
14. John Tyler (1809-1811) and James Polk (1818-1820), with Randolph and Grundy.
15. Thomas Jefferson (1763-1765), as had John Marshall and Henry Clay.
16. Woodrow Wilson (1911), as governor of New Jersey.
17. Calvin Coolidge (1919), as governor, calming a senator who had been told to go there.

Law Schools (answers)

1. Rutherford Hayes (1845) and Bill Clinton (1973), respectively.
2. Thomas Jefferson and James Monroe, the former the professor and the latter the student.
3. Gerald Ford (1941) and Bill Clinton (1973)

4. Which president had graduated from Harvard Law School?
5. Which president had graduated from the University of Virginia Law School?
6. Which president had graduated in his law school's first graduating class?
7. Which two presidents had dropped out of law school?
8. From which law school did Abraham Lincoln and Stephen Douglas graduate?

Letters

1. Which president was notorious for never dating his letters?
2. Which president introduced writing stationery to the Executive Mansion?
3. Which president first used stationery with "The White House" as a heading?
4. Which president most effectively used letters to convey his views to citizens?
5. Which president first spoke of a "United States of Europe" in a letter to a European figure?
6. Which president wrote out *all* his letters longhand, perhaps the last one who did so?
7. Which president's love letters are among the greatest in the English language?
8. Which president wrote love letters to a merchant's wife in Georgia?
9. Which president put the most literary quality into his letters?
10. What is the greatest amount paid for a letter written by a president?
11. What is the greatest amount paid for a letter written by a living person?
12. Whom did twelve-year-old Fidel Castro write asking for "a ten dollars bill green american"?
13. Which president wrote more letters regularly to friends than any other?
14. Who stated in a letter, "If I could save the Union without freeing any slave, I would do it"?
15. Which presidents wrote about 19,000 and 100,000 letters during their lifetimes?
16. How many letters does a president receive today, on average?

Libraries

1. Which president first collected his presidential papers for posterity in a private library?
2. Which presidential library was the first one organized and opened to the public?
3. Which president first established a *new* library to hold all his papers and memorabilia?
4. Which presidential library was first built on a university campus?
5. Which president first decided where to build his presidential library early into his tenure?
6. Which president's personal library formed the core holdings of the Library of Congress?
7. Which presidents were buried at their presidential libraries?
8. Since which year have all presidential libraries been built entirely with private funds?
9. Where is Richard Nixon's original letter of resignation?
10. Which president's library is separated from his presidential museum?
11. In which presidential library can one receive a televised answer to dozens of questions?
12. Which president last failed to attend opening ceremonies for his presidential library?

4. Rutherford Hayes (1845)
5. Woodrow Wilson (1882)
6. Richard Nixon (1937), from Duke University Law School.
7. Grover Cleveland (Albany Law School) and Woodrow Wilson (The University of Virginia)
8. Neither one attended law school.

Letters (answers)

1. William Henry Harrison
2. Abraham Lincoln
3. Theodore Roosevelt
4. Abraham Lincoln
5. George Washington, writing to the Marquis de Lafayette.
6. Grover Cleveland
7. Woodrow Wilson's
8. Dwight Eisenhower, some of which letters were *forty* pages long!
9. Thomas Jefferson, but often did not begin a sentence with a capital letter.
10. $800,000 (1991), for a letter written by Abraham Lincoln to a general.
11. $12,500 (1981), for Ronald Reagan's letter to Frank Sinatra.
12. Franklin Roosevelt (1940), from Santiago, Cuba.
13. Woodrow Wilson, with the possible exception of Thomas Jefferson.
14. Abraham Lincoln, who made that declaration to Horace Greeley.
15. George Washington and Theodore Roosevelt, respectively.
16. More than 7,000,000 per year!

Libraries (answers)

1. Ulysses Grant (1880)
2. The Rutherford Hayes Library (1916)
3. Franklin Roosevelt (1941). Beforehand, they had been kept at the Library of Congress.
4. The Lyndon B. Johnson Presidential Library (1971), at the University of Texas at Austin.
5. George Bush (1991), at Texas A&M University, in College Station, Texas.
6. Thomas Jefferson's (1815). Congress paid $23,950 for 6,487 volumes.
7. Franklin Roosevelt, Herbert Hoover, Dwight Eisenhower, Harry Truman, and Richard Nixon
8. Since 1955, by federal law.
9. In the Ford Library, a research facility at the University of Michigan at Ann Arbor.
10. Herbert Hoover's
11. In the Ford Presidential Library
12. Richard Nixon (1990)

13. Which presidential library's dedication marked the first gathering of five U.S. presidents?
14. Which president was the last one who did *not* have to raise private funds for his library?
15. Where is the Carter Presidential Center located?
16. Which of the modern presidential library complexes are the smallest and largest?
17. Which presidential library has a copy of the Declaration of Independence?
18. Which presidential library contains an exact replica of the Oval Office?
19. How many persons have visited the twelve presidential libraries under federal control?
20. Which presidential library does *not* charge admission?
21. Which presidential library is the most visited one in the nation?
22. Which states have more than one presidential library?
23. Which president's library was built while he was still in office?
24. Which two presidential libraries are closest to each other geographically?
25. Which president helped put out a fire at the Library of Congress?

Magazines

1. Which president had been pictured in an advertisement for a Vermont ski resort in *Look*?
2. Which president was first featured on the cover of *Life*?
3. Which president's favorite magazine was *Bassmaster*?
4. Which president wrote an article that was featured in *Boy's Life*?
5. Which president was a director of *National Review*, founded by William F. Buckley?
6. Who claimed to have been an aide to LBJ but was disproved by Lynne Cheney?
7. Which president's first published article was in the *Nassau Literary Magazine*?
8. Which president posed for the cover of the ladies' magazine *Cosmopolitan*?
9. Which presidents appeared on the covers of *Life* and *Time* more than any other?
10. Which presidents were the first and last ones selected as *Time*'s "Man of the Year"?
11. Which president since 1945 first failed to be selected *Time*'s "Man of the Year"?
12. Which president stated in a *Playboy* interview that he "committed adultery in my heart"?
13. Which magazine first used the political term "dark horse" in print?
14. Which managing editor of *Fortune* co-managed a presidential campaign?
15. Which presidents wrote articles that were featured in *National Geographic*?
16. Who led *Life*'s investigation into Kennedy's death and wrote *Six Seconds in Dallas*?
17. Between which president and a mobster did a woman claim she had been a courier?
18. Which president first wrote an article for *The Saturday Evening Post*?
19. Which president wrote more articles for *The Saturday Evening Post* than any other?
20. Which president first received a review in *Variety*?
21. Which magazine pictured Thomas Dewey as "The next President of the United States"?
22. Who said he had grown up with a "Bible in my right hand and the *Geographic* in my left"?

13. The Ronald Reagan Presidential Library's (1991), in Simi Valley, California.
14. Richard Nixon
15. Atlanta, Georgia. It opened in 1986.
16. The Harry S Truman and Lyndon B. Johnson Presidential Libraries, respectively.
17. The Richard Nixon Library and Birthplace, one of thirty-two known remaining copies.
18. The Lyndon B. Johnson Presidential Library
19. Over 30,000,000 since 1975, when the National Archives began keeping such records.
20. The Lyndon B. Johnson Presidential Library
21. The John F. Kennedy Library in Boston, Massachusetts, more than 200,000 visitors per year.
22. California (Nixon's and Reagan's) and Texas (Johnson's and George Bush's)
23. Franklin Roosevelt's
24. Richard Nixon's and Ronald Reagan's (87.1 miles, between Yorba Linda and Simi Valley)
25. Millard Fillmore (1851)

Magazines (answers)

1. Gerald Ford (1939), as the handsome "Yale boyfriend" of the woman pictured.
2. Franklin Roosevelt (1937)
3. George Bush's
4. Theodore Roosevelt (1913), who wrote "About Man Eating Lions."
5. Ronald Reagan
6. John Naisbitt, in a magazine article.
7. Woodrow Wilson's, about Otto von Bismarck, the "iron hand" of the German Empire.
8. Gerald Ford
9. John Kennedy (25 times) and Richard Nixon (64 times), respectively.
10. Franklin Roosevelt (1932) and George W. Bush (2000), respectively.
11. Gerald Ford (1974-1977)
12. Jimmy Carter (1976), as governor of Georgia and presidential candidate.
13. *Century Magazine* (1876), referring to Rutherford Hayes.
14. Russell Davenport (1940), who managed the presidential campaign of Wendell Willkie.
15. William Taft (1915 and 1917), Theodore Roosevelt (1916), and Woodrow Wilson (1917)
16. Josiah Thompson (1964-1967), former philosophy professor and now private detective.
17. John Kennedy and Sam Giancana
18. Benjamin Harrison (1902). Ronald Reagan was the first since Harrison *not* to write one.
19. Grover Cleveland (18), followed by Dwight Eisenhower (14) and Herbert Hoover (11).
20. Richard Nixon (1952), after his "Checkers" speech.
21. *Life* (1948), like the *Chicago Tribune*'s printing the headline "Dewey Defeats Truman."
22. Lyndon Johnson, speaking to Melville Grosvenor, editor of *National Geographic*.

Marriage Geography

1. Which president had married on New York City's Fifth Avenue?
2. Which president had been engaged in the "White House"?
3. Which president was married inside the White House?
4. Which presidents had been married outside the American colonies and outside the U.S.A.?
5. Where were John and Jacqueline Kennedy married?
6. Which president and his wife spent their honeymoon in Acapulco, Mexico?
7. Which president was married at the Schuyler Mansion in Albany, New York?
8. Which president was married at the foot of his house's staircase?
9. What can any descendant of the Washington family do?

Marriages

1. Which presidents' courtships were the shortest and longest?
2. Which president married on a Friday because he wanted to watch football on Saturday?
3. Which presidents proposed to their future wives on their first dates?
4. Which president first re-enacted his wedding on an anniversary?
5. Which presidents became widowers *before* becoming president?
6. Which presidents became widowers while president?
7. Which presidents became widowers *after* leaving the White House?
8. Which president's wedding probably had the most guests in attendance?
9. Which president married his cabinet member's twenty-year-old daughter?
10. Which president married the same woman twice *without* divorcing her?
11. Which president married Sarah Jane Fulks, whose ex-husband was Myron Futterman?
12. Which president sent his fiancée a list of her "Faults, Imperfections, [and] Defects"?
13. Which presidents survived their wives by the least and most amounts of time?
14. Which president still was persuading his fiancée to marry as they arrived at church?
15. Which *future* presidents re-married?
16. Which *incumbent* presidents re-married?
17. Which *former* presidents re-married?
18. Which president married a woman who had been fired as a waitress at a coffee shop?
19. Which president's parents refused to attend his wedding?
20. Which presidents married women older than they were?
21. Which presidents celebrated golden wedding anniversaries?
22. Which presidents were youngest and oldest when marrying firstly, respectively?
23. Which presidents were youngest and oldest when marrying secondly, respectively?
24. Which president did not even buy his fiancée a wedding ring for their wedding?
25. Which presidents married first cousins, a third cousin, and a fourth cousin, respectively?

Marriage Geography (answers)

1. John Tyler (1844), at the Church of the Ascension.
2. George Washington (1759), on the Custis plantation, in Virginia.
3. Grover Cleveland (1886), in the Blue Room.
4. John Quincy Adams (1797) and Theodore Roosevelt (1886), both in London, England.
5. St. Mary's Catholic Church in Newport, Rhode Island.
6. Jimmy and Rosalynn Carter (1946)
7. Millard Fillmore (1858)
8. Warren Harding (1891)
9. Marry at the estate of Mount Vernon

Marriages (answers)

1. Lyndon Johnson's (two months) and Harry Truman's (fifteen years), respectively.
2. Gerald Ford (1948)
3. Lyndon Johnson (1934) and Richard Nixon (1938)
4. Rutherford Hayes (1877), for his silver anniversary.
5. Thomas Jefferson (1782), Andrew Jackson (1828), and Chester Arthur (1880)
6. John Tyler (1842), Benjamin Harrison (1892), and Woodrow Wilson (1914)
7. Millard Fillmore (1853) and Richard Nixon (1993)
8. John Kennedy's (1952), with about 1,500 guests.
9. John Tyler (1844), who married the daughter of his secretary of the navy.
10. Andrew Jackson (1794), because his wife had not been divorced from her first husband.
11. Ronald Reagan (1940), who married Jane Wyman.
12. John Adams (1759)
13. Richard Nixon (304 days) and Thomas Jefferson (49 years, 125 days), respectively.
14. Lyndon Johnson (1934)
15. Theodore Roosevelt (1886) and Ronald Reagan (1952)
16. John Tyler (1844) and Woodrow Wilson (1915)
17. Millard Fillmore (1858) and Benjamin Harrison (1896)
18. Ronald Reagan (1940), whose wife Jane Wyman could not cut a pie into six equal pieces.
19. Ulysses Grant's (1848), because his fiancée, Julia Dent, was the daughter of slaveholders.
20. Washington (1759), Fillmore (1826), Harrison (1853), Harding (1891), and Nixon (1940)
21. John Quincy Adams, Truman, Eisenhower, Bush, Carter, Ford, and Reagan
22. Andrew Johnson (18 years, 127 days) and Grover Cleveland (49 years, 76 days)
23. Theodore Roosevelt (28 years, 36 days) and Benjamin Harrison (62 years, 229 days)
24. Lyndon Johnson (1934)
25. B. Harrison (1853) and Van Buren (1807), J. Adams (1764), and F. Roosevelt (1905)

26. Which presidents' first marriages lasted the shortest and longest, respectively?
27. Which presidents' second marriages lasted the shortest and longest, respectively?
28. Which presidents' first wives were the youngest and oldest at marriage, respectively?
29. Which presidents' second wives were the youngest and oldest at marriage, respectively?
30. Which president divorced at any time in his life?
31. Which presidents married a divorcée?
32. Which president's wife died at the youngest age?
33. Which presidents had married on their birthdays?
34. Which presidents' wives lived shortest and longest after their husbands, respectively?
35. Which president had promised his wife that he would not remarry after her death?
36. Which president had married the niece of a former president?
37. Which president married his recently-deceased wife's niece?
38. Which president had married his secretary?
39. Which presidents had been rejected on two and three different marriage proposals?
40. Which president had signed a pre-nuptial agreement with his fiancée?
41. Which president was the first one who had been married in a Roman Catholic ceremony?
42. During which president's Administration was the first person married in the White House?
43. Which president had eloped with his girlfriend?
44. Which president, with his wife and Cabinet, attended the wedding of General Tom Thumb?
45. Which president refused to use the word "obey" in his wedding vows?
46. Which president ordered all federal employees living out of wedlock to marry quickly?
47. Which president told his wife that he loved his country far more than he could love her?
48. Which president never wore a wedding band?
49. Which president's best man later became British ambassador to the U.S.A.?
50. Which president first had been accused of marital infidelity?
51. Which president first had been known to have an extramarital affair?
52. Which president was so eager to leave his wedding that he forgot to take the certificate?
53. Which president granted amnesty to Mormons who renounced polygamy?
54. Who lectured American Indian chief Quanah Parker, who had five wives, on polygamy?
55. Which president did the media follow on his honeymoon retreat, to Deer Park, Maryland?
56. Which president's cousin presided at the marriage of his successor?
57. At which president's wedding did John Philip Sousa and the Marine Corps Band perform?
58. According to historian Edward Pessen, which presidents married "below" themselves?
59. Which president owned only a uniform and some suits and books when he married?
60. Which president said he had delayed marriage "waiting for my wife to grow up"?
61. Which president translated Dante's *Inferno* on his honeymoon?
62. Which president married on the day he was promoted to first lieutenant?
63. Which two presidents married for the first time in their forties?

26. Theodore Roosevelt's (3 years, 110 days) and George Bush's (58 years and counting)
27. Woodrow Wilson's (8 years, 47 days) and Ronald Reagan's (51 years and counting)
28. Andrew Johnson's (16 years, 213 days) and Harry Truman's (34 years, 135 days)
29. John Tyler's (24 years, 53 days) and Millard Fillmore's (44 years, 112 days)
30. Ronald Reagan (1949), who divorced future *Falcon Crest* star Jane Wyman.
31. Andrew Jackson (1791), Warren Harding (1891), and Ronald Reagan (1940)
32. Theodore Roosevelt's first wife, Alice Hathaway Lee (22 years, 192 days).
33. John Tyler (1813) and Theodore Roosevelt (1880)
34. William McKinley's (1 year, 124 days) and James Garfield's (36 years, 25 days)
35. Thomas Jefferson, who kept his promise but likely had a relationship with Sally Hemings.
36. James Polk (1824), whose wife, Sarah Childress, was the niece of Andrew Jackson.
37. Benjamin Harrison (1896), who married Mary Scott Lord Dimmick.
38. James Polk (1824)
39. George Washington and Warren Harding, respectively.
40. Millard Fillmore (1858), whereby he became administrator of her fortune.
41. Herbert Hoover (1899), by Father Mestres from the Monterey Mission, California.
42. James Madison's (1812), when the sister of Mrs. Lucy Payne Washington was married.
43. William Henry Harrison (1796)
44. Abraham Lincoln
45. Grover Cleveland (1886), perhaps because she was twenty-seven years younger!
46. Jimmy Carter (1978)
47. John Quincy Adams
48. Franklin Roosevelt
49. Theodore Roosevelt's, Cecil Spring-Rice.
50. George Washington
51. Grover Cleveland
52. Lyndon Johnson (1934). He retrieved it twenty years later!
53. Benjamin Harrison (1893)
54. Theodore Roosevelt (1905)
55. Grover Cleveland (1886)
56. Abraham Lincoln's, when Squire Mordecai Lincoln officiated for Andrew Johnson (1827).
57. Grover Cleveland's (1886)
58. Richard Nixon, Gerald Ford, and Jimmy Carter
59. Harry Truman (1919)
60. Grover Cleveland (1886), who was twenty-seven years old when she was born.
61. Calvin Coolidge (1905)
62. Dwight Eisenhower (1916)
63. James Madison and Grover Cleveland

64. Which president had worn very "loud" orange gloves at his wedding?
65. After which president had refused to divorce his wife for her did a woman commit suicide?

Media

1. Which president technically is considered to have held the first press conference?
2. Who gave a reporter the Nazi Iron Cross after being asked an impertinent question?
3. Which president first made a science of manipulating the press?
4. During which Administration did reporters first camp on the White House grounds?
5. Which president first held regular White House press conferences?
6. Which presidents would answer reporters' questions only in writing?
7. Which president's press conferences were known as "walkie-talkies"?
8. Which president held the most press conferences?
9. Which president used his influence to have some newspaper reporters fired?
10. Which president first taped a presidential press conference?
11. Which president's Administration coined the term "photo opportunity"?
12. Which president became famous for wearing Hawaiian shirts to press conferences?
13. Which president first allowed direct quotations to be used at a press conference?
14. Which president frequently limited press-conference questions to specific policy areas?
15. Which president refused to allow reporters to quote him?
16. Which president first rallied public opinion by exploiting the press?
17. Which president introduced formal press conferences and held them twice a week?
18. Which president required all press-conference questions to be submitted in advance?
19. Which president first allowed casual rather than previously submitted, written questions?
20. Which president's press conferences were almost all held around his desk?
21. Which president first went completely "on the record" during press conferences?
22. Which president's farewell address originally contained an attack on the press?
23. Which president often held press conferences while swimming bare-chested?
24. Which president had press conferences like "question time" in the House of Commons?
25. Which president first had his press conference transcribed by a stereotypist?
26. Which president requested a list of "homosexuals . . . in the Washington press corps"?
27. Which reporter, when told a president had died, said, "How can they tell?"
28. Which presidents created the first informal and formal White House Press Corps?
29. How many press conferences has George W. Bush held since taking office?

Meetings

1. Which president had met his wife when she saw his family move to town?
2. Which president had met his wife shortly after moving to Delaware, Ohio?

64. Theodore Roosevelt
65. Warren Harding

Media (answers)

1. Grover Cleveland, although Woodrow Wilson (1913) held the first "real" press conference.
2. Franklin Roosevelt (1940)
3. Theodore Roosevelt
4. William McKinley's, in order to get news bits.
5. Woodrow Wilson (1914)
6. Calvin Coolidge and Herbert Hoover
7. Lyndon Johnson's, because reporters walked with Johnson while he talked.
8. Franklin Roosevelt (996 during 4,422 days in office)
9. Theodore Roosevelt
10. Harry Truman (1951)
11. Richard Nixon's
12. Harry Truman
13. Dwight Eisenhower (1952)
14. Richard Nixon
15. Calvin Coolidge
16. Theodore Roosevelt
17. Woodrow Wilson (1914), who held them regularly until the sinking of the *Lusitania*.
18. Calvin Coolidge
19. Franklin Roosevelt
20. Franklin Roosevelt's, because he was crippled with polio.
21. Dwight Eisenhower, as opposed to "not for attribution" or "on background."
22. George Washington's (1796)
23. Harry Truman
24. Woodrow Wilson (1914-1919), whereby reporters asked him questions rapid fire.
25. Dwight Eisenhower
26. Richard Nixon (1970)
27. Dorothy Parker (1933), speaking about Calvin Coolidge.
28. Theodore Roosevelt (1902) and Dwight Eisenhower (1950), respectively.
29. Nine, compared to about 70 for Clinton and 90 for George Bush at similar times.

Meetings (answers)

1. Andrew Johnson
2. Rutherford Hayes

3. Which president had met his wife when Colonel Richard Chamberlayne introduced them?
4. Which president had met his wife through his instructor, Dr. Alpheus S. Packard?
5. Which president had met his wife through his professor at Farmer's College?
6. Which president had met his wife when they were students at Geauga Seminary?
7. Which president had met his wife when she was working at her father's inn?
8. Which president had met his wife through his friend Richard Cranch's fiancée?
9. Which president had met his wife in New York City through her cousin Dabney Herndon?
10. Which president had met his wife through her brother, a West Point roommate?
11. Which president had met his wife when he became her student at an academy?
12. Which president had met his wife when his cousin introduced them to each other?
13. Which president had met his wife at the First National Bank of Canton, where she worked?
14. Which president had met his wife when she saw him through a boardinghouse window?
15. Which president had met his wife in Williamsburg, Virginia?
16. Which president had met his wife while sharing a bobsled at a party in Cincinnati, Ohio?
17. Which president had met his wife when their friend Dr. Alexander Duke introduced them?
18. Which president had met his wife, his law partner's daughter, on the day she was born?
19. Which president had met his wife through his physician, Admiral Cary Travers Grayson?
20. Which president had met his wife when he asked Aaron Burr to arrange a meeting?
21. Which president had met his wife at his next-door neighbors' home?
22. Which president had met his wife in Sunday school when he was six years old?
23. Which president had met his wife while students of Samuel Black?
24. Which president had met his wife at his cousin Jesse Bones's home in Rome, Georgia?
25. Which president had met his wife through the wife of one of his fellow officers?
26. Which president had met his wife in New York, as a delegate to the Continental Congress?
27. Which president had met his wife while filming *Brother Rat*, in which they both appeared?
28. Which president had met his wife while sharing the same classes and major in college?
29. Which president had met his wife at the home of Eugene Lasseter in Austin, Texas?
30. Which president had met his wife through Charles Bartlett of the *Chattanooga Times*?
31. Which president had met his wife while he was a law student in Virginia?
32. Which president had met his wife while they attended law school together?
33. Which president had met his wife through Peg Neuman, a mutual friend?
34. Which presidents had met their wives through their sisters?
35. Which president had met his wife in the play "The Dark Tower"?
36. Which president had met his wife when she accompanied him on a walking tour?
37. Which president had met his future wife in Nantes, France, when he was twelve years old?
38. Which president had met his wife defending her against smears of communist sympathy?
39. Which president had met his wife in Lexington, Kentucky, while there on military business?
40. Which presidents had met their wives at dances?

3. George Washington, who postponed a trip in order to do so.
4. Franklin Pierce, whose future wife was Packard's sister-in-law.
5. Benjamin Harrison, whose future wife was the professor's daughter.
6. James Garfield, in Chester, Ohio.
7. Andrew Jackson, at Donelson's Blockhouse, where Jackson had been a boarder.
8. John Adams
9. Chester Arthur
10. Ulysses Grant
11. Millard Fillmore, in New Hope, New York.
12. Woodrow Wilson, in Washington, DC.
13. William McKinley
14. Calvin Coolidge, shaving in front of a mirror.
15. Thomas Jefferson
16. William Taft
17. Zachary Taylor
18. Grover Cleveland
19. Woodrow Wilson
20. James Madison
21. Theodore Roosevelt, at the home of Harvard classmate Richard Saltonstall.
22. Harry Truman
23. James Polk, in Murfreesboro, Tennessee.
24. Woodrow Wilson
25. Dwight Eisenhower
26. James Monroe
27. Ronald Reagan
28. Herbert Hoover
29. Lyndon Johnson
30. John Kennedy
31. John Tyler
32. Bill Clinton
33. Gerald Ford
34. Theodore Roosevelt and Jimmy Carter
35. Richard Nixon
36. Franklin Roosevelt, of New York City's East Side slums.
37. John Quincy Adams
38. Ronald Reagan
39. William Henry Harrison
40. Abraham Lincoln and George Bush

Middle Names

1. What was George Washington's middle name?
2. Which presidents were the first and last ones who had a middle name?
3. Which president was the last one who did *not* have a middle name?
4. Which president's middle name became slang for a toilet?
5. Which presidents had middle names that were the same as their mothers' maiden names?

Military

1. Which president had served in the Mexican War *and* the Civil War?
2. Which president had served in World War I *and* World War II?
3. Which president almost always wore an American Legion lapel pin?
4. Which president got a letter from a colonel asking that he make himself king by force?
5. Which president did the Veterans of Foreign Wars endorse?
6. Which president allegedly had had an affair with his military driver?
7. Which president first heard the Marine Band and first called it "The President's Own"?
8. Which president first failed to attend the encampment of the Grand Army of the Republic?
9. Which president refused to appear as a defense witness at his assistant's court-martial?
10. Which president selected the site for the Marine Barracks in Washington, DC?
11. Which presidents fired Colonel Arthur MacArthur and General Douglas MacArthur?
12. Who told his general, "If you don't want to use the army, I should like to borrow it"?
13. Which president first ordered racially-integrated military fighting units?
14. What is the official gun salute for a president?
15. Which president's military chief of staff headed an inquiry into the Bay of Pigs invasion?
16. Which modern president abolished the peacetime draft?
17. Which president asked Congress to innoculate half of the army against smallpox?
18. Which president met the CEO of Bristow Helicopters, a former British commando?
19. Who was the first soldier executed in U.S. military history?
20. Which president presided at the inauguration of the Tomb of the Unknown Soldier?
21. Which military president had presented his aide-de-camp with a locket of his hair?
22. Which president chose the color for the "Green Berets"?
23. Which president said a general had "his headquarters where his hindquarters should be"?
24. Which president regularly lectured at the Naval War College in Washington, DC?
25. Which presidents had been recruiters for the army, in Pennsylvania and in Kentucky?
26. Which president nominated George Washington to be commander-in-chief of the army?
27. Which president's father had written all bulletins to George Washington in battle?
28. Which president had been a major in the army assigned to Fort Howard, Wisconsin?
29. What is the name of the briefcase with nuclear-strike codes kept near the president?

Middle Names (answers)

1. He did not have one.
2. John Quincy Adams and George Walker Bush, respectively.
3. Theodore Roosevelt
4. John Quincy Adams's, because he installed the first toilet in the White House.
5. Polk, Wilson, F. Roosevelt, Kennedy, L. Johnson, Nixon, Reagan, and George Bush

Military (answers)

1. Ulysses Grant
2. Dwight Eisenhower
3. Harry Truman
4. George Washington
5. Richard Nixon
6. Dwight Eisenhower, with Kay Summersby.
7. Thomas Jefferson (1801), at a New Year's Day reception.
8. Grover Cleveland (1887). The organization of Union soldiers had been founded in 1865.
9. Ulysses Grant (1875), at the court-martial of his favored assistant, Orville Babcock.
10. Thomas Jefferson (1801), at 8th and I Streets, SE, the home of every commandant.
11. William Taft and Harry Truman, respectively, both for insubordination.
12. Abraham Lincoln (1862), to General George McClellan, a reference to his inability to fight.
13. Harry Truman (1948)
14. Twenty-one guns, four ruffles, and four flourishes, two guns fewer for a vice president.
15. Dwight Eisenhower's (1961), General Maxwell Taylor, head of the Taylor Commission.
16. Jimmy Carter (1978), only to re-instate it less than a year later.
17. George Washington, when he learned that the other half had it.
18. Richard Nixon (1980), to plan a second attempt to rescue the Iranian hostages.
19. Thomas Hickey (1776), for trying to kill George Washington with poisoned peas.
20. Warren Harding (1921), at Arlington National Cemetery, in Arlington, Virginia.
21. George Washington (1793), who gave it to Colonel John Trumbull.
22. John Kennedy (1961). Green Berets pay homage to Kennedy annually on November 22.
23. Abraham Lincoln (1862), about General Joseph "Fighting Joe" Hooker.
24. Theodore Roosevelt (1887-1897)
25. William Henry Harrison and Zachary Taylor, respectively.
26. John Adams (1775), using terms so effusive that Washington left the room in shame.
27. William Henry Harrison's, Benjamin Harrison (1777), from the Continental Congress.
28. Zachary Taylor (1832), at the site of present-day Green Bay.
29. The "football," which has followed every president since John Kennedy (1962).

30. Against which president were remarks made that resulted in an Article 88 court-martial?

31. Which president's father had gotten the military to take a fake certificate of good health?

32. Whom did Harry Truman say had "a propaganda machine . . . almost equal to Stalin's"?

Military Academies

1. Which president set a horse-jumping record at West Point that stood for a generation?

2. Which president who had attended a military academy graduated highest in his class?

3. Which president founded the Naval Academy?

4. Which president had attended the Naval Academy?

5. Which president lectured at the Naval Academy?

6. Who was president when the Military Academy at West Point started training officers?

7. Which presidents had attended the Military Academy at West Point?

8. Which president signed a bill giving commissions to all graduates of West Point?

Military Craft

1. What was George Bush's mission when he was shot down over the Bonin Islands?

2. Which president pressed Congress for the construction of the first all-steel battleships?

3. Which president created an elephant "stampede" when he buzzed a girl's house?

4. Which presidents had been a navy PT operator and instructor?

5. What did George Bush name his navy fighter plane?

6. Which president, without a large naval force, proposed "renting" the Portuguese Navy?

Military Honors

1. Who established the Badge of Military Merit, the oldest military decoration in current use?

2. Which president re-established the Order of the Purple Heart?

3. Which president had received a Purple Heart?

4. For which president are chapters of the Military Order of the Purple Heart named?

5. To which future president did General Douglas MacArthur award a Silver Star?

6. Which president had won the Marine Corps Medal for his gallantry?

7. Which president did P. T. Barnum offer $100,000 to display military honors and gifts?

8. Which president first awarded the Congressional Medal of Honor in person?

9. Who first awarded the Congressional Medal of Honor "In the Name of the Congress?"

10. Who said he would rather wear the Congressional Medal of Honor than be president?

11. Who assembled the largest gathering of recipients of the Congressional Medal of Honor?

12. Which presidents received and declined Congressional Medals of Honor?

13. In which presidential election had two nominees received a Distinguished Flying Cross?

30. Lyndon Johnson (1965), by Second Lt. Henry Howe, for using "contemptuous" words.
31. John Kennedy's (1942), from a family doctor.
32. The United States Marines (1950)

Military Academies (answers)
1. Ulysses Grant (1842)
2. Jimmy Carter (59th out of 820)
3. James Polk (1845), on the site of an old army fort.
4. Jimmy Carter (1943-1946). He also spent one year (1942-1943) at Georgia Tech.
5. Theodore Roosevelt (1906)
6. Thomas Jefferson (1802)
7. Ulysses Grant (1839-1843) and Dwight Eisenhower (1911-1915)
8. Grover Cleveland (1885)

Military Craft (answers)
1. To bomb a Japanese communications center 600 miles south of Japan (1944)
2. Chester Arthur (1883), resulting in the construction of the *Atlanta*, *Boston*, and *Chicago*.
3. George Bush (1943), who frightened a nearby circus elephant.
4. John Kennedy (1943) and Gerald Ford (1942-1946), respectively.
5. *Barbara* (1944), after then girlfriend and future wife Barbara Pierce.
6. James Monroe (1823), in order to back up the Monroe Doctrine.

Military Honors (answers)
1. George Washington (1782), now called the Purple Heart, for exemplary military service.
2. Herbert Hoover (1932), to commemorate persons wounded or killed during war.
3. John Kennedy (1942), for the sinking of his PT-109 boat during World War II.
4. George Washington, by chapters in Connecticut and Virginia.
5. Lyndon Johnson (1942), to curry favor with Franklin Roosevelt, Johnson's mentor.
6. John Kennedy (1942)
7. Ulysses Grant, who declined.
8. Abraham Lincoln (1863)
9. Theodore Roosevelt (1905)
10. Harry Truman (1945), while awarding the Medal of Honor to Paul Bolden.
11. John Kennedy (1963), who gathered 240 recipients at the White House.
12. Theodore Roosevelt (2001) and Harry Truman, respectively.
13. The 1988 presidential election (George Bush and Lloyd Bentsen)

Military Posts

1. Which president had been stationed at Humboldt Bay, California?
2. Which naval base in Puerto Rico was named for Franklin Roosevelt?
3. Which president had been stationed in the Panama Canal Zone?
4. For which president was the first "infantry school of practice" named?
5. Which army post was at some point home to Generals Grant, Sheridan, and Patton?
6. Which president drank so much in a dreary post that he decided to quit the army?
7. From where did General George A. Custer and the 7th Cavalry leave, never to return?
8. Which president had held command of a fort named for another president?
9. Which president smoked about 10,000 cigars while stationed in a remote military post?
10. Who received a proposal to send actor Errol Flynn to secure bases in Southern Ireland?
11. Which presidents first and last had an American Legion post named for them?
12. Where was Confederate President Jefferson Davis jailed for two years after the Civil War?
13. Where were Dr. Samuel Mudd and many Confederate POWs sent to prison?

Military Ranks

1. Who promoted future president James Monroe to captain, for his bravery?
2. Which president had his general's insignia placed on his pajamas and golf clubs?
3. Which president had been a colonel in the National Guard?
4. Which president had been the first person to hold the rank of lieutenant colonel?
5. Who first held the rank of lieutenant general since George Washington?
6. Which president said he was prouder to have been a private in the army than president?
7. Which army generals were the first and last ones who became president?
8. Which Republican and Democratic presidents were the first ones who had been a general?
9. Who was the first person promoted to brevet major, the first brevet rank in the army?
10. Who was Ulysses Grant's aide who was an army major at the age of twenty-three years?
11. Which president had helped invade Canada as a major general?
12. Which president's nurse became the first female brigadier general in the army?
13. Which presidents had held the military title "general of the army"?
14. Which president was appointed the military title "general of the armies"?
15. Which president had marched from Atlanta to the sea with General William T. Sherman?
16. Which president preferred to be addressed as "Colonel," even while he was president?
17. Which president had been military commander of the Federal District?
18. Which *former* president was commissioned as commander-in-chief of military forces?
19. Which president had been the first four-star general in the army?
20. Which general ran for president against his former commander-in-chief, the president?
21. Which presidential election was between two nominees who had been military generals?
22. Which president probably elevated the first American Indian to the rank of general?

Military Posts (answers)

1. Ulysses Grant (1849)
2. Roosevelt Roads (1943)
3. Dwight Eisenhower (1922-1924)
4. Thomas Jefferson (1826), in St. Louis, Missouri. Taylor and Grant were stationed there.
5. Fort Clark, in Brackettville, Texas.
6. Ulysses Grant (1852), at Fort Vancouver, Oregon (later Washington) Territory.
7. Fort Abraham Lincoln (1876), near present-day Mandan, North Dakota.
8. William Henry Harrison (1796), of Fort Washington, near present-day Cincinnati, Ohio.
9. Ulysses Grant (1854), from Fort Humboldt, near present-day Eureka, California.
10. Franklin Roosevelt (1942), from William "Wild Bill" Donovan, the founder of the OSS.
11. George Washington and Richard Nixon, respectively. Posts are named for the deceased.
12. Fort Monroe, Virginia, near present-day Hampton, Virginia.
13. Fort Jefferson, Florida, called "America's Devil's Island," in the Dry Tortugas island chain.

Military Ranks (answers)

1. George Washington (1776)
2. Dwight Eisenhower
3. Harry Truman (1905-1911), for the Missouri National Guard.
4. Ulysses Grant (1861)
5. Ulysses Grant (1864), promoted by Abraham Lincoln for his numerous victories.
6. Rutherford Hayes (1877)
7. George Washington (1776-1781) and Dwight Eisenhower (1941-1945), respectively.
8. Ulysses Grant (1861-1869) and Andrew Jackson (1802-1814), respectively.
9. Zachary Taylor (1812), for his defense of Fort Harrison in Indiana Territory.
10. Major James T. West
11. William Henry Harrison (1813), during the War of 1812, against the British.
12. Dwight Eisenhower's, Anna Mae Hays (1970), in the Army Nurse Corps.
13. Ulysses Grant (1866-1869) and Dwight Eisenhower (1944-1946)
14. George Washington (1976), posthumously, effective July 4, 1776, by Gerald Ford.
15. Benjamin Harrison (1864)
16. Theodore Roosevelt (1901-1909)
17. James Monroe, appointed by James Madison.
18. George Washington (1798), on Independence Day.
19. Ulysses Grant (1866), for his remarkable military acumen and victory during the Civil War.
20. General George McClellan (1864), against Abraham Lincoln, as the Democratic nominee.
21. The 1880 presidential election, between James Garfield and Winfield S. Hancock.
22. Ulysses Grant (1869), who made Ely Parker a brevet general and personal secretary.

Ministers

1. Which presidents were the first and last ones who had been foreign ministers?
2. Which president was secretary to the minister to Russia, at the age of *fourteen* years?
3. Which president had been minister plenipotentiary to The Netherlands?
4. Which president had been an ambassador to a Latin American country?
5. Which president had been the first minister to the Court of St. James's?
6. Which president suspected his host country of spying on him at his post overseas?
7. Which president had negotiated the Louisiana Purchase as special minister to France?
8. Which *former* president represented the U.S.A. at The Hague, in The Netherlands?
9. Which president had been minister to Spain?
10. Which president had been minister to Russia?
11. Which president had been rebuked for his overly effusive praise for his host country?

Mount Rushmore

1. Which president's facsimile was first unveiled on Mount Rushmore?
2. Which other presidents' facsimiles are carved into Mount Rushmore?
3. What are these sixty-foot likenesses on Mount Rushmore meant to represent?
4. Who designed and sculpted the majority of the Mount Rushmore monument?
5. How much did the Mount Rushmore sculpting cost?
6. How much stone was removed during the Mount Rushmore sculpting?
7. How much did Congress budget for cleaning the four faces of Mount Rushmore?
8. In which state is Mount Rushmore located?

Mountains

1. For which president is the highest peak in North America named?
2. Which mountaineer named Denali for William McKinley after nearing the mountain edge?
3. When were the first unsuccessful and successful attempts to scale Mount McKinley made?
4. In which state are Mount Cleveland and Mount Harding located?
5. Which country named its highest unscaled peak for John Kennedy?
6. What did Theodore Roosevelt choose as the nation's first national monument?
7. Which *future* president climbed Mount Vesuvius?
8. Which president had climbed the legendary Matterhorn in Europe?
9. Which president first visited Mount Rainier National Park?
10. Which president was the first one who visited Mount Washington?
11. Which *incumbent* president last climbed a mountain peak?
12. Which president selected Yucca Mountain for the first nuclear-waste storage site?
13. Which *incumbent* president last visited the Canadian Rockies?

Ministers (answers)

1. John Adams and James Buchanan, respectively, both to the Court of St. James's.
2. John Quincy Adams (1781)
3. John Adams (1781-1788)
4. William Henry Harrison (1828-1829), as U.S. ambassador to Colombia.
5. John Adams (1785-1788)
6. George Bush (1975), in China, after his wife griped about glue and it emerged a day later.
7. James Monroe (1803), with the assistance of Robert Livingston.
8. Benjamin Harrison (1899), at a conference.
9. James Monroe (1805)
10. John Quincy Adams (1809-1814)
11. James Monroe (1794-1796), while minister to France.

Mount Rushmore (answers)

1. George Washington's
2. Thomas Jefferson's, Abraham Lincoln's, and Theodore Roosevelt's
3. The nation's founding, political philosophy, preservation, and conservation, respectively.
4. John Gutzon Borglum. Actually, son Lincoln finished it after the elder Borglum had died.
5. $990,000, $800,000 of which were donated by the federal government.
6. 450,000 tons of granite
7. $350,000 (1988)
8. South Dakota, near the mysterious Black Hills.

Mountains (answers)

1. William McKinley, for whom Alaska's Mt. McKinley (20,270 feet) was named.
2. W. A. Dickey (1897). The mountain is in Denali National Park, Alaska.
3. 1903 and 1913 (by Rev. Hudson Stuck, et al.), respectively.
4. Montana
5. Canada (1964). Robert Kennedy was the first person who scaled that peak (1965).
6. Devil's Tower (1906), in Wyoming.
7. John Kennedy (1940)
8. Theodore Roosevelt (1881), with his brand new bride, Alice.
9. Theodore Roosevelt (1903). Mount Rainier is North America's largest volcano.
10. Ulysses Grant (1868)
11. George W. Bush (2001), who climbed 6,500-foot Moro Rock, in Sequoia National Park.
12. Jimmy Carter (1978)
13. George W. Bush (2002), in Kananaskis, Alberta, for the G-8 Economic Summit.

Movies

1. Which president had first acted in films?
2. Who was Ronald Reagan's former roommate who played a munchkin in *The Wizard of Oz*?
3. Who portrayed Ulysses Grant in the movie *The Legend of the Lone Ranger*?
4. Which presidents were first filmed on "silent pictures" and "talking pictures"?
5. Which president, fascinated with movies, showed the first film at the White House?
6. Which was Ronald Reagan's only "bad guy" movie, the first movie made for television?
7. Which movie was a take-off on Jackie Onassis's wedding to Aristotle Onassis?
8. Which two Democratic presidential nominees did the movie *Sunrise at Campobello* feature?
9. Which president liked Western and Civil War movies?
10. Which president wrote a movie script based upon the story of the USS *Constitution*?
11. Which "president" did actor Peter Sellers portray in the movie *Dr. Strangelove*?
12. Whom did Burgess Meredith and Ginger Rogers portray in the movie *Magnificent Doll*?
13. For how many Academy Awards was Ronald Reagan nominated during his long career?
14. Which actor did George Bush say he wanted to portray him in a movie about his life?
15. Which presidents' likenesses appeared in Alfred Hitchcock's movie *North by Northwest*?
16. Which president "dumped" AT&T after it continued to sponsor a movie critical of him?
17. Which two presidents made guest appearances in *Womanhood: The Glory of a Nation*?
18. Which president has been portrayed in more films than any other?
19. Which movie did John Hinckley, Jr., say motivated him to attempt his heinous act?
20. Which living president was first featured in a major movie?
21. Which president said the best movie he had ever seen was *High Noon*?
22. Which president installed a movie theater in the East Colonnade of the White House?
23. Which president watched more movies in the White House than any other?
24. Who made *Wilson* to sway the U.S.A. "to avoid the isolationism that followed World War I"?
25. Which movie about a U.S. president was shown in Hong Kong under the title *The Big Liar*?
26. Which movie about Andrew Johnson's Senate trial is probably the only one on the subject?
27. What was the name of the protagonist in *The Distinguished Gentleman*?

Music

1. Which president started the tradition of following a state dinner with a musicale?
2. Which president described rock-and-roll as "that damned noise they're playing today"?
3. Which president had a strict rule never to pay musicians performing at the White House?
4. Which president had sung in a Methodist choir?
5. Which president liked to hear music coming from under his White House bed?
6. Which First Lady said her husband danced a waltz no matter what tune was played?
7. Which president first hosted a night of musical theater in the White House?

Movies (answers)

1. Theodore Roosevelt, in a one-reeler comedy by Matty Roubert.
2. Mickey Carroll (1939)
3. Jason Robards (1952)
4. Theodore Roosevelt (1898) and Calvin Coolidge (1924), respectively.
5. Woodrow Wilson (1916), who watched *Birth of a Nation* and others with close friends.
6. *The Killers* (1964), one of fifty-three movies in which Reagan played a role.
7. *The Greek Tycoon* (1978)
8. Alfred Smith and Franklin Roosevelt (1960)
9. John Kennedy
10. Franklin Roosevelt
11. Merkin Muffley (1964)
12. James Madison and Dolley Madison, respectively (1946).
13. None, although *Kings Row* (1942) is considered to have been his best performance.
14. Charlton Heston
15. Washington's, Jefferson's, Lincoln's, and Roosevelt's (1959), on Mount Rushmore.
16. Richard Nixon
17. Theodore Roosevelt and Woodrow Wilson (1917)
18. Abraham Lincoln (60), including *Abraham Lincoln* (1930) and *Young Mr. Lincoln* (1939).
19. *Taxi Driver* (1976), in which Jodie Foster, the object of Hinckley's obsession, appeared.
20. Franklin Roosevelt, in *Yankee Doodle Dandy* (1942), as himself.
21. Bill Clinton
22. Franklin Roosevelt (1942)
23. Ronald Reagan (1981-1989), a former actor, who watched dozens them.
24. Darryl F. Zanuck (1944), during the height of World War II.
25. *Nixon* (1995), starring Anthony Hopkins as President Richard Nixon.
26. *Tennessee Johnson* (1942), starring Van Heflin as President Andrew Johnson.
27. Thomas Jefferson Johnson (1992), portrayed by Eddie Murphy.

Music (answers)

1. William Taft
2. Harry Truman
3. William Taft, a tradition that has been followed ever since then.
4. William McKinley
5. John Kennedy
6. Barbara Bush
7. Dwight Eisenhower

8. Which incumbent presidents last made appearances on Broadway?
9. Which president was signaled by his wife's chief of staff when a classical piece had ended?

Names

1. What was the name of the baron who controlled 75% of the tobacco market in 1910?
2. Into what units did the Americans fighting the fascists in the Spanish Civil War organize?
3. Who threw the ball to Babe Ruth when he hit the longest home run in baseball history?
4. Which ship went to Nicaragua to give the elected president two days to leave power?
5. Who played lead in a movie based upon Edgar Rice Burroughs's *Tarzan, King of the Apes*?
6. At which high school did Miss Brooks teach in the television series *Our Miss Brooks*?
7. Which American folk singer had been named for Woodrow Wilson?
8. Which heavyweight boxing champion had been named for a president?
9. Which person with a presidential surname got partial credit for inventing the computer?
10. Which high school did television's "Laverne and Shirley" attend?
11. When Depression-era Texans turned their pockets inside out, what were they called?
12. What was referred to as a "Hoover hog" in Texas?
13. Which non-Masonic president does Masonic Lodge #166 in Kiddville, Kentucky, honor?
14. What was the name of the airport in the movie *Airport*, based upon Arthur Haley's novel?
15. Which signer of the Texas Declaration of Independence had been named for a president?
16. What was the full name of New York financier "Diamond Jim" Brady?
17. What was the name of Cornelius Vanderbilt's fourth child?
18. What was the name of the airport where "The Beatles" made their famous "invasion"?
19. What was the full name of the inventor of the Ferris wheel?
20. For whom was Cleveland, Ohio, named?
21. Whose real name was Richard M. Dixon, which he changed due to its similarity to Nixon's?
22. Which professional athletes with the same presidential name played tennis and football?
23. What was the name of the fort in the movie *The Devil's Brigade*?
24. Who served thirty-three years as Dallas County treasurer and Texas state treasurer?
25. Which Western name, after Jesus Christ and Elvis Presley, is most recognizable in China?
26. Which commander of the U.S. sector of Berlin had a presidential name?
27. Whose first names mean "enclosure of wild animals," "bald one," and "spear carrier"?
28. Which high school did the characters in television's *Happy Days* attend?
29. Whose name did financier J. P. Morgan absolutely forbid being mentioned in his home?
30. Which poet had three brothers named for Washington, Jefferson, and Jackson?
31. Which British university has a Lincoln College?
32. What was the name of the doctrine that established the U.S.A. as a world power?
33. Who was the army physician who tended to Zachary Taylor in the latter's final days?

8. Dwight Eisenhower (1955) and Bill Clinton (1997), in *Something Funny Happened* . . . .
9. John Kennedy's, in order to prevent his rushing on stage to congratulate the musicians.

Names (answers)

1. James Buchanan Duke (1856-1925)
2. Abraham Lincoln brigades (1936-1939)
3. Ulysses Simpson Grant "Lil" Stoner (1899-1966)
4. The *Cleveland* (1936)
5. Elmo Lincoln, who starred in *Tarzan of the Apes* (1918).
6. Madison High School
7. Woodrow Wilson "Woody" Guthrie (1912-1967)
8. William Henry Harrison "Jack" Dempsey (1895-1983)
9. Vannevar Bush (1890-1974)
10. Millard Fillmore High School (1976-1983)
11. Hoover flags
12. An armadillo, used for food during the Depression.
13. Zachary Taylor
14. Lincoln International Airport (1970)
15. Thomas Jefferson Rusk (1803-1857)
16. James Buchanan Brady (1856-1917)
17. William Henry Vanderbilt (1821-1885), named for William Henry Harrison.
18. John Fitzgerald Kennedy International Airport (1964), in New York, New York.
19. George Washington Gale Ferris (1859-1896)
20. Moses Cleveland (1754-1806), Connecticut surveyor and not related to Grover Cleveland.
21. Entertainer James LaRoe
22. John Fitzgerald (1960–) and John Fitzgerald (1975–), respectively.
23. Fort William Henry Harrison (1968)
24. Warren Harding (not the same man who became president)
25. Richard Nixon
26. Major General James Polk
27. Warren Harding's, Calvin Coolidge's, and Gerald Ford's, respectively.
28. Jefferson High School in Kenosha, Wisconsin.
29. Franklin Roosevelt's
30. Walt Whitman (G. W. Whitman, T. J. Whitman, and A. J. Whitman)
31. Oxford University (1427–), founded by the bishop of Lincoln, England.
32. The Monroe Doctrine (1823), which warned Europeans to stay out of Latin America.
33. Dr. Richard Coolidge (1850)

34. Who was the oldest freshman U.S. senator, at the age of eighty-seven years?

35. According to *Prophone*™, which presidents have the fewest and most living namesakes?

36. What was the name of the correspondent who filed dispatches from San Juan Hill, Cuba?

37. Who was the Mount St. Helen's resident who refused to leave his home after it erupted?

38. What was the full name of the founder of the American Nazi Party?

39. What was the full name of Senate leader Everett Dirksen?

40. What was the full name of one of the most influential journalists of the twentieth century?

41. Who was the chief engineer of the Panama Canal and first governor of the Canal Zone?

42. Which presidents' full names contain all the letters needed to spell the word "criminal"?

Newspapers

1. Which president first visited regularly with newspaper reporters?

2. Which city's newspapers reported "Hughes Elected," *à la* "Dewey Defeats Truman"?

3. Which newspaper besides the *Chicago Tribune* wrongly stated "Dewey Defeats Truman"?

4. Which president's *hometown* paper compared him to "the greatest butchers of antiquity"?

5. Which president first gave an exclusive interview to a member of the newspaper medium?

6. Who created the hoax that Millard Fillmore had installed the first White House bathtub?

7. Which president canceled his subscription to *The Washington Post* several times?

8. Which political cartoonist invented the Democratic donkey and Republican elephant?

9. Which president called a newspaper columnist an "S.O.B.," originating the term?

10. Which president refused to provide any news to one newspaper?

11. Which president brought poet Philip Freneau to Philadelphia to edit the *National Gazette*?

12. Which president ordered postmasters to secure subscribers for the *Extra Globe*?

13. Which columnist claimed that John Kennedy had not written *Profiles in Courage*?

14. Which newspaper's cartoon of Roosevelt sparing a bear cub inspired the "Teddy bear"?

15. Who got his friend Samuel H. Smith to start the first newspaper in Washington, DC?

16. Who set up a political newspaper with a $35,000 advance from the U.S. Treasury?

17. Which president read *The New York Times* every morning at the age of thirteen years?

18. Who purchased ads offering money for the best architectural plan for the new capital?

19. Which newspaper told readers how many days they had "to save your country"?

20. According to George Will, what first changed the relation of the citizen to the government?

21. Who got his start in politics running for the House after responding to a newspaper ad?

22. What fate did the *Louisville Courier-Journal* say should befall all former presidents?

Nicknames

1. Which presidents were first and last called by their nicknames?

2. Which president was disparagingly called "Jacobin," a radical of the French Revolution?

34. Andrew Jackson Houston (1854-1941), son of Sam Houston.
35. William Henry Harrison (0) and John Adams (3,591), respectively.
36. Richard Harding Davis (1864-1916)
37. Harry Truman (1980)
38. George Lincoln Rockwell (1918-1967)
39. Senator Everett McKinley Dirksen (D-IL) (1896-1969)
40. Franklin Pierce Adams (1881-1960), who wrote for four different New York newspapers.
41. George Washington Goethals (1858-1928)
42. Richard Milhous Nixon's and William Jefferson Clinton's

Newspapers (answers)

1. Grover Cleveland (1885)
2. Boston's (1916)
3. *The New York Times* (1948)
4. Abraham Lincoln's
5. Martin Van Buren (1839), to James Gordon Bennet.
6. H. L. Mencken (1917). He admitted the hoax, which was in the *New York Evening Mail*.
7. Richard Nixon (1969-1974), because he did not like Herblock's cartoons of him.
8. Thomas Nast (1870 and 1874, respectively), in *Harper's Weekly*.
9. Harry Truman, referring to Drew Pearson of *The Washington Post*.
10. Theodore Roosevelt, for reporting negatively and excessively about his children.
11. Thomas Jefferson (1792), as a rival to Alexander Hamilton's *United States Gazette*.
12. Martin Van Buren (1840). That newspaper supported his candidacy for president.
13. Drew Pearson (1957), who alleged that an aide, Ted Sorensen, had written it.
14. *The Washington Evening Star*'s (1902), inspiring Morris Mitchom to name his fuzzy toy.
15. Thomas Jefferson (1800), called the *National Intelligencer*.
16. James Polk, called *The Washington Globe*.
17. John Kennedy (1930)
18. Thomas Jefferson (1792), who offered a $500 prize.
19. The *Chicago Tribune* (1936), by voting against Franklin Roosevelt.
20. The New Deal (1933), whereby citizens became dependent upon government benefits.
21. Richard Nixon (1946)
22. Public execution

Nicknames (answers)

1. James Earl "Jimmy" Carter (1977) and William Jefferson "Bill" Clinton (2001), respectively.
2. Thomas Jefferson

3. When did Richard Nixon first become known as "Tricky Dick"?
4. Who was nicknamed "Unconditional Surrender" for refusing a proposed armistice?
5. Which president was nicknamed "Gloomy Gus" for his glumness while in law school?
6. Which president was nicknamed "Rubbers" for his enthusiastic support of family planning?
7. Which president was nicknamed "The Little Beauty" for his effeminate look?
8. Which president was nicknamed "Judas Johnson" for acquiescing to demands after a war?
9. Which president was nicknamed "Boy Scout in the White House" for his honesty?
10. Which president was nicknamed "The Flying Dutchman" for his ancestry?
11. Which president was nicknamed "The White House Iceberg" for his haughtiness?
12. Which president was nicknamed "Andy the Sot" for being drunk at his swearing-in?
13. Which president was nicknamed "The Hero of Two Wars" for his military genius?
14. Which president was nicknamed "Sir Veto" for his inclination to veto bills?
15. Which president was nicknamed "General Mum" for avoiding taking a position on issues?
16. Which president was nicknamed "Kansas Cyclone" for his prowess on the football field?
17. Which president was nicknamed "Old 8 to 7"?
18. Which president was nicknamed "Old Man Eloquent" for his oratorical skill?
19. Which president was nicknamed "The Sphinx of the Potomac" for his silence?
20. Which president was nicknamed "Old Hickory" for his toughness?
21. Which president was nicknamed "Mr. Nice Guy" for his amiability?
22. Which president was nicknamed "Slick Willie" for his dodging difficult questions?
23. Which president was nicknamed "The Grim Presence" for his dourness?

Nominations
1. Which president first sought his political party's nomination for a third term?
2. Which elected presidents were *not* re-nominated by their political parties?
3. Which president had been nominated for president on St. Valentine's Day?
4. Whom did historian George Bancroft put forth for nomination at a national convention?
5. Who received majorities of delegate votes and yet were *not* nominated for president?
6. Which presidents were first and last nominated by a congressional caucus?
7. Who was sent news of his nomination by mail but refused to pay two cents postage due?
8. Who beat his opponents in almost every primary yet was *not* nominated for president?
9. Who supposedly was nominated in order to appeal to newly-enfranchised voters?
10. Which president was in Rome, Italy, when he learned of his nomination for president?
11. Which president had received his nomination in a railroad car in San Diego, California?
12. Which *former* presidents did different parties first and last nominate for president?
13. Who placed New York Governor Alfred Smith's name in nomination three times?
14. When did Republicans first and last re-nominate an identical national ticket?

3. During a campaign for the Senate (1950), in the *Independent Review*.
4. Ulysses Grant (1862), from the Confederate commander at Fort Donelson.
5. Richard Nixon (1933-1937), at Duke University Law School.
6. George Bush, by House Ways and Means Committee Chairman Wilbur Mills.
7. Ulysses Grant
8. Andrew Johnson (1865-1869)
9. Gerald Ford
10. Martin Van Buren
11. Benjamin Harrison
12. Andrew Johnson (1865)
13. Andrew Jackson
14. Andrew Johnson (1865-1869)
15. William Henry Harrison
16. Dwight Eisenhower (1911)
17. Rutherford Hayes (1877), for winning an electoral dispute by that margin of votes.
18. John Quincy Adams
19. Calvin Coolidge
20. Andrew Jackson
21. Gerald Ford
22. Bill Clinton, by Arkansas newspaper columnist Paul Greenberg.
23. Andrew Johnson

Nominations (answers)

1. Ulysses Grant (1876), and came sixty-six delegates short of re-nomination.
2. Democrat Franklin Pierce (1856) and Republican Ulysses Grant (1876)
3. Theodore Roosevelt (1904)
4. James Polk (1844)
5. Martin Van Buren (1844) and Champ Clark (1912), lacking two-thirds votes.
6. Thomas Jefferson (1804) and John Quincy Adams (1824), respectively.
7. Zachary Taylor (1848)
8. Theodore Roosevelt (1912), overlooked for William Taft by 566-107 delegate votes.
9. Warren Harding (1920), on the theory that his good looks would appeal to women.
10. Millard Fillmore (1856), by the Know-Nothing Party.
11. Franklin Roosevelt (1944)
12. Martin Van Buren (1848) and Theodore Roosevelt (1912), respectively.
13. Franklin Roosevelt (1920, 1924, and 1928), for president, but then had a bitter split.
14. 1912 (Taft and Sherman) and 1992 (Bush and Quayle), respectively.

15. When did Democrats first and last re-nominate an identical national ticket?
16. Which presidents had been nominated by acclamation (without a single ballot)?
17. Who was nominated twice for president, lost both times, and was nominated a third time?
18. Who learned about his nomination for president while enjoying Egyptianite sepulchres?

Outdoors

1. Which president once had his underclothes eaten by a steer while on a camping trip?
2. Which famous explorer duplicated Theodore Roosevelt's "charge" up San Juan Hill?
3. Which president enjoyed bone-fishing in Islamorada, Florida?
4. Which president frequently camped with Messrs. Ford, Firestone, and Edison?
5. Which president greeted Antarctic explorer Sir Ernest Shackleton at the White House?
6. Which president began the tradition of flying the U.S. flag from public buildings?
7. Which president wrote on outdoor sports for *Collier's* and *The Saturday Evening Post*?
8. Which president had first fought in a duel?
9. Which conservationist was influential in Theodore Roosevelt's conservation policies?
10. Which president fished for tuna and swordfish but caught a 100-pound turtle instead?
11. Which president signed the Appalachian Trail Bill?
12. Through how many counties named for presidents does the Appalachian Trail pass?
13. Which national forest named for a president does the Appalachian Trail cross?
14. Which president regularly rode his bicycle in Rock Creek Park?
15. Which president first walked outdoors in the District of Columbia with a bodyguard?
16. Which president first used the presidential retreat Camp David, in Maryland?
17. Whose bust was carved from the largest sapphire, a 2,303-carat stone from Australia?
18. Whose bust is the largest cut sapphire in the world, cut from a 2,097-carat stone?
19. Which president was an amateur ornithologist?
20. For which president did frontiersman Davy Crockett have a burning hatred?
21. Which president was an enthusiastic duck hunter?
22. Which president amassed a collection of antique firearms?
23. Which president was an enthusiastic member of Trouts Unlimited?

Paper Money

1. Which *living* president first appeared on U.S. paper money?
2. Which president is pictured on the $1 bill?
3. Which president was pictured on the $2 bill?
4. Which president is pictured on the $5 bill?
5. Which president is pictured on the $20 bill?
6. Which president is pictured on the $50 bill?

15. 1916 (Wilson and Marshall) and 1996 (Clinton and Gore), respectively.

16. George Washington (1789), Franklin Roosevelt (1936), and Lyndon Johnson (1964)

17. William Jennings Bryan (1896, 1900, and 1908), by the Democrats.

18. Franklin Pierce (1852), at Mt. Auburn, the first major cemetery unrelated to a church.

Outdoors (answers)

1.   Theodore Roosevelt (1914), in Mato Grosso, Brazil.

2.   Richard Halliburton (1933)

3.   George Bush (2001)

4.   Warren Harding (1916-1923)

5.   William Taft (1910). Shackleton had shipwrecked and made an epic voyage to rescue.

6.   Benjamin Harrison

7.   Grover Cleveland

8.   Andrew Jackson (1805), who killed Charles Dickinson over a petty horse bet.

9.   John Burroughs (1901-1909)

10. Franklin Roosevelt

11. Jimmy Carter (1978), creating the longest continuously-marked footpath in the world.

12. Seven

13. The George Washington National Forest

14. Theodore Roosevelt (1901-1909)

15. Andrew Jackson (1829)

16. Franklin Roosevelt (1942). The original name for Camp David was "Shangri-la."

17. Abraham Lincoln's

18. Dwight Eisenhower's

19. Theodore Roosevelt

20. Andrew Jackson, a fellow Tennessean, in part for his ambivalence on states' rights.

21. Benjamin Harrison

22. Ronald Reagan

23. Jimmy Carter

Paper Money (answers)

1.   Abraham Lincoln (1861), on a $10 demand note.

2.   George Washington (1869–)

3.   Thomas Jefferson (1928 and 1976-1995)

4.   Abraham Lincoln (1928–)

5.   Andrew Jackson (1928–)

6.   Ulysses Grant (1928–)

7. Which president was pictured on the $500 bill?
8. Which president was pictured on the $1,000 bill?
9. Which president was pictured on the $5,000 bill?
10. Which president was pictured on the $1 silver certificate?
11. Which president was pictured on the $5 silver certificate?

Pardons

1. Which president first used the presidential pardon?
2. Whom did Gerald Ford pardon on his last day in office?
3. Which "qualification" must a president consider before issuing a pardon?
4. Who pardoned Dr. Mudd, the doctor who had set the leg of John Wilkes Booth?
5. Who pardoned Cassie Bigley, a con artist posing as Andrew Carnegie's daughter?
6. Who pardoned David Udall, the grandfather of presidential candidate Morris Udall?
7. Where did Gerald Ford go right after issuing his presidential pardon of Richard Nixon?
8. Who pardoned Yankees owner George Steinbrenner for federal election-law violations?
9. Which presidents pardoned Confederate Jefferson Davis and restored his U.S. citizenship?
10. Which president pardoned the bold-yet-inept train robber Al Jennings?
11. Which president pardoned all Vietnam War draft dodgers unconditionally?
12. In what circumstance can a president *not* pardon somebody?
13. Who commuted Jimmy Hoffa's thirteen-year sentence for jury tampering and mail fraud?
14. Which president made a federal pardon for a bank robber so that he could be executed?
15. Which presidents received pardons from an incumbent president?
16. Which president commuted Patricia Hearst's seven-year prison term for armed robbery?
17. Which presidents made the fewest and most acts of clemency during their tenures?
18. Which presidents had the lowest and highest average annual number of acts of clemency?
19. Which president made the most individual acts of clemency in a single day?
20. Which president pardoned the most persons at one time and the most during his tenure?
21. Which presidential pardon is probably history's most controversial one?

Parks

1. What is Reservation #1 of the Department of the Interior's National Capital Parks?
2. Which president signed the Act that created the first national park?
3. Which president signed the Act that created the first national forest?
4. Where are Franklin Delano Roosevelt State Parks?
5. Where is Theodore Roosevelt National Park?
6. Where is the James Buchanan State Forest?
7. Where is the Dixie National Forest?

7. William McKinley (1928-1945). The bill is still legal tender, but is no longer printed.
8. Grover Cleveland (1928-1969). The bill is still legal tender, but is no longer printed.
9. James Madison (1928-1969). The bill is still legal tender, but is no longer printed.
10. George Washington (1928-1963)
11. Abraham Lincoln (1928-1963)

Pardons (answers)

1. George Washington (1789), who pardoned two Whiskey Rebellion insurrectionists.
2. Iva Ikuko Toguri d'Aquino (1977), "Tokyo Rose," a Japanese agent during World War II.
3. The person must have committed a federal crime.
4. Andrew Johnson (1869), for battling yellow fever in prison.
5. William McKinley (1893), as governor of Ohio.
6. Grover Cleveland (1887), for trumped-up charges by Apaches to evict him from Arizona.
7. To the Burning Tree Golf Club (1974), to play nine holes while the furor spread.
8. Ronald Reagan (1989)
9. Andrew Johnson (1868) and Jimmy Carter (1978), respectively.
10. Theodore Roosevelt (1907)
11. Jimmy Carter (1977)
12. A president may not pardon a person impeached and convicted by Congress.
13. Richard Nixon (1971)
14. Calvin Coolidge (1925). With a federal pardon, he was prosecuted for murder.
15. Richard Nixon (1974), for Watergate, and Bill Clinton (1977), for draft resisting.
16. Jimmy Carter (1979)
17. W. H. Harrison and James Garfield (0) and Franklin Roosevelt (3,687), respectively.
18. George Washington (2) and Herbert Hoover (346), respectively, of those who made one.
19. Richard Nixon (1972), with 204 individual pardons on December 20.
20. Andrew Johnson (1868), pardoning millions who had supported the Confederacy.
21. Gerald Ford's pardoning Richard Nixon (1974), which might have cost him his job.

Parks (answers)

1. The White House
2. Ulysses Grant (1872), creating Yellowstone Park, in Wyoming.
3. Benjamin Harrison (1891), creating Shoshone National Forest, in Wyoming.
4. Yorktown Heights, New York, and Pine Mountain, Georgia.
5. Near Medora, North Dakota.
6. Near Chaneysville, Pennsylvania.
7. Garfield County, Utah.

8. Who made 104,000,000 acres of Alaskan wilderness part of the national-park system?
9. Which *incumbent* president first visited Sequoia National Park, in California?

Photographs

1. Which *incumbent* and *former* presidents were the first ones photographed, respectively?
2. Which president first had a daguerreotype made of himself?
3. Which presidential assassin was first photographed?
4. Which deceased president was first photographed in his coffin?
5. Which president was the first one of whom autographed photographs are known to exist?
6. Which president-elect's inauguration was first photographed?
7. Which presidential couple were first photographed voting at the polls?
8. Which president liked cigars but was never photographed while smoking one?
9. Which president was urged by his supporters not to be photographed playing golf?
10. Which president first asked sports champions to be photographed at the White House?
11. Which president was first photographed in an automobile?
12. Which president hated shaking hands and insisted on taking photographs instead?
13. Which president was the first one who was photographed with his Cabinet?
14. Which president probably personally signed more photographs than any other?
15. Which president was in a famous photograph, wearing an American Indian headdress?
16. When were photographs of the White House first made available to the public?
17. Who said on the campaign trail that his "Presbyterian face" did not photograph well?

Physiognomy

1. Which president's complexion was described as "strawberries and cream"?
2. Which multi-millionaire aristocrat had a striking resemblance to Chester Arthur?
3. Which Democratic and Republican presidents weighed the most?
4. Which president weighed the least in adulthood?
5. Which president had a scar above his right eye from fighting with burglars?
6. Which president's nose was permanently scarred from a case of frostbite?
7. Which president had been in a high-school soccer accident that scarred his forehead?
8. Which president had been in a cotton-gin accident that left one finger permanently bent?
9. Which presidents were left-handed?
10. Which president was born a left-hander but learned to write with his right?
11. Which president was the fourth oldest, fourth tallest, and fourth born in Massachusetts?
12. Which president was famous for falling asleep unexpectedly, at funerals and parades?
13. Which president nicknamed his genitals "Jumbo"?
14. Which presidents were notorious for their limp handshakes?

8. Jimmy Carter (1980), by signing the Alaskan National Interest Lands Conservation Act.
9. George W. Bush (2001)

Photographs (answers)

1. John Tyler (1841), by Matthew Brady, and John Quincy Adams (1843), by Josiah Dawes.
2. Andrew Jackson (1845), just seven weeks before his death.
3. Charles Guiteau (1881)
4. Abraham Lincoln (1865), at New York City Hall, during a funeral procession to Springfield.
5. Millard Fillmore (1850), on a "carte de visite," a 2" x 4" precursor of modern post cards.
6. James Buchanan's (1857)
7. President and Mrs. Warren Harding (1920)
8. William McKinley, because he thought it would set a bad example for children.
9. William Taft (1912), because it bolstered accusations that he was a do-nothing president.
10. George Bush (1989), instead of telephoning them in their locker rooms.
11. Theodore Roosevelt (1908), in a Cadillac.
12. Herbert Hoover (1929-1933)
13. James Buchanan (1857), by future Civil War photographer Matthew Brady.
14. Harry Truman
15. Calvin Coolidge
16. Andrew Johnson's Administration (1865-1869)
17. Woodrow Wilson

Physiognomy (answers)

1. Chester Arthur's
2. John Jacob Astor, III.
3. Grover Cleveland (260 pounds) and William Taft (300 pounds), respectively.
4. James Madison (100 pounds, sometimes less)
5. Abraham Lincoln
6. James Madison's
7. George Bush
8. Jimmy Carter
9. Garfield, Hoover, Truman, Ford, George Bush, and Clinton (only one elected to two terms)
10. Ronald Reagan
11. George Bush
12. William Taft
13. Lyndon Johnson
14. Benjamin Harrison and Woodrow Wilson, the latter's "pickled mackerel in brown paper."

15. Which president was famous for his freckles?
16. Which president had an uncanny likeness to the Duke of Wellington?
17. Which president was probably the ugliest, with a rough, scowling countenance?
18. Which president had one leg three-fourths of one inch shorter than the other one?
19. Which president last measured less than six feet tall?
20. Which presidents became famous for their wide grins?
21. Which president had a very slow heartbeat and unusually low blood pressure?
22. Which president had a bad habit of slobbering as a child?
23. Which president had a large wart on his right cheek above his mouth?
24. Which president had a physical breakdown from the intensely long hours that he worked?
25. Which president had chronic laryngitis?
26. Which president probably had the largest ears?

Piano

1. Which president's childhood ambition was to become a concert pianist?
2. Who designed the American eagle pedestals for the White House East Room grand piano?
3. Which actress sat seductively atop a piano in a famous photograph with a president?
4. Who personally delivered Harry Truman's piano to Independence as a gift for his library?
5. Which song was Richard Nixon's favorite, which he often played on the piano?
6. Which song was Harry Truman's favorite, which he often played on the piano?
7. Which president insisted that only Steinway pianos be played in the White House?
8. Which president awoke at 5:00 A.M. each morning as a boy to practice the piano?
9. Which president played "Happy Birthday" on the piano to former Governor John Connally?
10. Which president played the piano to calm himself while waiting for election-night returns?
11. Which president first placed a musical instrument in the White House?
12. Which president installed a small Kimball piano on the presidential yacht *Sequoia*?

Platforms

1. Which platform was first published?
2. During which national convention could delegates not decide on a platform?
3. Which presidential nominee openly repudiated his party's national platform?
4. Which political party first announced its platform at a national convention?
5. Who had no platform in order not to upset Southern planters or Northern manufacturers?
6. Which political party first promulgated a substantial platform?
7. Which president's political platform was nicknamed "New Freedom"?
8. Which political party's platform was the most explicit of the early platforms?
9. What was the closest margin of victory in any national-convention vote?

15. Thomas Jefferson
16. Andrew Jackson
17. Andrew Johnson
18. John Kennedy, prompting him to wear corrective shoes most of his life.
19. Richard Nixon
20. Dwight Eisenhower and Jimmy Carter
21. Harry Truman
22. Andrew Jackson
23. Abraham Lincoln
24. Benjamin Harrison
25. Bill Clinton
26. Lyndon Johnson

Piano (answers)

1. Harry Truman's
2. Franklin Roosevelt
3. Lauren Bacall, with Harry Truman.
4. Richard Nixon
5. "Home on the Range"
6. "Missouri Waltz"
7. William Taft
8. Harry Truman
9. Richard Nixon
10. Harry Truman
11. Theodore Roosevelt (1901), a $428 piano-forte.
12. Harry Truman

Platforms (answers)

1. The 1840 Democratic platform
2. The 1840 Whig National Convention
3. George McClellan (1864), because it called for an immediate peace in the Civil War.
4. The Anti-Masonic Party (1832)
5. William Henry Harrison (1840) and Zachary Taylor (1848)
6. The Democrats (1840), with nine planks.
7. Woodrow Wilson's (1912)
8. The 1852 Democratic platform
9. 4/5ths of one vote out of 1,086 votes cast (0.0007%), defeating an anti-Klan plank.

10. Which platform urged "an immediate and drastic reduction in government expenditures"?
11. Which former president was nominated on a platform of religious bigotry?
12. Which platform contained a condemnation of "hyphenated Americanism"?
13. Which Democratic presidents co-opted Republicans by asking Congress to pass their bills?
14. Which major-party national convention first included a significant platform fight?
15. Which major-party platform was the longest?
16. What did the 1856 Republican platform call the "twin relics of barbarism"?
17. Which major-party platform first recognized women's rights?
18. Which major-party platform pushed for a "railroad to the Pacific Ocean"?

Poetry

1. Which president first published a book of poetry?
2. Which president's death do two of Walt Whitman's best poems address?
3. Which poem did Franklin Roosevelt send to Winston Churchill to reassure England?
4. Which president wrote "Dermott McMorrogh," about Cromwell's conquest of Ireland?
5. About whom did William Cullen Bryant write, "Go, wretch! Resign the Presidential chair"?
6. Who wrote a book of poetry about possum hunting, barefoot fishing, and the homeless?
7. Who did e.e. cummings say could make "six errors in one sentence"?

Political Parties

1. Which political party holds the record for the most consecutive years in the White House?
2. Who changed the Republican Party more than any other person in the last 100 years?
3. Which third party is the oldest one that still runs candidates for president?
4. Which U.S. political party was the fastest growing and most successful from inception?
5. Which Federalist last ran for president?
6. Which division in the Republican Party foreshadowed the Goldwater-Rockefeller split?
7. Who said, "the existence of [political] parties is not necessary to free government"?
8. Which organized third party was the first one that fielded a presidential candidate?
9. In which presidential election did the Communist Party first field national candidates?
10. Which third party first received more than one million votes?
11. Which two persons were on the last bipartisan national ticket?
12. Which party's nominee for president was pediatrician and activist Dr. Benjamin Spock?
13. Which presidents had been courted arduously by both major political parties?
14. Which political party used the raccoon as its symbol?
15. Which president and his vice president were from opposing political factions?
16. Which president had served as state chairman of his political party?
17. Which president had served as national chairman of his political party?

10. The 1932 Democratic platform, ironic because the New Deal was about to begin.
11. Millard Fillmore (1856), by the Know-Nothing Party, bigoted towards Roman Catholics.
12. The 1916 Democratic platform
13. Harry Truman and Bill Clinton both "triangulated" the Republican Party.
14. The 1860 Democratic National Convention, over slavery and war.
15. The 1980 Democratic platform, about 40,000 words long.
16. Slavery and polygamy
17. The 1872 Republican platform
18. The 1856 Republican platform

Poetry (answers)
1. James Madison
2. Abraham Lincoln's (1865), "O Captain!" and "When Lilacs Last in the Dooryard Bloom'd."
3. "The Building of the Ship" (1940). Churchill's ended "westward, look, the land is bright."
4. John Quincy Adams (1832)
5. Thomas Jefferson (1808), in "Embargo."
6. Jimmy Carter (1994), in *Always a Reckoning*, sparked by a meeting with Miller Williams.
7. Warren Harding

Political Parties (answers)
1. The Republican Party (1861-1885). The Democratic record is twenty years (1933-1953).
2. Ronald Reagan (1980), mainly through appeals to Democrats and blue-collar voters.
3. The Prohibition Party, formed in 1869.
4. The Republican Party, formed in 1856 and victorious nationally just four years later.
5. Rufus King (1816)
6. The schism between Theodore Roosevelt and William Taft (1912)
7. James Monroe
8. The Anti-Masonic Party (1832), who nominated William Wirt against Andrew Jackson.
9. The 1932 presidential election. William Foster and James Ford were the national ticket.
10. The Populist Party (1892), with James Weaver and James Field as their national ticket.
11. Republican John Anderson and Democrat Patrick Lucey (1980), running as independents.
12. The Peace and Freedom Party's (1968)
13. Herbert Hoover and Dwight Eisenhower
14. The Whig Party, when portraying William Henry Harrison as a "backwoods good ol' boy."
15. John Adams and Thomas Jefferson (1797-1801)
16. Franklin Pierce, chairman of the New Hampshire Democratic Party.
17. George Bush (1972-1973), chairman of the Republican National Committee.

18. Which president quipped, "He serves his party who serves his country best"?
19. What was Ronald Reagan's "Eleventh Commandment"?

Polls

1. Which president's approval rating was the lowest since such polling began in 1939?
2. Which president's disapproval rating was the highest ever for any new president?
3. When was the electorate first polled about their presidential choices on a large scale?
4. Which presidential candidate had a net disapproval rating yet still won the election?
5. Which president regularly carried a card in his suit showing his popularity in the polls?
6. Which presidential election first featured "exit polling" to try to predict a winner?
7. Which president was the most admired man since Gallup began asking in 1948?
8. Which president had the highest approval rating in the Gallup poll at any time in office?
9. Which president had the highest approval rating in the Gallup poll upon *leaving* office?

Popular Vote

1. During which presidential election was the popular vote first recorded?
2. Which presidential nominee was 3,421 popular votes short of victory?
3. Which presidential nominee was 3,762 popular votes short of a fifty-state sweep?
4. Who got *nine* popular votes in Virginia, the only Southern state where he got *any* votes?
5. Which third-party nominee first received a popular-vote plurality in any state?
6. In which state did Bill Clinton place third in the popular vote?
7. By what amount of the national popular vote did Al Gore best George W. Bush?
8. Which president had first received more than one million popular votes?
9. Which president had received the most popular votes in his presidential election?
10. Which presidential nominee received the most popular votes in a losing effort?
11. Which president won re-election but got fewer popular votes than the previous time?
12. Which third-party presidential nominee received the most popular votes?
13. Which independent presidential candidate received the most popular votes?
14. In which state was the closest presidential contest ever recorded?
15. Which president had received the smallest popular-vote margin nationally?
16. Which president had received the largest popular-vote margin nationally?
17. Which presidents had first and last been elected *without* a popular-vote plurality?
18. Which presidents were elected twice yet never received a majority of the popular vote?
19. Which non-Southern Democratic president won a majority of the popular vote nationally?
20. Which president had been elected with the smallest percentage of the popular vote?
21. Which *incumbent* presidents got the smallest and largest percentages of popular votes?
22. Which Republican nominee received the highest percentage of popular votes in a state?

18. Rutherford Hayes
19. "Thou shalt not speak ill of a fellow Republican," especially in the general election.

Polls (answers)

1. Jimmy Carter's (22%), in 1979.
2. Bill Clinton's (32%), in 1998. Ronald Reagan's was second highest (13%).
3. In 1920, via postcards distributed by *The Literary Digest*.
4. George Bush (1988)
5. Lyndon Johnson, to brag to Congressmen when his approval rating was high.
6. The 1972 presidential election
7. George W. Bush (2001), who 39% said was the country's "most admired man."
8. George W. Bush (2001), with a 90% approval rating ten days after the terrorist attacks.
9. Ronald Reagan (1989), with a 63% approval rating as he left Washington for California.

Popular Vote (answers)

1. The 1824 presidential election
2. Charles Evans Hughes (1916), in California.
3. Ronald Reagan (1984), in Minnesota.
4. Martin Van Buren (1848), as presidential nominee of the Free Soil Party.
5. Millard Fillmore (1856), in Missouri, as presidential nominee of the Know-Nothing Party.
6. Utah (1992), behind George Bush and Ross Perot.
7. 543,614 votes, in the 2000 presidential election.
8. William Henry Harrison (1840), with 1,275,612 votes.
9. Ronald Reagan (1984), who won 54,455,075 votes nationwide.
10. Al Gore (2000), who won 50,999,897 votes nationwide (48.4%).
11. Franklin Roosevelt (1940), from 27,751,841 to 27,243,466 votes.
12. George Wallace (1968), who won 9,906,473 votes nationwide (13.5%).
13. Ross Perot (1992), who won 19,741,048 votes nationwide (19.0%).
14. Maryland (1832), where Henry Clay won by *four* votes!
15. James Garfield (1880), who won by 7,018 votes nationwide (0.0007628%).
16. Richard Nixon (1972), who won 17,998,810 votes more than George McGovern.
17. John Quincy Adams (1824), 31.9%, and George W. Bush (2000), 47.9%, respectively.
18. Cleveland (1884 and 1892), Wilson (1912 and 1916), and Clinton (1992 and 1996)
19. Franklin Roosevelt (1932, 1936, 1940, and 1944)
20. John Quincy Adams (1824), with 31.9%. The race was decided in the House.
21. William Taft (1912), with 23.2%, and Lyndon Johnson (1964), with 61.0%, respectively.
22. William McKinley (1896), who garnered 80.1% in Vermont.

23. Which Democratic nominee received the highest percentage of popular votes in a state?
24. Who had the largest margins of victory in the percentage of the popular vote?
25. During which presidential election did fewer than 1% of eligible voters participate?
26. In which presidential election did more than 70% of eligible voters last participate?
27. Which president had received the largest percentage of voters who were eligible to vote?

Portraits
1. Which president's facsimile appears on a state flag?
2. Which president owned a portrait of actress Jane Russell's mother?
3. Which president, of whom there are several famous paintings, hated sitting for portraits?
4. Which painter's portraits of the first five presidents hang in the National Gallery of Art?
5. Which portrait is missing from the Hall of Presidents in the National Portrait Gallery?
6. Who placed his wife's portrait bedside so that she would "meet his eyes in the morning"?
7. Which portrait has hung in the White House almost continuously since it was built?
8. Which famous American inventor painted James Monroe's official portrait?
9. Which president called his portrait "the ugliest thing I ever saw in my whole life"?

Primaries
1. Who organized the first Republican primary in Midland, Texas, which drew *three* votes?
2. During which presidential campaign was the first presidential primary held?
3. Which Republican won 35.5% of the New Hampshire primary vote *as a write-in candidate*?
4. Which Democratic and Republican presidents last failed to win the New Hampshire primary?
5. Which *incumbent* president first participated in a presidential primary?
6. Which president first participated in his home state's primary?
7. What disparity between a candidate with most primary votes and the nominee is smallest?
8. What disparity between a candidate with most primary votes and the nominee is largest?
9. Who received the highest percentage of primary votes but *not* his party's nomination?
10. Who won the smallest plurality of primary votes and did not win his party's nomination?
11. Who won the largest percentage of overall primary votes ever recorded?
12. Whom did the AFL-CIO first endorse for president *before* the presidential primaries?
13. When are the first and last primaries for the 2004 presidential campaign?

Printed Word
1. Which files was Andrew Johnson sure to take with him when he left the White House?
2. Which president first used a typewriter in the White House?
3. Which president's typewriter could be adapted to type in Greek?

23. Andrew Jackson (1832), who garnered 99.9% in Alabama.
24. Warren Harding (1920), at 26.4%, followed by Calvin Coolidge (1924), at 25.2%.
25. The 1820 presidential election, because James Monroe was the only legitimate candidate.
26. The 1900 presidential election
27. William Henry Harrison (1840), with 42.5%.

Portraits (answers)

1. George Washington's, for the State of Washington.
2. Woodrow Wilson, because she looked like his first wife.
3. George Washington
4. Gilbert Stuart's, in Washington, DC.
5. Rutherford Hayes's
6. Andrew Jackson
7. The Gilbert Stuart portrait of George Washington (1801–), except during the War of 1812.
8. Samuel F. B. Morse (1820), the inventor of Morse Code.
9. Lyndon Johnson (1967), commenting on his portrait by Peter Hurd.

Primaries (answers)

1. George Bush (1950)
2. The 1904 presidential campaign, in Florida.
3. Henry Cabot Lodge (1964), an amazing feat since write-ins usually tally in single digits.
4. Bill Clinton (1996) and George W. Bush (2000), respectively.
5. William Taft (1912), in North Dakota.
6. Woodrow Wilson (1916), in New Jersey, where he won 100% of the primary vote.
7. 0.4% (1972), when Ronald Reagan got 37.9% and Richard Nixon got 37.5%.
8. 62.7% (1952), when Estes Kefauver got 64.3% and Adlai Stevenson got 1.6%.
9. Senator Estes Kefauver (D-TN) (1952), with 64.3% of primary votes.
10. Earl Warren (1948), with 29.1%.
11. Woodrow Wilson (1916), with 98.8%.
12. Walter Mondale (1984)
13. January 13 (District of Columbia) and June 8 (Montana and New Jersey), respectively.

Printed Word (answers)

1. Those detailing his impeachment trial (1869)
2. Rutherford Hayes (1877), a Fairbanks and Company Improved Number Two Typewriter.
3. Woodrow Wilson's

4. Which president took a typewriter with him everywhere, even on hunting and fishing trips?
5. Which president admired author Charles Dickens and frequently attended his lectures?
6. Which president met British novelist and poet Rudyard Kipling?
7. Which president did lexicographer Noah Webster ardently defend after harsh criticism?
8. Which president was at the deathbed of author Nathaniel Hawthorne?
9. Which grandson of Benjamin Trumbull helped save Andrew Johnson from conviction?
10. Which presidents were involved in a libel suit against Joseph Pulitzer?
11. Who used George Washington's cherry-tree legend to satirize the evil of telling the truth?
12. Which president is often considered to have been the most literate?
13. Who created the Simplified Spelling Board guidelines, changing the way Americans spell?
14. Which president could read 2,000 words per minute with near complete comprehension?
15. Which president thought American English would become a separate language?
16. Which president printed and painted his own Christmas cards?
17. Which president coined the term "chiseler"?
18. Which president coined the term "war hawk"?
19. Which president coined the term "lunatic fringe"?
20. Which president coined the term "Founding Fathers"?

Quotations

1. Which president said, "the first want of man is his dinner, and the second his girl"?
2. Which president called Woodrow Wilson a "Byzantine logothete"?
3. Which president said, "You can fool all of the people some of the time, some of the . . ."?
4. Which president toasted "the great people of the government of Israel"?
5. Which president quipped, "I like to go out into the country and bloviate"?
6. What did George Bush tell Margaret Thatcher after attending three Soviet funerals?
7. Who said, "I don't expect to be the best president, but I hope to be the best-loved one"?
8. Who described the presidency as "the greased pig in the field game of American politics"?
9. Which president said, "We stand at Armageddon, and we battle for the Lord"?
10. Who said, "When more and more people are thrown out of work, unemployment results"?
11. Who said, with extreme frustration, "Now that damn cowboy is in the White House"?
12. Which president said, "Victory has a hundred fathers, and defeat is an orphan"?
13. Which president said chewing tobacco gives a man "time to think between sentences"?
14. Who said to his doctors after a gunshot wound, "I hope you're all Republicans"?
15. Which president said, "Facts are stubborn things"?
16. Which president said, "Sensible and responsible women do not want to vote"?
17. Which president said, "The ballot is stronger than the bullet"?
18. Which president bragged that he "killed a Spaniard with my own hand like a jackrabbit"?

4. Herbert Hoover
5. James Garfield
6. Theodore Roosevelt
7. John Adams
8. Franklin Pierce (1864)
9. Lyman Trumbull (1868)
10. Theodore Roosevelt and William Taft (1909), after he had made allegations of corruption.
11. Playwright Oscar Wilde (1905), in a play entitled "The Decay of Lying."
12. Abraham Lincoln, even though he had almost no formal education whatsoever!
13. Theodore Roosevelt (1906). Congress challenged his changing American orthography.
14. John Kennedy
15. Thomas Jefferson
16. Dwight Eisenhower
17. Franklin Roosevelt
18. Thomas Jefferson (1798), for Federalists who wanted war with France.
19. Theodore Roosevelt (1913), when he said, "Every reform movement has a lunatic fringe."
20. Warren Harding (1921), in his inaugural address.

Quotations (answers)

1. John Adams
2. Theodore Roosevelt (1915)
3. Abraham Lincoln (1864)
4. Gerald Ford (1975), while toasting Egyptian President Anwar Sadat.
5. Warren Harding (1920), meaning "to hang around and shoot the breeze."
6. "See you here next year" (1985).
7. Warren Harding
8. American writer Ambrose Bierce (1911)
9. Theodore Roosevelt (1912)
10. Calvin Coolidge (1923)
11. Senator Mark Hanna (R-OH), about Theodore Roosevelt (1901).
12. John Kennedy (1961), borrowed from Mussolini's foreign minister, Count Galeazzo Ciamo.
13. Woodrow Wilson (1912)
14. Ronald Reagan (1981)
15. John Adams
16. Grover Cleveland (1905), in *Ladies Home Journal*.
17. Abraham Lincoln (1856)
18. Theodore Roosevelt (1898)

19. Which president said, "I am the last president of the United States"?

20. Who heard economists saying, "on the one hand . . ." and "on the other hand . . ."?

21. What did Martin Van Buren say when asked if he believed the sun rises in the East?

22. What did Calvin Coolidge say when asked how many people work at the White House?

23. Who wrote, "The world will take care of Houston's fame," Sam Houston's epitaph?

24. Which president called the Masonic Order "organized treason"?

25. Which president said he regretted not shooting Henry Clay and hanging John Calhoun?

26. Which president said, "A statesman is a politician who's been dead ten or fifteen years"?

27. Who said, "I was told that anybody could become President. I'm beginning to believe it"?

28. Which president said, "Show me a good loser, and I'll show you a loser"?

29. Which president-elect quipped, "I am no longer a political accident"?

30. Who said his successor offered him "unsolicited advice for six years, all of it bad"?

31. Which president promised to rid the government of "Communists and pinks"?

32. Who did George Creel say was "distinguishable from the furniture only when he moved"?

33. Who told Orson Welles there were "two great actors in America . . . you are the other one"?

34. Who was the first person to use "lame duck" to refer to politicians' terms ending?

35. Whom did an Indian chief tell, "Watch your immigration laws — we got careless with ours"?

36. Who said, "My God! It's as bad as Eisenhower. The worse I do, the more popular I get"?

37. Which day did Gerald Ford say was "the lowest and loneliest" day of his presidency?

38. Who told a boy, "I wish for you that you may never be president of the United States"?

39. Which president, awe struck, said, "This is the greatest thing in history!"

40. Which president quipped, "I'm not smart enough to lie"?

41. Which president raged, "Let them impeach and be damned!"

42. Which president said somberly, "Our long national nightmare is over"?

43. Who said he thought "this country could run itself domestically without a president"?

44. Who said making love outdoors, with the "thermometer at zero, is a Yankee invention"?

Radio

1. Which president first spoke on the radio?

2. Which president first owned a radio?

3. Which president had first made a public address over the radio?

4. Which president's election results were first broadcast by radio?

5. Which president installed the first radio in the White House?

6. Which Republican National Convention was first broadcast by radio?

7. Which president first made a radio broadcast heard on the West Coast?

8. In which presidential election did candidates first buy radio time for political purposes?

9. Which president first made a radio broadcast nationwide from the White House?

19. James Buchanan (1861), because he feared the permanent dissolution of the Union.

20. Harry Truman, who responded, "I'll get a one-handed economist."

21. "As I never get up until after dawn, I can't really say."

22. "About half of them."

23. Fellow Tennesseean Andrew Jackson (1845), eighteen years before Houston's death.

24. Millard Fillmore, even though his uncle was a Mason.

25. Andrew Jackson

26. Harry Truman, after being praised for his elder statesmanship.

27. Warren Harding

28. Jimmy Carter (1976), after losing re-election to the presidency.

29. Theodore Roosevelt (1904), after winning a term in his own right.

30. Calvin Coolidge, speaking about Herbert Hoover.

31. Dwight Eisenhower

32. Calvin Coolidge

33. Franklin Roosevelt (1941)

34. Abraham Lincoln. A stockbroker defaulting was said to "waddle like a lame duck."

35. James Buchanan

36. John Kennedy (1961), referring to the Bay of Pigs invasion.

37. The day his wife got a mastectomy (1974)

38. Grover Cleveland (1889), who told that to Franklin Roosevelt, who served longest.

39. Harry Truman (1945), talking about the bombing of Hiroshima.

40. Ronald Reagan

41. Andrew Johnson (1868)

42. Gerald Ford (1974), after pardoning Richard Nixon.

43. Richard Nixon

44. John Quincy Adams

Radio (answers)

1. Woodrow Wilson (1919), from a ship, to troops on other ships, returning from Europe.

2. Warren Harding (1919)

3. Warren Harding (1920), at the Minnesota State Fair.

4. Warren Harding's (1920)

5. Warren Harding (1922)

6. The 1924 Republican National Convention

7. Calvin Coolidge (1924), at the Chamber of Commerce Building in Washington, DC.

8. The 1924 presidential election, between Calvin Coolidge and John Davis.

9. Calvin Coolidge (1924), on the anniversary of George Washington's birthday.

10. Which president first broadcast a Christmas message nationwide from the White House?
11. Which presidential inauguration was first broadcast on a radio station in Washington, DC?
12. In which presidential election did political parties first buy radio time?
13. Which presidential inauguration was first broadcast nationwide on a radio network?
14. Which president became famous for his "fireside chats" broadcast on radio?
15. Which president first made a radio broadcast in a foreign language?
16. Which president first held a press conference broadcast by radio?
17. Which president first made a radio broadcast worldwide via satellite?
18. Which president first held a press conference broadcast *live* by radio?
19. How many radio addresses did Woodrow Wilson make?
20. How many football games did Ronald Reagan broadcast by radio?
21. Which president made the most radio addresses?

Receptions

1. Which president first held a public White House reception?
2. Which president first shook hands instead of bowing at official receptions?
3. Which presidents first and last held public White House receptions on New Year's Day?
4. Which presidents first and last held an "Open House" after their inaugurations?
5. Which president first received a delegation of Japanese diplomats?
6. Which president first received a major foreign head of state?
7. Which president first restricted the number of persons attending public receptions?
8. Which president first received a female ambassador to the U.S.A.?
9. Which president first hosted a state dinner outside the White House grounds?
10. Which president first welcomed a European Community president to the White House?
11. Which president first hosted an arts festival at the White House?
12. Which president hosted the first state dinner that was televised?
13. Which president first welcomed a pope to the White House?
14. Which president set a hand-shaking record by pressing 4,816 palms in 1.75 hours?
15. Which president set a record by shaking hands with 8,513 persons, in a reception?
16. Which president rejected an ambassador when he presented his credentials on a Sunday?
17. Which president ended a sword fight between British and French ministers to the U.S.A.?
18. Which president's children were the only very young ones who attended state dinners?
19. Which president used emerald finger bowls at White House functions?
20. Who broke the tradition that a president escorts the secretary of state at a formal dinner?
21. Which president referred to his White House guests as "customers"?
22. Which president often greeted foreign emissaries while in his slippers?
23. Which president excused the rest of his White House guests after one of them had died?

10. Calvin Coolidge (1925)
11. Calvin Coolidge's (1925)
12. The 1928 presidential election
13. Herbert Hoover's (1929)
14. Franklin Roosevelt (1933-1945)
15. Franklin Roosevelt (1942), in French.
16. Dwight Eisenhower (1953)
17. Dwight Eisenhower (1958), delivering a Christmas message.
18. John Kennedy (1961)
19. One (1923), regarding the importance of Armistice Day.
20. One (1932), between Michigan and Iowa, with Gerald Ford playing for Michigan.
21. Ronald Reagan (1981-1989)

Receptions (answers)

1. Thomas Jefferson (1801), on Independence Day.
2. Thomas Jefferson (1801), starting a tradition.
3. Thomas Jefferson (1802) and Herbert Hoover (1932), respectively.
4. Thomas Jefferson (1805) and Andrew Jackson (1829), respectively.
5. James Buchanan (1860)
6. Ulysses Grant (1876), who received Brazilian Emperor Dom Pedro I.
7. William McKinley (1897), by requiring presentation of an invitation for admission.
8. Harry Truman (1952), who received the ambassador from India.
9. John Kennedy (1961), at Mount Vernon, for the president of Pakistan.
10. John Kennedy (1963), who welcomed Walter Hallstein.
11. Lyndon Johnson (1965)
12. Gerald Ford (1976), for Queen Elizabeth II.
13. Jimmy Carter (1979), who greeted Pope John Paul II.
14. William McKinley (1900)
15. Theodore Roosevelt (1907), during a New Year's Day reception at the White House.
16. James Polk (1845), who rejected the ambassador from Austria-Hungary.
17. John Adams (1797)
18. Abraham Lincoln's, William "Willie" Lincoln (1850-1862) and Tad Lincoln (1853-1871).
19. Martin Van Buren
20. William McKinley (1897), who opted for his wife instead because she was an invalid.
21. Harry Truman (1945)
22. Thomas Jefferson (1801-1809)
23. Chester Arthur, after the Haitian dean of the diplomatic corps passed away.

24. Who danced with Queen Elizabeth II as the band struck up "The Lady is a Tramp"?
25. Who hosted a delegation of Sac, Fox, and Osage American Indians at the White House?
26. Who introduced pêle-mêle to the White House, whereby guests seated wherever possible?
27. Which president introduced dignitaries to *any* member of the White House staff?
28. Which president hosted a White House jazz festival, with more than thirty entertainers?
29. Who was warned at a reception that chains holding chandeliers could snap any moment?
30. Which president received Japanese Emperor Hirohito at the White House?
31. Which president welcomed his inaugural visitors at Octagon House?
32. Who held a White House reception Tuesdays and a congressional dinner Thursdays?
33. Whose receptions featured dishes such as pâté, duck, partridge, venison, and terrapin?
34. Which president initiated the tradition of Sunday night hymn-singing in the White House?
35. Who began the "Speaker's Dinner," hosted by the president for the House speaker?
36. Which president hosted Charles Dickens in the White House?
37. Who ironically played both "Yankee Doodle" and "Dixie" at his last White House reception?
38. Who hosted a birthday party for Duke Ellington but mistook him for Cab Calloway?
39. Who asked his Cabinet member, "How are you, Mr. Mayor? I'm glad to meet you"?

Recreation

1. Which president liked to play poker, especially with many wild cards?
2. Which president liked playing bridge with his wife and another couple?
3. Which president liked playing card games, especially solitaire?
4. Which president's favorite card game was cribbage?
5. Which president hated playing bridge and resolved never to play it again in his life?
6. Which president admitted that he enjoyed swimming nude in the White House pool?
7. Which president was a daily skinny-dipper in the Potomac River?
8. Which president regularly swam in the near-frozen Potomac River?
9. Which president was the first one who took swimming lessons?
10. Which president enjoyed raffles and lotteries?
11. Which president applied to hold a lottery himself?
12. Which First Couple said they wished that opera were "one act shorter"?
13. What did Cabinet member Dean Acheson say was "one of [Herbert Hoover's] true joys"?
14. Which president first installed a horseshoe pit at the White House?
15. Which vice president organized for his boss a whip-cracking and sheep-herding show?
16. Which president liked to exercise on a $36 rowing machine?
17. Which president thought walking was the best possible form of exercise?
18. Which president was serious about his painting?
19. Which president had been a prizefighter?

24. Gerald Ford (1976), at the White House Bicentennial Ball.
25. President and Mrs. James Madison
26. Thomas Jefferson (1801)
27. Harry Truman (1945-1953), even to the cook or housekeeper.
28. Jimmy Carter (1978)
29. Herbert Hoover (1928)
30. Gerald Ford (1975), inflaming the passions of World War II veterans.
31. James Monroe (1817), because the British had burned the White House.
32. George Washington
33. Abraham Lincoln's
34. Rutherford Hayes (1877)
35. Theodore Roosevelt (1908), after Joseph Cannon disliked a seat assignment.
36. John Tyler (1842)
37. James Buchanan (1861), ironically because such ambivalence hastened the Civil War.
38. Richard Nixon (1969), at Ellington's seventieth birthday party.
39. Ronald Reagan (1981), to HUD Secretary Samuel Pierce, at a reception for mayors.

Recreation (answers)

1. Franklin Roosevelt
2. Dwight Eisenhower
3. Franklin Roosevelt
4. William McKinley's
5. Herbert Hoover
6. Lyndon Johnson. Richard Nixon converted the pool area into office space (1969).
7. John Quincy Adams (1825-1829). A reporter once sat on his clothes to get an interview.
8. Theodore Roosevelt (1901-1909)
9. John Quincy Adams (1827), in Boston, Massachusetts.
10. George Washington
11. Thomas Jefferson
12. President and Mrs. George Bush
13. Fly-fishing
14. Harry Truman. George Bush also enjoyed the sport.
15. Lyndon Johnson, at the LBJ Ranch, near Stonewall, Texas, on the day Kennedy was shot.
16. Benjamin Harrison
17. Thomas Jefferson
18. Dwight Eisenhower
19. James Buchanan

20. Which presidents were cockfighting enthusiasts?
21. Which presidents juggled to keep in shape?
22. Which president enjoyed tossing the medicine ball?
23. Which president attended the nation's first complete circus performance?
24. Which presidents collected marbles?
25. Which president especially enjoyed playing croquet?
26. Which president was adept at spitting contests?
27. Whose alleged 161-year-old slave did P. T. Barnum feature in his circus shows?
28. Which presidents were probably our most avid billiards players?
29. Which president was the first one who was an avid jogger, going for a run daily?
30. Which president hosted a stag party every Tuesday night?
31. Which president often used a scythe for exercise?
32. Which president often vacationed in Key West, Florida?
33. Which president forbade his wife, an accomplished dancer, to dance in public?
34. What percentage of his time did *Trivial Pursuit*® say Ronald Reagan spent on vacation?
35. Which president was an ardent dominoes player?
36. Which president was probably the most avid chess player?
37. Which president had led a local chapter of the YMCA?
38. Which president loved to window-shop, believing it calmed him?
39. Which president had Frank Sinatra listed as a reference on an application?
40. What was Richard Nixon's first public appearance after resigning?
41. Which president completed a marathon at any time in his life?

Religion

1. Which presidents were *not* members of an organized church?
2. Which president was a clergyman while in office?
3. Which president signed a charter for a synagogue?
4. Which president first allowed non-Christian clergymen to serve as military chaplains?
5. Which *incumbent* president first attended a synagogue service?
6. Which *incumbent* president first attended a Seder?
7. Which president first guaranteed Jewish federal employees observance of the Sabbath?
8. Which president first officially called for a homeland for the Jewish people?
9. For which president was a national Jewish award named?
10. Which president decided not to be baptized, which disappointed his parents greatly?
11. Which president was baptized for the first time *after* becoming president?
12. Which president converted to another denomination only one week before he died?
13. Which president had opposed the Episcopal Church as the official religion in his state?

20. George Washington and Andrew Jackson
21. James Garfield and Calvin Coolidge, with Indian clubs.
22. Herbert Hoover
23. George Washington (1793), by John Bill Ricketts, a well known showman, in Philadelphia.
24. George Washington, John Adams, and Thomas Jefferson
25. Rutherford Hayes. Chester Arthur installed a croquet lawn at the White House.
26. Andrew Jackson
27. George Washington's
28. George Washington and John Quincy Adams
29. Theodore Roosevelt. Also, George W. Bush was in the top 2% shape due to regular jogs.
30. George Washington
31. Calvin Coolidge
32. Harry Truman
33. Calvin Coolidge
34. 25%
35. Lyndon Johnson
36. James Madison
37. William McKinley (1862)
38. Calvin Coolidge
39. Ronald Reagan (1963), for a gambling license in Las Vegas, Nevada.
40. Dedicating the Richard M. Nixon Recreation Center in Hyden, Kentucky (1978).
41. George W. Bush (1993), who completed the Houston Marathon in 3:44:52.

Religion (answers)

1. Thomas Jefferson, Abraham Lincoln, and Andrew Johnson
2. James Garfield (1881)
3. Franklin Pierce (1856), for Washington Hebrew Congregation, the first one in the capital.
4. Abraham Lincoln (1862), who signed a congressional act.
5. Ulysses Grant (1874), for the dedication of Adas Israel Congregation in the capital.
6. William Taft (1912), at the home of Colonel Harry Cutler in Providence, Rhode Island.
7. Rutherford Hayes (1877)
8. Warren Harding (1922), who signed a joint resolution endorsing the Balfour Declaration.
9. John Kennedy (1963), the Kennedy Peace Award of the Synagogue Council of America.
10. Chester Arthur (1847)
11. Dwight Eisenhower (1953), who became a member of the National Presbyterian Church.
12. James Polk (1849), who became a Methodist.
13. James Monroe (1782), as a state representative.

14. Which president lighted the first National Christmas Tree for the Pageant of Peace?
15. Which two presidents issued particularly strong praise of the Roman Catholic Church?
16. Which *incumbent* presidents first and last met with a pope in the Vatican, respectively?
17. Which *incumbent* president was the last one who did *not* have a papal audience?
18. Which president, regarding his demeanor, said that he "would have made a good pope"?
19. Which president first established U.S. diplomatic relations with the Vatican?
20. Which four modern world leaders has the Vatican publicly condemned?

Revolutionary War

1. Who sent ships to France to retrieve John Paul Jones's corpse from an unmarked grave?
2. Which president had served Lord Stirling, a British general fighting for the Americans?
3. How long did George Washington believe the Revolutionary War would last?
4. Who followed George Washington everywhere, even in dirty, disease-ridden situations?
5. Which president had watched the Battle of Bunker Hill from atop nearby Penn's Hill?
6. Which president had served Edward Braddock, commander of British forces in America?
7. Which president was one of only two Americans wounded at the Battle of Trenton?
8. Who was George Washington's cavalry leader's son?
9. Who received the sword of capitulation from British General Charles O'Hara at Yorktown?
10. Which president had survived the cruel winter in Valley Forge with George Washington?

Royalty

1. Which president and his wife and son ate dinner at Windsor Castle with Queen Victoria?
2. Which president and royal debated who could best recite "The Shooting of Dan McGrew"?
3. Which president was it rumored had intended to start a royal dynasty?
4. Which president thought that Queen Elizabeth II was a good horseback rider?
5. How many times has the man of royal descent lost in a presidential election?
6. Which president escorted the future king of England on a tour of the Naval Academy?
7. Which British monarch asked Harry Truman for his autograph?
8. Which president was godfather to Prince Michael, first cousin of Queen Elizabeth II?
9. Which presidents were most closely related to the late Diana, Princess of Wales?
10. Which president, known for promiscuity, did the king of Saudi Arabia give harem clothes?
11. Which European prince's great-great-grandfather had been an aide to Ulysses Grant?
12. Which president helped open the Saint Lawrence Seaway?
13. Which president did the czar of Russia say was the best U.S. minister to his country?
14. Which president met Czar Nicholas II of Russia, the last czar of the Russian Empire?
15. Which president first received a queen?
16. Which president first received a king?

14. Dwight Eisenhower (1954)

15. Andrew Johnson and William Taft, the latter for its positions against socialism and anarchy.

16. Woodrow Wilson (1919), with Benedict XV, and George W. Bush (2002), with John Paul II.

17. Harry Truman (1945-1953), perhaps because he was a steadfast Mason.

18. Richard Nixon

19. Ronald Reagan (1984), who appointed William Wilson as the first U.S. ambassador.

20. Fidel Castro, Moammar Ghaddafi, Saddam Hussein, and Bill Clinton (1996)

Revolutionary War (answers)

1. Theodore Roosevelt (1905), for burial in a tomb in Annapolis, today a national shrine.

2. James Monroe (1777)

3. A few weeks

4. Martha Washington (1777-1781)

5. John Quincy Adams (1775), as an eight-year-old child.

6. George Washington (1755)

7. James Monroe (1776), where Americans routed the British and mercenary Hessians.

8. Robert E. Lee, who would marry Martha Washington's great-granddaughter.

9. General Benjamin Lincoln (1781), George Washington's subordinate.

10. James Monroe (1777-1778)

Royalty (answers)

1. Ulysses Grant (1877)

2. Ronald Reagan (1984) and the late Queen Mother, during a visit to London, England.

3. John Adams, by marrying his son to a daughter of King George III of England.

4. Ronald Reagan

5. Only once (1992), when George Bush lost to Bill Clinton.

6. Assistant Secretary of the Navy Franklin Roosevelt (1919)

7. King George VI (1945), aboard HMS *Renown*, after the Potsdam Conference.

8. Franklin Roosevelt. Prince Michael was given Roosevelt's first name as his fourth.

9. Washington, both Adamses, both Roosevelts, and Calvin Coolidge

10. Franklin Roosevelt

11. Prince Michael's (of Greece)

12. Dwight Eisenhower (1959), with Queen Elizabeth II.

13. James Buchanan

14. William Taft (1905)

15. Andrew Johnson (1866), who received Queen Emma of Hawaii.

16. Ulysses Grant (1874), who received King David Kalakuaa of Hawaii.

17. Which president first received a ruling European monarch?
18. Which president first received an absolute, not a constitutional, monarch?
19. Which president offered a British prince the Lincoln Bedroom while he slept on a sofa?
20. Which European queen strongly defended her country's rights against Woodrow Wilson?
21. Which *former* president attended the funeral of King Edward VII of England?
22. Which president hosted the Duke and Duchess of Windsor at the White House?
23. Which president appointed a special ambassador to the coronation of King George V?
24. Who said no monarch "would entitle him to be elected a vestryman"?
25. Which president did Queen Victoria say was the most handsome man she had ever seen?
26. Which president owned the only baseball autographed by a king?
27. Who was the only man to kiss the Queen Mother on the lips after her husband's death?

Salaries

1. Which president accepted his salary but returned it to the federal government?
2. Which president accepted his salary but donated it to charity?
3. Which president refused his salary?
4. Which Founding Father suggested that the president not have a salary?
5. What was the original presidential salary?
6. Who first earned $50,000 per year as president?
7. Who first earned $75,000 per year as president?
8. Who first earned $100,000 per year as president?
9. Who first earned $200,000 per year as president?
10. Who first earned $400,000 per year as president?
11. Which president first received a pension from the government?
12. Which former presidents first received annual lifetime pensions?
13. Which former president receives the highest annual lifetime pension?
14. On what is the president's annual lifetime pension income based?

Scandals

1. Which president had been an usher at his best friend's wedding and seduced his wife?
2. For whom did a strip-tease bar in Washington, DC, build a special viewing booth?
3. Which president allegedly had a thirty-eight-year romance with a woman?
4. Which presidents were involved in Teapot Dome, Watergate, Irangate, and Filegate?
5. Which president had been so upset by Teapot Dome that he became a public servant?
6. Which senators led investigations into the Harding Administration's iniquities?
7. Which scandal resulted in the Ghanian minister's being invited to the White House?
8. Which president's brokerage firm failed, throwing the U.S.A. into a small financial crisis?

17. Woodrow Wilson (1919), who received King Albert of Belgium.

18. Herbert Hoover (1931), who received Prajadhipoek, King of Siam.

19. James Buchanan (1860), to the future King Edward VII.

20. Queen Marie of Romania (1919), at the Paris Peace Conference.

21. Theodore Roosevelt (1910), at Windsor Castle, England.

22. Richard Nixon (1970)

23. William Taft (1911), who appointed John Hays Hammond, a gold magnate.

24. Thomas Jefferson (1788)

25. Millard Fillmore (1857)

26. Woodrow Wilson, autographed by King George V.

27. Jimmy Carter

Salaries (answers)

1. George Washington (1789-1797)

2. Herbert Hoover (1929-1933)

3. John Kennedy (1961-1963)

4. Benjamin Franklin

5. $25,000 per year

6. Ulysses Grant (1873)

7. William Taft (1909)

8. Harry Truman (1949)

9. Richard Nixon (1969)

10. George W. Bush (2001). The best paid chief executive is Singapore's (US $520,380).

11. James Monroe (1826), who received a one-time sum of $30,000 from Congress.

12. Herbert Hoover (1958-1964) and Harry Truman (1958-1972), $25,000 per year.

13. Bill Clinton (2001–), who receives $171,000 per year.

14. The salary of a Cabinet member

Scandals (answers)

1. Thomas Jefferson (1768), who seduced John Walker's wife, Betsey.

2. Warren Harding (1921-1923), to watch the show without being seen himself.

3. Thomas Jefferson (1788-1826), with his deceased wife's part-slave half-sister.

4. Warren Harding, Richard Nixon, Ronald Reagan, and Bill Clinton, respectively.

5. Richard Nixon, telling his mother that he would become a lawyer who could not be bribed.

6. Senator Thomas Walsh (D-MT) and Senator Burton Wheeler (D-MT) (1923-1924)

7. He was denied service at a restaurant (1957), so Eisenhower fed him at the White House.

8. Ulysses Grant's (1884), Grant & Ward, after the presidency. Ward had conned Grant.

9.   Whose aides considered using the Constitution to declare him incapable of serving?
10. Which president was arrested for jaywalking, in the District of Columbia?
11. Which president already was under investigation upon entering the presidency?

Science
1.   Which president received a U.S. patent?
2.   Which president is known as "The Father of the American Patent System"?
3.   Which president ordered that scale models held in the Patent Office be sold?
4.   Which president invented the dumbwaiter, thumbtack, pedometer, and calendar clock?
5.   Who invented the Lazy Susan, a revolving tray in a cabinet or on a table sharing food?
6.   Who invented the hand-cranked closing doors still seen in many yellow school buses?
7.   Which president first promised manned flight to the Moon?
8.   Who said, "This is the greatest week in the history of the world since Creation"?
9.   Which president's name is on the Moon?
10. Which president had filed a report with the Center for Unidentified Flying Objects Studies?
11. Which solar comet do some believe signaled the assassination of John Kennedy?
12. Which comet was the only one named for a president?
13. Which president's experiments helped the U.S.A. become a leader in rice production?
14. Which president signed the act creating the National Science Foundation?

Scouting
1.   Which president was the first one who had been a Boy Scout, chronologically?
2.   Which president was the first one who had been a Boy Scout, sequentially?
3.   Which president was an Eagle Scout?
4.   Which president first entered the White House with a record as an active Scout leader?
5.   Which other president had been a Boy Scoutmaster?
6.   Which president served on the national executive board of the Boy Scouts of America?
7.   Which president first became honorary president of the Boy Scouts of America?
8.   Which presidents first and last drafted messages to be read at Boy Scout Jamborees?
9.   Which presidents had attended or did attend Jamborees?
10. Which president first failed to address a Jamboree either in person or in writing?
11. Which president hosted the first annual meeting of the Boy Scouts of America?
12. Which president hosted the First National Explorer Presidents' Congress?
13. Which president helped establish a Scout post for pageboys working in Congress?
14. Which president signed the bill granting the Boy Scouts of America federal incorporation?
15. Which president was the only person ever designated "Chief Scout Citizen"?
16. Whom did journalist Walter Lippmann prematurely describe as "an amiable Boy Scout"?

9. Ronald Reagan's (1987), after Irangate, in *Landslide: The Unmaking of the President*.
10. Calvin Coolidge, mistakenly, by Captain Charles Findlay, the future governor of Maryland.
11. Bill Clinton (1993), for his potential role in the Whitewater scandal.

Science (answers)

1. Abraham Lincoln (1849), Patent #6469, a device to lift vessels over shoals more easily.
2. Thomas Jefferson
3. Calvin Coolidge (1928), after a fire destroyed half of them.
4. Thomas Jefferson, along with the folding bed, swivel chair, and revolving music stand.
5. Thomas Jefferson
6. Thomas Jefferson
7. Richard Nixon (1960), running for president. Kennedy called for it *as* president (1961).
8. Richard Nixon (1969), talking about the Moon landing.
9. Richard Nixon's (1969–), along with the Apollo 11 mission astronauts' names.
10. Jimmy Carter (1969), claiming he had seen a UFO in Leary, Georgia. It was Venus.
11. Comet Pereyra (1963)
12. Comet Hooveria (1920), by Austrian Johann Palisma, for his post-war food-relief efforts.
13. Thomas Jefferson's
14. Harry Truman (1950)

Scouting (answers)

1. Gerald Ford (1924-1927), with Troop 15, in Grand Rapids, Michigan.
2. John Kennedy (1929-1931), with Troop 2, in Bronxville, New York.
3. Gerald Ford (1927), also the only one who got the Distinguished Eagle Award (1970).
4. Franklin Roosevelt (1924-1928), as president of the Greater New York Councils.
5. Jimmy Carter, who also had been a troop committee chairman and Explorer Advisor.
6. Dwight Eisenhower (1948)
7. William Taft (1910). Bill Clinton is the only one since Taft *not* to serve in that capacity.
8. Franklin Roosevelt (1937) and Ronald Reagan (1985)
9. Truman (1921), Eisenhower (1960), Johnson (1964), and Bush (1989)
10. Bill Clinton (1994)
11. William Taft (1911), at the White House.
12. Richard Nixon (1971), at the White House.
13. Lyndon Johnson (1963), who helped form Post 1200, in Washington, DC.
14. Woodrow Wilson (1916)
15. Theodore Roosevelt (1910)
16. Franklin Roosevelt (1932)

Senate

1. Which senator-elect was elected president?
2. Which senator resigned three minutes after being sworn in?
3. Which *incumbent* senators were elected president?
4. Which *incumbent* senator last received a presidential nomination by a major party?
5. When were two occupants of the exact same Senate seat both on a national ticket?
6. Which *former* president became a senator?
7. Which presidents were the first and last ones who had been a senator?
8. Which president had headed a special Senate committee?
9. Which presidents first and last had been Senate committee chairmen?
10. Which president had been a party whip in the Senate?
11. Which Senate minority and Senate majority leaders last became president, respectively?
12. Which president had been the youngest Senate majority leader ever?
13. Which president had been elected president pro tempore of the Senate?
14. Who voted not to convict Andrew Johnson even though *he* would have become president?
15. When do all branches of the federal government work *simultaneously* in the same forum?
16. Which protections generally are *not* allowed to an impeached federal official?
17. What is the term used to refer to an impeached federal official during a Senate trial?
18. Which president had been an intern for Senator William Fulbright, while in college?
19. Which late Democratic senator had been a presidential assistant in the Nixon White House?
20. Which vice president never presided over the Senate as prescribed by the Constitution?
21. Which senator led the opposition to Woodrow Wilson's League of Nations?
22. Which president consulted personally with senators regarding foreign treaties?
23. Which president very remorsefully had left the Senate for the vice-presidency?
24. Who sits in the exact same Senate desk that John Kennedy did until 1961?
25. Which Southern senator opposed secession, swore fealty to the Union, and kept his seat?
26. Who dictated how many times messengers had to bow upon entering the Senate?
27. Which president had the Senate denied a ministerial appointment to a foreign country?
28. For which crucial vote were two seriously ill senators brought into the Senate chamber?
29. Which president had received less than 3% of the black vote in a Senate race?
30. How many of the Republican senators who acquitted Andrew Johnson kept their seats?
31. Which former president's rent income did the Senate inspect?
32. Which president had carried pistols onto the Senate floor?
33. Which president resigned from the Senate because his wife despised the capital city?
34. Which senator first resigned rather than make potentially embarrassing decisions?
35. Which senator had shot Andrew Jackson in a duel in Nashville, Tennessee?
36. Who nominated the father-in-law of General William Tecumseh Sherman for the Cabinet?
37. Which senator was the only member of his party to support the Louisiana Purchase?

Senate (answers)

1. James Garfield (1880), elected in summer and nominated for president shortly thereafter.
2. Lyndon Johnson (1961), to be sworn in as vice president seventeen days later.
3. Senator Warren Harding (R-OH) (1920) and Senator John Kennedy (D-MA) (1960)
4. Senator George McGovern (D-SD) (1972)
5. In 1960, with John Kennedy and his predecessor Henry Cabot Lodge on opposing tickets.
6. Andrew Johnson (1875), representing Tennessee. He had served there (1857-1862).
7. James Monroe (1790-1794) and Richard Nixon (1950-1953), respectively.
8. Harry Truman (1941), to investigate corruption in the National Defense Program.
9. James Buchanan (Foreign Relations) and Franklin Pierce (Pension), respectively.
10. Lyndon Johnson (1951-1953)
11. Lyndon Johnson, minority leader (1953-1954) and majority leader (1955-1960).
12. Lyndon Johnson (1955), at the age of forty-six years.
13. John Tyler (1835-1836)
14. Senator Benjamin Wade (R-OH), first in line if Johnson had been thrown out of office.
15. A trial of the president in the Senate, with the Supreme Court chief justice presiding.
16. Double jeopardy, self-incrimination, rules limiting evidence, burden of proof, and appeal
17. "Respondant," not "defendant."
18. Bill Clinton (1966-1967), then attending Georgetown University.
19. Senator Daniel Patrick Moynihan (D-NY) (1970-1973), as an urban-affairs adviser.
20. Rufus King (1853), because he died right after his term had begun.
21. Senator Henry Cabot Lodge (R-MA) (1919), father of Nixon's running mate (1960).
22. George Washington (1789-1790). All others have sent letters outlining their positions.
23. Harry Truman (1945), who said the "happiest ten years" of his life were in the Senate.
24. Senator Ted Kennedy (D-MA) (1961–), his brother.
25. Senator Andrew Johnson (R-TN) (1860), the only one who did so.
26. John Adams (1789-1797), as presiding officer.
27. Martin Van Buren (1832), as ambassador to the Court of St. James's, by one vote.
28. The vote to convict President Andrew Johnson (1868), which failed by a single vote.
29. George Bush (1964), a potential record low for a major-party nominee.
30. None out of seven
31. Theodore Roosevelt's (1910), which amounted to $10,000 per year.
32. Martin Van Buren (1836), as protection from Whig Senator George Poindexter.
33. Franklin Pierce (1842), only to return eleven years later as president.
34. Senator Andrew Jackson (1798), representing Tennessee.
35. Future Senator Thomas Hart Benton (D-MO) (1813)
36. Andrew Johnson (1868), who picked Thomas Ewing but was unable to gain confirmation.
37. John Quincy Adams (1803), because expansion meant more commerce.

38. Who was the only senator against a bill providing military enforcement of revenue laws?
39. Which senator is credited with wrecking Franklin Roosevelt's "court packing" plan?
40. Which president had actress Helen Gahagan Douglas opposed in a Senate race?
41. Which president urged life terms for senators as a check on the regularly-elected House?
42. Who said former presidents should be permanent, non-voting members of the Senate?
43. Which president walked onto the Senate floor and sat at his old desk?
44. Which *former* president made an appearance on the Senate floor?
45. Which president, in his maiden Senate speech, had "frozen" at the rostrum?
46. Which president had sponsored a rule opening the Senate chamber to the public?
47. Where were 200 votes allegedly "stuffed" in favor of Lyndon Johnson in a Senate race?
48. Which president since the Civil War *re*-gained a Senate majority during a midterm election?

Senate Composition

1. Which presidents were the first and last ones with a majority in the Senate?
2. Which presidents were the first and last ones *without* a majority in the Senate?
3. Which presidents were the first and last ones with a veto-proof majority in the Senate?
4. Which presidents were the first and last ones *without* a veto-proof majority in the Senate?
5. Which presidents were the only ones with a veto-proof majority of the opposition party?
6. Which Democratic presidents had the fewest and most Senate Democrats?
7. Which Democratic presidents had the fewest and most Senate Republicans?
8. Which Republican presidents had the fewest and most Senate Democrats?
9. Which Republican presidents had the fewest and most Senate Republicans?
10. Which Democratic presidents had the tiniest and largest portions of Senate Democrats?
11. Which Democratic presidents had the tiniest and largest portions of Senate Republicans?
12. Which Republican presidents had the tiniest and largest portions of Senate Democrats?
13. Which Republican presidents had the tiniest and largest portions of Senate Republicans?

Ships

1. Which U.S. warship first circumnavigated the globe?
2. Which ship sank while transporting 6,500 American troops to the Pacific Theater?
3. On which aircraft carrier did Gerald Ford serve during World War II?
4. Which president had an impressive collection of naval prints and ship models?
5. Which ship was supposed to pick up the Apollo 11 crew after splashdown?
6. Which former president argued at the Supreme Court to free fifty-three slave mutineers?
7. Which president officially opened the Panama Canal?
8. Who remotely fired a cannon to mark the opening of the Houston Ship Channel?
9. Which ship carried Woodrow Wilson to the Paris Peace Conference after World War I?

38. John Tyler (1832). President Andrew Jackson had sponsored the bill.
39. Senator Burton K. Wheeler (R-MT)
40. Richard Nixon (1950), who said, "She's pink right down to her underwear."
41. John Adams (1779), whose draft of the Massachusetts Constitution included such terms.
42. Harry Truman (1935), with privileges of speaking on the floor and in committee.
43. Harry Truman (1947). The astonished presiding officer recognized him to speak.
44. Harry Truman (1964), a year after the Senate allowed former presidents to debate there.
45. Martin Van Buren (1831), speaking about a land transaction in Louisiana.
46. James Monroe (1794), before which time it always had been closed to the public.
47. Alice, Texas (1948). Dozens of persons, some dead, voted *in alphabetical order*!
48. George W. Bush (2002), when Republicans won two seats and a majority, 51-48-1.

Senate Composition (answers)

1. George Washington (1789-1791) and George W. Bush (2003-2005), respectively.
2. John Quincy Adams (1827-1829) and George W. Bush (2001-2003), respectively.
3. Thomas Jefferson (1803-1809) and Lyndon Johnson (1965-1967), respectively.
4. George Washington (1789-1791) and George W. Bush (2001-2005), respectively.
5. None
6. Andrew Jackson (20) and Franklin Roosevelt (76), respectively.
7. Franklin Pierce (15) and Bill Clinton (55), respectively.
8. Abraham Lincoln (9) and Dwight Eisenhower (64), respectively.
9. Abraham Lincoln (31) and Theodore Roosevelt/William Taft (61), respectively.
10. Grover Cleveland (44.2%) and Franklin Roosevelt (79.2%), respectively.
11. Franklin Roosevelt (16.7%) and Grover Cleveland (55.8%), respectively.
12. Ulysses Grant (16.4%) and Dwight Eisenhower (65.3%), respectively.
13. Gerald Ford (37.0%) and Ulysses Grant (83.6%), respectively.

Ships (answers)

1. The USS *Vincennes* (1829-1831), sent by Andrew Jackson to protect Pacific commerce.
2. The USS *President Coolidge* (1942), near the New Hebrides, with the loss of two lives.
3. The USS *Monterey* (1943-1945)
4. Franklin Roosevelt
5. The USS *John F. Kennedy* (1969), but Nixon ordered the USS *Hornet* to go instead.
6. John Quincy Adams (1841), from the *Amistad*. Incumbent Martin Van Buren opposed it.
7. Woodrow Wilson (1914)
8. Woodrow Wilson (1914). The Houston Ship Channel is our third most important port.
9. The USS *George Washington* (1919), which ship Harry Truman later sent to war.

10. Which president signed the Atlantic Charter on board the HMS *Prince of Wales*?

11. Who was sent to England to bring home American survivors of the SS *Athenia* sinking?

12. Which ship's manifest listing munitions sent to England did Woodrow Wilson order hidden?

13. Which president swam 300 yards offshore to inspect the Confederate ironclad *Merrimac*?

14. Which ship took Arctic explorer Admiral Robert Peary to the North Pole?

15. For which presidents were U.S. ships named?

16. Which U.S. ships were named for living former presidents?

17. Which *incumbent* presidents spent the night on board an aircraft carrier?

18. Who said he doubted "that there has been anything in heroism equal to this"?

Signatures

1. Which president first used secretarial (proxy) signatures for official documents?

2. Which president was the *last* one required to sign ships' papers personally?

3. Which presidents first and last used rubber-stamp signatures for official documents?

4. Which president first complied with requests for autographs?

5. Which president first and last used rubber-stamp signatures for official correspondence?

6. Which president first used proxy signatures for official correspondence?

7. Which *former* president last used the presidential franking privilege extensively?

8. Which president first used the mechanical signature, or "autopen"?

9. Which president first used the mechanical signature, or "autopen," on a daily basis?

10. Whose "frank," the signature granting him free postage, is probably the most valuable?

11. Which presidents' autographs had the lowest and highest *average* retail price in 1998?

12. Which president first complained about the deluge of documents requiring his signature?

13. Which president almost never signed his full name but just his first initial and last name?

14. Which presidents were the only ones who were autograph collectors?

Sleep

1. Who always went to sleep at 9:00 P.M. and made White House guests leave at that time?

2. Which president could get by with only four hours of sleep each night?

3. Which president always rose at dawn?

4. Which president could fall asleep in minutes, and often did so in public?

5. Which president slept eleven hours a day and frequently needed a nap?

Slogans

1. Which presidential campaign featured the slogan "In your heart, you know he's right"?

2. Which presidential campaign featured the slogan "In your guts, you know he's nuts"?

10. Franklin Roosevelt (1941)
11. John Kennedy (1939), by his father, Ambassador Joseph P. Kennedy.
12. The *Lusitania*'s, in the Treasury, wanting it to appear the ship was carrying only civilians.
13. Theodore Roosevelt (1916), from Havana, Cuba, to inspect the ruins.
14. The *Roosevelt* (1909)
15. Washington, Lincoln, T. Roosevelt, Truman, Eisenhower, Reagan, and George Bush
16. The USS *Ronald Reagan* (2001) and the USS *George H. W. Bush* (2002)
17. Bill Clinton (1993) and George W. Bush (2003)
18. Harry Truman (1945), about chaplains' giving life jackets to GIs as the *Dorchester* sank.

Signatures (answers)
1. Andrew Jackson
2. Abraham Lincoln
3. Andrew Johnson and Theodore Roosevelt, respectively.
4. Rutherford Hayes, with autographed cards and "Executive Mansion" engraved at the top.
5. Theodore Roosevelt and Herbert Hoover, respectively.
6. Warren Harding
7. Dwight Eisenhower, although he used a printed frank, not a signature frank.
8. Dwight Eisenhower
9. John Kennedy (1961-1963)
10. James Polk's
11. Gerald Ford's ($88) and George Washington's ($4,750), respectively.
12. John Adams (1797)
13. Zachary Taylor
14. Franklin Roosevelt and John Kennedy

Sleep (answers)
1. George Washington. George W. Bush is also well known for going to sleep early.
2. Gerald Ford
3. John Quincy Adams
4. William Taft (1909-1913), who fell asleep at funerals several times.
5. Calvin Coolidge (1923-1929)

Slogans (answers)
1. The 1964 Republican presidential campaign
2. The 1964 Democratic presidential campaign

3. Which presidential campaign featured the slogan "A Full Dinner Pail for All"?
4. Which presidential campaign featured the slogan "New Frontier"?
5. Which presidential campaign featured the slogan "Free Wool"?
6. Which presidential campaign featured the slogan "Life, Liberty, and Landon"?
7. Which presidential campaign featured the slogan "Fifty-Four Forty or Fight!"
8. Which presidential campaign featured the slogan "Win with Whiskers"?
9. Which presidential campaign featured the slogan "Rugged Individualism"?
10. Which presidential campaign featured the slogan "Had Enough?"
11. Which presidential campaign featured the slogan "Grant Us Another Term"?
12. Which presidential campaign featured the slogan "Roosevelt for Ex-President"?
13. Which presidential campaign featured the slogan "Get This Country Moving Again"?
14. Which presidential campaign featured the slogan "Where's the Beef?"
15. Which presidential campaign featured the slogan "Come Home, America"?
16. Which presidential campaign featured the slogan "America First"?
17. Which presidential campaign featured the slogan "Two Chickens in Every Pot"?
18. Which presidential campaign featured the slogan "Thousand Points of Light"?
19. Which presidential campaign featured the slogan "Grits and Fritz"?
20. Which presidential campaign first included a labor slogan?
21. What was Gerald Ford's anti-inflation slogan, which led to a slogan fad?
22. Who invented the term "New Deal"?
23. How did Theodore Roosevelt's "Square Deal" term originate?
24. In which city did the term "Give 'em hell, Harry!" originate?
25. Which presidents used the slogan "Don't swap horses in the middle of the stream"?

Smoking

1. Which president was the first one who was a regular smoker?
2. Which president was the first one who smoked cigarettes regularly?
3. Which presidents smoked three and four packs of cigarettes per day?
4. Which president smoked cigarettes often but always hid them from photographers?
5. Which president was the first one who smoked cigars regularly?
6. Who requested his aides carry his cigars wrapped in tin foil to prevent bending?
7. Which president maintained a significant pipe collection?
8. Which president was the most renowned pipe-smoking president?
9. Which president particularly enjoyed chewing tobacco?
10. Which presidents were first thought to and known to have smoked marijuana?
11. Which president smoked occasionally from the age of *eight* years?
12. Which president banned smoking inside the White House, even at state dinners?
13. Which modern president strongly disapproved of women's smoking?

3. The 1892 Democratic presidential campaign
4. The 1960 Democratic presidential campaign
5. The 1888 Democratic presidential campaign, urging free trade, not protective tariffs.
6. The 1936 Republican presidential campaign
7. The 1844 Democratic presidential campaign, for acquisition of Oregon to that parallel.
8. The 1916 Republican presidential campaign, referring to their candidates' hirsuteness.
9. The 1928 Republican presidential campaign
10. The 1944 Republican presidential campaign
11. The 1872 Republican presidential campaign
12. The 1940 Republican presidential campaign
13. The 1960 Democratic presidential campaign
14. The 1984 Democratic presidential campaign
15. The 1972 Democratic presidential campaign
16. The 1920 Democratic presidential campaign. Patrick Buchanan used it in 1992 and 1996.
17. The 1928 Republican presidential campaign
18. The 1988 Republican presidential campaign, meaning persons serving their fellow man.
19. The 1976 Democratic presidential campaign
20. The 1840 Whig presidential campaign, "No reduction of the price of labour."
21. WIN (1974), an acronym for "Whip Inflation Now."
22. Mark Twain (1889), in Chapter XIII of *A Connecticut Yankee in King Arthur's Court*.
23. From efforts to give striking coal miners a "square deal" in resolving their labor dispute
24. Albuquerque, New Mexico (1948), when somebody yelled it out during a campaign stop.
25. Abraham Lincoln (1864), Herbert Hoover (1932), and Franklin Roosevelt (1944)

Smoking (answers)

1. John Quincy Adams, which he started while contemplating John Milton's *Paradise Lost*.
2. Chester Arthur (1881)
3. Lyndon Johnson (until 1959) and Dwight Eisenhower (until 1949), respectively.
4. Herbert Hoover (1929-1933)
5. Ulysses Grant (1869-1877), who, like William McKinley, smoked up to twenty cigars daily!
6. John Kennedy (1961-1963)
7. Andrew Jackson
8. Gerald Ford (1974-1976), often smoking ten bowls each day.
9. Zachary Taylor
10. John Kennedy (1961) and Bill Clinton (1992), respectively.
11. John Adams (1743-1826)
12. Bill Clinton (1993-2001), perhaps as a political statement against "Big Tobacco."
13. Herbert Hoover (1929)

Songs

1. In whose honor was "Wreaths for the Chieftain," precursor of "Hail to Chief," first played?
2. Which incumbent president first heard "Wreaths for the Chieftain," by the Marine Band?
3. Who renamed it "Hail to the Chief" and asked that it be played when a president appears?
4. Which president replaced "Hail to the Chief" with "Presidential Polonaise," by Sousa?
5. Which president banned any rendition of "Hail to the Chief" during his tenure?
6. What was the name of the nation's first national anthem?
7. Which president signed the act making "The Star-Spangled Banner" the national anthem?
8. Which president made Sousa's "Stars and Stripes Forever" our official national march?
9. Why do the Beach Boys not play their song "Warmth of the Sun" anymore?
10. Who said he knew two tunes, "one . . . is 'Yankee Doodle' and the other one isn't"?
11. For which president did black composer Al Jolson create a unique tune?
12. Which song was Lyndon Johnson's favorite?
13. Which president sang a song with jazz great Dizzy Gillespie at the White House?

Spanish-American War

1. Who was in charge of the "Rough Riders" in Cuba during the Spanish-American War?
2. Which one of Roosevelt's "Rough Riders" was Thomas Edison's brother-in-law?
3. Where were most of the "Rough Riders" trained?
4. Up which hill did Theodore Roosevelt and his "Rough Riders" charge in Cuba?
5. How did Theodore Roosevelt charge up Kettle Hill?
6. Who said before the Spanish-American War began that the U.S.A. would not invade Cuba?

Speeches

1. Who was the first person who devoted most of his time to presidential speech writing?
2. For which president was author John Steinbeck a speechwriter?
3. For which president was Peter Benchley, the author of *Jaws*, a speechwriter?
4. Which president first had speechwriters called by that title?
5. Which president liked to type at least the first draft of all his speeches?
6. Which president last wrote and delivered his own speeches?
7. Who delivered the first commencement address at George Washington University?
8. Who delivered the inaugural address at American University in Washington, DC?
9. Which post-Civil War president first advocated black civil rights while in the South?
10. Who delivered his acceptance speech for president from Leland Stanford Coliseum?
11. Where did John Kennedy deliver his "Ich bin ein Berliner" speech?
12. Where did Lyndon Johnson unveil his "Great Society" domestic program?

Songs (answers)

1. George Washington (1815), in Boston, Massachusetts, on the anniversary of his birth.
2. John Quincy Adams (1828), at a ceremony for the Chesapeake and Ohio Canal.
3. First Lady Julia Tyler (1844), based upon Sir Walter Scott's poem "The Lady of the Lake."
4. Chester Arthur (1881). It never caught on, his successors reverted to "Hail to the Chief."
5. Jimmy Carter (1977-1981), because he thought it was too ostentatious.
6. "God Save Great Washington" (1776), set to the British anthem "God Save the King."
7. Herbert Hoover (1931)
8. Ronald Reagan (1987). The national anthem also received congressional recognition.
9. Released in 1964, it reminds them too much of John Kennedy's death (1963).
10. Ulysses Grant
11. Warren Harding (1920), entitled "Harding, You're the Man for Us."
12. "The Yellow Rose of Texas" (1853)
13. Jimmy Carter (1978), with whom he sang "Salt Peanuts" (1945).

Spanish-American War (answers)

1. Colonel Leonard Wood (1898). Theodore Roosevelt was second in command.
2. Theodore Westwood Miller, who died in Cuba fighting in the Spanish-American War.
3. On the old fair grounds in San Antonio, Texas (1898).
4. Kettle Hill, not San Juan Hill as is commonly believed.
5. On horses, not afoot as is commonly believed.
6. William McKinley (1898), five days before the invasion began.

Speeches (answers)

1. Judson Welliver (1921), for Warren Harding.
2. Franklin Roosevelt (1937)
3. Lyndon Johnson (1967-1969)
4. Richard Nixon (1969), including Pat Buchanan, David Gergen, and Ben Stein.
5. Woodrow Wilson (1915-1921)
6. Herbert Hoover (1933)
7. James Madison (1821)
8. Woodrow Wilson (1914)
9. Warren Harding (1921), at the University of Alabama.
10. Herbert Hoover (1928)
11. At the Free University of Berlin in Berlin, Germany (1963).
12. The University of Michigan at Ann Arbor (1964), in a commencement speech.

13. Which presidents made commencement addresses at the University of Texas at Austin?
14. Who delivered the address at the Masonic fraternity's centennial of Washington's death?
15. Which presidents first and last spoke before the United Nations General Assembly?
16. Which president first addressed a joint session of the British Parliament?
17. Which president first addressed the Russian Parliament?
18. Which president first addressed a national convention of the Jaycees?
19. Which president first addressed a national meeting of Future Farmers of America (FFA)?
20. Which president had won a debate prize defending the Catholic Church?
21. Who was the only person to vote against war after Roosevelt's "day of infamy" speech?
22. Which president first appeared with Richard Nixon in the capital after his resignation?
23. Which president often began his speeches with "My fellow Americans . . ."?
24. Which presidents spoke at the Rebild festival for Danish and American independence?
25. Which president's public speaking was the worst, in terms of mangling the language?
26. Who coined the phrases "read my lips" and "kinder, gentler nation"?
27. Which Democratic president said he would cut spending and balance the federal budget?
28. Which president spoke where Churchill had delivered his "curtain of iron" speech?
29. Who said there is the "Mother Hubbard" speech covering everything?
30. To which president did Dan Quayle compare himself while debating Lloyd Bentsen?
31. Where did Richard Nixon make his first major appearance after leaving office?
32. Which president holds a world record for the highest speed of public speaking?
33. Which president's public speaking was the dullest, rarely lifting his eyes from his text?
34. Which president counted the times he got applause during a speech to Congress?
35. How many debates did Lincoln and Douglas have during their Senate campaign?
36. Which *incumbent* president first addressed a major homosexual gathering?
37. Which president first gave a speech timed for a prime-time audience in another country?
38. Which president's speech was the first one recorded for posterity?
39. Which presidential campaign was the first one with recorded campaign speeches?
40. When did James Monroe make his famous "Monroe Doctrine" speech before Congress?
41. Which president found James Monroe's speeches so "vacuous" that he parodied them?
42. Which president is probably the only one who offered a full-length speech in French?
43. Which president knew the St. Crispin's Day speech from *King Henry V* by heart?
44. Which president took pride in memorizing Martin Luther King's "I Have a Dream" speech?
45. Which president delivered a speech at the San Jacinto Battleground?
46. Which president probably was the first one who 100,000 persons heard speak in person?

Sports
1. Which president received the MacMillan Cup for winning the College Sailing Championship?
2. Which president founded the NCAA to make football "a rather less homicidal pastime"?

13. Lyndon Johnson (1973) and George Bush (1990)
14. William McKinley (1899), himself a Mason, initiated in 1865, in Winchester, Virginia.
15. Dwight Eisenhower (1953) and George W. Bush (2003), respectively.
16. Ronald Reagan (1982)
17. Bill Clinton (2000)
18. Dwight Eisenhower (1953)
19. Dwight Eisenhower (1953). Ford, Carter, Reagan, and George Bush did so as well.
20. Woodrow Wilson (1879), at the University of Virginia.
21. Representative Jeanette Rankin (R-MT) (1941), who had voted against World War I also.
22. George Bush (1992), at the Four Seasons Hotel.
23. Lyndon Johnson
24. Richard Nixon (1962), Ronald Reagan (1972), and George Bush (1983)
25. Warren Harding's
26. White House speechwriter Peggy Noonan (1988)
27. Franklin Roosevelt (1932), before the largest growth ever of the federal government.
28. Ronald Reagan (1990), at Westminster College, in Fulton, Missouri.
29. Lyndon Johnson, and the "bikini" speech covering the essential points.
30. John Kennedy (1988), prompting Bentsen to retort, "Dan, you're no Jack Kennedy."
31. At a meeting of the American Society of Newspaper Editors (1984), for a speech.
32. John Kennedy (1961), at 327 words per minute, almost six words per second!
33. Herbert Hoover's (1929-1933)
34. Lyndon Johnson (1965), who counted to eighty and bragged about it later!
35. Seven (1858)
36. Bill Clinton (1997), for the Human Rights Campaign.
37. Ronald Reagan (1983), to influence European opinion about ballistic missiles in Germany.
38. Benjamin Harrison's (1889)
39. The 1908 presidential campaign
40. December 2, 1823
41. Theodore Roosevelt, in parlor readings.
42. John Kennedy (1961)
43. Franklin Roosevelt
44. Bill Clinton
45. Franklin Roosevelt (1936), where the Texas Army defeated the Mexicans.
46. Ulysses Grant (1877), in Newcastle, England, during his world tour.

Sports (answers)

1. John Kennedy (1939), for Harvard University, with his brother, Joseph Kennedy, Jr.
2. Theodore Roosevelt (1906), after eighteen deaths.

3. Which *future* presidents officially inaugurated Olympiads?

4. Which *incumbent* president officially opened a Winter Olympiad?

5. Which presidents officially opened Summer Olympiads?

6. Who won respect from the Clark's Grove Boys gang by beating its leader at wrestling?

7. Which president had been a college wrestling champion for two years?

8. Which president arm-wrestled Dan Lurie, publisher of *Muscle Training Illustrated*?

9. Which president was the most ardent polo player?

10. Who started the presidential tradition of calling champions in their locker rooms?

11. Which president invented the "obstacle walk" for hiking parties?

12. Which president had been a champion track runner?

13. Which president had outrun the fastest man in town with a handicap of half the distance?

14. Which *incumbent* president first attended a professional hockey game?

15. Which president probably was the one only who had earned a belt in judo?

16. Which *incumbent* president attended a running of the Kentucky Derby?

17. For which president was a popular athletic game named?

18. Which president is the only one who called play-by-play in any professional competition?

Stamps

1. During which president's tenure were U.S. postage stamps first issued?

2. Which president first appeared on a U.S. stamp?

3. Which president first appeared on a U.S. stamp derived from a photograph?

4. Which president by far appears on more U.S. postage stamps than any other?

5. Which president's residence first appeared on a U.S. stamp?

6. Which president's quotation first appeared on a U.S. stamp?

7. Which presidents' signatures appear on U.S. stamps?

8. Which president first appeared on a U.S. airmail stamp?

9. Which president mailed the first letter on the first regular U.S. airmail service?

10. Which president first appeared on an official government issue of "mourning stamps"?

11. Who is runner-up for the most different "mourning stamps" issued in his honor?

12. Which presidents first appeared on Confederate postage stamps?

13. Which foreign country first issued a stamp commemorating a U.S. president?

14. Which presidents had the fewest commemorative stamps issued by foreign countries?

15. Which president has been commemorated on the most foreign stamps?

16. Which South American country first issued a stamp commemorating a U.S. president?

17. Which Asian country first issued a stamp commemorating a U.S. president?

18. Which African country first issued a stamp commemorating a U.S. president?

19. Which Communist country first issued a stamp commemorating a U.S. president?

3. Franklin Roosevelt (1932, in Lake Placid) and Richard Nixon (1960, in Squaw Valley)
4. George W. Bush (2002, in Salt Lake City)
5. Ronald Reagan (1984, in Los Angeles) and Bill Clinton (1996, in Atlanta)
6. Abraham Lincoln
7. William Taft (1878), for Yale University, in the heavyweight division.
8. Ronald Reagan (1984)
9. Theodore Roosevelt, reducing the players from four to three for more action.
10. Richard Nixon (1969)
11. Theodore Roosevelt, going from one point to another in a line no matter the obstacle.
12. Rutherford Hayes (1843), at Kenyon University.
13. Andrew Jackson
14. Bill Clinton (1998), when the Sabres defeated the Capitals at MCI Center, in Washington, DC.
15. Theodore Roosevelt (1904), who had earned a brown belt.
16. Richard Nixon (1969). Others who attended include Truman and both Bushes.
17. Herbert Hoover (1928), for whom "Hooverball," a game similar to volleyball, was named.
18. Ronald Reagan (1988), who called an inning from Wrigley Field, in Chicago, Illinois.

Stamps (answers)

1. James Polk's (1847)
2. George Washington (1847), on the first stamp issued by the federal government.
3. Abraham Lincoln (1861)
4. George Washington (143)
5. George Washington's, Mount Vernon.
6. Abraham Lincoln's (1948), "That government of the people, by the people . . . ."
7. George Washington's, Thomas Jefferson's, and Abraham Lincoln's
8. Abraham Lincoln (1866), on a fifteen-cent postage stamp.
9. Woodrow Wilson (1918)
10. Warren Harding (1923), on a two-cent, black postage stamp.
11. John Kennedy, on 183 stamps and 32 miniature sheets, second only to Winston Churchill.
12. Thomas Jefferson, George Washington, and Andrew Jackson (1861)
13. France (1927), of George Washington and the Marquis de Lafayette.
14. William Henry Harrison, Tyler, Buchanan, Benjamin Harrison, Coolidge, and Hoover (1)
15. John Kennedy (175), followed by Washington, Lincoln, and Franklin Roosevelt.
16. Paraguay (1928), of Rutherford Hayes, for his part in mediating the Gran Chaco War.
17. The Philippines (1935), of George Washington.
18. Liberia (1945), of Franklin Roosevelt, for reviewing troops there on his way to a summit.
19. Cuba (1965), of Abraham Lincoln, for the centenary of his death.

20. Which foreign country has issued the most stamps commemorating presidents?
21. Which European countries have issued the most stamps commemorating presidents?
22. Which South American country has issued the most stamps commemorating presidents?
23. Which Asian country has issued the most stamps commemorating presidents?
24. Which president was first honored on "mourning stamps" issued by a foreign country?
25. Which foreign country commemorated every president in a single stamp issue?
26. Which foreign countries have issued stamps of a president with his stamp collection?
27. Which president was commemorated on a stamp by an Arab political entity?
28. Which president took at least one stamp album with him *everywhere*?
29. With which collector and future Cabinet member did Franklin Roosevelt correspond?
30. Which president's collection had more than 1,200,000 stamps and sold for $228,000?
31. Which president approved the design and color of the stamps issued during his tenure?
32. Which president used breaks in Cabinet meetings to consider proposals for new stamps?
33. Which president is pictured with Dr. Sun Yat-Sen in a three-cent blue U.S. airmail stamp?
34. Which U.S. stamp with a likeness of a president is the highest denomination?
35. Which presidents were in the first pictorial stamp series with different motifs per value?
36. During which Administration did the cost of a regular first-class stamp actually *decrease*?

State of the Union

1. Which president first presented an Annual Message?
2. Which presidents did *not* deliver an Annual Message?
3. Which president first delivered an Annual Message in the new Capitol Building?
4. Which president first delivered an Annual Message in person?
5. Which president first broadcast an Annual Message on radio?
6. Which president first broadcast a State of the Union Address on television?
7. Which president first broadcast a State of the Union Address live on the Internet?
8. Which presidents made the shortest and longest Annual Messages in number of words?
9. Which presidents made the shortest and longest Annual Messages in number of minutes?
10. Which president first delivered a State of the Union Address by that name?
11. Which president since then called his State of the Union Address something different?
12. Which president called a State of the Union Address the "State of *My* Union Address"?
13. Which president termed the Annual Message "a speech from the throne"?
14. Which president often edited his State of the Union Address in the ride to the Capitol?
15. Which president first recognized a guest while making a State of the Union Address?
16. Who must stay away from the Capitol during a president's State of the Union Address?
17. Which president's State of the Union Address first drew a response from the opposition?
18. Which woman first offered her party's response to a State of the Union Address?

20. Liberia (51)
21. Poland and Turkey (4)
22. Ecuador (23)
23. The Philippines (13)
24. Franklin Roosevelt (1945), by Greece, Haiti, Honduras, Hungary, and Nicaragua.
25. Liberia (1981), which issued the series honoring Washington through Reagan, inclusive.
26. Monaco, Nicaragua, and American Samoa, featuring Franklin Roosevelt.
27. John Kennedy, by Ajman, Dubai, Fujeira, Sharjah, Jordan, and Qatar.
28. Franklin Roosevelt (1933-1945)
29. Robert F. Kennedy, attorney general (1961-1965).
30. Franklin Roosevelt's
31. Franklin Roosevelt, who approved 134 commemoratives and forty-nine regular stamps.
32. Franklin Roosevelt
33. Abraham Lincoln (1955)
34. Calvin Coolidge (1938), on a $5 stamp.
35. George Washington and Abraham Lincoln (1869)
36. Chester Arthur's (1881-1885), from three cents to two cents.

State of the Union (answers)

1. George Washington (1789)
2. William Henry Harrison and James Garfield, dying before their first full years in office.
3. John Adams (1800)
4. Woodrow Wilson (1913), whose predecessors had chosen written argument or debate.
5. Calvin Coolidge (1923)
6. Harry Truman (1947)
7. George W. Bush (2002)
8. George Washington (1790), at 833, and Harry Truman (1946), at 25,000, respectively.
9. George Washington (1790), at 4, and Bill Clinton (2000), at 89, respectively.
10. Harry Truman (1947)
11. Bill Clinton (1993), who called his speech "An Address to the Nation."
12. Lyndon Johnson
13. Thomas Jefferson (1801), starting its demise for 110 years.
14. Bill Clinton
15. Ronald Reagan (1982), a tradition followed by each of his successors as president.
16. One Cabinet member goes on "Doomsday duty" to preserve the presidential succession.
17. Lyndon Johnson's (1966), delivered by Senator Everett Dirksen and Rep. Gerald Ford.
18. Governor Christine Whitman (1995), to Bill Clinton's State of the Union Address.

19. Which president delivered a State of the Union Address from the White House?
20. Which president did Bob Hope say gave a State of the Union Address in sign language?

States

1. Which president proposed the creation of and mapped fourteen new states?
2. Which presidents first and last followed a president from the same state, respectively?
3. Who was the first president of the forty-eight contiguous states?
4. Who sent William Tecumseh Sherman to survey in New Mexico, Arizona, and California?
5. Which president opened up Oklahoma American Indian territory to whites?
6. Which president gave part of Texas back to Mexico?
7. For which president was the State of Colorado originally named?
8. During which president's Administration was the District of Columbia first a territory?
9. Which president first represented a state West of the Mississippi River?
10. Which president's Administration saw more states admitted to the Union than any other?
11. Which president said that California and Arizona were too distant to become states?

Statues and Memorials

1. Who designed the Jefferson Memorial and created the statue of him inside it?
2. Which president dedicated the Jefferson Memorial on the bicentennial of Jefferson's birth?
3. Who designed the Lincoln Memorial and created the statue of him inside it?
4. Which president dedicated the Lincoln Memorial?
5. Which president often made a pilgrimage to the Lincoln Memorial on Lincoln's birthday?
6. Which president specifically requested that no statues be dedicated to him?
7. At which president's tomb is it considered good luck to rub the nose of his statue?
8. Which equestrian statue in Washington, DC, is the second-largest one in the world?
9. Of which famous president was only one statue sculpted while he posed?
10. Of which president was Jimilu Mason commissioned to make an official bust?
11. Which presidents' busts have been inducted into the Hall of Fame for Great Americans?
12. Which president's statue in Athens, Greece, was bombed by militant leftists?
13. Which presidential monument, the world's largest masonry structure, stands tallest?
14. Which president's statue has a left ear intentionally omitted by its sculptor?
15. Which presidential monument's dedication took place on July 4?
16. Which president's hometown took fifty years after his death to honor him with a statue?
17. Which president's bust appears in the private dining room of the secretary of state?
18. Which president's statue stands in London's Grosvenor Square, near the U.S. Embassy?
19. Which president's statue was ridiculed when it appeared bare-chested in a Roman toga?
20. Which president's statue stands in front of the city hall of Buffalo, New York?

19. Franklin Roosevelt (1944), after having contracted the flu.
20. Calvin Coolidge (1925)

States (answers)

1. Thomas Jefferson (1801-1809)
2. James Madison (1809), from Virginia, and James Garfield (1881), from Ohio.
3. William Taft (1912)
4. Zachary Taylor (1849)
5. Benjamin Harrison (1889)
6. Lyndon Johnson (1964), a strip of land along the Rio Grande that had shifted.
7. Thomas Jefferson (1860), named the State of Jefferson.
8. Ulysses Grant's (1871), so that a territorial government could be established for DC.
9. Zachary Taylor (1849), who was from Louisiana.
10. Benjamin Harrison's (1893-1897), when ID, MT, ND, SD, WA, and WY were admitted.
11. Zachary Taylor (1849), to James Polk, suggesting they become an independent country.

Statues and Memorials (answers)

1. John Russell Pope (1936) and Rudulph Evans (1942), respectively.
2. Franklin Roosevelt (1943)
3. Henry Bacon (1914) and Daniel Chester French (1920), respectively.
4. Warren Harding (1922)
5. Harry Truman (February 12)
6. Franklin Roosevelt (1945). It was honored for decades but eventually overlooked.
7. Abraham Lincoln's, in Springfield, Illinois.
8. Ulysses Grant's, on the Mall. The largest one is Victor Emmanuel's, in Rome, Italy.
9. George Washington, at the State Capitol Building in Richmond, Virginia.
10. Lyndon Johnson (1959). Mason used photos because Johnson was always so busy.
11. Washington's, Adams's, Jefferson's, Lincoln's, and Grant's, at New York University.
12. Harry Truman's (1987), even though he had helped Greece escape Soviet domination.
13. The Washington Monument (555 feet, 5.5 inches), constructed between 1848 and 1888.
14. Abraham Lincoln's, to represent his unfinished life.
15. The Washington Monument's (1850), attended by Zachary Taylor, who died afterwards.
16. Franklin Pierce's (1919), from Concord, New Hampshire.
17. James Madison's, in the Harry S Truman State Department Building.
18. Franklin Roosevelt's (1948–)
19. George Washington's (1841), moved from the Capitol to the Smithsonian Institution.
20. Millard Fillmore's (1875–)

21. Which president had his federal memorial approved while he was still alive?
22. Who ordered that perpetually-illuminated U.S. flags encircle the Washington Monument?
23. Who dedicated Washington's statue at the Washington Masonic National Memorial?
24. Which president dedicated the Washington Monument?
25. Where was the first statue of Abraham Lincoln erected in the former Confederacy?
26. Which president renamed the island where the Statue of Liberty stands?
27. Which president's statue was the only one ever to stand on the White House grounds?

Submarines
1. Which president first submerged in a submarine?
2. Which president first submerged in an atomic submarine?
3. Which presidents helped construct and launched the world's first nuclear submarine?
4. What was the name of the world's first ballistic-missile submarine?
5. For which recent president was a nuclear submarine named?
6. Which sub found George Bush after he had ejected from a plane during World War II?
7. Which president had served on board a submarine while in the navy?

Suits
1. Which president changed his impeccably clean white vest several times each day?
2. Which president always had a silk handkerchief showing from his vest pocket?
3. Which president wore a red carnation in his lapel buttonhole at all times?
4. Which president last wore four-button suits regularly?
5. Which men's clothing stores were George Bush's favorites, especially for suits?
6. Which president made a suit as a gift for the neighboring governor of Kentucky?
7. Who was the tailor for John Kennedy, Lyndon Johnson, and Ronald Reagan?
8. Which president never removed his suit coat while in the Oval Office out of respect?

Supreme Court
1. Which presidents first and last made a Supreme Court appointment?
2. Which presidents first and last failed to make a Supreme Court appointment?
3. Which presidents first and last served a full term without a Supreme Court appointment?
4. Which president served *at least* one full term and never made a Supreme Court appointment?
5. What is the most time during which no president made a Supreme Court appointment?
6. Which president made the most Supreme Court appointments?
7. Which president made the most Supreme Court appointments other than the original six?
8. Who attempted to "pack" the Supreme Court by expanding the number of justices?

21. George Washington (1783), taking more than a century to build and open to the public!
22. Richard Nixon (1971), and that they fly day and night, in Executive Order #4064.
23. Harry Truman (1950)
24. Chester Arthur (1885)
25. Richmond, Virginia (2003), almost 150 years after the Civil War had ended!
26. Dwight Eisenhower (1957), from Bedloe's Island to Liberty Island, the current name.
27. Thomas Jefferson's (1848-1875), a bronze by David d'Engers later moved to the Capitol.

Submarines (answers)

1. Theodore Roosevelt (1905), in the USS *Plunger*, for one hour.
2. Dwight Eisenhower (1957), in the USS *Seawolf*.
3. Jimmy Carter and Harry Truman (1953), respectively. The sub was the USS *Nautilus*.
4. The USS *George Washington* (1959)
5. Jimmy Carter (1998), the USS *Jimmy Carter* SSN-23, due to be delivered in 2003.
6. The USS *Finback* (1944)
7. Jimmy Carter (1948-1953), chosen to serve under famed Admiral Hyman Rickover.

Suits (answers)

1. William McKinley (1897-1901)
2. Chester Arthur (1881-1885), and a flower in his buttonhole.
3. William McKinley (1897-1901), because it was his home state's (Ohio's) state flower.
4. Theodore Roosevelt (1909). Since then, the three-button suit has been more popular.
5. Arthur A. Adler in Washington, DC, and Norton Ditto in Houston, Texas.
6. Andrew Johnson, while governor of Tennessee.
7. Alex Klein
8. Harry Truman (1945-1953), appropriate since he had been a haberdasher.

Supreme Court (answers)

1. George Washington (1790) and Bill Clinton (1994), respectively.
2. William Henry Harrison (1841-1841) and George W. Bush (2001-2003), respectively.
3. James Madison (1813-1817) and Bill Clinton (1997-2001), respectively.
4. Jimmy Carter (1977-1981)
5. Eleven years, 7 months, 210 days (February 3, 1812, to September 1, 1823)
6. George Washington (10)
7. George Washington (4), who also appointed the original six members of the Court.
8. Franklin Roosevelt (1937), from nine to fifteen. Congress did not approve the plan.

9.   Which president accepted an appointment to the Supreme Court?

10. Which presidents first and last declined an appointment to the Supreme Court?

11. Who was the first black Supreme Court justice?

12. Who was the first Hispanic Supreme Court justice?

13. Who was the first Supreme Court justice of Italian descent?

14. Who was the first female Supreme Court justice?

15. Who was the first Roman Catholic Supreme Court justice?

16. Who was the first Jewish Supreme Court justice?

17. Who was the only Lutheran Supreme Court chief justice?

18. Who was the only Quaker Supreme Court justice?

19. Who was the first disabled Supreme Court justice?

20. Which nominee for Supreme Court chief justice was the first one rejected?

21. Which Supreme Court nominee was rejected for confirmation by the most senators ever?

22. Which Supreme Court justice had been opposed by the most senators for confirmation?

23. Which president had two nominees for Supreme Court justice rejected by the Senate?

24. Which president first witnessed the swearing-in of his Supreme Court justice appointee?

25. Which president lobbied for the construction of a building for the Supreme Court?

26. Which presidential elections were decided by a single Supreme Court justice?

27. Which president had argued a case before the Supreme Court?

28. Which *incumbent* president was the only one who addressed the full Supreme Court?

29. Who was the last major Federalist in public office?

30. Which Supreme Court justice ardently defended Andrew Johnson against impeachment?

31. Which Supreme Court justice did Harry Truman ask to become a presidential candidate?

32. Who lead the "official" investigation into the assassination of John Kennedy?

33. Which female Supreme Court justice inaugurated a president or vice president?

34. Which president said famously, "Presidents come and go, but the Court goes on forever"?

35. Which president tried to impeach a Supreme Court justice for opposing other nominees?

36. Which president kept the Supreme Court standing for hours as he greeted well-wishers?

37. Who began the tradition that seniority not determine the Supreme Court chief justice?

38. Who said the biggest mistake that he made was an appointment to the Supreme Court?

39. Which Supreme Court justice served longest and wrote the most opinions?

40. Which Supreme Court justice was the first one who resigned?

41. Which Supreme Court justice was impeached but not convicted for attacks on a president?

42. Which Supreme Court justice lived longest, to the age of ninety-five years?

43. Who was the first Southerner on the Supreme Court since the Civil War had ended?

44. Which Supreme Court justice had the same first name as the president who picked him?

45. When did the Supreme Court last accept an appeal directly from a district court?

46. Which president was suspended from practicing law before the Supreme Court?

47. Which president ordered the arrest of a Supreme Court chief justice?

9. William Taft (1921-1930), nominated by Warren Harding.

10. John Quincy Adams (1811) and William Taft (1901-1904), respectively.

11. Thurgood Marshall (1967-1989), nominated by Lyndon Johnson.

12. No Hispanic has ever been confirmed to the Supreme Court.

13. Antonin Scalia (1986–), nominated by Ronald Reagan.

14. Sandra Day O'Connor (1981–), nominated by Ronald Reagan.

15. Edward D. White (1894-1910), nominated by Grover Cleveland.

16. Louis D. Brandeis (1916-1939), nominated by Woodrow Wilson.

17. William H. Rehnquist (1986–), nominated by Ronald Reagan.

18. Noah H. Swayne (1862-1881), nominated by Abraham Lincoln.

19. Ward Hunt (1873-1882), nominated by Ulysses Grant.

20. John Rutledge (1789), nominated by George Washington, on the grounds of insanity.

21. Robert H. Bork (1987), nominated by Ronald Reagan and opposed by 58 senators.

22. Clarence Thomas (1991–), nominated by George Bush and opposed by 48 senators.

23. Richard Nixon, Clement Haynsworth (1969) and G. Harold Carswell (1970).

24. Harry Truman, for the inauguration of Harold H. Burton (1945-1958).

25. William Taft (1925). The building was completed on October 7, 1935.

26. 1876 (by Joseph Bradley) and 2000 (one-vote majority gave Florida electors to Bush)

27. Richard Nixon (1967), in *Time, Inc. v. Hill*.

28. Richard Nixon (1969)

29. John Marshall (1801-1835), nominated by John Adams.

30. Benjamin R. Curtis (1851-1857), nominated by Millard Fillmore.

31. Fred Vinson (1946-1953), who responded with an irrevocable "No."

32. Supreme Court Chief Justice Earl Warren (1953-1969)

33. Sandra Day O'Connor (1981–), who inaugurated Dan Quayle (1989).

34. William Taft

35. Gerald Ford (1970), for William O. Douglas's (1939-1975) opposing Nixon's nominees.

36. Bill Clinton, during a visit to the Supreme Court for a reception.

37. George Washington (1789)

38. Harry Truman, who regretted having nominated Thomas C. Clark (1949-1967).

39. William O. Douglas (1939-1975), nominated by Franklin Roosevelt.

40. Thomas Johnson (1791-1793), nominated by George Washington, for failing health.

41. Samuel Chase (1796-1811), nominated by George Washington, on Thomas Jefferson.

42. Stanley F. Reed (1938-1957), nominated by Franklin Roosevelt.

43. William B. Woods (1881-1887), nominated by Rutherford Hayes.

44. Thomas Todd (1807-1826), nominated by Thomas Jefferson.

45. *U.S. v. Nixon* (1974), ordering Nixon to relinquish tapes to congressional investigators.

46. Bill Clinton (2002), as a result of the suspension of his law license in Arkansas.

47. Abraham Lincoln (1861), for Roger Taney's opposing his suspension of habeus corpus.

Surnames

1. Which letter begins more presidents' surnames than any other?
2. Which four presidents' surnames end in a vowel?
3. Which presidents' surnames are first and last alphabetically?
4. Which presidents' first and last names began with the same letter?
5. Which five presidents' surnames are only four letters long?
6. Which national ticket had the same number of letters in their first names and last names?
7. Which president's surname became a verb in the English language?
8. Which president's surname became a noun synonymous with corruption and nepotism?
9. Which president's surname became a slang term for "political evasiveness"?
10. Which anti-communist president employed a ghostwriter whose surname was "Moscow"?
11. Which president's name did the longest-living survivor of the mutiny on the *Bounty* adopt?
12. What was Stan Laurel's real name?
13. Which presidents with identical surnames were runaways ninety-nine years apart?
14. Which presidential surnames have been shared by more than one president?
15. Which president appointed two Cabinet members with the same surname?
16. When since 1960 was the major-party loser's surname shorter than the winner's?
17. Which syndicated advice columnist had a presidential surname?
18. Which famous physicist had a presidential surname?
19. Which citizen had a presidential surname in Shakespeare's *Merry Wives of Windsor*?
20. Which pair of brothers served as governors of Maine and Massachusetts simultaneously?
21. Which surgeon who operated on Abraham Lincoln had a presidential surname?
22. Which vice president's surname fits *exactly* into a president's full name?
23. Which actress, born Baker, chose a presidential surname as her "acting" name?
24. Which president's surname was the same as populist Huey Long's middle name?
25. Which states' postal abbreviations form anagrams of a president's first and last names?
26. Whose female descendants married men with the surnames of eight presidents?
27. Which political appointee's first *and* last names were the same as a presidential surname?
28. Which two presidents' middle names are presidential surnames?

Teeth

1. Which president first wore false teeth?
2. Which president mailed the last of his real teeth to his dentist?
3. Where were George Washington's long-lost teeth finally found?
4. At what ages did George Washington lose his first and last teeth?
5. How many of his own teeth did George Washington have upon becoming president?
6. Which president talked with a lisp because he refused to wear dentures?
7. Who introduced toothpicks to the White House, placing them at convenient locations?

Surnames (answers)

1. "H" (Harrison, Hayes, Harrison, Harding, and Hoover)
2. James Monroe's, Millard Fillmore's, Franklin Pierce's, and Calvin Coolidge's
3. John Adams's and John Quincy Adams's are first, Woodrow Wilson's is last.
4. Herbert Hoover's and Ronald Reagan's (Wilson and Coolidge went by middle names)
5. James Polk's, William Taft's, Gerald Ford's, George Bush's, and George W. Bush's
6. Gerald Ford and Robert Dole (1976)
7. Herbert Hoover's. To "hooverize" is to save food during war, to "hoover" is to vacuum.
8. Ulysses Grant's, "Grantism."
9. Martin Van Buren's
10. Richard Nixon, who employed Alvin Moscow to write his bestseller *Six Crises* (1962).
11. John Adams's. Adams lived until 1829, and his descendants still populate Pitcairn Island.
12. Arthur Stanley Jefferson
13. Andrew Johnson, escaping an apprenticeship, and Lyndon Johnson, driving to California.
14. Adams, Harrison, Roosevelt, Johnson, and Bush
15. Benjamin Harrison (Charles Foster and John W. Foster)
16. In 1976, 1992, and 1996
17. Abigail Van Buren
18. William Coolidge
19. Frank Ford
20. Enoch Lincoln (1827-1829) and Levi Lincoln (1825-1834), respectively.
21. Acting Assistant Surgeon Charles S. Taft (1865)
22. Hannibal Hamlin's, which fits exactly into the name of his president, Abra*ham Lin*coln.
23. Marilyn Monroe
24. Franklin Pierce's
25. Alabama's (AL), California's (CA), and Delaware's (DE)
26. Thomas Jefferson's (Harrison, Tyler, Taylor, Pierce, Lincoln, Wilson, Coolidge, Kennedy)
27. Assistant Secretary of Labor Ford Ford, nominated by Ronald Reagan.
28. William Jefferson Clinton's and Ronald Wilson Reagan's

Teeth (answers)

1. George Washington, made from hippopotamus teeth set in gold by patriot Paul Revere.
2. George Washington, to John Greenwood, for use as a model in making new dentures.
3. In a storage room at the Smithsonian Institution (1982)
4. At the ages of twenty-two years (1754) and sixty-five years (1797), respectively.
5. One, his lower left pre-molar.
6. John Adams
7. Warren Harding (1921)

Telegrams

1. Which president's nomination was the first one news of which was sent by telegraph?
2. Which candidate on a national ticket was first notified of his nomination by telegraph?
3. Which president received the first transatlantic telegram?
4. Which president received the first transcontinental telegram?
5. Which president received the first aerial telegram, in his White House office?
6. Who was the first person to command troops by telegraph?
7. Which First Lady was told mistakenly that her husband had been killed in battle?
8. Which president installed the first White House telegraph?
9. Who received a telegram lamenting, "the rope with which Judas hung himself is mislaid"?
10. Which future president proposed to his wife via telegram from Australia?
11. Which president sent the first official wireless transatlantic telegram?
12. Which president participated in the first two-way transatlantic communication?
13. Which president sent the first telegram message around the world?
14. Whom did Robert Peary telegram, "Have Honor to place North Pole at your disposal"?
15. Who sent Dwight Eisenhower a telegram saying, "Dear Ike, today I spat in the Seine"?
16. What was Ronald Reagan's last official act?

Telephones

1. Which president first spoke on a telephone?
2. Where was the first telephone in the country installed?
3. Which president first obtained a public telephone number?
4. Which president was first interviewed over the telephone?
5. Which president regularly picked up the White House telephone himself?
6. Which president first used a telephone for campaign purposes?
7. Which president first placed a transcontinental telephone call from the White House?
8. Which president first had a telephone on his desk at the White House?
9. Which president telephoned the inaugural session of the United Nations?
10. Which president first conversed on a "hot line" to Moscow?
11. Which president had a telephone at his White House dining-room table?
12. Which president placed a floating telephone in his pool in order to work in the water?
13. Which president first made a long-distance telephone call by satellite?
14. Which president first made a telephone call to the Moon?
15. Which president participated in a national phone-in?
16. For which television station were "1-900" telephone numbers first created?
17. How many telephone calls can a current U.S. president expect to receive?
18. Which president created the Federal Universal Service Fee for everybody's phone bills?
19. Which president installed telephone lines in the White House for political purposes?

Telegrams (answers)

1. James Polk's (1844), by Samuel F. B. Morse himself, the inventor of Morse Code.
2. Senator Silas Wright (D-NY) (1844), who declined a chance to run for VP as a Democrat.
3. James Buchanan (1858), from Queen Victoria of England.
4. Abraham Lincoln (1861), from California Supreme Court Chief Justice Stephen J. Field.
5. Abraham Lincoln (1861), from Dr. Thaddeus Lowe in a balloon above the White House.
6. Ulysses Grant (1862), at the Battle of Iuka, Mississippi.
7. Lucy Hayes (1862), by telegram, in the Battle of South Mountain, Maryland.
8. Andrew Johnson (1866)
9. Senator Edmund Ross (R-KS) (1868), after he voted to acquit Andrew Johnson.
10. Herbert Hoover (1898), who received the one-word response "Yes."
11. Theodore Roosevelt (1903), to King Edward VII of England, at Poldhu Station, England.
12. Theodore Roosevelt (1903), on the same day, from South Wellfleet, Massachusetts.
13. Theodore Roosevelt (1903). The message took twelve minutes to complete.
14. William Taft (1909), who responded, "I do not know exactly what I could do with it."
15. George Patton (1944). He had crossed the French river at Melun, outflanking Paris.
16. To send a telegram to British Prime Minister Margaret Thatcher (1989)

Telephones (answers)

1. Rutherford Hayes (1877), who asked Alexander Graham Bell to "speak . . . more slowly."
2. In the Treasury Building (1877), as a private line from the White House, a block away.
3. Rutherford Hayes (1879), whose telephone number "1" lasted for thirty years!
4. Grover Cleveland (1885)
5. Grover Cleveland (1885-1889), unsure how to delegate the responsibility for the novelty.
6. William McKinley (1896)
7. Woodrow Wilson (1915), who called San Francisco, California, from the Oval Office.
8. Herbert Hoover (1929). Before that, one had been located in a telephone booth.
9. Harry Truman (1945), which took place in San Francisco, California.
10. John Kennedy (1963), on a now traditional red telephone.
11. Lyndon Johnson (1964-1969)
12. Lyndon Johnson (1964-1969), at his Texas ranch.
13. Lyndon Johnson (1965), who called British Prime Minister Harold Wilson.
14. Richard Nixon (1969), to Astronauts Buzz Aldrin and Neil Armstrong.
15. Jimmy Carter (1977), when forty-two participants called to literally talk to the president.
16. ABC (1980), to receive immediate response to the Reagan-Carter presidential debates.
17. About 15,000,000 per year!
18. Bill Clinton (1996), to help wire schools and libraries for the Internet.
19. Bill Clinton (1998), prompting a federal investigation and calls for campaign reform.

Television

1. Which president took part in the first long-distance demonstration of television?
2. Which president first made a television broadcast, opening the New York World's Fair?
3. Which president first made a television broadcast from the White House?
4. Which president had been the first emcee of *Francis the Talking Mule*?
5. Which presidential candidate first used television spots and ads during his campaign?
6. Which president first put press conferences on television after White House approval?
7. Which president first held a press conference broadcast by television?
8. Which president first simulcast a press conference on radio and television?
9. Which president first used make-up for his television appearances?
10. Which president's press conference was first televised and "newsreeled"?
11. Which president first appeared on color television?
12. Which television reporter first interviewed President and Mrs. Harry Truman?
13. Which president had first addressed the Soviet people on their own television?
14. Which election was the first one with presidential nominees debating on television?
15. Which president moved his press conferences to the State Department auditorium?
16. Which president offered the first live telecast of a presidential press conference?
17. What was the first television broadcast of a courtroom verdict?
18. Which president first appeared on the television show *Meet the Press*?
19. Which president was first lampooned on television's *Saturday Night Live*?
20. Which other actors were well known for portraying U.S. presidents on *Saturday Night Live*?
21. Which president first made the first live, televised, phone-in television broadcast?
22. Which president first gave a press conference from an Eastern-bloc nation?
23. Who made the first television interview with an incumbent president *and* vice president?
24. Which president gave a major television address from a moving ship?
25. Who required reporters to state their names and affiliations before asking a question?
26. Whom did Ronald Reagan label "the ayatollah of the [Washington] press corps"?
27. Which words always signal the end of a presidential press conference?
28. Which president did Paul Keyes, producer of *Laugh-In*, consider a good friend?
29. For which president was a "muppet" named on television's *Sesame Street*?
30. Which president gave one of the 732 "Bicentennial Minutes" on CBS?
31. Which First Couple made a cameo appearance on the television series *Dynasty*?
32. Which president called *Nightline* host Ted Koppel "Dan" three times during one episode?
33. Who installed televisions in the Oval Office to view himself on three networks at once?
34. Which president hated televisions and had all of them removed from the White House?
35. With what did Groucho Marx often end his television show, hoping nobody would miss it?

Television (answers)

1. Herbert Hoover (1927), when his image was transmitted 200 miles over telephone lines.
2. Franklin Roosevelt (1939), at the Fair's Federal Building, on NBC.
3. Harry Truman (1947), who pled to New York and Pennsylvania for food for Europe.
4. Ronald Reagan (1949). It was the first television show to win a PATSY award (1950).
5. Dwight Eisenhower (1952), entitled "Eisenhower Answers America."
6. Dwight Eisenhower (1953), using delayed recording and film.
7. Dwight Eisenhower (1953), and also first tape-recorded a press conference.
8. Dwight Eisenhower (1953)
9. Dwight Eisenhower (1953), often applied by his actor-friend Robert Montgomery.
10. Dwight Eisenhower's (1955)
11. Dwight Eisenhower (1955)
12. Mary "Margaret" Truman (1955), on Edward R. Murrow's show, *Person to Person*.
13. Richard Nixon (1959), as vice president, during a trip to open a U.S. exhibition.
14. The 1960 presidential election between Kennedy and Nixon, in four hour-long debates.
15. John Kennedy (1961)
16. John Kennedy (1961), to announce the release of two RB-47 fliers from prison in Russia.
17. The trial of Jack Ruby (1964), who had killed Lee Harvey Oswald in Dallas, Texas.
18. Gerald Ford (1975), on the show's twenty-eighth anniversary.
19. Gerald Ford (1975), by Dan Aykroyd.
20. Chevy Chase, Phil Hartman, Dana Carvey, Will Farrell, and Darrell Hammond.
21. Jimmy Carter (1977), entitled *Ask Mr. Carter*. Clinton considered hosting a TV show.
22. Jimmy Carter (1977), from Warsaw, Poland, during a seven-nation tour.
23. Larry King (1995), who interviewed Bill Clinton and Al Gore on *Larry King Live*.
24. George W. Bush (2003), about Operation Iraqi Freedom, from USS *Abraham Lincoln*.
25. John Kennedy (1961-1963)
26. Sam Donaldson
27. "Thank you, Mr. President."
28. Richard Nixon, who was the only president to appear on that show (1968).
29. Franklin Roosevelt (1969), for whom "Roosevelt Franklin" was named.
30. Gerald Ford (1976), helping to explain the events that shaped our country.
31. President and Mrs. Gerald Ford (1983)
32. George Bush (1988), confusing him with Dan Rather, the anchor for CBS.
33. Lyndon Johnson
34. John Kennedy (1961), returning one after daughter Caroline's plea to watch *Lassie*.
35. "Who's buried in Grant's Tomb?" always ended *What's My Line?* (1950-1961).

36. What did television journalist Walter Cronkite say made television journalism come of age?
37. Whom did Jimmy Carter cite as his advisor on nuclear weapons during televised debate?
38. Which television anchor incorrectly announced a Reagan-Ford deal for the national ticket?

Tenure

1. Which presidents purchased Florida from Spain and Alaska from Russia?
2. Which presidents' foreign policies added the most territory to the U.S.A.?
3. Which president was the first one who did *not* treat Indian chiefs as foreign diplomats?
4. Which president helped issue the Ostend Manifesto?
5. Which president recognized the Republic of Texas?
6. Which president arbitrated a boundary dispute between Venezuela and Great Britain?
7. Whose first act was to recognize the Chinese Republic?
8. With which president did Vietnamese nationalist Ho Chi Minh once request an audience?
9. Which president signed a bill granting citizenship to all American Indians?
10. Which president ordered the encampment of tens of thousands of Japanese-Americans?
11. Which president approved the Marshall Plan?
12. Which president was renowned for his "conference diplomacy"?
13. Which president first attended a peacetime "summit" with the Soviets?
14. Which president met with a Soviet premier for a "summit" in Glassboro, New Jersey?
15. Which president first signed a nuclear-arms reduction treaty with the Soviet Union?
16. Which president was the only one who suggested the division of the City of Jerusalem?
17. Which president created the largest cabinet department?
18. Which amendment limited an elected president's tenure to two four-year terms?
19. Which president and vice president combinations served a full eight years in a row?
20. Which Republican presidents served two full four-year terms?
21. Which presidents had the shortest and longest tenures?
22. Which president recommended a single six- or seven-year term for the president?
23. Which president proposed a one-term presidency, but took two terms?
24. Since when have the first 100 days of a presidency been viewed as a "honeymoon"?
25. Which presidents served at least part of their terms while no former presidents lived?
26. Which president was the only one who paid off the national debt?
27. During which Administrations did the national debt first reach $1 billion and $1 trillion?
28. Which presidents' budgets first spent $1 million and $1 billion per day?
29. Which president's budget spent the least money per day?
30. Which Administration first received unsolicited money from guilt-ridden tax-evaders?
31. Which president approved a $1.6 billion loan to save New York City from bankruptcy?
32. Which president first warned about large public debt and about special-interest groups?

36. The coverage of John Kennedy's assassination and funeral (1961)

37. Amy Lynn Carter (1980), his teenage daughter.

38. Dan Rather (1980), at the Republican National Convention in Detroit, Michigan.

Tenure (answers)

1. James Monroe (1819) and Andrew Johnson (1867), respectively.

2. James Polk's (1845-1849), followed by Thomas Jefferson's (1801-1809).

3. Franklin Pierce (1853)

4. James Buchanan (1854), advocating the annexation of Cuba as a slave state.

5. Andrew Jackson (1836), the only one who recognized a republic later part of the U.S.A.

6. Benjamin Harrison (1899), in Paris, France, after leaving the presidency.

7. Woodrow Wilson's (1919), which republic had toppled a millennia-old royal dynasty.

8. Woodrow Wilson (1919), at the Versailles Peace Conference. Wilson declined the request.

9. Calvin Coolidge (1924)

10. Franklin Roosevelt (1941), affecting about 115,000 persons.

11. Harry Truman (1948), pumping billions of dollars into a starved post-war Europe.

12. Dwight Eisenhower (1953-1961)

13. Dwight Eisenhower (1955), with Nikita Khrushchev, in Geneva, Switzerland.

14. Lyndon Johnson (1967), with Aleksei Kosygin.

15. Ronald Reagan (1987), the Intermediate-Range Nuclear Forces Treaty.

16. Bill Clinton (2001)

17. George W. Bush (2002), who created the Department of Homeland Security.

18. The Twenty-Second Amendment (1951), but a VP becoming president can serve more.

19. Eisenhower/Nixon (1953-1961), Reagan/Bush (1981-1989), Clinton/Gore (1993-2001)

20. Grant (1869-1877), Eisenhower (1953-1961), and Reagan (1981-1989)

21. William Henry Harrison (30 days) and Franklin Roosevelt (4,422 days), respectively.

22. Jimmy Carter, at various times since he left the presidency.

23. Andrew Jackson (1828)

24. Franklin Roosevelt's Administration (1933-1945)

25. Washington, John Adams, Grant, Theodore Roosevelt, Hoover, and Nixon

26. Andrew Jackson (1834), only to have it reappear permanently after the Panic of 1837.

27. Woodrow Wilson's (1916) and Ronald Reagan's (1981), respectively.

28. Abraham Lincoln's (1861) and Gerald Ford's (1975), respectively.

29. George Washington's ($20,548), which the current Administration spent in 0.29 seconds.

30. James Madison's (1809-1817), when he received a letter with five dollars inside it.

31. Jimmy Carter (1978)

32. George Washington (1797)

33. Which president signed the first federal income-tax law?
34. During which president's first two years did the stock market lose the most value?
35. Which president established the United States Weather Bureau?
36. Which president "fathered" the Smithsonian Institution by starting its collection?
37. Which president accepted the donation of the Freer Gallery to the government?
38. Which president signed the Pure Food and Drug Act?
39. Which president established the parcel-post system?
40. Which president established the Federal Narcotics Control Board?
41. Which president signed the Social Security Act?
42. Which president established the Atomic Energy Commission?
43. Which president created Volunteers in Service to America (VISTA)?
44. Which president issued the first executive order?
45. Which president issued the most executive orders?
46. Which presidents made executive orders declared unconstitutional by the Supreme Court?
47. Which president first observed an official Thanksgiving Day?
48. Which president changed the official observance of Thanksgiving?
49. Which president first hosted an annual White House Thanksgiving Day dinner?
50. Which president first realized the power of the presidency?
51. Which president first "grew" into the responsibilities of the presidency?
52. Who signed the Flag Act, making the "Stars and Stripes" the official flag of the country?
53. Which president expanded the wording of the Pledge of Allegiance?
54. Who dissolved the Maryland Legislature by fiat?
55. Which president first took a strong stand on an issue and asked voters to go the polls?
56. Which president signed the first civil-rights legislation in eighty-two years?
57. Which president changed the national seal to make the eagle face the olive branches?
58. Which Administration was the most corrupt, in terms of the number of persons involved?
59. Which president since James Monroe first had known his four immediate predecessors?
60. Which president first expected regular reports from each agency?
61. Which president last "witnessed" a constitutional amendment?
62. Which president initiated the biggest public-works project in U.S. history?
63. Which president first displayed the official presidential flag?
64. During which Administration did all the astronauts who ever stepped on the moon do so?
65. Which president publicized the Gold Rush?
66. Which president first represented forty-nine states and first represented fifty states?
67. Which president endorsed phrenology, the study of the head to predict personality?
68. Which president first celebrated Independence Day with fireworks?
69. Which president created the term "Mr. President" as a form of address for the president?
70. Which president's Administration had the largest percentage increase in population?

33. Woodrow Wilson (1913)

34. George W. Bush's (33%), more than Herbert Hoover's 29% before the Great Depression.

35. John Tyler (1845), now called the National Weather Service, to monitor the weather.

36. John Quincy Adams (1846). James Polk signed the bill creating the Smithsonian.

37. Theodore Roosevelt (1904)

38. Theodore Roosevelt (1906), prompted by Upton Sinclair's *The Jungle*.

39. William Taft (1912), beginning the home delivery of small commodities and products.

40. Warren Harding (1922), with the power to prohibit importation of non-medicinal narcotics.

41. Franklin Roosevelt (1935), creating the first large-scale federal entitlement.

42. Harry Truman (1946), to exercise control over atomic research and development.

43. Lyndon Johnson (1964), as the domestic equivalent of the international Peace Corps.

44. Abraham Lincoln (1862), authorizing military commanders to protect U.S. property.

45. Franklin Roosevelt (1933-1945), who issued 3,728 executive orders.

46. Harry Truman (1952) and Bill Clinton (1996)

47. Abraham Lincoln (1863)

48. Franklin Roosevelt (1939), who briefly changed it to the third Thursday in November.

49. James Polk (1854)

50. Theodore Roosevelt (1901-1909), or, arguably, Abraham Lincoln (1861-1865).

51. James Monroe (1817-1825)

52. James Monroe (1818). Harry Truman signed the bill making June 14 Flag Day (1949).

53. Dwight Eisenhower (1954), by adding the words "Under God," the last change made.

54. Abraham Lincoln (1861), who also jailed civilians without trial and banned newspapers.

55. Andrew Jackson (1832), regarding the Second Bank of the United States.

56. Dwight Eisenhower (1957), for powers to guarantee every citizen's right to vote.

57. Harry Truman (1946), instead of the arrows. He also renamed the War Department.

58. Ulysses Grant's (1869-1877), with the possible exception of Bill Clinton's (1993-2001).

59. Lyndon Johnson (Roosevelt, Truman, Eisenhower, and Kennedy)

60. John Kennedy (1961), on its problems and decisions made.

61. Richard Nixon (1971), the Twenty-Sixth Amendment, at the National Archives.

62. Dwight Eisenhower (1956), the interstate-highway system, which took fifty years to finish!

63. Woodrow Wilson (1916), by Executive Order #2390.

64. Richard Nixon's (1969-1974)

65. James Polk (1848-1849), in order to help settle recently-acquired American territories.

66. Dwight Eisenhower (1959), after the admission of Alaska and Hawaii, respectively.

67. Chester Arthur (1881)

68. John Adams (1797)

69. James Madison (1787), at the Constitutional Convention, in Philadelphia, Pennsylvania.

70. Thomas Jefferson's

71. Which president left office with fewer federal employees than when he had taken office?
72. What has every vice president who succeeded to the presidency failed to do?
73. Who were the youngest *former* presidents in U.S. history?
74. Which Administration issued the most new pages in the Federal Register in one year?

Tombs

1. Which president's tomb is the most visited tomb *in the world*?
2. At which president's tomb did a Prince of Wales ceremoniously plant a tree?
3. Beside which president's grave was a vine planted from Napoleon's tomb on St. Helena?
4. Which president dedicated Grant's Tomb?
5. Who is buried in Grant's Tomb?
6. What is inscribed on Grant's Tomb?

Trains

1. Which *non-incumbent* and *incumbent* presidents first traveled by train?
2. Which president ordered an armor-plated railroad car for his personal use?
3. Which president's railroad car was named *Mayflower*?
4. What was the name of the official presidential train car?
5. Which president first conducted a "whistle-stop tour"?
6. Which president first traveled in a diesel train?
7. Which president conducted the longest "whistle-stop tour," making 351 speeches?
8. From which train did Truman display the erroneous headline "Dewey Defeats Truman"?
9. Who used the same railroad car and route that Harry Truman had during his tour?
10. Which engine carried a deceased Franklin Roosevelt from Warm Springs to Washington?
11. Which president brought criminal proceedings against striking engineers?
12. Which president first advanced the idea of federal responsibility for interstate commerce?
13. Which president had been dragged from a train by an angry mob and almost hanged?
14. Which president first used Union Station in Washington, DC?
15. Which president was involved in the first fatal train wreck in U.S. history?
16. Which two presidents had dreamed of becoming railroad engineers?
17. Which president completed the Alaskan Railroad by driving home a golden spike?

Transportation

1. Which subway stops on the Los Angeles Subway are named for presidents?
2. For which presidents are subway stops on the New York City Subway system named?
3. Which subway stops on the Paris Metro are named for presidents?

71. Herbert Hoover (1933)
72. Get elected to a second *full* four-year term (Theodore Roosevelt tried to do so in 1912)
73. Theodore Roosevelt (50), followed by Grover Cleveland (51).
74. George W. Bush's (2002), with 75,606 pages, but fewer rules than in prior years.

Tombs (answers)

1. John Kennedy's, at Arlington National Cemetery, in Arlington, Virginia.
2. George Washington's (1860). The future King Edward VII did so, with James Buchanan.
3. Ulysses Grant's (1885), by President Grover Cleveland and other dignitaries.
4. William McKinley (1897), with more than one million well-wishers.
5. President *and* Mrs. Ulysses S. Grant, buried in 1885 and 1902, respectively.
6. "Let us have peace."

Trains (answers)

1. John Quincy Adams (1831) and Andrew Jackson (1833), respectively, on the B&O.
2. Abraham Lincoln (1861), later used to carry his cadaver from Washington to Springfield.
3. Woodrow Wilson's (1913-1921)
4. The *Ferdinand Magellan* (1928), now at the Gold Coast Railroad Museum in Miami.
5. Theodore Roosevelt (1904)
6. Franklin Roosevelt (1937)
7. Harry Truman (1948), who traveled 31,473 miles in thirty-six states.
8. The *Ferdinand Magellan* (1948)
9. Ronald Reagan (1984)
10. *Engine 1401* (1945), now at the Smithsonian Institution.
11. Rutherford Hayes (1877), of the Boston & Maine Railroad, for obstructing the mail.
12. Grover Cleveland (1894), after the Pullman strike.
13. Andrew Johnson (1860), in Lynchburg, Virginia, for opposing secession from the Union.
14. William Taft (1909), for whom a custom-built chair was provided in the presidential suite.
15. John Quincy Adams (1833), on the Camden & Amboy Railroad. Two passengers died.
16. Dwight Eisenhower, who had grown up with railroads, and Richard Nixon.
17. Warren Harding (1923), at Nenana, Alaska, with future president Herbert Hoover present.

Transportation (answers)

1. "Fillmore" and "Washington"
2. Washington, Jefferson, Jackson, Grant, Roosevelt, Wilson, Kennedy, and Clinton
3. "Franklin D. Roosevelt" and "Kennedy Radio France"

4. For which presidents are subway stops on the Washington Metro named?
5. Where are the Eisenhower and Kennedy Expressways located?
6. Where are the Lyndon B. Johnson Freeway and President George Bush Turnpike located?
7. Which president first promoted the building of canals?
8. Which president received the first flag to fly above U.S. soil?
9. Which president designed his own White House transportation?
10. Which *incumbent* president was arrested for running over an elderly woman?
11. Which other *incumbent* president was arrested for speeding?
12. Which president's law firm opened public transportation to blacks in New York City?
13. Which president was fond of sleigh rides down Pennsylvania Avenue?
14. Which president first attended the launching of a manned space flight?

Travels

1. Who sent Zebulon M. Pike, for whom Pike's Peak is named, to explore the West?
2. Which president's hometown was the Eastern terminus of the Oregon Trail?
3. Which president first visited White Sulphur Springs, West Virginia, a famous retreat?
4. Which *future* and *incumbent* presidents first visited Texas?
5. Which *incumbent* president first made an extended trip around the country?
6. Which *incumbent* president first traversed the North American continent?
7. For which president was the first coast-to-coast, paved highway in the U.S.A. named?
8. Which *incumbent* president first visited Hawaii?
9. Which president traveled to the top of the Gateway Arch in St. Louis, Missouri?
10. Which president was *not* in the country during Memorial Day?
11. Which *incumbent* president technically first left the country?
12. Who could have become the first *incumbent* president to leave the country?
13. Which *incumbent* president first took a trip to another country?
14. Which *incumbent* president first crossed the Atlantic Ocean?
15. Which *incumbent* president first left the U.S.A. during wartime?
16. Which *incumbent* president's trip probably took the longest amount of time?
17. Which president left his White House office for a total of six weeks during his tenure?
18. Which *incumbent* president spent more time outside the U.S.A. than any other?
19. Which *incumbent* president made more trips abroad than any other?
20. Which *incumbent* president visited more foreign countries than any other?
21. Which *incumbent* president visited one country the most times?
22. Which presidents traveled farthest north and south in the world, respectively?
23. Where did George Washington go on his only trip outside continental North America?
24. Which president occasionally vacationed in Bermuda with Mark Twain?

4. George Washington, Grover Cleveland, Dwight Eisenhower, and Ronald Reagan
5. Chicago, Illinois, and environs.
6. Dallas, Texas, and environs.
7. George Washington (1785), from the Chesapeake Bay to the Ohio River Valley.
8. George Washington (1793), from Frenchman Jean Pierre Blanchard, after a balloon flight.
9. Thomas Jefferson (1801-1809)
10. Franklin Pierce (1853), who had run over Mrs. Nathan Lewis while on his horse.
11. Ulysses Grant (1870), for "speeding" with a team of horses. He was fined $20.
12. Chester Arthur's (1856)
13. Chester Arthur (1881-1885)
14. Richard Nixon (1969), to watch Apollo 12 lift off from Cape Canaveral, Florida.

Travels (answers)

1. Thomas Jefferson (1805)
2. Harry Truman's, in Independence, Missouri. The Trail ended in Oregon City, Oregon.
3. Andrew Jackson (1829), as a summer retreat from the capital.
4. Rutherford Hayes (1840), to the Brazos River, and Ulysses Grant (1874), to Denison.
5. James Monroe (1817), to inspect military defenses in the North after the War of 1812.
6. Rutherford Hayes (1880), when he traveled to San Francisco and the West Coast.
7. Abraham Lincoln (1913). The Lincoln Highway went from New York City to San Francisco.
8. Franklin Roosevelt (1934), when he landed on the Hawaiian island of Hilo.
9. Dwight Eisenhower (1968), who took a tram to the top of the 630-foot monument.
10. George W. Bush (2002), who spent Memorial Day on the beaches of Normandy, France.
11. Grover Cleveland (1897), fishing outside the three-mile boundary off the Atlantic coast.
12. William McKinley (1901), standing on a bridge to Canada, at Niagara Falls, New York.
13. Theodore Roosevelt (1906), to inspect progress on the Panama Canal.
14. Woodrow Wilson (1918), aboard the SS *George Washington*, bound for Europe.
15. Franklin Roosevelt (1943), who visited Casablanca, Morocco, for a conference there.
16. Rutherford Hayes's (1880), a trip to the West Coast lasting almost three months.
17. James Polk (1845-1849), probably the least of any president.
18. Bill Clinton (1993-2001), at least 229 days (8%) outside the country.
19. Bill Clinton (1993-2001), with at least 133 trips overseas.
20. Bill Clinton (1993-2001), with trips to seventy-five foreign countries.
21. Franklin Roosevelt (8 trips to Canada and 18 trips to the British Commonwealth)
22. Nixon (1973) and Reagan (1986), to Iceland, and Clinton (1999), to New Zealand.
23. Barbados (1751), with his half-brother Laurence Washington.
24. Woodrow Wilson

25. Which presidents since Warren Harding did *not* visit Canada?
26. Which *incumbent* presidents first and last visited Mexico, respectively?
27. Which presidents since Franklin Roosevelt did *not* visit Mexico?
28. Which North American country has no U.S. president ever visited at any time?
29. Which president visited five Central American countries *in one day*?
30. Which president first visited the Panama Canal?
31. Which president-*elect* had visited ten Latin American countries before being inaugurated?
32. Which future First Couple visited Americana, Brazil, founded in 1865 by ex-Confederates?
33. Which president sought the "River of Doubt" in the Brazilian Amazon?
34. Which South American countries has no U.S. president ever visited at any time?
35. Which president had cut some wood from Shakespeare's chair at Stratford-upon-Avon?
36. Which president had met French philosopher Voltaire?
37. Which president crossed the European Alps in a mule train, from France to Italy?
38. Which president bailed out newspaper editor Horace Greeley from jail in Paris for debts?
39. Which presidents met Prussian dictator Otto von Bismarck and Nazi dictator Adolf Hitler?
40. Which *incumbent* presidents have been to the magnificent Palace of Versailles in France?
41. Which presidents since Woodrow Wilson did *not* visit the United Kingdom?
42. Who was the first foreigner to stand on Lenin's Tomb in Red Square?
43. Which *incumbent* president was the first one who visited Russia?
44. Whom did Ronald Reagan ask to greet the Iranian hostages in West Germany?
45. Which president visited Northern Ireland?
46. Which president engaged political parties face-to-face in Belfast, Northern Ireland?
47. Which European countries has no U.S. president ever visited at any time?
48. Which presidents first and last had visited Jerusalem and the Holy Land?
49. Which *future* and *incumbent* presidents first visited India?
50. Which president traveled to Agra, India, and rudely screamed inside the Taj Mahal?
51. Which presidents first visited China, Communist China, and Taiwan, respectively?
52. Which president met Chinese Communist revolutionary Mao Tse-Tung?
53. Which presidents first and last visited the Great Wall of China?
54. Which president allegedly was the first person to shake the hand of a Japanese emperor?
55. Which president was denied a state visit to Japan?
56. Which *incumbent* president first met a Japanese ruling monarch, in Anchorage, Alaska?
57. Which *incumbent* presidents first and last visited Japan?
58. Which *incumbent* president first visited Africa?
59. Which presidents visited sub-Saharan Africa?
60. Which president first visited Egypt at any point of his life?
61. Which president first visited Liberia at any point of his life?
62. Which president first visited South Africa at any point of his life?

25. Calvin Coolidge, Harry Truman, Gerald Ford, and Jimmy Carter

26. William Taft (1909), in Ciudad Juárez, and George W. Bush (2002), in Los Cabos.

27. None

28. Belize, at least among mainland North American countries.

29. Lyndon Johnson (1968), Guatemala, El Salvador, Honduras, Nicaragua, and Costa Rica.

30. Theodore Roosevelt (1906), who visited Colón, Panama City, and the Canal Zone.

31. Herbert Hoover (1928)

32. Jimmy and Rosalynn Carter (1978), who discovered her great uncle's grave site there!

33. Theodore Roosevelt (1913). He survived the trip but had health difficulties thereafter.

34. Bolivia, French Guiana, Guyana, and Paraguay

35. John Adams (1786), during his time as ambassador to the Court of St. James's.

36. John Adams (1778), in Paris, France.

37. Thomas Jefferson (1787), to smuggle rice from the Piedmont to take back to the U.S.A.

38. Millard Fillmore (1855), even though Greeley had vilified him in the press.

39. Ulysses Grant (1877) and Herbert Hoover (1938), respectively, both in Berlin, Germany.

40. Woodrow Wilson (1918), John Kennedy (1961), and Ronald Reagan (1982)

41. Calvin Coolidge, Lyndon Johnson, and Gerald Ford

42. Dwight Eisenhower (1945), reviewing a gymnastics event.

43. Richard Nixon (1972), who visited Moscow, for a state visit.

44. Jimmy Carter (1981)

45. Bill Clinton (1995 and 1998), who visited Belfast in order to advance peace talks.

46. George W. Bush (2003), at Hillsborough Castle, to advance the Good Friday Agreement.

47. Albania, Andorra, Estonia, Lichtenstein, Luxembourg, Moldova, and Slovakia

48. Theodore Roosevelt (1872) and George W. Bush (1994), respectively.

49. Herbert Hoover (1905) and Dwight Eisenhower (1959), respectively.

50. Lyndon Johnson (1961), to hear his echo. Bill Clinton also visited the Taj Mahal (2000).

51. Herbert Hoover (1899), Richard Nixon (1972), and Dwight Eisenhower (1960)

52. Richard Nixon (1972), during the first U.S. presidential visit to Communist China.

53. Richard Nixon (1972) and Bill Clinton (1998), respectively, during presidential visits.

54. Former President Ulysses Grant (1878), meeting Emperor Mutsuhito while on world tour.

55. Dwight Eisenhower (1960), since his safety was not guaranteed after anti-American riots.

56. Richard Nixon (1971). It was the first time in 2,000 years that a monarch had left Japan!

57. Gerald Ford (1974) and George W. Bush (2003), respectively.

58. Franklin Roosevelt (1943), who visited Morocco to attend the Casablanca Conference.

59. Jimmy Carter (1978), Bill Clinton (1998), and George W. Bush (2003)

60. Ulysses Grant (1878). Franklin Roosevelt (1943) was the first incumbent to do so.

61. Franklin Roosevelt (1943), who visited Monrovia. Jimmy Carter (1978) also visited there.

62. Herbert Hoover (1909). Bill Clinton (1998) was the first incumbent to do so.

63. Which president visited the Horn of Africa?
64. Which president led a year-long safari to Africa?
65. Which *incumbent* presidents first and last visited Australia?
66. Which presidents first and last visited a Communist country after World War II?
67. Which First Couple took a famous world tour after his presidency, to rave reviews?
68. Who can order the president *not* to travel somewhere and the president must obey?

Vetoes

1. Which presidents first and last used a regular veto?
2. Which presidents first and last did *not* use a regular veto, respectively?
3. Which president vetoed not a single bill during at least one full, four-year term?
4. Which presidents with at least one regular veto utilized it least and most?
5. Which presidents first and last used a "pocket veto," respectively?
6. Which presidents first and last did *not* use a pocket veto?
7. Which presidents with at least one pocket veto utilized it least and most?
8. Which presidents first and last had at least one veto overridden?
9. Which presidents with at least one veto first and last had no veto overridden?
10. Which president had more of his vetoes overridden than any other president?
11. Which presidents had the smallest and largest percentages of regular vetoes overridden?
12. Which presidents had the smallest and largest percentages of total vetoes overridden?
13. Which president first vetoed a general-revenue bill?

War of 1812

1. Which president had been military commander of the District of Columbia?
2. Whom did Andrew Jackson defeat at the Battle of New Orleans?
3. Who was the last U.S. general who defeated the British in battle?
4. Which president had been commander at the British defeat of the Battle of the Thames?
5. Which president received 160 acres of land in Sioux City, Iowa?

Wars

1. Which military conflict was the last one in which the president had declared war?
2. Which president was perhaps the only one who had fought against the French?
3. Which president did not enlist blacks until it became obvious his white troops were losing?
4. Which president had been a prisoner of war, and refused to shine his captor's boots?
5. Which president was asked to head a provisional army in case war broke out?
6. Who said, "First in war, first in peace, first in the hearts of his countrymen"?

63. George Bush (1992-1993), who visited Mogadishu, Somalia.
64. Theodore Roosevelt (1909), to Kenya, Uganda, Zaire, and Sudan.
65. Lyndon Johnson (1966) and George W. Bush (2003), the latter with an armed air escort.
66. Richard Nixon (1969), to Rumania, and Jimmy Carter (2002), to Cuba, respectively.
67. President and Mrs. Ulysses Grant (1877-1879), to Europe, Africa, and Asia.
68. The director of the United States Secret Service, currently W. Ralph Basham.

Vetoes (answers)

1. George Washington (1792) and Bill Clinton (2000), respectively.
2. John Adams (1797-1801) and George W. Bush (2001-2003). Five others did not do so.
3. John Quincy Adams (1825-1829)
4. James Monroe (1) and Franklin Roosevelt (372), respectively.
5. James Madison (1812) and Bill Clinton (2000), by not signing a bill and allowing it to die.
6. George Washington (1789-1797) and George W. Bush (2001-2003), respectively.
7. Van Buren, Polk, Hayes, and Harding (1) and Franklin Roosevelt (263), respectively.
8. John Tyler (1845) and Bill Clinton (1997), respectively.
9. George Washington (1789-1797) and Lyndon Johnson (1963-1969), respectively.
10. Andrew Johnson (1865-1869), with fifteen overrides.
11. Grover Cleveland (2.02%) and Andrew Johnson (71.43%), respectively.
12. Dwight Eisenhower (1.10%) and Franklin Pierce (55.56%), respectively.
13. Franklin Roosevelt (1944), who vetoed a $2.3 billion tax bill.

War of 1812 (answers)

1. James Monroe (1813-1815), after the repulsion of the British from American soil.
2. General Edward Pakenham (1814-1815), two weeks *after* the peace treaty had been signed!
3. Andrew Jackson (1815), at the Battle of New Orleans, on January 8.
4. William Henry Harrison (1813), in which battle Tecumseh was killed.
5. John Tyler (1850), for his service during the War of 1812, two generations earlier!

Wars (answers)

1. None. Only Congress has a constitutional authority to declare war.
2. George Washington (1754), at Fort Necessity, during the French and Indian Wars.
3. George Washington (1776), at which point he called up 5,000 black recruits.
4. Andrew Jackson (1781), at the age of fourteen years!
5. George Washington (1798), who was asked by John Adams.
6. Henry "Light Horse Harry" Lee (1799), talking about George Washington.

7. Who wrote that he had won one of the greatest victories since the Pilgrims had landed?
8. Which president often rode sidesaddle in battle, a method usually only ladies used?
9. Who received the famous message "We have met the enemy and they are ours"?
10. Which president first faced enemy gunfire while in office?
11. Which president had canoed down the Mississippi River on the way to war?
12. Which president received Chief Black Hawk as a prisoner during the Black Hawk Wars?
13. Which president twice had fainted in battle?
14. Who demanded a president show where "American blood was shed on American soil"?
15. Which was the "most unjust war ever waged by a stronger nation against a weaker"?
16. Which president first ordered his generals *not* to allow Congressmen to serve in battle?
17. In which war did the most future presidents serve?
18. Which president visited more battle sites during wartime than any other president?
19. Which president appointed the youngest general in U.S. military history?
20. Who signed "General Order No. 11" expelling Jews from the Treasury Department?
21. Who summarized his pax americana policy as, "Speak softly and carry a big stick"?
22. Which president offered to raise volunteers to fight with the Allies in France?
23. Who was a tank commander while Douglas MacArthur burned "Coxey's Army" campsites?
24. Who was in a combat zone for thirteen minutes yet said he had "months in active duty"?
25. Which president ordered bats dropped over enemy territory in Operation X-Ray?
26. What did "the man who built the atomic bomb" say to Harry Truman after Hiroshima?
27. Which former president opposed U.S. involvement in the Korean War?
28. Which president ordered that "Democracy Kits" be dropped on the enemy?
29. Which president was responsible for the creation of Presidential Joke Day, August 11?
30. Which president accepted direct financial assistance from other countries to fight a war?
31. Which president proposed a federal budget cutting taxes while preparing for war?

Watergate

1. Which Watergate conspirator was last released from jail?
2. Who replaced Attorney General John Mitchell during Watergate, but resigned afterwards?
3. Who defended President Nixon during the Watergate crisis?
4. Which reporters for *The Washington Post* followed the Watergate break-in and cover-up?
5. Who portrayed journalists Woodward and Bernstein in the movie *All the President's Men*?
6. Who was appointed to fill FBI Chief J. Edgar Hoover's position after he had died?
7. What was the "Saturday Night Massacre"?
8. Who was the Watergate's janitor who noticed the break-in at the Democratic offices?
9. Which District of Columbia judge controlled the Watergate judicial hearings?
10. How many persons were convicted in the Watergate scandal?

7. William Henry Harrison (1811), referring to the Battle of Tippecanoe.
8. Zachary Taylor (1812-1848)
9. William Henry Harrison (1813), from Oliver Hazard Payne, after the Battle of Lake Erie.
10. James Madison (1814), near Bladensburg, Maryland, to delay the capture of Washington.
11. Abraham Lincoln (1831), from Pekin to Havana, Illinois, to fight in the Black Hawk Wars.
12. Zachary Taylor (1832), after the Battle of Bad Axe River, Wisconsin.
13. Franklin Pierce (1846), during the Mexican War, in the Battle of Churubusco.
14. Abraham Lincoln (1846), disbelieving President James Polk's pretext for the Mexican War.
15. The Mexican War (1846-1848), according to Ulysses Grant.
16. Abraham Lincoln (1861), after Senator Edward Baker died in the Battle of Ball's Bluff.
17. The Civil War (1861-1865), by Johnson, Grant, Hayes, Garfield, Harrison, and McKinley.
18. Abraham Lincoln (1861-1865)
19. Abraham Lincoln (1865), who appointed twenty-year-old Galusha Pennypacker.
20. Ulysses Grant (1862), because Jews shipped commodities to the North for triple prices.
21. Theodore Roosevelt (1905), also referred to as "gunboat diplomacy."
22. Theodore Roosevelt (1917), during World War I, but was declined by Woodrow Wilson.
23. Dwight Eisenhower (1932), blocking the Anacostia Bridge from the advancing veterans.
24. Lyndon Johnson (1940)
25. Franklin Roosevelt (1944), in order to start thousands of fires.
26. "Mr. President, I feel I have blood on my hands" (1945), by J. Robert Oppenheimer.
27. Herbert Hoover (1952)
28. Richard Nixon (1970), of brooches and pen-pencil sets, upon the North Vietnamese.
29. Ronald Reagan (1984), after joking on live radio that he would start bombing Russia.
30. George Bush (1991), during the Persian Gulf War.
31. George W. Bush (2003), eliminating taxes on dividends before Operation Iraqi Freedom.

Watergate (answers)

1. John N. Mitchell (1979). He had been attorney general (1969-1972).
2. Richard G. Kleindienst, attorney general (1972-1973).
3. James St. Clair (1974), his private defense attorney.
4. Bob Woodward and Carl Bernstein (1972-1974), winning the Pulitzer Prize (1973).
5. Robert Redford and Dustin Hoffman (1976), respectively.
6. L. Patrick Gray (1972-1973), who resigned because of the Watergate scandal.
7. When Richard Nixon told Elliot Richardson to fire Special Investigator Archibald Cox.
8. Frank Wills, who found it on June 17, 1972. The press initially panned it as a "caper."
9. U.S. District Judge John J. Sirica (1973-1974)
10. Twenty

11. Which Republican senator first called for Richard Nixon's resignation?
12. How many minutes were missing from Richard Nixon's Oval Office tapes?
13. Which two persons planned the Watergate break-in of the Democratic campaign offices?
14. Which Watergate figure had been the youngest marine corps company commander?
15. Which Watergate figure had been a strategist for the invasion of the Bay of Pigs?
16. What resulted in the heaviest telegram traffic in the history of Western Union?
17. Which one of the Watergate conspirators served the longest jail term?
18. Which Watergate figure had been the CIA station chief in Montevideo, Uruguay?
19. Which Watergate figure appeared on television series such as *Miami Vice* and *MacGyver*?
20. Which Watergate figure became the subject of author Norman Mailer's *Harlot's Ghost*?
21. Which Watergate figure drove a Corvette with the license plate "H20-GATE"?
22. Which Watergate figure became the chairman of Prison Fellowship Ministries?
23. Which Watergate figure said, "The president *is* the government"?
24. Who was "Deep Throat," the mysterious source claimed by *The Washington Post*?

Weapons

1. Where is the 6.5-millimeter Mannlicher-Carcano rifle that Lee Harvey Oswald used?
2. Where is the bullet from the Bulldog pistol Charles Guiteau used to kill James Garfield?
3. Where is the Derringer that John Wilkes Booth used to assassinate Abraham Lincoln?
4. Who has the gun that John Hinckley, Jr., used in his assassination attempt?
5. Which two would-be presidential assassins' weapons are displayed by the Secret Service?
6. Where did Jack Ruby purchase the gun that he used to kill Lee Harvey Oswald?
7. What type of weapon did William McKinley's assassin use?
8. Which president, challenged to a duel, chose "cavalry broad swords of the largest size"?
9. Which president renounced his life membership in the National Rifle Association (NRA)?
10. Which doctrine urged selling weapons to friendly governments to defend themselves?
11. What did Harry Truman know about the atomic bomb upon assuming office in 1945?
12. What was the nickname of Grover Cleveland's rifle?
13. Which First Couple kept a pair of pistols under their pillows at night?

White House

1. What was the address of the first presidential "mansion"?
2. Which president selected the site of the new capital in Washington, DC?
3. Which president appointed a black man to help survey the new capital?
4. Who designed the White House, the largest house in the U.S.A. until after the Civil War?
5. When was the cornerstone laid for the White House?
6. What was the original color of the White House?

11. Senator James Buckley (C-NY), an ornithologist and first third-party senator since 1940.

12. 18½ minutes, on June 20, 1972. He had been speaking with H. R. Haldeman.

13. G. Gordon Liddy and Howard Hunt (1972)

14. Chuck Colson (1953)

15. E. Howard Hunt (1961)

16. The "Saturday Night Massacre," which took place on October 20, 1973.

17. G. Gordon Liddy (fifty-two months out of a 258-month sentence)

18. E. Howard Hunt (1957-1960)

19. G. Gordon Liddy, in 1984 and 1985, respectively.

20. E. Howard Hunt (1991)

21. G. Gordon Liddy (1997)

22. Chuck Colson (1978), who was born again and hosted Pat Robertson's *700 Club* show.

23. John Ehrlichman

24. Hal Holbrook, at least in the film *All the President's Men* (1976).

Weapons (answers)

1. In the National Archives, and a replica is used in the tour through the FBI building.

2. At the Historical Society of Washington, DC.

3. The Lincoln Museum of Ford's Theater, in Washington, DC.

4. The Federal Bureau of Investigation (FBI)

5. Giuseppe Zangara's .32 revolver and Sarah Jane Moore's .38 pistol

6. At a pawn shop in Dallas, Texas, for $75. It is now worth more than $250,000.

7. A .32 Iver Johnson revolver

8. Abraham Lincoln (1842), in a duel with Illinois State Auditor James Shields that was nixed.

9. George Bush (1995), after he believed it had become too anti-government.

10. The Nixon Doctrine (1969), in order to avoid U.S. intervention.

11. Absolutely nothing, it had been kept secret from him.

12. "Death and Destruction," a prized hunting rifle.

13. President and Mrs. Franklin Roosevelt (1933-1945), nicknamed "His" and "Hers."

White House (answers)

1. 1 Cherry Street, New York City, first occupied by George Washington on April 23, 1789.

2. George Washington (1790), in "The Indian Maid" tavern, in Bladensburg, Maryland.

3. George Washington (1791), who appointed Benjamin Banneker (1731-1806).

4. James Hoban (1792). Thomas Jefferson submitted a design under the pseudonym "A.Z."

5. October 13, 1792, by Freemasons and the commissioners of the District of Columbia.

6. Gray. Calcimine used to obscure burns from the War of 1812 turned it white (1817).

7. What is the full address and telephone number of the 55,000-square-foot White House?

8. Which president added the East and West Terraces of the White House?

9. Which president added the South Portico of the White House?

10. Which president added the North Portico of the White House?

11. Which president added the West Wing to the White House?

12. Which president added the East Wing to the White House?

13. Which president added the Oval Office to the White House?

14. Which ones of the 132 rooms in the White House are named for colors?

15. Which president first decorated the Green Room in that color?

16. Whose prayer to his wife is inscribed over the fireplace in the State Dining Room?

17. Which president gave the State Dining Room its name?

18. Which president allowed a painter to use the State Dining Room as his studio?

19. Which president let the Marquis de Lafayette's pet alligator stay in the East Room?

20. Which president established the first press room in the White House?

21. Which president established the first "war room" in the White House?

22. Which president intentionally locked himself in White House bathrooms?

23. Which president made love in a five-by-five-foot closet near the Cabinet Room?

24. Which president did not like seeing servants in the hallways of the White House?

25. Until when could any American citizen walk into the White House and roam the halls?

26. Where is there an exact but 3/5ths life-size replica of the White House?

27. Which president almost built a new White House, with plans drawn and scale models built?

28. Which president had servants flick light switches and slept with all the lights on?

29. Who remotely turned on electricity for the Columbian Exposition, in Chicago, Illinois?

30. Which president fanatically turned off all White House lights not absolutely necessary?

31. Which presidents were forced to move out of the White House for long periods of time?

32. Where did those presidents live instead of at the White House?

33. Which president almost always carried a basket of official-looking documents?

34. Who billed the King of England for the British burning of the White House?

35. Who said the White House could fit "two emperors, one pope, and the grand lama"?

36. What did Margaret Truman and Lynda and Luci Johnson call the White House?

37. To which president did a law first apply banning removal of items from the White House?

38. Which president was the only one who participated in a séance in the White House?

39. Which president dressed as Santa Claus for his grandchildren in the White House?

40. Which president prayed every morning and night on his knees while in the White House?

41. Who first paid for his own White House meals, while billing the government for his guests'?

42. When was the White House accredited as a "museum"?

43. Which president recycled paper, glass, and aluminum from the White House trash?

44. What is "The White House" in Auckland, New Zealand?

7. 1600 Pennsylvania Avenue, Washington, DC 20500, (202) 456-1414.
8. Thomas Jefferson (1807), first used regularly by J. Q. Adams and Jefferson, respectively.
9. James Monroe (1824). Andrew Jackson (1829) first used it regularly.
10. Andrew Jackson (1830). Calvin Coolidge (1923) first used it regularly.
11. Theodore Roosevelt (1902), for business functions.
12. Franklin Roosevelt (1942), after the U.S.A. had entered World War II.
13. William Taft (1909), during the enlargement of the West Wing.
14. The Blue (1837), Green (1818), Red (1845), and Yellow Oval (1809) Rooms
15. James Monroe (1818), choosing a distasteful shade to keep women out of it, a parlor.
16. John Adams's (1800), "May none but honest and wise men ever rule under this roof."
17. Andrew Jackson (1829), although it had been used for formal dining by prior presidents.
18. Abraham Lincoln (1864), so Francis Carpenter could paint him manumitting the slaves.
19. John Quincy Adams (1826)
20. William McKinley (1897). Richard Nixon built the modern Press Briefing Room (1970).
21. John Kennedy (1961), during the Cuban Missile Crisis.
22. Rutherford Hayes (1877-1881), to avoid having to engage in small talk with guests.
23. Warren Harding (1921-1922), with his mistress, Nan Britton.
24. Herbert Hoover (1929-1933), making them scurry when bells announced his presence.
25. Since Pearl Harbor (1941), the White House has never been as cavalierly protected.
26. La Porte, Texas, with a similar one in Irving owned by *Trinity Broadcasting Corporation*.
27. Benjamin Harrison (1890), at the head of 16th Street in Washington, DC.
28. Benjamin Harrison (1891-1893), because he was horrified by electricity.
29. Grover Cleveland (1893), from the White House.
30. Jimmy Carter (1977-1981). LBJ did so also, earning the moniker "Light Bulb Johnson."
31. James Monroe (1814), due to war, and Harry Truman (1947), due to disrepair.
32. James Monroe lived at Octagon House, and Harry Truman lived at Blair House.
33. Chester Arthur (1881-1885), in order to give the appearance that he was hard at work.
34. Calvin Coolidge, who billed King George V of England more than a century after the fact!
35. Thomas Jefferson (1792), disliking Hoban's design, but the original was four times larger!
36. "The Great White Jail" and "A Great White Mausoleum," respectively.
37. John Kennedy (1961), although some presidents have had items placed in their libraries.
38. Abraham Lincoln (1863). Mrs. Nettie Maynard tried to contact his deceased son Willie.
39. Benjamin Harrison (1891), who encouraged other parents to do so in their homes.
40. Woodrow Wilson (1913-1921), who was a devout Presbyterian.
41. George Washington (1789-1797), a tradition every president has followed since then.
42. In 1988, by the American Association of Museums.
43. Bill Clinton (1993-2001)
44. A brothel (2003–)

White House Events

1.   Which presidents lay in state in the East Room of the White House?
2.   Which president first invited a black person to perform inside the White House?
3.   What is the most famous document signed inside the White House?
4.   What is the most notable event that took place inside the Red Room?
5.   Which presidents celebrated silver wedding anniversaries at the White House?
6.   Who first invited a black person to present a musical program at the White House?
7.   Which president first made a "command performance" at the White House?
8.   What is the most notable event that took place inside the Blue Room?
9.   What is the most notable event that took place inside the Yellow Oval Room?
10. What are the most notable events that took place inside the Treaty Room?
11. What are the most notable events that took place inside the Diplomatic Reception Room?
12. Which president had a "dojo," or training school, perform in the White House?
13. Which musician performed at the wedding of Lynda Bird Johnson and Charles Robb?
14. Which would-be presidential assassin had performed at the White House?
15. Whose outdoor wedding was the first one ever at the White House?
16. What is the most notable event that took place inside the East Room?

White House Firsts

1.   Which president first lived in the White House?
2.   Which president installed the first billiards table in the White House?
3.   Which president ordered twenty spittoons upon moving into the White House?
4.   Which president installed the first plumbing in the White House?
5.   Which president installed the first central heating in the White House?
6.   Which president installed the first bathtub in the White House?
7.   Which president installed the first natural-gas lighting in the White House?
8.   Which president installed the first cooking stove in the White House?
9.   Which president installed the first central plumbing in the White House?
10. Which president first erected a Christmas tree at the White House?
11. Which president installed the first telephone in the White House?
12. Which presidents installed the first hydraulic and electric elevators in the White House?
13. Which president installed the first air conditioning in the White House?
14. Which president first signed vignettes of the White House on small cards as souvenirs?
15. Which president removed public baths in the White House?
16. Which president first ordered the U.S. flag to fly over the White House, and every school?
17. Which president installed the first "modern" tiled bathroom in the White House?
18. Which president installed the first electric lighting in the White House?
19. Which president first placed electric lights on the White House Christmas tree?

White House Events (answers)

1. W. H. Harrison, Taylor, Lincoln, Garfield, McKinley, Franklin Roosevelt, and Kennedy
2. James Buchanan (1859), who invited pianist Thomas Greene "Blind Tom" Bethune.
3. The Emancipation Proclamation (1863), in the Lincoln Bedroom, at that time an office.
4. The swearing-in of Rutherford Hayes (1877) after an election decided three days prior
5. Hayes (1877), Taft (1911), Clinton (2000), and Bush (2002)
6. Rutherford Hayes (1878), who invited Marie "Selika" Williams, a coloratura soprano.
7. Chester Arthur (1882), for whom soprano Adelina Patti performed.
8. The only president's marriage inside the White House (1886), Grover Cleveland's.
9. Benjamin Harrison's display of the first family Christmas tree in the White House (1889)
10. The ending of the Spanish-American War (1898) and the atomic-test ban treaty (1963)
11. Franklin Roosevelt's "fireside chats" (1933-1945), radio broadcasts lifting U.S. spirits.
12. Theodore Roosevelt (1904), when Professor Yoshiaki Yamashita arrived from Japan.
13. Pianist Peter Duchin (1967), at the White House.
14. Lynette "Squeaky" Fromme, as part of the "Dancing Lollipops," for Richard Nixon.
15. Tricia Nixon's (1971), marrying Edward R. F. Cox. The reception was in the East Room.
16. The Intermediate Nuclear Force (INF) Treaty (1987), signed by Reagan and Gorbachev.

White House Firsts (answers)

1. John Adams (1800). Therefore, George Washington was the only one who did *not* live there.
2. John Quincy Adams (1825), which fact was used against him in the next election.
3. Andrew Jackson (1829)
4. Andrew Jackson (1833), during a $45,000 modernization of the White House.
5. Andrew Jackson (1835). Hot air was forced up from fires below the White House.
6. Martin Van Buren (1837), criticized by political foes for using warm water instead of cold!
7. James Polk (1848), replacing candles and oil lamps.
8. Millard Fillmore (1850), and nobody was quite sure how to use it.
9. Franklin Pierce (1853). It was even pumped to the second floor!
10. Franklin Pierce (1856)
11. Rutherford Hayes (1877), from the White House to the Treasury Department.
12. James Garfield (1881) and William McKinley (1898), respectively.
13. James Garfield (1881), forcing air past screens wet with ice water.
14. Chester Arthur (1881), which were periodically re-issued by the Bureau of Engraving.
15. Chester Arthur (1882), as part of a massive renovation.
16. Benjamin Harrison (1889). A new flag flies each and every day at the White House.
17. Benjamin Harrison (1891), to serve the entire White House!
18. Benjamin Harrison (1891), but electricity had been used ad hoc since Hayes (1877).
19. Grover Cleveland (1895)

20. When was "The White House" first the official name for the president's residence?
21. When was the first notable political protest at the White House?
22. Which president installed the first electric-powered steed at the White House?
23. Which president first lighted a White House Christmas tree personally?
24. Which president installed the first electric refrigerator in the White House?
25. Which president installed the first fully electric kitchen in the White House?
26. Which president installed the first swimming pool at the White House, heated and indoors?
27. Which president first secretly taped conversations in the Oval Office?
28. Which president installed the first bomb shelter and movie theater in the White House?
29. Which president installed the first bowling alley in the White House?
30. Which president first extensively recorded his meetings in the Oval Office?
31. Which president first regularly recorded his telephone calls in the Oval Office?
32. Which president first used a voice-activated recorder for conversations in the Oval Office?
33. Which president installed the first fully-automated White House office?
34. Which president installed the first "Golden Carrot" refrigerator in the White House?

White House Flora

1. Which president grew red geraniums inside his office at the White House?
2. Which president lined Pennsylvania Avenue with Lombardy poplar trees?
3. Who reduced the White House grounds to bring the people closer to the White House?
4. Which president installed the first flower garden on the White House grounds?
5. Which president planted American elms on the White House grounds?
6. Which president planted magnolias on the White House grounds as a tribute to his wife?
7. Which president planted a blue-flowered bush, the "Ageratum," on White House grounds?
8. Which presidents began, ended, and revived the Easter Egg Roll at the White House?
9. Which president first held a large auction and garage sale on the White House lawn?
10. Which president grew more than 100 types of roses on the White House grounds?
11. Which president first closed the White House gates?
12. Which president removed the greenhouses covering most of the White House lawn?
13. Which president let a tobacco-chewing sheep "mow" the White House lawn?
14. Which president created what became the Rose Garden at the White House?
15. Which president planted European white birches on the White House lawn?
16. Who had shrubs trimmed to give the Jefferson Memorial statue a view into the Oval Office?

White House Furnishings

1. Which president ordered a round table for the White House?
2. Which president started a nationwide paint-by-numbers fad?

20. In 1901, when Theodore Roosevelt put that name on official presidential stationery.
21. In 1917, Woodrow Wilson jailed 97 female suffragists without due process for six months!
22. Calvin Coolidge (1923), for exercise.
23. Calvin Coolidge (1923)
24. Calvin Coolidge (1926)
25. Franklin Roosevelt (1933)
26. Franklin Roosevelt (1933). Because of his polio, it was one of his only forms of exercise.
27. Franklin Roosevelt (1940), during a press conference, to ensure accurate coverage.
28. Franklin Roosevelt (1942), after Pearl Harbor. He also hired the first sharpshooters.
29. Harry Truman (1947). Richard Nixon (1969-1974) used it the most.
30. John Kennedy (1961), by a hidden microphone.
31. John Kennedy (1961)
32. Richard Nixon (1969)
33. George Bush (1991), who also first used a computer regularly while in the White House.
34. Bill Clinton (1994). It is CFC free and allegedly the most efficient refrigerator available.

White House Flora (answers)
1. Thomas Jefferson (1801-1809), brought from France. Coolidge grew pink geraniums.
2. Thomas Jefferson (1803), four rows' worth.
3. Thomas Jefferson (1804), creating Lafayette Park, a haven for protestors, in the process.
4. John Quincy Adams (1825). A flower garden is still in use today at the White House.
5. John Quincy Adams (1826), but they all died.
6. Andrew Jackson (1830), one of which is the oldest tree at the White House today.
7. James Buchanan (1857)
8. Hayes (1878), Franklin Roosevelt (1941), and Eisenhower (1953), respectively.
9. Chester Arthur (1881), who sold twenty-four wagonloads of furniture and bric-a-brac.
10. Chester Arthur (1881-1885), in the massive White House greenhouses.
11. Grover Cleveland (1894), because his daughter, Ruth, had been lost amid well-wishers.
12. Theodore Roosevelt (1902), replacing them with long-windowed galleries.
13. Woodrow Wilson (1913), named "Old Ike," in order to save money on labor.
14. Woodrow Wilson (1913), although John Kennedy (1961) made it what it is today.
15. Calvin Coolidge (1924)
16. Franklin Roosevelt (1943)

White House Furnishings (answers)
1. Thomas Jefferson (1801), to end fights about seating privileges.
2. Thomas Jefferson (1801), after using a White House room for painting.

3. Which pieces of White House furniture have been in the home continuously the longest?
4. Which presidents involved themselves in questions of White House furniture?
5. Which president purchased the first pressed glassware for the White House?
6. Which president often sat at his White House desk for ten to twelve hours continuously?
7. Whose desk has been used by every president since him, except Kennedy through Ford?
8. Which president undertook a massive Victorian redecoration of the White House?
9. Which president removed White House chandeliers because their clinking kept him awake?
10. Which president rocked in his rocking chair on the White House porch on a regular basis?
11. How much money does Congress allow each presidential family for redecorating?
12. Which president first put bedroom furniture in the Lincoln Bedroom?
13. Which president's family donated a painting by Monet to the White House in his memory?
14. Who decorated the back Oval Office rooms with Catlin paintings and Remington bronzes?
15. Which president first made a complete catalogue of all White House furnishings?
16. Which president appointed the first White House curator, in an executive order?
17. Which president's desk did Richard Nixon return to the Oval Office for his own use?
18. Which president hosted the first White House art exhibit?
19. Which president used the same "The Buck Stops Here" sign that Harry Truman had used?
20. Which presidents' portraits did Jimmy Carter remove from the White House?

White House Staff

1. Which president first hired a full-time White House gardener?
2. Which president first hired a full-time White House bodyguard?
3. Which president first hired a full-time White House physician?
4. Which president first hired a full-time White House typist?
5. Which president first hired a professional White House rat catcher?
6. Which president hired the first female White House staff member?
7. Which president hired the first black White House staff member?
8. Which president first appointed a full-time White House surgeon?
9. Which president ended the tradition that White House butlers serve food in tails?
10. Which president was criticized for outfitting the White House guard in plumes and pomp?
11. Which president canceled White House limousine service for his staff members?
12. Which president got convicted murderer Mary Fitzpatrick to live in the White House?

Wills

1. Which presidents were broke at death?
2. Which presidents left estates of more than $1 million?
3. Which presidents did *not* leave wills?

3. A mahogany marble-top table and a pier table purchased by James Monroe in 1817.
4. James Monroe (1817-1825) and Chester Arthur (1881-1885)
5. Martin Van Buren (1837)
6. James Polk (1845-1849), who claimed to have been the hardest-working president ever.
7. Rutherford Hayes's (1878), the "Resolute Desk," a gift from Queen Victoria of England.
8. Chester Arthur (1882), who went to live with Senator John P. Jones (R-NV) (1873-1902).
9. Theodore Roosevelt (1901)
10. Calvin Coolidge (1923-1924), until too many people gawked.
11. $50,000 per Administration, *not* per year, a sum unchanged since 1925!
12. Harry Truman (1952). It had been an office (1830-1902) and Lincoln's Cabinet Room.
13. John Kennedy's (1963), who donated "Morning on the Seine, Good Weather" (1897).
14. Lyndon Johnson (1963-1969) and Gerald Ford (1974-1977)
15. Lyndon Johnson (1964), something each president has followed since Johnson.
16. Lyndon Johnson (1964), in EO #11145. James Ketchum was the first official one.
17. Woodrow Wilson's (1969)
18. Richard Nixon (1970), displaying twenty-one paintings by Andrew Wyeth.
19. Jimmy Carter (1977-1981), on his desk as Truman had.
20. Jefferson's and Truman's, replaced by Coolidge's and Eisenhower's (Republicans!).

White House Staff (answers)
1. James Monroe (1825), who hired Charles Bizet.
2. Franklin Pierce (1853), who established the two-tiered security structure still used.
3. James Buchanan (1857), who hired Jonathan Messersmith Foltz and is buried near him.
4. Rutherford Hayes (1880)
5. Benjamin Harrison (1889)
6. Benjamin Harrison (1889), who hired Alice B. Sanger, a stenographer.
7. Dwight Eisenhower (1955), who hired E. Frederic Morrow, assistant for special projects.
8. William McKinley (1897), who appointed General Presley M. Rixey.
9. John Kennedy (1961)
10. Richard Nixon (1970), in outlandish Graustarkian outfits.
11. Jimmy Carter (1977), deeming it an extravagance while Americans waited in line for gas.
12. Jimmy Carter (1977), to care for his daughter, Amy. Fitzpatrick had been serving life.

Wills (answers)
1. Jefferson (1826), Monroe (1831), William Henry Harrison (1841), and Grant (1885)
2. F. Roosevelt (1945), Kennedy (1963), Hoover (1964), and L. Johnson (1973)
3. Lincoln (1865), Andrew Johnson (1875), Garfield (1881), and Grant (1885)

4. Which president's will was the shortest?
5. Which three persons witnessed John Kennedy's will?
6. Which president instructed that his estate be liquidated and invested in bonds?
7. Which president first wrote a "living will" specifying end-of-life medical care?

World War II
1. Which president was in the reserve cavalry when World War II broke out?
2. Which president had been the first congressman to volunteer for service in World War II?
3. Which mission in World War II was so secret that President Roosevelt was not notified?
4. Which president had been part of the First Motion Picture Unit of the army air force?
5. Which president had flown 1,228 hours in fifty-eight combat missions during World War II?
6. Who was Dwight Eisenhower's chief of staff during World War II?
7. Which president had served forty-seven months in the Pacific Theater of World War II?
8. Which Japanese destroyer rammed John Kennedy's PT-109 in the South Pacific?
9. Which two island natives saved John Kennedy's life after his PT boat had sunk?
10. Which president almost died in World War II when his ship was caught in a huge typhoon?
11. Who won a shooting match between Winston Churchill and General Dwight Eisenhower?
12. Who repatriated two million anti-communists after World War II, many to be executed?
13. Which two U.S. presidents visited Hiroshima, Japan, after August 6, 1945?
14. Who restored Charles Lindbergh to the U.S. Air Force Reserve as a brigadier general?

Yachts
1. Which president first had a presidential yacht?
2. Where was William McKinley during the dedication ceremony for Grant's Tomb?
3. Which president utilized the third presidential yacht to travel to his summer retreat?
4. Which presidential yacht was secretly outfitted to carry post-World War II Jewish refugees?
5. Which presidential yacht served every president from Herbert Hoover to Jimmy Carter?
6. What was the name of Harry Truman's presidential yacht?
7. What was the name of Dwight Eisenhower's presidential yacht?
8. Which president spent his last birthday party on board the *Sequoia*?
9. Which president ordered a bar, big televisions, and large doorknobs for the *Sequoia*?
10. Which presidential yacht did Elvis Presley purchase?
11. Which president spent the most time aboard the *Sequoia*?
12. Which president decommissioned the presidential yacht since it was "no longer needed"?

4. Calvin Coolidge's (1933), twenty-three words long, leaving everything to his wife.
5. Evelyn Lincoln, Ted Reardon, and Theodore Sorensen (1963)
6. Millard Fillmore (1874)
7. Richard Nixon (1994)

World War II (answers)

1. Ronald Reagan (1937-1941), as a second lieutenant in the 14th Cavalry.
2. Lyndon Johnson (1942), although President Roosevelt convinced him not to go through.
3. "Doolittle's Raid" (1942), the first fully-loaded bombers to take off from an aircraft carrier.
4. Ronald Reagan (1942-1945), producing morale-building and propaganda films.
5. George Bush (1942-1945), World War II's youngest navy pilot, in the Pacific Theater.
6. General Walter Bedell-Smith (1942-1945), ambassador to the USSR (1946-1948).
7. Gerald Ford (1942-1946), in the U.S. Navy.
8. The *Amigiri* (1943), resulting in two deaths and Kennedy's legendary rescue of his crew.
9. Biuku Gasa and Eroni Kumana (1943), who discovered the shipwrecked crew.
10. Gerald Ford (1944), on the aircraft carrier USS *Monterrey*, which ship lost 800 men.
11. Churchill got nine out of ten bull's eyes, Eisenhower none (1945).
12. Dwight Eisenhower (1945), in Operation Keelhaul, as commander of occupation forces.
13. Richard Nixon (1985) and Jimmy Carter (1990), each as a former president.
14. Dwight Eisenhower (1954), after Franklin Roosevelt had prohibited it in World War II.

Yachts (answers)

1. Rutherford Hayes (1880-1881), the USS *Despatch* (1880-1891).
2. On board the USS *Dolphin* (1891-1902), the second presidential yacht.
3. Theodore Roosevelt, on board the USS *Sylph* (1898-1913), to Oyster Bay, New York.
4. The USS *Mayflower* (1902-1919), after being sold, from Europe to Palestine.
5. The USS *Sequoia* (1933-1977), commissioned and built by John Trumbull.
6. The USS *Williamsburg* (1945-1953), whose last known whereabouts are in Italy.
7. The USS *Lenore II* (1952-1971), which Kennedy named the *Honey Fitz* for his grandpa.
8. John Kennedy (1963)
9. Lyndon Johnson (1964)
10. The USS *Potomac* (1964). It had been the sixth presidential yacht (1933-1941).
11. Richard Nixon (1969-1974), mostly agonizing whether or not to resign the presidency.
12. Jimmy Carter (1977), to save money. Herbert Hoover did so with the *Mayflower* (1929).

Bibliography

Books

Acheson, Dean. *Present At The Creation: My Years in the State Department*. New York: W. W. Norton & Company, Inc., 1969.

Adams, Cecil. *The Straight Dope*. New York: Ballantine Books, 1984.

_____. *The Straight Dope*. New York: Ballantine Books, 1989.

Bailey, Thomas A. *Presidential Saints and Sinners*. New York: The Free Press (a division of MacMillan Publishing Co., Inc.), 1981.

Benford, Timothy B. *The Royal Family Quiz & Fact Book*. New York: Harper & Row, 1987.

Bettenton, Don. *Alma Mater*. Princeton: Peterson's Guides, Inc., 1988.

Blackman, John L., Jr. *Presidential Seizures in Labor Disputes*. Cambridge: Harvard University Press, 1967.

Boller, Paul F., Jr. *Congressional Anecdotes*. New York: Oxford University Press, 1991.

_____. *Presidential Anecdotes*. New York: Penguin Books, 1981.

_____. *Presidential Campaigns*. New York: Oxford University Press, 1985.

_____. *Presidential Wives: An Anecdotal History*. New York: Oxford University Press, 1988.

Bowan, Roy, and Brooke Janis. *First Dogs: American Presidents and Their Best Friends*. Chapel Hill, North Carolina: Algonquin Books, 1997.

Brooks, Stewart M. *Our Murdered Presidents: The Medical Story*. New York: Frederick Fell, Inc., 1966.

Brownstein, Ronald, and Nina Easton. *Reagan's Ruling Class: Portraits of the President's Top One Hundred Officials*. Washington: Presidential Accounting Group, 1982.

Bryan, C. D. B. *The National Geographic Society: 100 Years of Adventure and Discovery*. New York: Harry N. Abrams, Inc., 1988.

Calder, Nigel. *¡Que Viene El Cometa!* Barcelona: Salvat Editores, S.A., 1985.

Canning, John, ed. *100 Great Kings, Queens and Rulers of the World*. New York: Bonanza Books, 1985.

Caro, Robert A. *The Years of Lyndon B. Johnson: The Path to Power*. New York: Vintage Books, 1983.

_____. *The Years of Lyndon Johnson: Means of Ascent*. New York: Alfred A. Knopf, Inc., 1990.

Caroli, Betty Boyd. *First Ladies*. New York: Oxford University Press, 1987.

_____. *Inside the White House: America's Most Favorite Home The First 200 Years*. New York: Canopy Books, 1992.

Chatwin, Bruce. *In Patagonia*. New York: Summit Books, 1977.

Cheney, Richard B. and Lynne V. *Kings of the Hill*. New York: Continuum Publishing, 1983.

Collins, Herbert Ridgeway. *Presidents on Wheels: The Complete Collection of Carriages and Automobiles Used by Our American Presidents*. Washington: Acropolis Books, Ltd., 1971.

Cook, Rhodes. *Race for the Presidency: Winning the 2000 Presidential Nomination*. Washington: Congressional Quarterly Books, 1999.

Cunliffe, Marcus. *The Literature of the United States*. New York: Penguin Books, 1982.

Curley, Harold T. *Presidential Quiz*. Washington: Fraternity Press, 1951.

Darío, Rubén. *Cantos de Vida y Esperanza*. 6ª Edición. Colección Austral. Buenos Aires: Espasa-Calpe Argentina, S.A., 1946.

Da Silva, Dr. Manuel Luciano. *Os Pioneiros Portugueses e a Pedra de Dighton*. Porto: Brasília Editora, L.da, 1974.

DeGregorio, William A. *The Complete Book of U.S. Presidents*. Fourth Edition. New York: Barricade Books, Inc., 1993.

Denslow, William R. *10,000 Famous Freemasons*. Volumes I-IV. Richmond, Virginia: Macoy Publishing & Masonic Supply Co., Inc., 1957.

Devlin, L. Patrick, ed. *Political Persuasion in Presidential Campaigns*. New Brunswick, New Jersey: Transaction Books, 1987.

Diamond, Edwin, and Stephen Bates. *The Spot: The Rise of Political Advertising on Television*. Cambridge: The M.I.T. Press, 1984.

Diamond, Robert A., ed. *Congressional Quarterly's Guide to U.S. Elections*. Washington: Congressional Quarterly, Inc., 1975.

Dooley, Kirk. *The Book of Texas Bests*. Dallas: Taylor Publishing Company, 1988.

Dos Passos, John. *U.S.A.* New York: Penguin Books, 1983.

Downey, Morton, Jr. *Mort! Mort! Mort! No Place to Hide*. New York: Delacorte Press, 1988.

Durbin, Louise. *Inaugural Cavalcade*. New York: Dodd, Mead, & Company, 1971.

Fadiman, Clifton, ed. *The Little, Brown Book of Anecdotes*. Boston: Little, Brown And Company, 1985.

Fisher, Ken. *Isaac Asimov Presents Super Quiz III: The Fun Game of Q & A's*. New York: Dembner Books, 1987.

_____. *Isaac Asimov Presents Super Quiz IV: The Fun Game of Q & A's*. New York: Dembner Books, 1989.

Frank, Sid, and Arden Davis Melick. *The Presidents: Tidbits & Trivia*. Maplewood, New Jersey: Hammond, Inc., 1986.

Garvey, Edward B. *Appalachian Hiker II*. Oakton, Virginia: Appalachian Books, 1978.

Grun, Bernard. *The Timetables of History: A Horizontal Linkage of People and Events*. New York: Simon & Schuster, Inc., 1982.

Haas, Irvin. *Historic Homes of the American Presidents*. New York: David McKay Company, Inc., 1976.

Hake, Ted. *Encyclopedia of Political Buttons: United States 1896-1972*. New York: Dafran House, 1972.

Hardesty, Von. *Air Force One: The Aircraft That Shaped the Modern Presidency*. San Diego: Tehabi Books, 2003.

Harter, Eugene C. *The Last Colony of the Confederacy*. Jackson, Mississippi: University Press of Mississippi, 1985.

Hay, Peter. *All the President's Ladies: Anecdotes of the Woman Behind the Man in the White House*. New York: Viking, 1988.

Hayes, Carlton J. H. *Contemporary Europe Since 1870*. New York: The Macmillan Company, 1953.

Healy, Diana Dixon. *America's First Ladies: Private Lives of the Presidential Wives*. New York: Atheneum, 1988.

_____. *America's Vice Presidents*. New York: Atheneum, 1984.

High, Peter B. *An Outline of American Literature*. New York: Longman, Inc., 1986.

Hirsch, E. D., Jr., et al. *The Dictionary of Cultural Literacy: What Every American Needs To Know*. Boston: Houghton Mifflin Company, 1988.

Holland, Barbara. *Hail to the Chiefs*. New York: Ballantine Books, 1990.

Holt, Patricia Lee. *George Washington Had No Middle Name: Strange Historical Facts From The Days of the Greeks and Romans To The Present*. Secaucus, New Jersey: Citadel Press, 1988.

Hooper, John. *Los Españoles de Hoy*. Madrid: Javier Vergara Editor, S.A., 1987.

Huntford, Roland. *Shackleton*. New York: Ballantine Books, 1985.

Jensen, Amy LaFollette. *The White House and its Thirty-two Families*. New York: McGraw-Hill, 1958.

Johnston, Marguerite. *Houston: The Unknown City 1836-1946*. College Station: Texas A&M University Press, 1991.

Jones, Maldwyn A. *The Limits of Liberty: American History, 1607-1980*. The Short Oxford History of the
    Modern World. Oxford: Oxford University Press, 1983.

Kahler, James G. *Hail to the Chief: An Illustrated Guide to Political Americana*. Princeton: The Pyne Press, 1972.

Kane, Joseph Nathan. *Facts about the Presidents*. New York: H.W. Wilson, 1989.

_____. *Famous First Facts*. New York: H. W. Wilson Co., 1964.

Klepper, Michael, and Robert Gunther. *The Wealthy 100: From Benjamin Franklin to Bill Gates — A
    Ranking of the Richest Americans, Past and Present*. Secaucus, New Jersey: Carol Publishing
    Group, 1996.

Korda, Michael. *Power! How To Get It, How To Use It*. New York: Random House, 1975.

Levi, Steven C. *Making It! Personal Survival in the Corporate World*. Los Angeles: Price Stern Sloan, 1990.

Lindop, Edmund, and Joy Crane Thornton. *All About Democrats*. Hillside, New Jersey: Enslow Publishers,
    Inc., 1985.

_____. *All About Republicans*. Hillside, New Jersey: Enslow Publishers, Inc., 1985.

Longford, Elizabeth. *The Royal House of Windsor*. London: Weidenfeld and Nicolson, 1974.

Lorant, Stefan. *The Glorious Burden*. Lenox, Massachusetts: Authors Edition, Inc., 1976.

Louis, David. *2201 Fascinating Facts*. New York: Crown Publishers, Inc., 1983.

Mackay, James. *The Guinness Book of Stamps Facts & Feats*. London: Guinness Superlatives, Ltd., 1982.

Martin, Ralph G. *Ballots & Bandwagons*. New York: Rand McNally & Co., 1964.

Martínez Carreras, José U. *Introducción a la Historia Contemporánea Desde 1917*. Siglo XX. Colección
    Fundamentos 86. Madrid: Ediciones ISTMO, 1986.

Meyers, Joan, ed. *John Fitzgerald Kennedy . . . As We Remember Him*. New York: Atheneum, 1965.

Miller, Hope Ridings. *Great Houses of Washington, D.C.* New York: Bramhall House, 1969.

_____. *Scandals in the Highest Office: Facts and Fictions in the Private Lives of Our Presidents*. New York:
    Random House, 1973.

Miller, Merle. *Plain Speaking: an oral biography of Harry S. Truman*. New York: Berkley Medallion
    Books, 1999.

Moore, James, and Wayne Slater. *Bush's Brain*. New York: John Wiley & Sons, Inc., 2003.

Nash, Roy. *The Conquest of Brazil*. New York: Harcourt, Brace and Company, Inc., 1926.

O'Brien, Laurence F. *No Final Victories*. New York: Ballantine Books, 1974.

Olcott, William. *The Greenbrier Heritage*. Library of Congress Number 67-16176.

Olive, David. *Political Babble: The 1,000 Dumbest Things Ever Said by Politicians*. New York: John
    Wiley & Sons, 1992.

Paletta, Lu Ann, and Fred L. Worth. *The World Almanac of Presidential Facts*. New York: World
    Almanac, 1988.

Palm, Rita. *The Republican Passport: A Commemorative Publication for the 1992 Republican National
    Convention*. New Orleans: The Phoenix Media Group, Ltd., 1992.

Pérez Gallego, Cándido, et al. *Literatura Norteamericana Actual*. Madrid: Catedra, 1986.

Perloff, James. *The Shadows of Power: The Council on Foreign Relations And The American Decline*.
    Appleton, Wisconsin: Western Islands Publishers, 1990.

Pitch, Anthony S. *Congressional Chronicles*. Potomac, Maryland: Mino Publications, 1990.

_____. *Exclusively First Ladies Trivia*. Washington: Mino Publications, 1985.

_____. *Exclusively Presidential Trivia*. Washington: Mino Publications, 1985.

_____. *Exclusively Washington Trivia*. Washington: Mino Publications, 1985.

Quirk, John Patrick, et al. *The Central Intelligence Agency: A Photographic History*. Briarcliff Manor, New
    York: Stein and Day, 1986.

Randall, David. *Royal Follies: A Chronicle of Royal Misbehavior*. New York: Sterling Publishing Co.,
    Inc., 1988.

Ranelagh, John. *The Agency: The Rise and Decline of the CIA*. New York: Simon & Schuster, Inc., 1987.

Reagan, Ronald W. *An American Life*. New York: Simon & Schuster, 1990.

Reinsch, J. Leonard. *Getting Elected: From Radio and Roosevelt to Television and Reagan*. New York: Hippocrene Books, 1988.

Ripley, Randall B. *Party Leaders in the House of Representatives*. Washington: The Brookings Institute, 1967.

Roberts, Gary Boyd. *Ancestors of American Presidents*. Santa Clarita, California: Carl Boyer, 1989.

_____. *New England Ancestors of the Princess of Wales*. Boston: New England Historic Genealogical Society, 1982.

Rooks, George. *An Irresistible Litany of Failure Through the Ages*. New York: St. Martin's Press, 1980.

Roseboom, Eugene H., and Alfred E. Eckes, Jr. *A History of Presidential Elections From George Washington to Jimmy Carter*. 4th Edition. New York: Macmillan Publishing Co., Inc., 1979.

Ross, George E. *Know Your Presidents and Their Wives*. New York: Rand, McNally, 1960.

Ross, Shelley. *Fall from Grace: Sex, Scandal, and Corruption in American Politics from 1702 to the present*. New York: Ballantine Books, 1988.

Rowan, Roy, and Brooke Janis. *First Dogs*. New York: Algonquin Books, 1997.

Sadler, Christine. *Children in the White House*. New York: G. B. Putnam's Sons, 1967.

Sanders, Dennis. *The First of Everything: A compendium of important, eventful, and just-plain-fun facts about all kinds of firsts*. New York: Dell Publishing Co., Inc., 1981.

Sanford, Terry. *A Danger of Democracy: The Presidential Nominating Process*. Boulder: Westview Press, 1981.

Santangelo, Susan Hillebrandt. *Kinkaid and Houston: 75 Years*. Houston: Gulf Publishing Company, 1981.

Scammon, Richard M., and Alice V. McGillivray, eds. *America Votes 12*. Washington, DC: Election Research Center, Congressional Quarterly, 1977.

_____. *America Votes 14*. Washington: Election Research Center, Congressional Quarterly, 1985.

Seuling, Barbara. *The Last Cow on the White House Lawn & Other Little-Known Facts About the Presidency*. Garden City, New York: Doubleday & Co., Inc., 1978.

Shafer, Neil. *A Guide Book of Modern United States Currency*. Racine: Western Publishing Company, Inc., 1975.

Shaw, Mark. *The John F. Kennedys: A Family Album*. New York: Farrar, Straus and Company, 1964.

Shields-West, Eileen. *The World Almanac of Presidential Campaigns*. New York: World Almanac, 1992.

Silva, Michael, and Bertil Sjögren. *Europe 1992 and The New World Power Game*. New York: John Wiley & Sons, 1990.

Smith, A. Robert, and Eric Sevareid. *Washington: Magnificent Capital*. Garden City, New York: Doubleday & Company, Inc., 1965.

Smith, Dean. *The Goldwaters of Arizona*. Flagstaff: Northland Press, 1986.

Smith, Don. *Peculiarities of the Presidents — Strange and Intimate Facts Not Found in History*. Van Wert, Ohio: Wilkinson Press, 1938.

Smith, Hedrick. *The Power Game: How Washington Works*. New York: Random House, 1988.

Stimpson, George. *Why Do Some Shoes Squeak? and 568 Other Popular Questions Answered*. New York: Bell Publishing Company, 1984.

Tally, Steve. *Bland Ambition*. New York: Harcourt Brace Jovanovich, 1992.

Taylor, John M. *From the White House Inkwell: American Presidential Autographs*. Rutland, Vermont: Charles E. Tuttle Company, 1968.

Taylor, Tim. *The Book of Presidents*. New York: Arno Press, 1972.

Thorndike, Joseph J., Jr. *The Very Rich: A History of Wealth*. New York: American Heritage Publishing Co., Inc., 1976.

Trebek, Alex, and Merv Griffin. *The Jeopardy! Challenge: The Toughest Games from America's Greatest Quiz Show!* New York: HarperCollins, 1992.

Tripp, William R. *Presidential Campaign Posters*. New York: Drake Publishers, Inc., 1976.

Truman, Margaret. *Bess W. Truman*. New York: MacMillan Publishing Company, 1986.

_____. *White House Pets*. New York: David McKay Company, Inc., 1969.

Udall, Morris K. *Too Funny To Be President*. New York: Henry Holt and Company, 1988.

Ueberroth, Peter, Levin, Richard, and Amy Quinn. *Made in America: His Own Story*. New York: William Morrow and Company, Inc., 1985.

Vonada, Damaine. *Ohio Matters of Fact*. Wilmington, Ohio: Orange Frazer Press, 1987.

Wallace, Amy, David Wallechinsky, and Irving Wallace. *The Book of Lists #3*. New York: Bantam Books, 1983.

Ward, Susan M., and Michael K. Smith. *Biltmore Estate: A National Historic Landmark*. Asheville, North Carolina: The Biltmore Company, 1989.

Wead, Doug. *George Bush: Man of Integrity*. Eugene, Oregon: Harvest House Publishers, 1988.

White, Calvin Coolidge. *All The Things You Never Knew About Our American Presidents*. Louisburg, North Carolina: The Franklin Times, 1974.

Whitney, David C. *The American Presidents*. Garden City, New York: Doubleday & Co., Inc., 1985.

Will, George F. *The New Season: A spectator's guide to the 1988 Election*. New York: Simon & Schuster, 1988.

Williamson, David. *Debrett's Presidents of the United States of America*. Topsfield, Massachusetts: Salem House Publishers, 1989.

Worth, Fred L. *The Complete Unabridged Super Trivia Encyclopedia*. New York: Warner Books, 1978.

_____. *Complete Unabridged Super Trivia Encyclopedia Volume II*. New York: Warner Books, 1981.

_____. *The Presidential Quiz Book*. New York: Bell Publishing Company, 1988.

_____. *Questions: The Perfect Companion To Your Trivia Games*. New York: Warner Books, 1984.

Books Without Attribution

The American Heritage Book of the Presidents and Famous Americans. Volume 6. New York: American Heritage Publishing Company, Inc., 1967.

The American Land. Smithsonian Exposition Books. New York: W. W. Norton & Company, 1979.

The Best of Smithsonian. Smithsonian Exposition Books. New York: Harmony Books, 1981.

Burke's Presidential Families of the United States. 1st Edition. London: Burke's Peerage, Ltd., 1975.

Candidates '88. Washington: Congressional Quarterly, Inc., 1988.

The Complete Works of William Shakespeare. London: Octopus Books, Ltd., 1982.

Crónica del Siglo XX. Madrid: Plaza & Janes Editores, S.A.

Election 1972. New York: Encyclopedia Britannica, 1972.

The 1986 Information Please Almanac, Atlas, and Yearbook. 39th Edition. Boston: Houghton Mifflin Company, 1986.

The 1989 Information Please Almanac, Atlas, and Yearbook. 42nd Edition. Boston: Houghton Mifflin Company, 1989.

1989 Guinness Book of World Records. New York: Sterling Publishing Co., Inc., 1988.

1993 Guinness Book of World Records. New York: Sterling Publishing Co., Inc., 1992.

National Five-Digit Zip Code & Post Office Directory 1989. Washington: U. S. Postal Service, 1989.

Presidential Elections Since 1789. 3rd Edition. Washington: Congressional Quarterly, Inc., 1983.

Presidential Inaugural Bibles: Catalogue of An Exhibition. Washington: Washington Cathedral, 1969.

The Presidents . . . Their Inaugural Addresses. Chicago: Whitehall Company, 1968.

The Presidents: Their Lives, Families, and Great Decisions as Told by The Saturday Evening Post. Indianapolis: The Curtis Publishing Company, 1980.

Ripley's Believe It or Not! Book of Chance. New York: Ripley Books, 1982.

Scott's Standard Postage Stamp Catalogue. 67th Edition. Sidney, Ohio: Scott Publishing Co., 1988.

The Vision Shared: Uniting Our Family, Our Country, Our World. Houston: The Republican National Committee, 1992.

The Wall Street Journal, eds. *American Dynasties Today*. Homewood, Illinois: Dow Jones-Irwin, Inc., 1980.

The World Almanac and Book of Facts 1994. New York: World Almanac, 1993.

The World Almanac: Book of the Strange. New York: The New American Library, Inc., 1977.

World Book Encyclopedia. 1989 Edition. Volume 6. Chicago: World Book, Inc., 1989.

Internet

"Abe Lincoln: Who was this man?" *Jim Cheatham Home Page*. Online. World Wide Web. January 26, 2003. Available: http://www.cbt.net/jimcheat/lincoln.htm.

Aleixo, Chris. "File this under 'Fall Classic.'" *Newport this week*. Online. World Wide Web. November 8, 2001. Available: http://www.newportthisweek.com/News/2001/1108/Sports/038.html.

"The American Presidency." *Grolier Incorporated*. Online. World Wide Web. January 25, 2003. Available: http://gi.grolier.com/presidents/cards/back/09bharr.html.

"America's Caesar: The Decline and Fall of Republican Government in the United States of America." *Crown Rights Book Company*. Book Review. Online. World Wide Web. January 26, 2003. Available: http://www.crownrights.com/books/americas_caesar.htm.

"Augusta National slammed as 'Secret Golf Club.'" *NewsMax.com: America's News Page*. Online. World Wide Web. September 27, 2002. Available: http://www.newsmax.com/showinsidecover.shtml?a=2002/9/27/134935.

Barnes, Fred. "God and Man in the Oval Office." *The Weekly Standard*. Online. World Wide Web. Volume 8, Issue 26. March 17, 2003. Available: http://www.weeklystandard.com/Content/Public/Articles/000/000/002/335uuffd.asp.

"Believe it or not." *ansh.com*. Online. World Wide Web. 2003. Available: http://www.ansh.com/ALLPAGES/believe_it_or_not.htm.

Benedetto, Richard, and Susan Page. "Bush job approval lowest since 9/11 Though still high at 58%, rating reflects anxieties." *USA Today*. Online. World Wide Web. January 14, 2003. Available: http://www.usatoday.com/usatonline/20030114/4775840s.htm.

"Brothel irks US Embassy." *News Interactive*. Online. World Wide Web. July 7, 2003. Available: http://www.news.com.au/common/story_page/0,4057,6711381%255E13762,00.html.

Bursic, Mark. *USATrivia.com*. Online. World Wide Web. 2003. Available: http://www.usatrivia.com.

"Bush Attends Elite Alfalfa Club Dinner." *Austin American-Statesman*. Online. World Wide Web. January 25, 2003. Available: http://www.austin360.com/shared/news/ap/ap_story.html/Washington/AP.V8078.AP-Bush-Alfalfa.html.

"Bush, Staubach to take part in coin toss." *National Football League*. Online. World Wide Web. February 1, 2002. Available: http://ww2.nfl.com/xxxvi/ce/feature/0,3892,4933423,00.html.

"Bush to Address War on Terror, Economic Recession." *From China, About China*. Online. World Wide Web. January 25, 2003. Available: http://www.china.org.cn/english/26105.htm.

"By Popular Demand: Portraits of the Presidents and First Ladies 1789-Present." *Library of Congress, Prints and Photographs Division*. Online. World Wide Web. 2003. Available: http://lcweb2.loc.gov/ammem/odmdhtml/preshome.html.

Caltech Quiz Bowl Packet Archive. Online. World Wide Web. April 29, 2002. Available: http://quizbowl.caltech.edu/packs/q4/caltech_a.htm.

"Camelot Revisited." *Washington Life Magazine*. Online. World Wide Web. November 1999. Available: http://www.washingtonlife.com/backissues/99nov/mv_candlelight.htm.

Caple, Jim. "Dubya won't get this vote." *ESPN Network*. Online. World Wide Web. August 26, 2002. Available: http://espn.go.com/mlb/columns/caple_jim/1422878.html.

Carr, Stephen. "Fun and Amazing Facts . . . Concerning the United States." *StephenCarr.com*. Online. World Wide Web. January 27, 2003. Available: http://www.stephencarr.com/facts.html.

Chavez, Paul, and Alan Boyle. "Site blends tradition and technology." *MSNBC*. Online. World Wide Web. Official Inaugural World Wide Web Site. January 20, 1997. Available: http://www.msnbc.com.

"Clinton vows to use the Web to bring democracy closer to the people." *CNN*. Online. World Wide Web. July 8, 2000. Available: http://www.cnn.com/2000/ALLPOLITICS/stories/07/08/clinton.webcast/.

Columbia Encyclopedia. Sixth Edition. *InfoPlease.com*. Online. World Wide Web. June 14, 2003. Available: http://www.infoplease.com/ce6/people/A0802430.html.

"Commander-in-Chief's Trophy." *Air Force Falcons*. Online. World Wide Web. October 1, 2001. Available: http://www.usafa.af.mil/pa/factsheets/athletic.htm.

"Common Sense." *Morgan Commercial Structures*. Online. World Wide Web. Winter 2003 Newsletter. Available: http://www.morgancs.com/docs/morgan_winter03.pdf.

"The Council on Foreign Relations." *America's Apocalypse Now*. Online. World Wide Web. January 27, 2003. Available: http://www.angelfire.com/yt/angelz/cfr.html.

Dana, Rebecca, and Peter Carlson. "Harry Truman's Forgotten Diary: 1947 Writings Offer Fresh Insight on the President." *Washington Post*. Online. World Wide Web. July 11, 2003. Available: http://www.washingtonpost.com/wp-dyn/articles/A40678-2003Jul10.html.

Davies, Frank. "High-minded yet humble, Carter is often outspoken, unpredictable – and effective." *The Miami Herald*. Online. World Wide Web. May 12, 2002. Available: http://www.miami.com/mld/miami/3250014.htm.

Departments and Chapter Links. *Military Order of the Purple Heart*. Online. World Wide Web. July 2, 2003. Available: http://www.purpleheart.org/i112900-depchlist.htm.

"Did You Know?" *Jim Tatz Web Page*. Online. World Wide Web. April 22, 2001. Available: http://www.chemistry.ohio-state.edu/~jtatz/neat.html.

"Do your job as a citizen: Know the candidates and issues and VOTE." *The Examiner*. Online. World Wide Web. October 22, 1998. Available: http://www.theexaminer.com/archives/10-23-98/thisissue.cfm.

Dowling, Brian, Senan Molony, Tom Brady and Susan Garraty. "President Bush set for historic North visit as Provos finally ready to end struggle." *The Irish Independent*. Online. World Wide Web. April 5, 2003. Available: http://home.eircom.net/content/unison/national/489611?view=Eircomnet.

Easterbaby.com. Online. World Wide Web. January 27, 2003. Available: http://www.easterbaby.com/presidents/ike.htm.

Eichelberger, Greg. *Delphi Trivia Club*. Online. World Wide Web. February 18, 2001. Available: http://billp49.addr.com/triviaclub/quizzes/.

"Fact Sheets: Treasury Building." *Department of the Treasury*. Online. World Wide Web. July 6, 2003. Available: http://www.ustreas.gov/education/fact-sheets/building/history.html.

"Facts About Florence." *Friends of Harding Home and Memorial*. Online. World Wide Web. January 26, 2003. Available: http://www.hardingfriends.org/pages/research/mrsbio.htm.

Falwell, Jerry, Dr. "American Values Are Dying." *NewsMax.com*. Online. World Wide Web. July 3, 2003. Available: http://www.newsmax.com/archives/articles/2003/7/2/220328.shtml.

"The Fate of Liberty: Abraham Lincoln and Civil Liberties." *Amazon.com*. Book Review. Online. World Wide Web. January 26, 2003. Available: http://www.data4all.com/list/500/512000/0195080327.

Griener, Julie. "The Kentucky Derby." *visit-Louisville.com*. Online. World Wide Web. January 27, 2003. Available: http://kentucky-derby.visit-louisville.com/.

Grodin, Dana Heiss. "Flurry of activity opens College World Series." *USA TODAY Baseball Weekly*. Online. World Wide Web. June 8, 2003. Available: http://www.usatoday.com/sports/college/baseball/cws/2001-06-08-notebook.htm.

Hathaway, Dr. Griff. "Constitutional Powers of the President." *Towson University*. Online. World Wide Web. February 3, 2003. Available: http://www.towson.edu/users/hathaway/ExecLegisPowers.html.

Haupt, Wyatt. "Politicians ponder musical chairs." *North County Times*. Online. July 28, 2001. World Wide Web. Available: http://www.nctimes.com/news/2001/20010728/64147.html.

Hedges, Michael. "Ex-president honored for WWII stint as Navy flier." *Houston Chronicle*. World Wide Web. December 10, 2002. Available: http://www.chron.com/cs/CDA/ssistory.mpl/nation/1695430.

Herman, Dave. "Trivia." *First Masonic District, Grand Lodge of New Jersey, Chapter #201*. Online. World Wide Web. November 18, 1997. Available: http://www.2be1ask1.com/mendedhearts/lite/trivia.html.

Hibbetts, Bernard J. "Presidential Clemency Actions 1789-2001." *Jurist*. University of Pittsburgh School of Law. Online. World Wide Web. 2002. Available: http://jurist.law.pitt.edu/pardonspres1.htm.

"High Court Disbars Clinton: Former President Can Contest Ruling." *ABC News*. World Wide Web. October 1, 2002. Available: http://abcnews.go.com/sections/us/DailyNews/scotus011001.html.

"History & Tours." *The White House*. Online. World Wide Web. 2003. Available: http://www.whitehouse.gov/history/life/.

"History of Store County, Iowa." *Mark Christian's Home Page*. Online. World Wide Web. January 27, 2003. Available: http://genloc.com/1887/Display.mv?90.

"History of the Day for: November 5." *MisterGWorld.com*. Online. World Wide Web. January 26, 2003. Available: http://www.mistergworld.com/05-1105.htm.

"The History of the United States Flag." *Great Rivers Council, Boy Scouts of America*. Online. World Wide Web. January 25, 2003. Available: http://www.bsa-grc.org/flag/history_of_the_flag.htm.

"Inaugural History." *PoliticsNow. National Journal*. Online. World Wide Web. January 1997. Available: http://www.inaugural97.org/history/frame_r.html.

"Inaugurals of Presidents of the United States: Some Precedents and Notable Events." *The Architect of the Capitol*. Office of the Curator. Online. World Wide Web. April 2001. Available: http://www.aoc.gov/aoc/inaugural/inaug_fact.htm.

"Interesting Medal of Honor Facts." *Home of Heroes*. Online. World Wide Web. January 25, 2003. Available: http://www.homeofheroes.com/moh/history/history_facts.html.

"Interview with David Gergen." *Center for Strategic and International Studies*. Online. World Wide Web. August 6, 1997. Available: http://www.csis.org/ics/dia/intgerge.html.

"Jimmy Carter wins Nobel Peace Prize." *CNN.com/World*. Online. World Wide Web. October 11, 2002. Available: http://www.cnn.com/2002/WORLD/europe/10/11/nobel.peace/index.html.

Kiefer, Francine. "The private faith of a public man." *Christian Science Monitor*. Online. World Wide Web. September 6, 2002. Available: http://www.csmonitor.com/2002/0906/p01s03-uspo.html.

Knickmeyer, Ellen. "U.S. ties to Liberia reach back to mid-19th century." *The Associated Press*. Online. World Wide Web. July 3, 2003. Available: http://www.dfw.com/mld/dfw/news/world/6225968.htm.

Lane, Tim. "Net4TV Presents: FITNET 36." *net4tv.net*. Online. World Wide Web. August 9, 1999. Available: http://net4tv.com/voice/Story.cfm?storyID=1137.

"Larger than Life." *Los Angeles Times*. Letter to the Editor. Online. World Wide Web. December 30, 2001. Available: http://events.calendarlive.com/top/1,1419,L-LATimes-Books-!ArticleDetail-48965,00.html.

Lee, Christopher. "2002 Federal Register Is Longest Ever: Page Count of Regulations Grows Under GOP, Study Finds." *Washington Post*. Online. World Wide Web. July 8, 2003. Available: http://www.washingtonpost.com/wp-dyn/articles/A23316-2003Jul7.html.

Lee, Robert W. "Like Father, Like Son." *New American*. Online. World Wide Web. September 13, 1999. Available: http://www.thenewamerican.com/tna/1999/09-13-99/vo15no19_bush.htm.

Library of Congress, Prints and Photographs Division, Reference LC-USZ61-480 DLC, LC-USZ62-13002 DLC, LC-USZ62-13004 DLC, LC-USZ62-13008 DLC, LC-USZ62-13009 DLC, LC-USZ62-13010 DLC, LC-USZ62-13011 DLC, LC-USZ62-13012 DLC, LC-USZ62-13013 DLC, LC-USZ62-13014 DLC, LC-USZ62-13016 DLC, LC-USZ62-13017 DLC, LC-USZ62-13018 DLC, LC-USZ62-13019 DLC, LC-USZ62-13020 DLC, LC-USZ62-13021 DLC, LC-USZ62-13024 DLC, LC-USZ62-13025 DLC, LC-USZ62-13026 DLC, LC-USZ62-13027 DLC, LC-USZ62-13028 DLC, LC-USZ62-13029 DLC, LC-USZ62-13030 DLC, LC-USZ62-13036 DLC, LC-USZ62-13037 DLC, LC-USZ62-13038 DLC, LC-USZ62-13039 DLC, LC-USZ62-13040 DLC, LC-USZ62-24155 DLC, LC-USZ62-96357 DLC, LC-USZ62-98302 DLC, LC-USZ62-107700 DLC, LC-USZ62-117116 DLC, LC-USZ62-117117 DLC, LC-USZ62-117118 DLC, LC-USZ62-117119 DLC, LC-USZ62-117120 DLC, LC-USZ62-117121 DLC, LC-USZ62-117122 DLC, LC-USZ62-117123 DLC, LC-USZ62-117124 DLC.

Limbacher, Carl. "Bush's Carrier Visit Contrasts with Clinton's." *NewsMax.com*. Online. World Wide Web. May 2, 2003. Available: http://www.newsmax.com/showinsidecover.shtml?a=2003/5/2/71343.

"A man for all seasons." *South Coast Massachusetts News*. Online. World Wide Web. January 27, 2003. Available: http://www.s-t.com/millennium/people/kids.htm.

"Most Recent Recipients." *Congressional Medal of Honor Society*. Online. World Wide Web. November 7, 2002. Available: http://www.cmohs.org/recipients/most_recent.htm.

"Nice and Naughty." *evote.com*. Online. World Wide Web. December 24, 2001. Available: http://www. evote.com/features/insider/insider12242001.asp.

Noah, Timothy. "Gridiron Grotesquerie." *Slate.com*. Online. World Wide Web. March 22, 1999. Available: http://slate.msn.com/id/1002398/.

"The Outcast President." *The American President*. Online. World Wide Web. January 27, 2003. Available: http://www. americanpresident.org/KoTrain/Courses/JT/JT_Presidential_Moments.htm.

"Over 300,000 Attend 'One Jerusalem' Rally." *Torah Community Connections*. Online. World Wide Web. January 26, 2003. Available: http://www.torahcc.org/news/5761/14-01-01/jerusalem.htm.

Patterson, Kort E. "Burning The Reichstag in Oklahoma." *The Inspection Network*. Online. World Wide Web. June/July 1995. Available: http://www.hevanet.com/kort/BURN1.HTM.

Pawlak, Debra. "John Philip Sousa: The Leader of the Band." *The Media Drome*. Online. World Wide Web. 2000. Available: http://www.themediadrome.com/content/articles/history_articles/sousa.htm.

Peitz, Doug. "Let No Bitter Root Grow Up." *Baraboo Worldwide Church of God*. Online. World Wide Web. January 27, 2003. Available: http://www.baraboowcg.org/sermons/1999/bitter.html.

Pokorski, Doug. "Lincoln statue causes stir in South: To be unveiled in April at National Park Service site in Richmond, Va." *The State Journal-Register*. Online. Internet. March 27, 2003. Available: http:// showcase.netins.net/web/creative/lincoln/news/stir.htm.

"Postal Museum exhibit chronicles FDR's passion for stamps." *Associated Press*. CNN Travel News. Online. World Wide Web. February 16, 1998.

"President Bush Brings Port Shutdown to an End." *National Association of Convenience Stores*. Online. World Wide Web. October 10, 2002. Available: http://www.nacsonline.com/NACS/News/ Daily_News_Archives/October2002/nd1010023.htm.

"President Clinton urges world leaders to embrace global trade." *CNN.com*. Online. World Wide Web. January 29, 2000. Available: http://edition.cnn.com/2000/WORLD/europe/01/29/davos/.

"President Presents Medal of Honor to Captain Ed W. Freeman." *The White House*. Online. World Wide Web. July 16, 2001. Available: http://www.whitehouse.gov/news/releases/2001/07/20010716-1.html.

"Presidential Firsts." *Baseball Almanac*. Online. World Wide Web. July 18, 2003. Available: http:// baseball-almanac.com/firsts/prz_1st.shtml.

"Presidential St. Louis." *Washington University in St. Louis*, from *St. Louis Convention and Visitors Commission*. Online. World Wide Web. January 25, 2003. Available: http://debate.wustl.edu/ presidential.html.

"Presidential Transportation." *Mike King Home Page*. Online. World Wide Web. August 2, 2003. Available: http://home.rose.net/~dingdong/Yachts/Yachts.html.

"Presidential Trivia: Little Known Facts About Our Chief Executive Officer." University of Missouri at Kansas City. Instructional Materials Center. Online. World Wide Web. February 17, 2003. Available: http://www.umkc.edu/imc/prestriv.htm.

"Presidential Visits Abroad." *U.S. Department of State*. Online. World Wide Web. 2000. Available: http://www.state.gov/r/pa/ho/trvl/pres/.

"Presidents and Baseball." *The White House*. Online. World Wide Web. June 2002. Available: http://www. whitehouse.gov/kids/index.html.

"Presidents Trivia." *CASSAR Ladies Auxiliary*. Online. World Wide Web. May 19, 2003. Available: http://www.sar.org/cassar/ladaux/trivia.htm.

"Quill and Bugle Newsletter." *Florida Chapter of the Sons of the American Revolution*. Online. World Wide Web. February 26, 2001. Available: http://www.flssar.org/sarmr01.htm.

Rembert, Mark. "Golf in the White House." *Golf Today Magazine*. Online. World Wide Web. December 1, 1996. Available: http://www.golftodaymagazine.com/frames/backissues/dec96/guestcolumns/golfwhitehouse.html.

Root, Jay. "Access is name of game in Austin." *Fort Worth Star-Telegram*. Online. World Wide Web. January 19, 2003. Available: http://www.dfw.com/mld/dfw/news/legislature/4983610.htm.

Ruppe, David. "Monuments to the Gipper." *ABCNews.com*. Online. World Wide Web. January 27, 2003. Available: http://www.reaganlegacy.org/articles/abcnews.com.3.30.htm.

Seldowitz, Mark. "Lincoln and his Cabinet." *FontWorld.com*. Online. World Wide Web. 2002. Available: http://www.fontworld.com/lantern/lincoln1.html.

Seligman, Dan. "Executive Disorders." *Forbes*. Online. World Wide Web. July 3, 2000. Available: http://www.ncpa.org/pd/govern/pd062600e.html.

_____. *The Liberty Committee*. Online. World Wide Web. July 3, 2000. Available: http://www.thelibertycommittee.org/eomedia.07.03.00.forbes.htm.

Shih, Cheng-Feng. "American Policy Towards Taiwan: A Taiwanese Nationalist View." *Tamkang University*. Online. World Wide Web. November 7, 1998. Available: http://mail.tku.edu.tw/cfshih/Introduction.htm.

Showers, Steven S., ed. "Isaac Stern: Virtuoso Violinist?" *Homeward Bound – The Journal of Ascended Master Devotion*. Online. World Wide Web. January 27, 2003. Available: http://www.homewardboundjournal.com/2000/jan/fireside_briefs.htm.

Slater, Jim. "Bush Opens World Series game 3 at Yankee Stadium." *Agence France-Presse*. Online. World Wide Web. October 31, 2001. Available: http://www.inq7.net/brk/2001/oct/31/brkafp_5-1.htm.

Sloan, Allan. "Bush's Depressing Economy." *Newsweek*. Online. World Wide Web. February 10, 2003. Available: http://www.msnbc.com/news/866512.asp.

Sobel, Robert. "Coolidge: An American Enigma." *Ashbrook Center for Public Affairs*. Online. World Wide Web. July 19, 1998. Available: http://www.ashbrook.org/books/sobel.html.

Sommer, Joseph C. "President Adams and the Religious Right." *Humanism by Joe*. Online. World Wide Web. January 27, 2003. Available: http://www.humanismbyjoe.com/Adams_Family_Religion.htm.

Stein, Herbert. "Reading the Inaugurals: A primer on what presidents say after they take the oath." *On the Issues*. American Enterprise Institute for Public Policy Research. Online. World Wide Web. January 10, 1997. Available: http://www.aei.org/oti/oti7364.htm.

"The Story of Father's Day." *Studio Melizo*. Online. World Wide Web. June 2002. Available: http://www.holidays.net/father/story.htm.

"The Strange Military Career of Millard Fillmore." *Strategy Page*. Online. World Wide Web. January 26, 2003. Available: http://www.crownrights.com/books/americas_caesar.htm.

Stuchko, Chris. "Baseball and the Presidency: A Perfect Team." *SportsPages.com*. Online. World Wide Web. December 12, 2002. Available: http://www.sportspages.com/content/blog.php?p=224&more=1.

"Taiwan Speaks Up." *Wall Street Journal* Editorial. Online. World Wide Web. July 15, 1999. Available: http://expert.cc.purdue.edu/~iltc/WSJcomment.html.

"Trivia Collection." *Anderson Americana*. Online. World Wide Web. January 26, 2003. Available: http://my.erinet.com/~aaauctn/trivia.htm.

"Turnout could be lowest in 172 years." *Decision '96*. MSNBC. Online. World Wide Web. November 7, 1996.

"US Presidents and the Jews: From George Washington to George Bush." *Jewish Post of New York*. Online. World Wide Web. January 22, 2003. Available: http://www.jewishpost.com/jp 0803/jpn0803j.htm.

"Vice president will be governor's guest for Kentucky Derby." *The Oak Ridger*. Online. World Wide Web. April 28, 1999. Available: http://www.oakridger.com/stories/042899/spo_0428990028.html.

"Wambooli Factoids." *Wambooli Home Page*. Online. World Wide Web. January 27, 2003. Available: http://www.wambooli.com/fun/fyi/.

Wartenberg, Steve. "Exhibit features holiday cards from both Georges." *The Philadelphia Intelligencer-Record*. Online. World Wide Web. January 25, 2003. Available: http://www.phillyburbs.com/intelligencerrecord/news/columnists/wartenberg/1750017.htm.

"Weekly Update Archive – Week 19." *Run Chad Run*. Online. World Wide Web. October 20, 2001. Available: http://www.runchadrun.com/marathon2001/updates/update19.html.

White House Historical Association. Online. World Wide Web. 2003. Available: http://www.whitehousehistory.org/Default.asp.

"Who is Ken Collins?" *Ken Collins' Web Site*. Online. World Wide Web. January 27, 2003. Available: http://www.kencollins.com/about/about.htm.

"Who's Who in Judo." *Bushido Kai America*. Online. World Wide Web. January 26, 2003. Available: http://www.bushdiokai.bravepages.com/Who.htm.

"Who Was Harry S. Truman?" *Harry S Truman Lodge 1066, Free and Accepted Masons*. Online. World Wide Web. May 31, 2002. Available: http://www.harrystrumanfreemasons.org/who_was_harry_s.htm.

Wienerboard.com. Online. World Wide Web. January 8, 2003. Available: http://wienerboard.com/newreply.php/id=8676&postid=104946.

Wooster, Marvin Morse. "Monuments to Presidents? Then and now at America's presidential libraries." *Philanthropy*. Online. World Wide Web. July 1, 2002. Available: http://www.philanthropyroundtable.org/magazines/2001/july/wooster.html.

Magazine Articles

Allen, Henry. "Talking Fashion." *Vogue*, November 1989.

Baldridge, Letitia. "Corporate Gift-Giving Guide." *New York*, October 16, 1989.

Bayer, Peter J. "Bull Rush." *Vanity Fair*, May 1992.

Beschloss, Michael R. "How Nixon Came In from the Cold." *Vanity Fair*, June 1992.

Bhutto, Benazir. "The Education and Stormy Career of Islam's Leading Lady." *People*, March 6, 1989.

Blumenthal, Sidney. "So Long, Sununu." *Vanity Fair*, February 1992.

Borger, Gloria. "The politician at the Pentagon: Dick Cheney's calm surface conceals the tug of ambition." *U.S. News and World Report*, October 2, 1989.

Brock, Pope. "Chief Anderson." *People*, November 28, 1988.

Brookhiser, Richard. "Some Misconceptions about Transitions." *Time*, December 19, 1988.

Brower, Montgomery. "Was LBJ's Final Secret a Son?" *People*, August 3, 1987.

Brown, Christie. "Buyer beware, seller too." *Forbes*, March 1, 1993.

Burka, Paul. "John the Catalyst: A new biography of John Connally inflates his importance by making him the cause of great events." *Texas Monthly*, November 1989.

Bush, Barbara. "Let Me Tell You About The House I Live In . . ." *Parade Magazine*, September 29, 1991.

Carrascal, José María. "Bush aventaja ya a Dukakis en diecisiete puntos." *ABC* (Madrid), October 19, 1988.

Catchpole, Terry. "A Short History of Political Dirty Tricks: From the Time of our Founding Fathers, Cheap Shots Have Been a Proud Tradition." *Playboy*, October 1992.

Chua-Eoan, Howard G. "Power Mom: She's been a sister, lawyer, wife, activist and mother. What will she be as First Lady? Those who know Hillary Rodham Clinton best look at her spiritual center." *People*, January 25, 1993.

Cruz, Arturo, Jr. "Glory Past but Not Forgotten." *Insight*, August 6, 1990.

Davidson, Michael J., Lt. Col. *The Army Lawyer*, July 1999.

Dingus, Anne. "The Pet Set: Texans Have Always Doted on Their Animal Pals." *Texas Monthly*, June 2003.

Farnham, Alan. "And Now, Here's The Man Himself." *Fortune*, June 15, 1992.

Filler, Martin. "Designing President." *House & Garden*, April 1993.

⸻. "Food at the White House takes on an American accent." *House & Garden*, July 1993.

Fisher, Adam. "When Donna Shalala Ruled the World (Almost)." *George*, January 1998.

Freeman, Patricia, and Dirk Mathison. "Writer D'Arcy O'Connor, digging deep into 'money pit' lore, unearths a trove of mysteries." *People*, March 6, 1989.

Freund, Charles Paul. "That Proposed Closing of Pennsylvania Avenue: Thomas Jefferson Would Roll Over in His Grave." *The Washingtonian*.

Gates, David, Frank Gibney, Jr., and Robert Parry. "The Kennedy Conundrum: Still too many questions - and too many answers." *Newsweek*, November 28, 1988.

Geeslin, Ned, and Stanley Young. "Having collected 40,000 wacko gadgets, Cliff Petersen is patently one big mother of inventions." *People*, November 28, 1988.

Gormley, Myra Vanderpool, C.G. "Genealogy: Presidential Pedigrees." *Colonial Homes*, April 1995.

Harding, Christopher. "Yale quiz." *Yale Alumni Magazine*, April 1988.

⸻. "Yale quiz." *Yale Alumni Magazine*, October 1990.

Harrington, Walt. "Born to run: On the privilege of being George Bush." *The Washington Post Magazine*, September 28, 1986.

Heard, Alex. "To Live and Vote in L.A." *The Washington Post Magazine*, April 3, 1988.

Hewitt, Bill. "A Heartbeat Away." *People*, May 20, 1991.

Hitt, Jack, and Bob Mack. "Everybody's a Great Communicator: The Revolving Door Between Politics and the Press." *Spy*, November 1988.

Jackson, Bruce E. "Campaign Collectibles - From buttons to banners: U.S. political history in a nutshell." *Country Living*, November 1990.

Keller, W. Eric. "To Mr. President-simple gifts of, by and from the people." *Smithsonian*, December 1990.

Lambert, Pam. "The Reporter Who Would Be King." *People*, September 7, 1992.

Leibovitz, Annie. "Watergate." *Vanity Fair*, June 1992.

Leo, John. "On Granting an Iranscam Pardon: A debate grows over the President's power vs. the public good." *Time*, April 11, 1988.

Levitt, Shelley. "If You'll be my Bodyguard: The attraction between protectors and protected can be powerful—and risky." *People*, January 25, 1993.

Long, Steven. "Touring the LBJ ranch." *Texas, Houston Chronicle Magazine*, August 26, 1990.

Maguire, Jack. "Speaking of Texas." *Texas Highways*, June 1987.

Marin, Pamela. "Who Made Danny Run?" *Playboy*, 1991.

Mark, Erika Reider. "Test your Presidential IQ." "The Better Way," *Good Housekeeping*, November 1990.

Maxfield, David M. "Blacks and the Constitution: Is the Dream linked to that venerable document?" *Texas, Houston Chronicle Magazine*, June 12, 1988.

McFerran, Warren L. "Conspiracies: They have been with us from the beginning of time." *The New American*, December 4, 1989.

McLeod, Don, et al. "The Quick Dissolve: Image into Agenda." *Insight*, November 21, 1988.

McMurran, Kristin. "Shirley Temple Black taps out a telling memoir of child stardom." *People*, November 28, 1988.

Minton, Lynn. "Robert Schuller: 1000th Broadcast." *Parade Magazine*, April 2, 1989.

Mitgang, Herbert. "Dangerous Dossiers." *People*.

Morrison, Donald. "Ghost Dad." *Time*, July 30, 1990.

Morrow, Lance. "A Conjuration of the Past: Nixon's library enshrines his fight for vindication." *Time*, July 30, 1990.

Munson, Sammye. "Cavazos family." *Texas, Houston Chronicle Magazine*, February 5, 1989.

Myler, Kathleen. "George Bush's Other Home." *Texas, Houston Chronicle Magazine*, July 2, 1989.

Norquist, Grover. "The Coming Clinton Dynasty: Conservatives who think the Clinton Administration will be a short interregnum are making a disastrous mistake. For since Watergate, Democrats have learned to deal behind the scenes to ensure their re-election—with or without popular support." *The American Spectator*, November 1992.

Perney, Suzanne. "First Lady." *Boston Sunday Herald Magazine*, November 15, 1987.

Plummer, William, and David Grogan. "November 22, 1963." *People*, November 28, 1988.

Proctor, John Clagget. "New Year Receptions at the White House." *Washington Herald*, January 11 - January 24, 1988.

Ratnesar, Romesh. "The Battle Hymn of the Republicans." *Time*, November 10, 2002.

Reeves, Richard. "JFK: Secrets and Lies." *Reader's Digest*. April 2003.

Roberts, Gary Boyd, and Michael J. Wood. "Foreign Prime Ministers or Presidents with New England-Derived Forebears or Wives: Part II — Europe." *NEHGS NEXUS* (The Bimonthly Newsletter of The New England Historic Genealogical Society), Volume V, Number 3, June-July 1988.

Roberts, Gary Boyd. "Presidents, New England, and Kings." *NEHGS NEXUS* (The Bimonthly Newsletter of The New England Historic Genealogical Society), Volume V, Number 6, December 1988 - January 1989.

_____. "Some Ancestors, Presidential Kinships, and Royal Descents of President George Herbert Walker Bush." *NEHGS NEXUS* (The Bimonthly Newsletter of The New England Historic Genealogical Society), Volume VI, Number 1, February - March 1989.

Santelmann, Neal. "Armchair auctions." *Forbes*, May 29, 1989.

Schwartz, John, Ann McDaniel, Thomas M. DeFrank, and Sue Hutchison. "A 'Pussycat' for Chief." *Newsweek*, November 28, 1988.

Scott, Walter. "Personality Parade." *Parade Magazine*, February 24, 1991.

Shearer, Lloyd. "New Planes for President." *Parade Magazine*, February 5, 1989.

_____. "Perks and Privileges of the Veep." *Parade Magazine*, January 15, 1989.

_____. "The Reagans' Daughter." *Parade Magazine*, November 12, 1989.

Sheehy, Gail. "Born to please." *Zest Magazine, Houston Chronicle*, June 26, 1988.

Sherley, Connie. "The Sixth Floor: Tribute to a Fallen President." *Texas Highways*, November 1990.

Sidey, Hugh. "Present at the Construction." *Time*, November 20, 1989.

Simms, Paul. "How to Become President." *Spy*, November 1988.

Smith, Linda Joan. "The Victor and the Vanquished." *Country Home*, October 1988.

Sporkin, Elizabeth. "Practical Chic: Fashion doesn't come first for this First Lady, but with some help from Hollywood—and Little Rock—sensible Hillary has transformed her look." *People*, January 25, 1993.

Stone, Emerson. "The way we were in 'Poppy's' day." *Yale Alumni Magazine*, February 1989.

Vespa, Mary. "Alice Roosevelt Longworth" (book review). "Picks & Pans," *People*, March 28, 1988.

Wells, Melanie. "Alex the Tailor: He Needles Washington's VIPs But They're Still Coming Back." *The Washingtonian*.

Williams, Marjorie. "What We Know About George." *The Washington Post Magazine*, August 16, 1992.

Wills, Gary. "Dishonest Abe: America's most revered politician dissembled, waffled, told racist stories and consorted with corrupt politicians—all in his noble effort to free the slaves and save the Union." *Time*, October 5, 1992.

Winik, Lyric Wallwork. "World's Most Valuable Coin Can Be Yours." *Parade Magazine*, March 31, 2002.

Wood, Barry D. "America's Commitment to Europe: From the Marshall Plan Through the 1990s." *Europe*, July/August 1990.

Wong, Brant K. "The Unconventional Convention." *Rising Tide*, August 1996.

Magazine Articles without Attribution

"Ahead: The $3 Billion A Day Presidency." *U.S. News and World Report*, December 24, 1984.

"American Dreamer: The Memoirs of Ronald Reagan." *Time*, November 5, 1990.

"American Survey." *The Economist*, April 6, 1988.

"And Now There Are Five." *Time*, October 29, 1990.

"Architectural Digest Visits: President and Mrs. Ronald Reagan At The White House." *Architectural Digest*, December 1981.

"The Best Little Trailer in Texas." *The Washingtonian*.

"The Bush Era Begins." *Time*, January 30, 1989.

"Bush «premia» con la Secretaría de Estado al director de su campaña." *ABC* (Madrid), November 10, 1988.

"A Comic History: Savage Truths." *Time*, September 12, 1988.

"Country Home." *Country Gazette*, Volume VII, Issue Number V, October 1988.

"Dangerous Dossiers." "Picks & Pans," *People*.

"Doling out the odds." *U.S. News and World Report*, February 22, 1988.

"Election Special." *Time*, November 21, 1988.

"Executive Purrrvilege." "Picks & Pans," *People*, January 25, 1993.

"Exercising our right to vote?" *American Gas*, February 1989.

"Exxon plan to resume cleanup approved." *Oil & Gas Journal*, April 9, 1990.

"Farewell to a Flagging Firm." *Time*, November 5, 1990.

"Farewells." *Time*, December 26, 1988.

"Fear and Self-Loathing on the Far Right." *Regardie's*, March 1988.

"A Feel-Good Field Trip." *Newsweek*, December 11, 1995.

"The Fine Print." *Spy*, November 1988.

"From the Ronald Reagan Joke File." *Parade Magazine*, June 26, 1988.

"The Global President." *Parade Magazine*, January 20, 1991.

"González apoyó al perdedor." *ABC* (Madrid), November 10, 1988.

"GOP Convention Makes History (Again) with High-Tech, Grassroots Communications." *Rising Tide*, Special Convention Issue, 2000.

"Hammer and Sickle Seal of Approval." *Insight*, December 26, 1988 - January 2, 1989.

"Happy Birthday, Mr. President." *Parade Magazine*, January 31, 1988.

"Information Please." *The Washingtonian*, February 1986.

"Kale to the chief." *U.S. News & World Report*, November 13, 2000.

"Kemp Bids to Become Pro Ball's Quarterback." *Insight*, September 19, 1988.

"The 'Magellan' Rides Again." *Southern Living*, July 1987.

"Mr. Grocer Goes To Washington." *California Grocer*, February 1988.

"«National Geographic»: Cien Años por los senderos del mundo." *ABC* (Madrid), October 9, 1988.

"El Naufragio del 'President Coolidge.'" *Epoca* (Madrid), Number 79, September 15, 1986.

"A New Harmony." *Newsweek*, December 10, 1990.

"Oh, Sir Caspar." *The Economist*, February 6, 1988.

"Picking up the Pieces: Bobby Fischer, chess champ and brooding recluse, makes a comeback—playing an old foe for $5 million." *People*, September 7, 1992.

"Picks & Pans." *People*, March 28, 1988.

"Presidents on Parade." *U.S. News and World Report*, January 23, 1989.

"Roosevelts to Sing and Dance in a New $4 Million Musical." *The Washingtonian*, June 1985.

"Speaking of Texas." *Texas Highways*, December 1990.

"Staying Neutral." *U.S. News and World Report*, April 11, 1988.

"To the Contenders, Jews Seem to Hold Key to White House." *Insight*, May 16, 1988.

"20 Questions: How's Your Indy Trivia Knowledge?" *Parade Magazine*, May 10, 1992.

"Union Station Firsts." *Insight*, October 24, 1988.
"Updates: Naisbitt Changes His Resume; USA Today's String Is Broken." *The Washingtonian*, 1988.
"U.S. Embassies Hit Political Mass." *Parade Magazine*, October 19, 1997.
"Voting: The Making of an American Birthright." *Insight*, October 24, 1988.
"Was LBJ's Final Secret A Son?" *People*, August 3, 1987.
"What is a Pocket Veto?" *George*, January 1998.
"What Makes George Tick?" *The Washington Post Magazine*, September 28, 1986.

Magazine Articles without Attribution or Titles

ABC (Madrid), December 3, 1988.
Boston Sunday Herald Magazine, November 15, 1987.
Civil War Times Illustrated, September/October 1990, Volume XXIX, Number 4.
Dossier, November 1989.
The Economist, December 26, 1987.
The Economist, January 9-15, 1988.
Fortune, March 1988.
Fortune, April 18, 1988.
Insight, September 19, 1988.
Insight, September 26, 1988.
Insight, November 7, 1988.
Insight, December 5, 1988.
Insight, December 12, 1988.
Insight, February 6, 1989.
Insight, February 27, 1989.
Life, John F. Kennedy Memorial Edition, Winter 1988.
M, January 1989.
The New American, April 19, 1993.
Newsweek, May 19, 1986.
Newsweek, September 26, 1988.
Newsweek, Election Special, November 21, 1988.
Newsweek, December 19, 1988.
Parade Magazine, June 12, 1988.
Parade Magazine, June 19, 1988.
Parade Magazine, June 26, 1988.
Parade Magazine, January 1, 1989.
Parade Magazine, January 15, 1989.
Parade Magazine, January 22, 1989.
Parade Magazine, April 23, 1989.
Parade Magazine, June 4, 1989.
Parade Magazine, June 18, 1989.
Parade Magazine, November 5, 1989.
Parade Magazine, December 10, 1989.
Parade Magazine, December 26, 1993.
People, March 6, 1989.
Smithsonian, March 1989.
Smithsonian, April 1989.
Tiempo (Madrid), September 12-18, 1988.
Time, April 4, 1988.

Time, April 11, 1988.
Time, June 19, 1989.
Time, November 6, 1989.
U.S. News and World Report, February 22, 1988.
U.S. News and World Report, March 21, 1988.
U.S. News and World Report, April 11, 1988.
U.S. News and World Report, July 1988.
Washington Herald, January 11-24, 1988.
The Washingtonian, October 1986.
The Washingtonian, April 1987.
The Washingtonian, February 1988.
Yale Alumni Magazine, April 1988.
Yale Alumni Magazine, February 1989.
Zest Magazine, Houston Chronicle, January 1, 1989.

Newspaper Articles

Abram, Lynwood. "JFK made three Houston trips: His last visit, on day before Dallas trip, was to soothe Texas political tiff." *Houston Chronicle*, November 20, 1988.

Ackerman, Todd. "Bush library fight turns into subtle game of chess." *Houston Chronicle*, July 22, 1990.

Ahrens, Bill. "Judgment day coming Friday in Ruby feud: Family, attorney battle over estate." *Houston Chronicle*, October 15, 1989.

Apple, R. W., Jr. "In the Capital." *The New York Times*, March 29, 1989.

Armstrong, Kiley. "Quotes from his-story: New book collects 5,000 years of male-chauvinist opinion." *Houston Chronicle*, November 10, 1991.

Attlesey, Sam. "Bush fights to keep Texas on his side: Clinton a close 2nd; Perot a strong 3rd." *The Dallas Morning News*, November 4, 1992.

_____. "Texas' political weathervane: Reagan County tops in state in picking presidential winners." *The Dallas Morning News*, May 27, 1992.

Bailey, Doug. "1993 — The Year Congress May Pick a President." *The Wall Street Journal*, April 22, 1992.

Ballard, Steve. "Krygier's OT goal helps Capitals nip Sabres 3-2." *USA Today*, May 26, 1998.

Bark, Ed. "Even the good old days had mudslinging." *The Dallas Morning News*, July 13, 1992.

Barker, Leslie. "Pomp and Presidents: Each inauguration has had something different to offer." *The Dallas Morning News*, January 20, 1997.

Basterra, Francisco G. "A un latido de corazón de la Casa Blanca: Primer duelo televisado de Quayle y Bentsen, aspirantes a la vicepresidencia de EE UU." *El País* (Madrid), October 6, 1988.

_____. "El clan Kennedy prefiere no recordar el magnicidio." *El País* (Madrid), November 23, 1988.

_____. "Funcionarios de la Casa Blanca pensaron declarar incapaz a Reagan en 1987." *El País* (Madrid), September 16, 1988.

Becker, Jean. "Everything has 'clicked' for the Quayles." *USA Today*, International Edition, August 18, 1988.

Belknap, Linda. "Presidents' tastes for healthy food have varied." *Houston Chronicle*, September 24, 1989.

Bethell, "The Interview Ace." *The Wall Street Journal*, March 31, 1989.

Bleiberg, Larry. "The name rings a bell: But school monikers a challenge for DISD." *The Dallas Morning News*, September 1, 1994.

Boasberg, Leonard W. "Power study: Research portrays misuse of authority through Hoover's FBI career." *Austin American-Statesman*, January 15, 1989.

Booth, William. "Did poison kill Taylor in 1850?: Coroner to test remains of president for arsenic." *Dallas Times Herald*, June 15, 1991.

Bounds, Mary C. "Oswald's widow works hard at normal life." *Houston Chronicle*, November 20, 1988.

Bowden, Charles. "Goldwater presents himself as nice guy." *Houston Chronicle*, November 10, 1988.

Boyce, Joseph N. "Going for Broker: What Can Jackson Offer Dukakis?" *The Wall Street Journal*, March 14, 1988.

Boyd, L. M. "Informed Source." *The Houston Post*, July 4, 1992.

Bradley, Shannon. "Hill Scores Sweep in Iowa: Congressional Support Key to Dole, Gephardt Wins; Now, On to N.H." *Roll Call*, February 21, 1988.

Branch, Taylor. "MLK caught in power play pitting J. Edgar Hoover against Kennedys." *Houston Chronicle*, January 18, 1989.

Broder, David S. "Politicking in Texas with JFK." *Houston Chronicle*, November 20, 1988.

Brown, Chip. "Son of ex-president of Panama indicted in threat on Bush." *Houston Chronicle*, April 25, 1990.

Buchanan, Patrick J. "The Coming Resurrection of the GOP." *The Wall Street Journal*, 1993.

Burger, Warren E. "The Declaration and the Constitution." *Houston Chronicle*, The Mini-Page, June 25, 1988.

Burnes, Brian. "Even wimps can grow up to be presidents." *Houston Chronicle*, July 6, 1988.

Byers, Carlos. "Texas congressman is reservist, but exempt from active duty." *Houston Chronicle*, August 23, 1990.

Byers, Carlos, and Jo Ann Zúniga. "Bush may consider several Texans." *Houston Chronicle*, July 22, 1990.

Campion, Nardi Reeder. "The contents of Abe Lincoln's pockets." *The Washington Times*, April 14, 1988.

Chriss, Nicholas, and Cragg Hines. "Jewish leaders say they won't oppose Malek for summit post." *Houston Chronicle*, September 12, 1989.

Clayton, William E., Jr. "Bush takes oath with same Bible used by George Washington." *Houston Chronicle*, January 21, 1989.

_____. "Despite assassination attempt in 1981, Reagan lives through '20-year jinx.'" *Houston Chronicle*, January 21, 1989.

_____. "Glitter, expense of inaugurations continue to grow." *Houston Chronicle*, January 15, 1989.

Coffey, Jerry. "Exhibit traces rich heritage of lotteries." *Houston Chronicle*, October 7, 1990.

Compton, Robert. "Joe Coomer sets sail for Atlantic waters." Books Notes, *The Dallas Morning News*, April 20, 1992.

Conroy, Sara Booth. "Martha-bashing in vogue, but founding mother really cool." *The Washington Post*, 1988.

Cornell, George W. "Pews and politicians: Episcopalians strong in Congress, presidency." *Houston Chronicle*, January 14, 1989.

Coulter, Bill. "JFK's inner circle at New Frontier's forefront." *Houston Chronicle*, November 20, 1988.

Cox, Dan. "Manuscript of Lincoln speech for sale." *Houston Chronicle*, August 18, 1992.

Crowe, Adell. "Capital Line." *USA Today*, November 11, 1987.

Curran, Tim. "If Presidential Race Gets Thrown to House In 1993, Gov. Clinton Is the Likely Winner: In Curious Process, He Has 21 States Virtually Sewn Up, But Last Five Won't Be Easy." *Roll Call*, May 18, 1992.

Cutler, Lloyd N. "Election 1992: The Plot Thickens — You aren't going to believe this." *The Washington Post*, May 1992.

Dart, Bob. "Gail Sheehy's book looks at psyches of potential presidents." *Houston Chronicle*, May 17, 1988.

_____. "Trading glamour for Texas glitter: Inaugural features big-bucks pageantry." *Austin American-Statesman*, January 15, 1989.

Davis, William A. "Unpretentious Harry Truman home nothing like museum." *Houston Chronicle*, February 19, 1989.

Dean, Richard. "Bush latest in line of presidents chasing par." *Houston Chronicle*, May 19, 1990.

Debnam, Betty. *Houston Chronicle*, The Mini Page, January 18, 1997.

_____. *Houston Chronicle*, The Mini Page, January 21, 1989.

_____. *Houston Chronicle*, The Mini Page, January 14, 1989.

Dubin, Murray. "Kids ask president the darndest things." *Houston Chronicle*, December 26, 1993.

Edwards, John. "Odessa site salutes presidents." *Houston Chronicle*, February 19, 1989.

Ellerbee, Linda. "Profound thoughts: A lot can be said using just a few words." *Houston Chronicle*.

Elkind, Peter. "The welfare billionaire: A look at Perot's past turns up plenty of muck to rake: He lies, he cheats, he waffles, and he made his fortune on the public tab." *Dallas Observer*, April 16, 1992.

Elsasser, Glen. "Supreme Court judge cited in bid to discredit RFK." *Houston Chronicle*, February 11, 1990.

Ely, Jane. "Friends say Bush has mellowed." *Houston Chronicle*, 1989.

_____. "Libertarian Party: Candidate unfazed by certain loss, hopes 'truth wins.'" *Houston Chronicle*, November 2, 1988.

Emery, Glenn. "The Sequoia goes to work for its own future good." *The Washington Times*, April 26, 1988.

Evans, Harold. "The American Century." *Houston Chronicle*.

Farney, Dennis. "Carter Redux: The Former President A Bush Issue for 1988, Has New Champions." *The Wall Street Journal*, June 1988.

Farragher, Thomas. "Man who saved Ford from assassin dies." *Houston Chronicle*, February 5, 1989.

Feeney, Susan. "Making, breaking promises: Reality can thwart campaign pledges." *The Dallas Morning News*, October 27, 1991.

_____. "Vietnam's echoes defined unconventional Kerrey: Demands of politics won't change him, friends say." *The Dallas Morning News*, January 9, 1992.

Feldman, Claudia. "J.D. Tippit was love of Marie's life." *Houston Chronicle*, November 20, 1988.

Flick, David. "Fewer Medals of Honor awarded in modern war." *The Dallas Morning News*, April 21, 2003.

Flint, Peter B. "Frances Hammer, A Painter, Was 87; Wife of Industrialist." *The New York Times*, December 18, 1989.

Foxhall, Nene, and Judy Weissler. "Ann Richards reported chosen as Democrat keynote speaker." *Houston Chronicle*, June 26, 1988.

Frank, Jay. "Reagan gets into Dutch in broadcast booth." *Houston Chronicle*, July 12, 1989.

Germain, David. "New York governors rarely make leap to White House." *The Dallas Morning News*, January 20, 1991.

Gillan, T. Gregory. "Johnson building also place to meditate." *Houston Chronicle*, February 19, 1989.

Goodnow, Cecelia. "Is Bush's election a stroke of luck for lefties?" *Houston Chronicle*, January 25, 1989.

Gravino, Patrice. "Paging firm's owner shares Bush's name: No ad deception intended, he says." *Houston Chronicle*, December 10, 1989.

Greenberger, Robert S. and John Walcott. "The Pragmatist: Appointment of Baker May Signal a New Era in U.S. Foreign Policy." *The Wall Street Journal*, November 11, 1988.

Greene, A. C. "Famous Texans buried in some unlikely places." *The Dallas Morning News*, January 1991.

Greene, Fred. "Stamp collecting is a hobby for all ages." *The Dallas Morning News*, June 28, 1997.

Groer, Anne. "Presidential progeny find home a gilded cage." *Houston Chronicle*, November 29, 1992.

Hall, Mimi. "Secret Service is 'all for more women.'" *USA TODAY*, July 2, 1997.

Harlan, Doug. "Think Gramm's kidding? Then think again." *The Houston Post*, October 29, 1989.

Hanson, Christopher. "Reagan's word, hair color true, stylist says." *The Houston Post*.

Harris, Beverly. "A tribute from the heart: Gala honors Nellie Connally, raises funds for diabetes research." *Houston Chronicle*, March 13, 1989.

Hayes, Ron. "Remember when? A rundown of anniversaries worth remembering." *The Dallas Morning News*, January 26, 1993.

Hearst, William Randolph, Jr. "In our classrooms, an alarming situation." *Houston Chronicle*, September 24, 1989.

Heller, Jeffrey. "Bush is the Messing link to put British village on the map." *Houston Chronicle*, January 20, 1989.

Heymann, C. David. "Assassination and aftermath: Jackie seeks to emphasize JFK's place in history." *Houston Chronicle*, June 19, 1989.

_____. "Onassis deals for 'supertanker.'" *Houston Chronicle*, June 20, 1989.

_____. "'A Woman Named Jackie': JFK's adulteries didn't stop her from assuming a key political role." *Houston Chronicle*, June 18, 1989.

Hildebrand, Holly. "Patti does Nicaragua: Reagan daughter pens a naive tale of intrigue." *The Houston Post*, October 29, 1989.

Hines, Cragg. "Around the world in 110 days — a look back." *Houston Chronicle*, June 26, 1988.

_____. "Bush returns to posh roots by visiting his prep school." *Houston Chronicle*, November 6, 1989.

_____. "New day marked in old Soviet empire." *Houston Chronicle*, November 18, 1990.

_____. "Quayle plans strategic end to invisible man role." *Houston Chronicle*, January 15, 1989.

_____. "Winning the California vote is crucial to Bush in 1992." *Houston Chronicle*, October 15, 1989.

Horwitz, Tony. "Sex and Suicide In Sweden Aren't The Rage After All: Ingrid and Ingmar Bergman Gave a False Impression; Try Holland and Hungary." *The Wall Street Journal*, April 6, 1990.

Howe, Robert F. "His name is Mudd: Grandson wants doctor cleared in Lincoln's assassination." *Houston Chronicle*, March 2, 1991.

Howlett, Debbie. "Granddad fashioned an empire." *USA Today*, International Edition, August 18, 1988.

Hoyt, Mary Finch. "Former White House chef 'busier than ever.'" *Houston Chronicle*, January 17, 1989.

Hunt, Dianna. "Grandmotherly touch takes Barbara Bush far." *Houston Chronicle*, August 16, 1992.

Jackson, David. "Overcoming cancer added fire to Tsongas' ambition." *The Dallas Morning News*, January 6, 1992.

_____. "Perot fills ticket with former POW: He calls Stockdale an interim choice." *The Dallas Morning News*, March 31, 1992.

_____. "Perot's exit slowed efforts to reform Electoral College." *The Dallas Morning News*, August 27, 1992.

Jolidon, Laurence. "'We want to reach out': Bush son aids Armenians." *USA Today*, December 28, 1988.

Kanamine, Linda, and Leslie Phillips. "Zaccaro critics cry foul: Ferraro, others defend housing." *USA Today*, International Edition, August 18, 1988.

Karaim, Reed. "Sierra Club supports Clinton: Endorsement only 2nd in environmental group's history." *Houston Chronicle*, September 5, 1992.

Karkabi, Barbara, and Kathleen Myler. "Bush style-elect." *Houston Chronicle*, November 12, 1988.

Katz, Gregory. "Britain's most beloved royal dies in her sleep." *The Dallas Morning News*, March 31, 2002.

Kenney, Charles. "The way she was: Hillary Clinton in her college days." *The Dallas Morning News*, January 22, 1993.

Kilday, Anne Marie. "Krueger sworn in as senator, vows he'll walk in Bentsen's footsteps." *The Dallas Morning News*, January 22, 1993.

Kilpatrick, James. "What if Perot throws race into House?" *The Dallas Morning News*, April 6, 1992.

King, Larry. "Larry King's New Orleans." *USA Today*, International Edition, August 18, 1988.

Klein, Frederick C. "He's No. 2: The Veep as Sports Fan." *The Wall Street Journal*, May 22, 1992.

Kole, Bill. "Overdue process: After 203 years, states OK Congress pay limit." *The Dallas Morning News*, May 8, 1992.

Kruh, Nancy. "First Father: Bill Clinton's dad died before the president-elect was born, but the ties to his Texas roots remain strong." *Dallas Morning News*, January 4, 1993.

Lank, Avrum D. "A lesson rich in history: Book ranks individual wealth relative to GNP of chosen year." *Houston Chronicle*, 1997.

Lannon, Linnea. "Changing addresses will be costly for Reagans." *Houston Chronicle*, June 13, 1988.

Lash, Steve. "Clinton trial will be unlike anything public has seen." *Houston Chronicle*. December 21, 1998.

Leary, Warren E. "Cloned tissues of Abraham Lincoln may answer long-debated questions." *Houston Chronicle*, February 10, 1991.

Lee, Jessica, and Richard Prince. "Bush defends 'brown ones' remark." *USA Today*, International Edition, August 18, 1988.

Lee, Robert W. "Return of Congressional GOP." *The New American*, December 9, 1996.

Leubsdorf, Carl P. "Clinton's 1st day on the job clouded by Baird issue." *The Dallas Morning News*, January 22, 1993.

———. "Iowa's Harkin makes most of opportunities: Backers see senator as having remarkable political sense, but critics decry his approach." *The Dallas Morning News*, January 8, 1992.

———. "McCarthy's bitterness evident as he mounts another run for president." *The Dallas Morning News*, January 8, 1992.

———. "'The people have spoken,' Bush concedes: Perot finishes 3rd, wishes Democrat well." *The Dallas Morning News*, November 4, 1992.

Lewis, Joy Schaleben. "Denmark hails Stars and Stripes on Fourth of July." *Houston Chronicle*, July 1, 1990.

Lewis, Kathy. "Five U.S. Presidents help dedicate library." *The Dallas Morning News*, November 5, 1991.

———. "Nancy Reagan tells her side." *The Houston Post*, October 29, 1989.

Long, Steven. "Presidential landmarks fill new book." *Houston Chronicle*, August 1, 1992.

Louie, Edwin. "Reagan-era resumés." *Houston Chronicle*, August 16, 1992.

Marcus, Ruth. "The Jefferson example: Privilege claim cited in likely contest of North subpoenas." *Houston Chronicle*, January 2, 1989.

Marshman, Donald M., Jr. "Bush knows the game — and how to win at it." *Houston Chronicle*, January 15, 1989.

Marvel, Bill. "Clinton Standard Time: The new president tends to be tardy and it's a trend. But when the rest of us run late, it's just plain rude." *The Dallas Morning News*, January 26, 1993.

McDonald, Greg. "Hillary Clinton is first presidential wife under inquiry." *Houston Chronicle*, January 15, 1994.

McKenzie, J. Norman. "Rattling Skeletons in the White House." *The Washington Times*, May 10, 1984.

McNeely, Dave, and Seth Kantor. "LBJ war record is familiar tale to political foes." *Houston Chronicle*, November 3, 1989.

Means, Howard. "Inaugural festivities have a colorful history." *The Dallas Morning News*, January 20, 1997.

Means, Marianne. "Not even the most-secretive insiders' club of all should be above the law." *Houston Chronicle*, October 15, 1989.

Mintz, Bill. "'We made it,' shouts Quayle as VP parades past crowds." *Houston Chronicle*, January 21, 1989.

Minzesheimer, Bob. "Members maneuver for top spots." *USA Today*, December 28, 1988.

Mitgang, Herbert. "Trial transcript puts Lincoln's courtroom image in a new light." *Houston Chronicle*, February 10, 1989.

Morehead, Richard. "Big John: a tale of Connally and Texas: A one-sided but interesting look at ex-governor." *The Houston Post*, October 29, 1989.

Morley, Jefferson. "Bush and the Blacks: The president's Texas years taught him to put politics above principle." *Dallas Observer*, January 23, 1992.

Murray, Nancy. "First fashions: Clothes of presidents' wives preserved." *Houston Chronicle*, June 15, 1989.

Myler, Kathleen. "Bush-bash bonanza: Texas State Society focus of inauguration festivities." *Houston Chronicle*, January 19, 1989.

———. "Bush-bash! Frenzy on the Potomac and along Buffalo Bayou." *Houston Chronicle*, January 15, 1989.

———. "Still a first family to adoring public: Unceasing curiosity surrounds lives of Jackie, children." *Houston Chronicle*, November 20, 1988.

Parachini, Allan. "Actor Heston has top-level N-clearance." *Houston Chronicle*, November 9, 1989.

Parks, Louis B. "President-elect enjoys a good ribbing at Otto's." *Houston Chronicle*, November 11, 1988.

———. "You can bet lottery popular in 1800s." *Houston Chronicle*, November 2, 1989.

Patsilelis, Chris. "Mrs. Harding was a first lady to reckon with." *Houston Chronicle*, July 12, 1998.

Pearson, Rick. "Honest Abe seduced?: Mary Todd might have gotten pregnant to catch herself a husband, scholar claims." *Houston Chronicle*, October 22, 1995.

Peers, Alexandra, and Ken Bensinger. "We cannot tell a lie: The value of presidential autographs has taken off in recent weeks." *The Wall Street Journal*, Weekend Journal, November 27, 1998.

Perry, James M. "Buchanan, Shaped Early by Unchanneled Anger, Now Directs His Ire at Bush-Brand Intellectuals." *The Wall Street Journal*, December 30, 1991.

_____. "Hands Off: When it comes to honeymoons, some presidents have been luckier than others." *The Wall Street Journal*, January 20, 1993.

Phillips, Leslie, and Mary Benanti. "How those not picked got word." *USA Today*, International Edition, August 18, 1988.

Pierobon, James R. "Bush joins select group in winning presidency while holding No. 2 job." *Houston Chronicle*, January 21, 1989.

Pogatchnik, Shawn. "Black lawmakers again seek slavery reparations." The *Houston Chronicle*, 1990.

Posner, Michael. "Nixon revisits House for first time since '74." *The Houston Post*, March 9, 1990.

Powell, Michael. "Clinton not the first to use unpopular pardon," *The Dallas Morning News*, March 4, 2001.

Precker, Michael. "Engineer built niche in history with JFK eternal flame in '63." *Houston Chronicle*, November 25, 1990.

_____. "The left-hander-in-chief: The three leading candidates for president have a characteristic in common: They're all southpaws." *The Dallas Morning News*, July 13, 1992.

Pruden, Wesley. "An angry attack of killer vowels." *The Washington Times*, February 26, 1988.

_____. "The scarlet sins in a CIA cover-up." *The Washington Times*, April 29, 1988.

Queenan, Joe. "Why Political Editors Root for the Opposition." *The Wall Street Journal*.

Radcliffe, Donnie. "Re-evaluating her life: Barbara Bush reaches crossroads in mid-1970s." *Houston Chronicle*, November 14, 1989.

Ramstad, Evan. "Colleagues recall years of 'Mr. Sam.'" *Houston Chronicle*, September 16, 1990.

Reed, Steven R. "Day of pride turned to nightmare for Dallas DA." *Houston Chronicle*, November 20, 1988.

_____. "Important decisions ahead for George W." *Houston Chronicle*, July 2, 1989.

_____. "Police captain felt he had strong case on Oswald." *Houston Chronicle*, November 20, 1988.

_____. "Two seconds that live for eternity: Ruby shot down Oswald as hundreds of press cameras recorded moment." *Houston Chronicle*, November 20, 1988.

Reifenberg, Anne. "Virginia's Wilder relishes chance to defy political odds: Presidential hopeful has often overcome racial barriers." *The Dallas Morning News*, January 7, 1992.

Rice, John, ed. "The killing of Camelot." *Houston Chronicle*, November 20, 1988.

Riechmann, Deb. "Johnson's trial provided true test of patience." *Houston Chronicle*. December 21, 1998.

Rios, Delia M. "Clinton opens up to the public at the White House." *The Dallas Morning News*, January 22, 1993.

Rodriguez, Lori. "'The best our state has to offer.'" *Houston Chronicle*, July 13, 1988.

Roessing, Walter. "Presidents on Parade: Libraries reveal men behind leadership roles." *Houston Chronicle*. February 19, 1989.

Rosenfeld, Seth. "FBI kept 'sex deviate' files on public, private sector employees." *The Dallas Morning News*, January 20, 1991.

Rosenthal, Andrew. "Reagan not eager to hang up spurs of office: Active 'retirement' to include lecturing, lobbying, writing." *Austin American-Statesman*, January 15, 1989.

Rushing, J. Taylor. "Archive tapes a candid earful into presidents' power, tribulations." *Fort Worth Star-Telegram*, August 11, 2002.

Ryan, Kelly. "Presidential libraries tell tales of leaders' times and challenges: Repositories show positive, negative sides." *The Dallas Morning News*, October 26, 1997.

Safire, William. "Critiquing George Bush's inaugural address." *Houston Chronicle*, February 5, 1989.

_____. "Is 'summit' undergoing a 'sea change?'" *Houston Chronicle*, November 26, 1989.

_____. "Those nine little 'modified limited' words." *Houston Chronicle*, April 2, 1989.

Sallee, Rad. "Untermeyer picked to coordinate transition." *Houston Chronicle*, November 10, 1988.

Sartain, Sophie. "Astrology: Heavens to Nancy! Life's rough, who you gonna call?" *The Houston Post*, October 25, 1989.

Schob, David E. "The definitive history of the Mexican War." *Houston Chronicle*.

_____. "Truman's thoughts on the presidency: no equivocation." *Houston Chronicle*, December 24, 1989.

Schwartz, Matt. "Harding rise to top as GOP challenger to Sharp for comptroller." *The Houston Post*, March 14, 1990.

Selvin, Rick. "Secret ballot among '88 anniversaries." *Houston Chronicle*, January 10, 1988.

Sheehy, Gail. "Reagan grew up in a fantasy world." *Houston Chronicle*, June 28, 1988.

Shribman, David. "Boston Lawyer Who Is an Old Friend of Dukakis Plays Key Role in His Choice of a Running Mate." *The Wall Street Journal*, May 19, 1988.

_____. "Susan Estrich, Campaign Manager for Dukakis, Is, Like Her Candidate, Cerebral and Disciplined." *The Wall Street Journal*, July 14, 1988.

Simmon, Jim. "Obsessions: Author's exhaustive study focuses on men who wanted to be president." *Houston Chronicle*, 1992.

Slater, Wayne. "Early failures taught Clinton brutal lessons about politics: 1980 defeat called humbling to Arkansas governor." *The Dallas Morning News*, January 10, 1992.

Snyder, Richard A. "Presidents on Presidents: Square Pegs in the Oval Office." *The Wall Street Journal*, June 12, 1988.

Solomon, Burt. "Every inch Capt. Baker's grandson." *Houston Chronicle*, January, 1989.

Span, Paula. "Designer's favorite clotheshorse rides into the sunset: Award given for just saying yes to fashion." *Houston Chronicle*, January 12, 1989.

Sporkin, Elizabeth. "The Bush style: Down-home conservative comfort." *USA Today*, International Edition, August 18, 1988.

Stepp, Laura Sessions. "Bush's beliefs shaped by tradition." *Houston Chronicle*, November 12, 1988.

Stout, Hilary. "Hide and Seek: How to keep your job when others about you are losing theirs." *The Wall Street Journal*, January 20, 1989.

Swanson, Doug J. "Brown campaigning as man for the masses: He criticizes party 'elite' in 3rd presidential bid." *The Dallas Morning News*, January 13, 1992.

_____. "On the fringe: Parties outside mainstream U.S. politics provide an outlet for alienated electorate." *The Dallas Morning News*, May 10, 1992.

Trueheart, Charles. "Mud on your machismo: Foes' manhood long been target for politicians." *Houston Chronicle*, November 3, 1989.

Tutt, Bob. "1900 murder plot failed to derail Rice bequest." *Houston Chronicle*, July 8, 1990.

_____. "The '28 Dem convention — what a time they had!" *Houston Chronicle*, June 26, 1988.

_____. "Historians kinder to Eisenhower: But another scholar cites 'ploy' 30 years after presidency." *Houston Chronicle*, October 14, 1990.

Urban, Jerry. "Conspiracy theories abound; none proved." *Houston Chronicle*, November 20, 1988.

Vaidhyanathan, Siva. "Bush may find slim pickings on quail hunt." *The Dallas Morning News*, December 28, 1988.

Walton, David. "Turnabout's Fair Play: Details from the file on the FBI's J. Edgar Hoover." *The Dallas Morning News*, August 18, 1991.

Weeks, Jerome. "God rest ye rowdy gentlemen: How Christmas customs evolved from naughty to nice." *The Dallas Morning News*, December 15, 1996.

Weingarten, Gene. "Clinton's father had other son: Birth certificate records the event." *Houston Chronicle*, June 20, 1993.

Wentzel, Michael. "A look at LBJ: Interview offers glimpse of president's egomania." *Houston Chronicle*, May 4, 1990.

Wertheimer, Linda K. "SMU considered front-runner for Bush library." *The Dallas Morning News*, November 10, 2002.

White, Cecile Holmes. "God and the White House: Bush moves to mainstream, leaves evangelicals uneasy." *Houston Chronicle*, May 6, 1989.

Whittle, Richard. "Columnist Buchanan enters '92 GOP race for president." *The Dallas Morning News*, December 11, 1991.

Will, George F. "Is Bush Puzzled?" *Lubbock-Avalanche Journal*, February 22, 1992.

_____. "Narrowing it down to Dukakis." *Houston Chronicle*, February 9, 1989.

Wolf, Richard, and Richard Benedetto. "He's 'Boomer,' conservative and unknown." *USA Today*, International Edition, August 18, 1988.

Woodward, Bob, and David S. Broder. "Quayle's rise to vice president carefully planned, insiders say: He jockeyed for spot on Bush ticket for 6 months." *The Dallas Morning News*, January 5, 1992.

Wooster, Martin Morse. "Liberals Capture Private Foundations." *Human Events*, July 28, 1990.

Zuniga, Jo Ann. "New Alliance Party: Fulani seeks to turn around an 'underproductive' U.S." *Houston Chronicle*, November 2, 1988.

Newspaper Articles without Attribution

"Almanac talks turkey about Thanksgiving." *The Houston Post*, September 8, 1990.

"Amy Carter explains activism." *Houston Chronicle*.

"As the world turns." *Houston Chronicle*, January 13, 1989.

"Bad Signal." *Saint Paul Pioneer Press*, August 25, 1997.

"Barbara Bush says handguns scare her." *Houston Chronicle*, February 4, 1989.

"Better With Age." *The Dallas Morning News*, December 17, 1997.

"Biography reopens controversy about character of young LBJ." *The Houston Post*, March 9, 1990.

"Book claims LBJ helped by massive S. Texas voter fraud." *Houston Chronicle*, February 11, 1990.

"Breves." *El País* (Madrid), International Section, October 31, 1988.

"Bush aims to bridge Greek gap." *Dallas Times Herald*, July 19, 1991.

"Bush backs men's clubs." *Houston Chronicle*, February 5, 1989.

"Bush, el presidente que afrontará el «postreaganismo»." *La Gaceta* (Madrid), November 10, 1988.

"Bush era begins: Special Inauguration Report." *The Houston Post*, January 21, 1989.

"Bush plays host to his old war buddies." *Houston Chronicle*, January 19, 1989.

"Bush to visit Ukrainian capital after summit talks in Moscow." *Dallas Times Herald*, July 25, 1991.

"Bush warns Czechs of aggression threat." *San Antonio Express-News*, November 18, 1990.

"Bush will speak at UT graduation." *Houston Chronicle*, March 27, 1990.

"Business mogul, horseman C.V. Whitney dies at 93." *The Dallas Morning News*, December 14, 1992.

"Candidate's brother arrested." *Houston Chronicle*, June 6, 1988.

"Cap the knight." *The Washington Times*, February 24, 1988.

"A Carter Christening." *The Washington Post*, 1988.

"Carter, Ford to help monitor elections as Panama opposition predicts fraud." *Houston Chronicle*, May 6, 1989.

"China expedition will search for remains of Doolittle planes." *Houston Chronicle*, July 29, 1990.

"China talking about return of the 'Busher': President, first lady reflect on memorable times there." *The Washington Post*, February 25, 1989.

"Cinco Estados decidirán esta noche el ganador." *El País* (Madrid), November 8, 1988.

"Clinton resolved to lift gay ban despite dissent." *The Dallas Morning News*, January 26, 1993.

"Confidence before the fight." *Houston Chronicle*, June 28, 1988.

"Contradiction marked life of Oswald." *Houston Chronicle*, November 20, 1988.

"D.C. denies Hinckley's right to vote." *Houston Chronicle*, May 23, 1992.

"Doctor: Kitty Dukakis drank rubbing alcohol." *Houston Chronicle*, November 9, 1989.

"A Dukakis battalion is set to invade Iowa." *The Boston Globe*, January 30, 1988.

"Easter Eggscitement." *The Washington Times*, April 4, 1988.

"Eisenhower weds." *Houston Chronicle*, February 10, 1990.

"El bautizo de Tyson." *El País* (Madrid), November 29, 1988.

"Elliott Roosevelt." *Plano Star Courier*, October 28, 1990.

"Evangelicals debate spiritual politics." *The Denver Post*, May 26, 1996.

"Executive expletive." *Houston Chronicle*, May 4, 1989.

"Expert says Bush of royal lineage." *Houston Chronicle*, July 5, 1988.

"Family heirloom rare document." *The Galveston Daily News*, July 4, 1992.

"Ferraro to stand by husband." *Houston Chronicle*.

"A few roots in presidential history." *The Washington Times*, April 14, 1988.

"The First Family's Family Tree." *The Dallas Morning News*, August 19, 1993.

"First salmon from Maine river reserved for Reagan." *Houston Chronicle*, 1985.

"First times for inaugurals." *Houston Chronicle*, January 15, 1989.

"5 presidents lost Cabinet nominee fights." *Houston Chronicle*, March 5, 1989.

"For UNICEF." *Houston Chronicle*, 1987.

"Former presidents took a parting shot: Photograph deal could bring windfall." *Houston Chronicle*, October 16, 1993.

"Four living ex-presidents will be a record for 20th century." *Houston Chronicle*, January 14, 1989.

"France honors Reagan." *Houston Chronicle*, June 16, 1989.

"From the relatives, some inside stories." *The Boston Globe*, January 30, 1988.

"Fun financial facts." *Houston Chronicle*, December 24, 1991.

"Gente." *El País* (Madrid), November 14, 1988.

"Getting Personal." *The Wall Street Journal*, January 20, 1993.

"Good luck rub." *Houston Chronicle*, February 14, 1989.

"Great-grandson's plea nets Roosevelt Medal of Honor." *The Dallas Morning News*, January 14, 2001.

"Half of potential electorate voted." *Houston Chronicle*, November 11, 1988.

"He'll miss the party." *Houston Chronicle*, January 5, 1989.

"Hill Scores Sweep in Iowa." *Roll Call*, February 21, 1988.

"His loneliest moment." *Houston Chronicle*, April 9, 1989.

"Historian dies." *Houston Chronicle*, 1996.

"Historian notes Truman's racist statements." *The Dallas Morning News*, October 15, 1991.

"The Houston Century." *Houston Chronicle*, December 12, 1999.

"How's your political I.Q.?" *Human Events*, July 7, 1995.

_____. June 16, 2003.

_____. October 6 and 20, 2003.

"Hughes had 50 years in public life." *Houston Chronicle*, November 20, 1988.

"Hundreds visit home to see Christ image." *Houston Chronicle*, June 26, 1988.

"Ieoh Ming Pei: Cómo convertir el Louvre en el museo mayor del mundo." *El País* (Madrid), October 25, 1988.

"In the name of George: Forks of Tar River, N.C., got Washington's moniker first." *Houston Chronicle*, October 15, 1989.

"Inauguration gala to have country air." *Houston Chronicle*, January 6, 1989.

"Interior secretary backs Puerto Rican statehood." *The Houston Post*, July 28, 1990.

"It's never too late." *Houston Chronicle*, June 24, 1988.

"Jackie in the buff?" *Houston Chronicle*, April 28, 1989.

"Jack's on target." *The Washington Times*, March 1, 1988.

"Jackson named sexiest." *Houston Chronicle*, July 7, 1988.

"Jackson's half-brother gets 10 years." *Houston Chronicle*, January 29, 1989.

"Jacqueline Kennedy Onassis' mother, champion horsewoman, is dead at 81." *Houston Chronicle*, July 24, 1989.

"Jane Wyman, 'Angela Channing', trabaja por 'hobby' y destina el 75 por ciento de sus ingresos a obras benéficas." *La Gaceta Regional* (Madrid), 1988.

"Jokes better than par." *Houston Chronicle*, June 26, 1988.

"Justices revive custom of wearing skullcaps at ceremony." *Houston Chronicle*, January 21, 1989.

"Kennedy-Mafia tale brings teller $50,000." *The Washington Times*, February 24, 1988.

"Kopechne 'cover-up' still enrages parents." *Houston Chronicle*, June 16, 1989.

"Landon leaves hospital." *The Houston Post*, October 11, 1987.

"Law firm linked to Lincoln dissolves." *The Washington Times*, April 11, 1988.

"Los otros candidatos." *El País* (Madrid), November 7, 1988.

"Markets Closed For Nixon's Funeral, To Reopen Thursday." *The Dallas Morning News*, April 28, 1994.

"Martha Raye is given three months to live." *Houston Chronicle*, October 16, 1993.

"More equal than others." *Houston Chronicle*, November 11, 1988.

"Movies now and then." Washington Weekend. *The Washington Times*, April 7, 1988.

"My stars — 65 or 67?" *Houston Chronicle*, July 6, 1988.

"Nancy Reagan, una «primera dama» que gasta mucho en ropa, según los norteamericanos." *El Adelanto* (Madrid), October 23, 1988.

"Nancy Reagan's memoirs 'set the record straight.'" *Houston Chronicle*, October 15, 1989.

"New JFK museum planned." *Houston Chronicle*, April 2, 1989.

"A night to remember." *Houston Chronicle*, June 13, 1990.

"1992 elections draw record number of U.S. voters." *The Dallas Morning News*, November 5, 1992.

"Nixon follows through on threat, dumps AT & T." *Houston Chronicle*, November 2, 1989.

"Nixon leaves hospital." *Houston Chronicle*, July 9, 1988.

"Nixon made plan to free hostages, paper reports." *Houston Chronicle*, September 17, 1989.

"Nixon's other side." *Houston Chronicle*, June 11, 1988.

"No fielder's choice, this." *Houston Chronicle*, June 18, 1989.

"No kiss-and-tell here." *Houston Chronicle*, July 13, 1988.

"No system exists to tap ex-presidents' experience." *The Houston Post*, November 12, 1989.

"An oldie but goodie." *Houston Chronicle*, February 6, 1989.

"Organization of U.S. Education Department and Telephone Numbers of Key Officials." *The Chronicle of Higher Education*, April 13, 1988.

"Oswald's mom held firm in belief of son's innocence." *Houston Chronicle*, November 20, 1988.

"Pancreatic cancer discovered in Billy Carter; prognosis 'poor.'" *The Houston Post*, September 12, 1987.

"'Pleased' with holiday." *Houston Chronicle*, September 21, 1989.

"Poll finds split on Clinton performance." *The Dallas Morning News*, February 1, 1993.

"Pose of statue probably tells nothing of fallen hero's fate." *Houston Chronicle*, November 26, 1989.

"President Bush was made a captain in the Texas Rangers by Governor Bill Clements." *The Houston Post*, April 27, 1989.

"President Has a Half Sister, An Arizona Family Claims." *The New York Times*, August 6, 1993.

"President pardons oilman Hammer." *Houston Chronicle*, August 15, 1989.

"Presidents compared." *The Houston Post*, April 29, 1987.

"President's mother, Dorothy Bush, dies at 91 after stroke." *The Dallas Morning News*, November 20, 1992.

"Reagan crosses the line." *Houston Chronicle*, October 15, 1989.

"Reagan says 'I'll miss you' in radio talks sign-off." *Houston Chronicle*, January 15, 1989.

"Reagan tells talk show host that he's forgiven Hinckley." *Houston Chronicle*, January 12, 1990.

"Retired White House butler spills secrets." *The Galveston Daily News*, July 4, 1992.

"A Round of Hearty Yawns." *The Dallas Morning News*, January 7, 1993.

"Ruby's shot killed chance of learning Oswald's motive." *Houston Chronicle*, November 20, 1988.

"Scholars doubt Taylor poisoned." *Dallas Times Herald*, June 15, 1991.
"Secret ballot among '88 anniversaries." *Houston Chronicle*, January 10, 1988.
"The Sequoia goes to work for its own future good." *The Washington Times*, April 26, 1988.
"Shall I Compare Thee to a Peanut?" *The Dallas Morning News*, December 10, 1994.
"She might try green." *Houston Chronicle*, June 25, 1988.
"Smithsonian opens visitors' center with high-tech computer displays." *The Houston Post*, November 12, 1989.
"Some day far away." *The Dallas Morning News*, December 6, 1991.
"Some highlights of the Reagan years, 1981-88." *Houston Chronicle*, December 18, 1988.
"Spread the word — peanut butter turns 100 years old this month." *The Houston Post*, March 28, 1990.
"Steinbrenner pardoned." *Houston Chronicle*, January 20, 1989.
"Stormy history leaves mark on Democratic conventions." *Houston Chronicle*, July 12, 1992.
"Testifying for dolphins." *Houston Chronicle*, July 25, 1990.
"To Reagan without 'Sir': Queen bestows honorary knighthood." *Houston Chronicle*, June 15, 1989.
"A toast to its history." *The Houston Post*, 1995.
"Tyson, convertido a la Iglesia baptista." *La Gaceta* (Madrid), November 29, 1988.
"Waiting for Lefty." *USA Today*, December 28, 1988.
"We owe $3,000,000,000,000." *The Houston Post*, April 4, 1990.
"Weinberger kin cited in HUD inquiry." *Houston Chronicle*, June 20, 1989.
"White House teases Shultz." *Houston Chronicle*, November 8, 1989.
"White House turns 'green.'" *Houston Chronicle*, April 24, 1994.
"Who's in line for Oval Office." *USA Today*.
"Who's left?" *Houston Chronicle*.
"Zapruder film recorded assassination of president." *Houston Chronicle*, November 20, 1988.

Newspaper Articles without Attribution or Titles
Austin Chronicle, Interview with William Goetzmann, October 10, 1986.
Boston Globe, January 30, 1988.
The Chronicle of Higher Education, April 13, 1988.
The Dallas Morning News, People/Sports Section, The Quiz, April 6, 1992.
Houston Chronicle, Travel section, June 26, 1988.
Houston Chronicle, July 12, 1988.
Houston Chronicle, November 23, 1988.
Houston Chronicle, February 16 and 19, 1989.
Houston Chronicle, June 12, 1989.
Houston Chronicle, December 10, 1989.
El País (Madrid), July 23, 1988.
USA Today, November 11, 1987.
USA Today, October 19 and 26, 1988.
USA Today, November 9-10, 15, and 17, 1988.
USA Today, December 15, 21, and 30, 1988.
USA Today, January 4-6, 10-13, 17, 20, and 24, 1989.
The Wall Street Journal, July 13, 1988.
The Washington Times, February 26, 1988.
The Washington Times, April 12 and 14, 1988.

Radio
"Presidents' Usage of Radio," *National Public Radio (NPR)*, April 20, 1992.

Television

"Air Force One," *The History Channel with Roger Mudd*, September 27, 1997.
Booknotes, C-SPAN, December 26, 1993.
Brooks, Philip. Interview with Historian of the Presidential Inaugural Committee. C-SPAN.
"Clinton gets to cheer both sides at Army-Navy game," *All Politics*, CNN, December 7, 1996.
"Daughters of the President," *Prime Time Texas with Tracy Rowlett*, March 18, 1995.
Fox News Channel, August 22, 1997.
Headline News, CNN, July 4, 1988.
————, February 10, 1992.
Larry King Live, CNN, June 20, 1988.
————, June 24, 1988.
"Nathan Miller: Author, *Theodore Roosevelt: A Life*," *Booknotes*, C-SPAN, February 1992.
News7Late Edition, Washington, DC, February 9, 1988.
Nightly News, NBC, coverage of the presidential inauguration, January 20, 1989.
————, January 20, 1993.
Rather, Dan. *CBS News*, January 24, 1988.
Reagan, Ronald. *CBS News*, Interview by Tom Brokaw, January 18, 1989.
"Richard Norton Smith: Author, *Patriarch*," *Booknotes*, C-SPAN, February 1992.
Safire, William. *Nightline*, ABC.
Washington Week, Washington, DC, May 11, 2003.
Wimbledon Lawn Tennis Championships. Television coverage. 1988.
World News Tonight with Peter Jennings, ABC News, December 18, 2000.

Other Sources

Berthoud, John, and Demian Brady. "Bill Clinton: America's Best Traveled President, A Study of Presidential Travel 1953-2001," Washington, DC: National Taxpayers Union, March 16, 2001.
"Fact Sheet: The Presidents of the United States and the Boy Scouts of America," Irving, Texas: The Boy Scouts of America, 1992.
Hollywood Squares, May 26, 2003.
Hoy, Tim. Interview and Consultation, 2003.
Museum of the Badlands, Medora, North Dakota, 1993.
"Page-A-Day Calendar," New York: Workman Publishing, 1993.
"Presidential Fact Finder," Los Angeles, California: Perrygraf, 1991.
The Presidential Museum, Odessa, Texas.
Rand McNally Road Atlas. Suburbot Skokie, Illinois: Rand McNally & Co., 1995.
Republican National Committee, Official brochures and publications.
"Residents' Newsletter," Plano, Texas: The Highlands of Preston Apartments, July 1992.
Risky Strategy board game, Golden (Jim Bear Enterprises), 1992.
Texas Trivia board game.
The White House. Official North Lawn tape recording.

Appendix A

Presidential Portraits

Washington J. Adams Jefferson Madison

Monroe J. Q. Adams Jackson Van Buren

W. H. Harrison Tyler Polk Taylor

Fillmore   Pierce   Buchanan   Lincoln

A. Johnson   Grant   Hayes   Garfield

Arthur   Cleveland   B. Harrison   McKinley

T. Roosevelt   Taft   Wilson   Harding

Coolidge   Hoover   F. Roosevelt   Truman

Eisenhower   Kennedy   L. Johnson   Nixon

Ford   Carter   Reagan   G. Bush

Clinton   G. W. Bush

Appendix B
The Presidents

Name (Party)	Term	Birth State	Born	Died	Religion	Age at Inaug.	Death
1. George Washington (F)	1789-1797	VA	02/22/1732	12/14/1799	Episcopalian	57	67
2. John Adams (F)	1797-1801	MA	10/30/1735	07/04/1826	Unitarian	61	90
3. Thomas Jefferson (DR)	1801-1809	VA	04/13/1743	07/04/1826	Deist	57	83
4. James Madison (DR)	1809-1817	VA	03/16/1751	06/28/1836	Episcopalian	57	85
5. James Monroe (DR)	1817-1825	VA	04/28/1758	07/03/1831	Episcopalian	58	73
6. John Quincy Adams (DR)	1825-1829	MA	07/11/1767	02/23/1848	Unitarian	57	80
7. Andrew Jackson (D)	1829-1837	SC	03/15/1767	06/08/1845	Presbyterian	61	78
8. Martin Van Buren (D)	1837-1841	NY	12/05/1782	07/24/1862	Reformed Dutch	54	79
9. William H. Harrison (W)	1841-1841	VA	02/09/1773	04/04/1841	Episcopalian	68	68
10. John Tyler (W)	1841-1845	VA	03/29/1790	01/18/1862	Episcopalian	51	71
11. James Polk (D)	1845-1849	NC	11/02/1795	06/15/1849	Methodist	49	53
12. Zachary Taylor (W)	1849-1850	VA	11/24/1784	07/09/1850	Episcopalian	64	65
13. Millard Fillmore (W)	1850-1853	NY	01/07/1800	03/08/1874	Unitarian	50	74
14. Franklin Pierce (D)	1853-1857	NH	11/23/1804	10/08/1869	Episcopalian	48	64
15. James Buchanan (D)	1857-1861	PA	04/23/1791	06/01/1868	Presbyterian	65	77
16. Abraham Lincoln (R)	1861-1865	KY	02/12/1809	04/15/1865	Liberal	52	56
17. Andrew Johnson (U)	1865-1869	NC	12/29/1808	07/31/1875	————	56	66
18. Ulysses Grant (R)	1869-1877	OH	04/27/1822	07/23/1885	Methodist	46	63
19. Rutherford Hayes (R)	1877-1881	OH	10/04/1822	01/17/1893	Methodist	54	70
20. James Garfield (R)	1881-1881	OH	11/19/1831	09/19/1881	Disciples of Christ	49	49
21. Chester Arthur (R)	1881-1885	VT	10/05/1830	11/18/1886	Episcopalian	50	56
22. Grover Cleveland (D)	1885-1889	NJ	03/18/1837	06/24/1908	Presbyterian	47	71
23. Benjamin Harrison (R)	1889-1893	OH	08/20/1833	03/13/1901	Presbyterian	55	67
24. Grover Cleveland (D)	1893-1897	NJ	03/18/1837	06/24/1908	Presbyterian	55	71
25. William McKinley (R)	1897-1901	OH	01/29/1843	09/14/1901	Methodist	54	58
26. Theodore Roosevelt (R)	1901-1909	NY	10/27/1858	01/06/1919	Reformed Dutch	42	60
27. William Howard Taft (R)	1909-1913	OH	09/15/1857	03/08/1930	Unitarian	51	72
28. Woodrow Wilson (D)	1913-1921	VA	12/28/1856	02/03/1924	Presbyterian	56	67
29. Warren Harding (R)	1921-1923	OH	11/02/1865	08/02/1923	Baptist	55	57
30. Calvin Coolidge (R)	1923-1929	VT	07/04/1872	01/05/1933	Congregationalist	51	60
31. Herbert Hoover (R)	1929-1933	IA	08/10/1874	10/20/1964	Quaker	54	90
32. Franklin Roosevelt (D)	1933-1945	NY	01/30/1882	04/12/1945	Episcopalian	51	63
33. Harry Truman (D)	1945-1953	MO	05/08/1884	12/26/1972	Baptist	60	88
34. Dwight Eisenhower (R)	1953-1961	TX	10/14/1890	03/28/1969	Presbyterian	62	78
35. John Kennedy (D)	1961-1963	MA	05/29/1917	11/22/1963	Roman Catholic	43	46
36. Lyndon Johnson (D)	1963-1969	TX	08/27/1908	01/22/1973	Disciples of Christ	55	64
37. Richard Nixon (R)	1969-1974	CA	01/09/1913	04/22/1994	Quaker	56	81
38. Gerald Ford (R)	1974-1977	NE	07/14/1913	————	Episcopalian	61	—
39. Jimmy Carter (D)	1977-1981	GA	10/01/1924	————	Southern Baptist	52	—
40. Ronald Reagan (R)	1981-1989	IL	02/06/1911	————	Disciples of Christ	69	—
41. George Bush (R)	1989-1993	MA	06/12/1924	————	Episcopalian	64	—
42. Bill Clinton (D)	1993-2001	AR	08/19/1946	————	Southern Baptist	46	—
43. George W. Bush (R)	2001-	CT	07/06/1946	————	Methodist	55	—

(F) Federalist, (DR) Democratic-Republican, (D) Democratic, (W) Whig, (R) Republican, (U) Unionist

Source: *The Information Please Almanac* (Boston: Houghton Mifflin Company)

Appendix C
The Vice Presidents

Name (Party)	Term	Birth State	Born	Died	President(s) Served
1. John Adams (F)	1789-1797	MA	1735	1826	Washington
2. Thomas Jefferson (DR)	1801-1809	VA	1743	1826	John Adams
3. Aaron Burr (DR)	1801-1805	NJ	1756	1836	Jefferson
4. George Clinton (DR)	1805-1812	NY	1739	1812	Jefferson, Madison
5. Elbridge Gerry (DR)	1813-1814	MA	1744	1814	Madison
6. Daniel D. Tompkins (DR)	1817-1825	NY	1774	1825	Monroe
7. John C. Calhoun (DR,D)	1825-1832	SC	1782	1850	J. Q. Adams, Jackson
8. Martin Van Buren (D)	1833-1837	NY	1782	1862	Jackson
9. Richard M. Johnson (D)	1837-1841	KY	1780	1850	Van Buren
10. John Tyler (W)	1841-1841	VA	1790	1862	W. H. Harrison
11. George M. Dallas (D)	1845-1849	PA	1792	1864	Polk
12. Millard Fillmore (W)	1849-1850	NY	1800	1874	Taylor
13. William R. D. King (D)	1853-1853	NC	1786	1853	Pierce
14. John C. Breckinridge (D)	1857-1861	KY	1821	1875	Buchanan
15. Hannibal Hamlin (R)	1861-1865	ME	1809	1891	Lincoln
16. Andrew Johnson (U)	1865-1865	NC	1808	1875	Lincoln
17. Schuyler Colfax (R)	1869-1873	NY	1823	1885	Grant
18. Henry Wilson (R)	1873-1875	NH	1812	1875	Grant
19. William A. Wheeler (R)	1877-1881	NY	1819	1887	Hayes
20. Chester A. Arthur (R)	1881-1881	VT	1830	1886	Garfield
21. Thomas A. Hendricks (D)	1885-1885	OH	1819	1885	Cleveland
22. Levi P. Morton (R)	1889-1893	VT	1824	1920	B. Harrison
23. Adlai E. Stevenson (D)	1893-1897	KY	1835	1914	Cleveland
24. Garrett A. Hobart (R)	1897-1899	NJ	1844	1899	McKinley
25. Theodore Roosevelt (R)	1901-1901	NY	1858	1919	McKinley
26. Charles W. Fairbanks (R)	1905-1909	OH	1852	1918	T. Roosevelt
27. James S. Sherman (R)	1909-1912	NY	1855	1912	Taft
28. Thomas R. Marshall (D)	1913-1921	IN	1854	1925	Wilson
29. Calvin Coolidge (R)	1921-1923	VT	1872	1933	Harding
30. Charles G. Dawes (R)	1925-1929	OH	1865	1951	Coolidge
31. Charles Curtis (R)	1929-1933	KS	1860	1936	Hoover
32. John N. Garner (D)	1933-1941	TX	1868	1967	F. D. Roosevelt
33. Henry A. Wallace (D)	1941-1945	IA	1888	1965	F. D. Roosevelt
34. Harry S Truman (D)	1945-1945	MO	1884	1972	F. D. Roosevelt
35. Alben W. Barkley (D)	1949-1953	KY	1877	1956	Truman
36. Richard M. Nixon (R)	1953-1961	CA	1913	1994	Eisenhower
37. Lyndon B. Johnson (D)	1961-1963	TX	1908	1973	Kennedy
38. Hubert H. Humphrey (D)	1965-1969	SD	1911	1978	Johnson
39. Spiro T. Agnew (R)	1969-1973	MD	1918	1996	Nixon
40. Gerald R. Ford (R)	1973-1974	NE	1913	———	Nixon
41. Nelson A. Rockefeller (R)	1974-1977	ME	1908	1979	Ford
42. Walter F. Mondale (D)	1977-1981	MN	1928	———	Carter
43. George H. W. Bush (R)	1981-1989	MA	1924	———	Reagan
44. J. Danforth Quayle (R)	1989-1993	IN	1947	———	Bush
45. Albert Gore (D)	1993-2001	TN	1948	———	Clinton
46. Richard B. Cheney (R)	2001-	NE	1941	———	Bush

(F) Federalist, (DR) Democratic-Republican, (D) Democratic, (W) Whig, (R) Republican, (U) Unionist

Source: *The Information Please Almanac* (Boston: Houghton Mifflin Company)

Appendix D
Wives and Children of the Presidents

President	Wife's Name	Born	Birth State	Married	Died	Sons	Daughters
1. George Washington	Martha Dandridge Custis	1732	VA	1759	1802	—	—
2. John Adams	Abigail Smith	1744	MA	1764	1818	3	2
3. Thomas Jefferson	Martha Wayles Skelton	1748	VA	1772	1782	1	5
4. James Madison	Dorothy "Dolley" Payne Todd	1768	NC	1794	1849	—	—
5. James Monroe	Elizabeth "Eliza" Kortright	1768	NY	1786	1830	—	2
6. John Quincy Adams	Louisa Catherine Johnson	1775	England	1797	1852	3	1
7. Andrew Jackson	Mrs. Rachel Donelson Robards	1767	VA	1791	1828	—	—
8. Martin Van Buren	Hannah Hoes	1788	NY	1807	1819	4	—
9. William Henry Harrison	Anna Symmes	1775	NJ	1795	1864	6	4
10. John Tyler	Letitia Christian	1790	VA	1813	1842	3	4
	Julia Gardiner	1820	NY	1844	1889	5	2
11. James Polk	Sarah Childress	1803	TN	1824	1891	—	—
12. Zachary Taylor	Margaret Smith	1788	MD	1810	1852	1	5
13. Millard Fillmore	Abigail Powers	1798	NY	1826	1853	1	1
	Caroline Carmichael McIntosh	1813	NJ	1858	1881	—	—
14. Franklin Pierce	Jane Means Appleton	1806	NH	1834	1863	3	—
15. James Buchanan	(Unmarried)	—	—	—	—	—	—
16. Abraham Lincoln	Mary Todd	1818	KY	1842	1882	4	—
17. Andrew Johnson	Eliza McCardle	1810	TN	1827	1876	3	2
18. Ulysses Grant	Julia Dent	1826	MO	1848	1902	3	1
19. Rutherford Hayes	Lucy Ware Webb	1831	OH	1852	1889	7	1
20. James Garfield	Lucretia Randolph	1832	OH	1858	1918	5	2
21. Chester Arthur	Ellen Lewis Herndon	1837	VA	1859	1880	2	1
22. Grover Cleveland	Frances Folsom	1864	NY	1886	1947	2	3
23. Benjamin Harrison	Caroline Lavinia Scott	1832	OH	1853	1892	1	1
	Mary Scott Lord Dimmick	1858	PA	1896	1948	—	1
24. Grover Cleveland	Frances Folsom	1864	NY	1886	1947	2	—
25. William McKinley	Ida Saxton	1847	OH	1871	1907	—	2
26. Theodore Roosevelt	Alice Hathaway Lee	1861	MA	1880	1884	—	1
	Edith Kermit Carow	1861	CT	1886	1948	4	1
27. William Howard Taft	Helen Herron	1861	OH	1886	1943	2	1
28. Woodrow Wilson	Ellen Louise Axson	1860	GA	1885	1914	—	3
	Edith Bolling Galt	1872	VA	1915	1961	—	—
29. Warren Harding	Florence Kling DeWolfe	1860	OH	1891	1924	—	—
30. Calvin Coolidge	Grace Anna Goodhue	1879	VT	1905	1957	2	—
31. Herbert Hoover	Lou Henry	1875	IA	1899	1944	2	—
32. Franklin Roosevelt	Anna Eleanor Roosevelt	1884	NY	1905	1962	5	1
33. Harry Truman	Bess Wallace	1885	MO	1919	1982	—	1
34. Dwight Eisenhower	Mamie Geneva Doud	1896	IA	1916	1979	2	—
35. John Kennedy	Jacqueline Lee Bouvier	1929	NY	1953	1994	2	1
36. Lyndon Johnson	Claudia Alta "Lady Bird" Taylor	1912	TX	1934	—	—	2
37. Richard Nixon	Thelma Catherine "Pat" Ryan	1912	NV	1940	1993	—	2
38. Gerald Ford	Elizabeth "Betty" Bloomer Warren	1918	IL	1948	—	3	1

President	Wife's Name	Born	Birth State	Married	Died	Sons	Daughters
39. Jimmy Carter	Rosalynn Smith	1928	GA	1946	———	3	1
40. Ronald Reagan	Jane Wyman	1914	MO	1940	———	1	1
	Nancy Davis	1921	NY	1952	———	1	1
41. George Bush	Barbara Pierce	1925	NY	1945	———	4	2
42. Bill Clinton	Hillary Rodham	1947	IL	1975	———	—	1
43. George W. Bush	Laura Welch	1946	TX	1977	———	—	2

Source: *The Information Please Almanac* (Boston: Houghton Mifflin Company).

Index